IN-CLASS ACTIVITIES GUIDE

for

The Instructor's Survival Kit

to accompany

Marketing

Eighth Edition

Roger A. Kerin
Southern Methodist University

Steven W. Hartley
University of Denver

Eric N. Berkowitz
University of Massachusetts

William Rudelius
University of Minnesota

Prepared by
Michael J. Vessey

Boston   Burr Ridge, IL   Dubuque, IA   Madison, WI   New York   San Francisco   St. Louis
Bangkok   Bogotá   Caracas   Kuala Lumpur   Lisbon   London   Madrid   Mexico City
Milan   Montreal   New Delhi   Santiago   Seoul   Singapore   Sydney   Taipei   Toronto

McGraw-Hill
Irwin

In-Class Activities Guide for The Instructor's Survival Kit to accompany
MARKETING
Roger A. Kerin, Eric N. Berkowitz, Steven W. Hartley, William Rudelius

Published by McGraw-Hill/Irwin, an imprint of The McGraw-Hill Companies, Inc., 1221 Avenue of the Americas, New York, NY 10020. Copyright © 2006 by The McGraw-Hill Companies, Inc. All rights reserved.

1 2 3 4 5 6 7 8 9 0 BKM/BKM 0 9 8 7 6 5

ISBN 0-07-282886-2

www.mhhe.com

ACKNOWLEDGMENTS

We have been heartened by the enthusiastic reaction by marketing instructors to our *In-Class Activities Guide* and *Instructor's Survival Kit* that accompanied *Marketing, 5th, 6th and 7th Editions*. These reactions have caused us to expand and update the set of In-Class Activities (ICAs) for *Marketing, 8th Edition*, which includes 23 new and 22 significantly revised ICAs out of a total of 60.

The co-authors of *Marketing 8th Edition* wish to recognize the important contributions of the several individuals whose efforts, based on their own classroom experiences, has led to the new and updated In-Class Activities (ICAs) in this edition of the *In-Class Activities Guide*. We thank our ICA authors, which include faculty members Linda Rochford of the University of Minnesota-Duluth, Robert Hansen of the University of Minnesota-Twin Cities, and James Spiers of Arizona State University. Thanks also go to marketing executives Mary L. Brown and Kirk Hodgdon of Bolin Marketing, as well as David H. Gobeli, Amy Cox, Joann Peck, Mark Bergen, and Michael J. Vessey, who also wrote and/or contributed to these ICAs.

In developing these ICAs and our *Instructor's Survival Kit,* we received the continuing support of our McGraw-Hill/Irwin team—Marketing Manager Dan Silverberg, Sponsoring Editor Barrett Koger, Development Editor Sarah Crago, Production Supervisor Heather Burbridge, Media Project Manager Susan Lombardi, Media Technology Producer Damian Moshak, and Supplement Producer Carol Loreth.

We especially want to thank the people who generously provided the items and other resources in our *Instructor's Survival Kit* that give special life in the classroom to a number of our ICAs. These include Dr. Richard Beltramini, Nicholas Skally of Rollerblade, Karolyn Warfel and Betsy Boyer of Woodstream Corp. (Victor), Traci Moscowitz of hotjobs.com, Peggy Mathias of McNeil Nutritionals, LLC (Splenda), Leonard Fuld of Fuld & Company, Inc., Sharon Gibson of the University of St. Thomas (Employment Questions), Chris Gorley of Starbucks Coffee Company, Kelly Hulme of BzzAgent, Glenn Cheshire of Sprint, Dr. Aelred (Al) J. Kurtenbach, LaVetta Foster, and Nichole Bjerke of Daktronics, Inc., Kerri Miller of MINIUSA, Daniel Sutton of Crispin, Porter, and Bogusky (MINI Cooper), Lisa Castaldo of Pepsico, Jessica Benbow of Arbitron, Kimberly Crews and Tom Webster of the U.S. Census Bureau, Muffie Taggett and Denise Bosch of General Mills (Honey Nut Cheerios Milk 'n Cereal Bar and Cheerios), David Windorski of 3M, Keith Nowak of Nokia, Robert M. McMath of NewProductWorks, Chad Carney of 3M (VHB Tape), Greg Lee of Magnetic Poetry, Inc., Lynn Winter, Jane Fulton Suri, Scott Underwood, Whitney Mortimer, and Kelly Robinson of IDEO, Frank Lynch and Patty Serie of ConAgra Snack Foods (Act II Popcorn), Carol Watzke and Joanne Harms of CNS Inc., (Breathe Right), Greg Rodriguez and Nick Stein of Frito-Lay (Lay's Stax), Dave Ridley of Southwest Airlines, Karen McCall of Panasonic, Bob Robinson and Sue Carroll of Apple Computer, Willard Oberton of Fastenal Company, John Blodgett of Ketchum Communications (Kodak), Scott Wosniak and Jennifer Arnold of Toro, David Krane of Harris Interactive, Kim Eskro of Fallon Worldwide, Robin Grayson of TBWA/Chiat/Day (Apple), Patricia Hudson and Krystal Webber of Valassis Communications, Inc. (Advil), Tim Stauber of Wyeth Consumer Healthcare (Advil), Marsha Levine of A List Entertainment, Eric Fleming of Segway LLC, Dawn Knauer and Laura Richards of News America Marketing, Amanda Kelly of VML (Hill's Pet Nutrition), Teresa Bencivengo of BMW USA, Josselyn Simpson of *The McKinsey Quarterly*, and George Dierberger of 3M.

Additional thanks go to Karen Primak, Margie Brown, and Ken Neimeister of IPAK, who produced the ISK. Finally, Daniel Hundley of Token Media, digitized many of the video and TV ads contained in the *Instructor's CD* for the *Instructor's Survival Kit*.

We believe that the efforts, creativity, and knowledge of all those mentioned above will bring both excitement and enhanced understanding of key marketing concepts to your classroom.

Roger A. Kerin, Steven W. Hartley, Eric N. Berkowitz, William Rudelius, and Michael J. Vessey

CONTENTS

CONTENTS (Continued)

CONTENTS (Continued)

CONTENTS (Continued)

I.

USING THE IN-CLASS ACTIVITIES GUIDE

AND

INSTRUCTOR'S SURVIVAL KIT

I. USING THE *IN-CLASS ACTIVITES GUIDE* AND *INSTRUCTOR'S SURVIVAL KIT*

Student Involvement Matters

Research shows that students who participate actively in their own learning—who are challenged to think, debate, and discuss—often retain and apply much more than students who are less involved. This edition of our *In-Class Activities Guide* contains In-Class Activities (ICAs) for instructors using our textbook. These activities encourage classroom discussion and involvement by adding an experiential component to the education process.

Why a Separate In-Class Activities Guide?

An *In-Class Activities Guide* to accompany *Marketing, 8th Edition* is a result of the overwhelmingly positive reactions we have received from instructors using ICAs from previous editions. To facilitate their use, we have placed the ICAs in this separate *Guide* and provided detailed descriptions—often with some product samples and other "props," to enhance student involvement and learning. Also, most ICAs refer to websites, and for several accessing a website is integral to the ICA. Therefore, we encourage instructors to always recheck the websites and specific links referred to in each ICA before class since these are constantly changing.

Elements of Each In-Class Activity

Each ICA has nine (9) key elements to help instructors select and utilize these in-class activities:

1. **Learning Objectives**. While the activities seek to increase student involvement and participation in the classroom, the most fundamental goal is enhanced learning. Making the key learning objectives explicit helps instructors select activities that are appropriate for their students.

2. **Definitions**. From the glossary, these are provided for the key marketing terms mentioned in the activity. Occasionally, other terms are defined using other sources, as indicated.

3. **Nature of Activity**. This is a snapshot summary of what the activity is and does.

4. **Estimated Class Time**. Knowing the approximate time to complete an activity allows instructors to schedule the class period. Many of the ICAs can be edited to shorten or enhance as desired.

5. **Materials Needed**. This describes what is needed to successfully complete the ICA during the specified time period. In many cases, transparencies will need to be made, particularly if you choose not to use the PowerPoint slides developed for the ICA. Also, photocopies need to be made of handouts developed to give to students when specified in the ICA to facilitate their learning. Finally, inexpensive product samples or props may need to be purchased for the ICA in addition to the sample provided.

6. **Preparation Before Class.** This summarizes what instructors must do before conducting the activity in front of the class.

7. **Instructions.** To simplify preparation for busy instructors, this element provides a step-by-step sequence to follow to achieve genuine instructional value. As instructors gain experience with an activity, they will often find ways to modify it to achieve their own special objectives in light of their students' backgrounds and interests.

8. **Marketing Lessons.** This is the educational wrap-up—the "takeaways" for students.

9. **Websites.** This lists the websites used in the ICA or suggests others for student use.

Some In-Class Activities also have PowerPoint presentations and other resources associated with them. In addition, some of the activities, supplementary information is provided to elaborate on the organization involved.

Items in the *Instructor's Survival Kit*

Besides the *In-Class Activities Guide* and the *Instructor's CDs*, the *Instructor's Survival Kit* contains the following product samples, props, and other items that can be shown in class.

Sample Product or Item	ICA
■ Hershey's Milk Chocolate Candy Bar	1-1
■ The 2005 Rollerblade® Consumer Brochure	1-2
■ Original Wooden Victor® 'Metal Bait Pedal' Mousetrap	1-3
■ Victor® 'Live-Catch' Mousetrap	1-3
■ Victor® 'Easy Set®, Pre-Baited' Mousetrap with the "plastic cheese"	2-1
■ Victor® 'Quick-Kill' Mousetrap	2-1
■ Splenda Tip Card w/ 2 Packets	3-1
■ Fuld & Company Brochure	3-2
■ Starbucks House Blend Coffee Bag	5-1
■ Daktronics Video Display Brochure	6-2
■ The 2005 MINI Cooper Convertible Encyclopedia of Motoring Brochure	7-1
■ Howlin' Coyote® Chili Challenge Taste Test Questionnaire	8-2
■ U.S. Census Form D-61A	9-1
■ U.S. Census American Community Survey Form ACS-1	9-1
■ Honey Nut Cheerios® Milk 'N Cereal Bar	9-2
■ Starbucks Penza Caramel Dolce Bar	9-2
■ 3M Post-it® Flag Highlighter	9-3
■ Nokia 7610 Mobile Phone Brochure	10-1
■ Packet of 3M® VHB™ Tape Pull-Tabs	10-3
■ Original/Sequel Magnetic Poetry Kit	10-4
■ IDEO Method Cards	10-5

The *Instructor's CDs* for the *In-Class Activities* and *Instructor's Survival Kit*

For *Marketing, 8th Edition*, we have included two *Instructor's CDs*, each of which contains product shots, print ads, TV ads, etc. that either are integral to an ICA. The *Instructor's CDs* are organized by ICA. Because a number of ICAs include digital resources, we have produced two CDs: Disc 1 contains the ICAs for Chapters 1 – 11 and Disc 2 contains those for Chapters 12 – 22.

Organization of the *Instructor's CDs*

The *Instructor's CDs* contain the set of In-Class Activities developed for instructors and include the *In-Class Activity Guide* documents, PowerPoint slides, and the digital resources (image, audio, and video) that are part of the learning experience.

1. *In-Class Activity Guide* **documents.** The *In-Class Activity Guide* comes in both a 3-holed, perforated paper-based printed manual. The ICAs also come in digital form:

   a. **Microsoft Word document (.doc) files.** In-Class Activities are saved as Microsoft Word files (ICA01-1.doc) in their respective chapter folders located in the *Instructor's CD*.

   b. **Adobe Portable Document Format (.pdf) files.** Some ICAs require the use of a file saved in Portable Document Format ('pdf). These are also contained in a 'pdf' folder within the ICA folder for a given ICA. You will need the Adobe Acrobat Reader to view the PDF document. To download the latest version, go to www.adobe.com/products/acrobat.

   c. **PowerPoint presentation (.ppt) files.** Most ICAs have an accompanying PowerPoint presentation. This is also contained in the folder for a given ICA.

d. **Other files**. A select few ICAs have an Excel spreadsheet (.xls) or Flash animation (.swf) file associated with it. To use these, resources, you will need Microsoft Office or Excel and Macromedia's Flash Player, respectively.

2. **PowerPoint slides**. The *Instructor's CDs* contain all the image slides for the In-Class Activities. These resources will encourage classroom discussion and involvement by adding a multimedia dimension to the education process. The PowerPoint presentation developed for each ICA contains the following key elements:

a. **Slide Numbers**. Each slide in a PowerPoint presentation has a slide number placed in the lower right corner of the slide and **not on the master slide**.

b. **Icons**. The following four tools are used to navigate within a PowerPoint presentation.

- **"Web" icon**. When this icon is clicked, the classroom computer's default browser (such as Internet Explorer or Safari) will launch and go to the website address that is embedded within the icon.

- **"Excel" icon**. When this icon is double-clicked, it will launch the Excel application and open the Excel file in a separate window based on its location (or path) embedded within the icon.

c. **Types of Slides**. There are two types of slides within a PowerPoint presentation.

- **In-Class Activity Title Slide**. The chapter title image is always Slide 1 for each ICA.

- **Resource Slides**. These include slides that contain video, TV ads, print Ads, product shots, audio, handout images, etc.

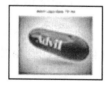

3. **Digital Resources**. Within each ICA folder, there are image files consisting of product shots, print ads, point-of-purchase display shots, handouts, etc. in JPEG (.jpg) format. These are contained in a 'pic' folder. Also within the ICA folder are the Word document (.doc), PowerPoint presentation (.ppt), as well as the video (.mpg), audio (.wav), and Excel (.xls) files that constitute the ICA. As indicated above, a few ICA folders will have a '.pdf' subfolder that contains handouts that should be copied for students. All of these resources are either contained within or linked to a PowerPoint slide.

System Requirements

The *Instructor's CDs* are intended for instructors that are somewhat familiar with:
(1) Microsoft's Windows operating system and how to locate file folders and files,
(2) Microsoft's PowerPoint (part of the Office Suite), and how it can be an effective tool to create and present marketing content to students, and (3) personal computer operations, such as installing software or transferring files from a CD-ROM to a computer's hard drive.

The *Instructor's CDs* are meant to run directly from either the CD-ROM or DVD drive of your classroom computer. However, if you prefer to run these presentations from the hard drive (the C:\ or root drive) on your classroom computer, we recommend the following hardware and software specifications (see below). If you have any questions, please contact McGraw-Hill/Irwin toll-free at **1-800-331-5094** or on the Internet at http://www.mhhe.com/support.

1. **Hardware Required**

We recommend that PC users have the following minimum hardware specifications to use the *Instructor's CDs*. **If you are not familiar with the technical capabilities of your classroom computer, please review this section with your institution's technical support personnel.** For Mac users, similar hardware requirements are recommended.

- **Processor**. To minimize delays in load times or playback of the digital resources contained in the *Instructor's CDs*, your classroom computer should have at least a 500 MHz Pentium (or equivalent) processor. NOTE: Faster is better!

- **RAM**. A minimum of 128 Mb of RAM (system memory) is required to run the *Instructor's CDs* for a given chapter since: (1) the size of a chapter's PowerPoint file can reach up to 50 Mb due to the number, type (higher resolution print ads or video) and size of digital resources involved, (2) PowerPoint itself can use up to 10 Mb of memory, and (3) the browser, the default media player (Windows Media Player or QuickTime Player), and other software (Adobe Acrobat Reader, Macromedia Flash Player, etc.) will all need memory allocated to run their programs.

- **Media Cards**. Your classroom computer should have at least a 16-bit stereo sound card and a 16-bit or higher video card with at least 8 Mb of memory.

- **CD-ROM/DVD Drive**. Your classroom computer should have at least a 4x or faster CD-ROM or DVD drive installed on your classroom computer to run the *Instructor's CDs* or load its contents onto the computer's hard drive.

- **Free Hard Disk Space**. To load the entire *Instructor's CDs* (Chapters 1-22) onto your classroom computer's hard drive requires about 1.0 giga byte (Gb) of free hard disk space. Please plan ahead and reserve enough time before class to load the *Instructor's CDs* onto the classroom computer.

- **Monitor Settings**. Since projection systems display at different pixel resolutions (640×480, 800×600, 1024×768, etc.) and levels of color (256, 16-bit high color, or 24-bit true color), it is important to set your classroom computer to the projection system's parameters before using the *Instructor's CDs*. If you experience problems with projection, check the "Control Panel" setting. In the Windows XP operating system, click and hold the mouse down on the "Start" button. Then, move the cursor over to the "Control Panel" icon. To open it, double-click on the icon. Next, go to the "Settings" tab and click on it. Finally, select the appropriate screen resolution and color quality settings. Also, you may also need to simultaneously hold down the "Function" and "F8" keys to display the image using the projection system.

- **Apple Macintosh Computers**. Although the presentation will work on a Macintosh using Mac OS 10.2 or higher with PowerPoint/Office 2001, PowerPoint/Office v. X, and PowerPoint/Office 2004 (Service Pack 1), the *Instructor's CDs* was developed to operate on PCs. If the Excel spreadsheet files and the playback of audio and video files do not work properly, you will have to manually "relink" each file within the PowerPoint slide (see the *PowerPoint CD Package Guide* that is part of the *Instructor's Resource CD*).

2. Microsoft Windows Operating System Required

We recommend that your classroom computer has at least Microsoft Windows 2000 or higher installed as the operating system (OS). The *Instructor's CDs* will also work on Microsoft Windows ME® (Millennium Edition), NT®, XP®, and any of these that run on a server. Microsoft Windows XP (Service Pack 2) is preferred since it is the OS that is being supported by Microsoft. We will endorse the next version of Microsoft Windows OS when it becomes available.

3. Microsoft PowerPoint/Office Required

We recommend that your classroom computer has at least Microsoft PowerPoint or Microsoft Office XP (a.k.a. PowerPoint/Office 2002 with Service Pack 3 plus updates) installed. The *Instructor's CDs* will also work on PowerPoint/Office that runs on a server. Microsoft PowerPoint/Office 2003 (Service Pack 1 plus updates) is preferred since it is being supported by Microsoft. We will endorse the next version of Microsoft PowerPoint/Office when it becomes available. Since PowerPoint uses Windows Media Player or QuickTime Player to play the videos we included, which are in "MPEG-1" format, earlier versions of PowerPoint/Office will not work or work well. Therefore, *we cannot recommend* that you use PowerPoint/Office '97® or earlier.

4. Microsoft Windows Media Player or QuickTime Player Required

We support Windows Media Player 9.0 or higher to pay audio and video files but recommend that classroom computers have the latest Windows Media Player (WMP 10) or QuickTime Player (QT 6 or 7) installed. Although WMP comes installed with Windows XP when a PC is purchased, newer and free editions of WMP are continually being released to provide better integration with the Windows XP and PowerPoint. Therefore, we recommend that you download the latest version of WMP by going to Microsoft's website, which is http://www.microsoft.com/windows/windowsmedia/mp10 or the latest version of QuickTime Player, which is http://www.apple.com/quicktime. If your computer is not set up to use this application to play video or audio files, your classroom computer *may* have to be reset to play them **within** the PowerPoint presentation. For instructions on how to do this, consult your institution's technical support personnel or call the toll-free McGraw-Hill/Irwin technical support telephone number at **1-800-331-5094**.

You can still play these video or audio files outside of the PowerPoint presentation. To do this, double-click on the desired file after you have located it in its folder. However, this will open the default media player in a separate window. Click the "play" button to start the audio or video. When finished, close the window to return to the PowerPoint presentation.

[NOTES: (1) The newest versions of WMP or QuickTime will have features that are different from older versions. Therefore, there may be some small differences when playing the audio and video files in the *Instructor's CDs*. (2) You may want your institution's technical support personnel update your classroom computer.]

5. Internet Browser Required

You may use either Microsoft's Internet Explorer (6.0 or higher), Apple's Safari (1.0 or higher), or other comparable Internet browser as the classroom computer's default browser to access the hyperlinks that are used in the PowerPoint presentations. The classroom computer must be connected to the Internet for the "Web" icon hyperlinks to work (see below). High-speed Internet connections are best.

6. Other Software Required

Many promotional websites (see Chapter 21) now use "rich media" (animations, audio, video, etc.) to communicate with their online consumers. Therefore, you should download and install the latest versions of Adobe's Acrobat Reader (see www.adobe.com/products/acrobat/) and Macromedia's Flash Player (see www.macromedia.com/software/flashplayer).

Technical Assistance

If you encounter any problems or would like technical assistance regarding the *Instructor's CDs*, please call the McGraw-Hill/Irwin toll-free technical support telephone number, which is **1-800-331-5094**. You may also seek online help at www.mhhe.com/support.

II.

IN-CLASS ACTIVITES (ICAs)

CHAPTER 1: CREATING CUSTOMER RELATIONSHIPS AND VALUE THROUGH MARKETING

ICA 1-1: IN-CLASS ACTIVITY

Designing a Candy Bar[1]

Learning Objectives. To have students: (1) define a target market segment and develop a simple marketing program for a product they are familiar with; (2) value the practice of working in a team when engaging in the aforementioned aspects of the marketing function; and (3) develop presentation skills they may need for later in the course.

Definitions. The following marketing terms are referred to in this in-class activity (ICA):

- Customer Value: The unique combination of benefits received by targeted buyers that includes quality, price, convenience, on-time delivery, and both before-sale and after-sale service.

- Market: People with both the desire and the ability to buy a specific product.

- Marketing: An organizational function and a set of processes for creating, communicating, and delivering value to customers and for managing customer relationships in ways that benefit the organization and its stakeholders.

- Marketing Mix: The marketing manager's controllable factors—product, price, promotion, and place—that can be used to solve a marketing problem.

  - Product: A good, service, or idea to satisfy the consumer's needs.

  - Price: What is exchanged for the product.

  - Promotion: A means of communication between the seller and the buyer.

  - Place (Distribution): A means of getting the product into the consumer's hands.

- Marketing Program: A plan that integrates the marketing mix to provide a good, service, or idea to prospective buyers.

- Points of Difference: Those characteristics of a product that make it superior to competitive substitutes.

- Target Market: One or more specific groups of potential consumers toward which an organization directs its marketing program.

Nature of the Activity. To have students design a candy bar by specifying its target market, marketing mix elements, and points of difference during the first class meeting.

Estimated Class Time. 30 minutes.

---

[1] The author wishes to thank Dr. Richard Beltramini, who inspired this ICA when he had him for a marketing principles course.

Materials Needed.

- The ICA01-1.doc Word and ICA01-1.ppt PowerPoint files contained in the ICA01-1 folder of the Instructor's CD #1 from the *Instructor's Survival Kit* box.

- Samples of candy bars that represent a variety of kinds (composition – chocolate, caramel, peanuts, etc.; form – bar, drop, bundle, etc.; sugar/nonsugar; etc.) sold in the U.S. and which students may be familiar with. Purchase one each of the following:

  - <u>Hershey's</u>: Milk Chocolate Bar, Kisses, Swoops, 1 Gram Sugar Carb Bar, Sugar Free Chocolate Candy, Reese's Pieces, etc.

  - <u>Mars</u>: M&Ms, Snickers, Milky Way Bar, etc.

  - <u>Nestlé's</u>: Milk Chocolate Bar, Crunch Bar, Buncha Crunch, Butterfinger, Baby Ruth, Skittles, etc.

  - Other candy bars of interest.

  To buy one candy bar in bulk (Hershey's Milk Chocolate bar or Nestlé's Crunch Bar), go to your local mass merchandiser (Wal-Mart or Target) or warehouse club (Sam's Club or Costco). Estimated cost: $13.00 per 36 count (Sam's Club).

- Copies of the Designing a Candy Bar Handout.

- Easel with markers or black/white board markers/chalk for students to write on/with.

Preparation Before Class. Follow the steps below:

1. Read pp. 10-17 of Chapter 1.

2. Print, read, and if necessary, edit ICA01-1.doc Word file.

3. Print and/or review the PowerPoint slides from ICA01-1.ppt PowerPoint file.

4. Get easels and markers of sufficient quantity for the number of student teams.

5. Make copies of the Designing a Candy Bar Handout for each student.

6. OPTIONAL: Bookmark the following websites on your classroom computer to view a variety of candy bars from the top three U.S. candy marketers:

   - Hershey's: www.hersheys.com/websites/index.shtml.
   - Mars: www.mars.com/The_Mars_Directory/Brand_search_results.asp?lstCountry=135.
   - Nestlé: www.nestleusa.com/consumerSite/brand/brand_home.asp.

Instructions. Follow the steps below to conduct this ICA:

1. Give the following mini-lecture about marketers and their responsibilities:

   "All of you purchase products and services every day, ranging from necessities, such as food, clothing, and shelter, to discretionary items, such as candy, music, and education. And marketers develop many of these products and services with you specifically in mind—just look at the stores in and around campus that cater to you!

   To offer these products and services, marketers must first understand your needs and wants. Then, they must:

   - develop the features and benefits for the products and services that you desire;
   - charge a price that you are able and willing to pay;
   - inform you that the product or service exists, where it can be purchased, and perhaps offer you a small inducement to try it;
   - make it available at locations where you are likely to buy it;
   - ensure that it is superior to similar offerings available from competitors; and
   - earn a profit for the organization."

2. Form students into 4-person teams.

3. Give the following mini-lecture on the candy industry:

   "Let's take a look at one product that you are all familiar with: the candy bar. According to *Candy Industry*, the confectionery market for the U.S. reached $10.4 billion in 2004. Chocolate candy consumption (bars, boxes, bags, snack sizes, etc.) reached $4.2 billion in dollar sales and 3.3 billion in unit sales in 2004. Diet candy (low-carb and sugar free) was the fastest growing category in 2004, increasing 36 percent from 2003 to $257.5 million. The top four channels where candy is sold are grocery, drug, mass merchandiser, and convenience stores.

   Globally, the top confectionery marketers were Mars ($9.1 billion), Nestlé ($8.2 billion), and Cadbury Schweppes ($7.0 billion). The top three chocolate candy marketers in the U.S. for 2004, in terms of dollar sales, were Hershey's ($1.8 billion; 44%), Mars ($1.1 billion; 26%), and Nestlé ($369 million; 9%). The top candy bars sold are Mars M&Ms Chocolate Candies, Hershey's Milk Chocolate bar, Hershey's Kisses, Hershey's Reese's Peanut Butter Cups, and Mars Snickers Bar."[2]

4. **Spend 3 minutes** and ask students the following questions about their candy purchasing behavior:

   - Question 1: How many of you buy candy? Why?

     Answer: Students buy candy for a variety of reasons (taste, energy, holiday, etc.).

   - Question 2: What candy brands have you bought within the past week/month?

     Answer: Students will have bought candy from Hershey's, Mars, and Nestlé.

---

[2] "U.S. State of the Industry," *Candy Industry*, March 2005 (Stagnito Communications). See http://www.candyindustry.com/library.php?iss=2005/03.

• <u>Question 3</u>: Have you tried any new candy within the past 1-3 months? If so, what was it? Did you like it? How did you find out about it?

  <u>Answer</u>: Most likely, students will have tried a new candy product.

Designing a Candy Bar Handout

Slide 2

5. **Show Slide 2** and pass out the Designing a Candy Bar Handout.

6. Begin the ICA with the following statement:

   "Because teams are used marketing, what I'd like you to do now is get into the teams that we formed earlier."

7. Give the following instructions to complete this ICA:

"For the next **15 minutes**, your team will design a candy bar based on your personal experiences as candy bar consumers, the class discussion we had about the candy industry, and your new role as potential marketers. When designing your candy bar, be as creative as you can. However, the candy bar you design must answer the following questions:

a. **Where and to whom will your candy bar be sold?** The answer to this question will specify the geographic location (U.S., Europe, etc.) and the characteristics (age, gender, income, health-consciousness, etc.) of your target market segments. Provide a rationale for market segments you select.

b. **What is the product?** The answer to this question will specify the features, such as the ingredients, form, size, packaging, etc. and benefits of the candy bar you think are important to consumers. Provide a rationale for the product you create.

c. **How much will consumers pay for it?** The answer to this question will specify the price paid for the quantity received by consumers. Provide a rationale for the price you want to charge.

d. **How will consumers find out about it?** The answer to this question will specify the advertising methods and message you will use to communicate to consumers about the candy bar and the kinds of inducements (coupons, samples, etc.) you will offer them to try it. Provide a rationale for the promotions you want to use.

e. **Where will consumers buy it?** The answer to this question will specify the types of retail outlets or "place" where consumers in your target market are likely to buy the candy bar. Provide a rationale for the distribution channels you want to use.

f. **How is your candy bar different from those already on the market?** The answer to this question will specify the significant points of difference of your candy bar. Provide a rationale for why your candy bar is superior to those offered by the competition."

8. When the 15-minute time is up, **spend 5 minutes** and have one student from each of these teams take a marker/chalk and go to the easel and/or black/white board and write down their answers to the six sets of questions asked in the Designing a Candy Bar Marketing Program Handout.

9. **Spend 10 minutes** and discuss and compare the marketing programs that the student teams developed for their candy bars. Ask the following questions of the entire class for discussion and probe their responses:

    a. **What is the target market you selected?** Is it attractive enough (large, growing, etc.) to warrant the expense of a marketing effort?

    b. **What are the key features and benefits of your product?** Are they important to prospective customers? Can they form the basis of a message that can be effectively communicated?

    c. **What will you charge?** What is the price based on? Do you want to recover marketing costs quickly by charging a higher price or do you want to achieve larger sales earlier by charging a lower price?

    d. **How will you communicate to consumers?** What relatively inexpensive actions could you use to inform and induce prospective customers to try your product?

    e. **What retail outlets will sell your product?** Will you sell your product over the Internet? Why?

    f. **What are the significant points of difference of your product?** Does your product provide overall customer value?

Marketing Lessons. This ICA introduces students to the essential concepts of marketing that marketing and product managers deal with on a daily basis. Students should conclude that when developing a marketing program for a product, marketers must: (a) select a set of market segments to target; (b) specify the marketing mix; and (c) identify significant points of difference.

Websites. The three major candy marketers' websites are: Hershey's: www.hersheys.com; Mars: www.mars.com; and Nestlé: www.nestleusa.com.

Designing a Candy Bar Handout

MARKETING PROGRAM AND POINTS OF DIFFERENCE	WHERE AND TO WHOM WILL IT BE SOLD? (TARGET MARKET SEGMENTS)	
	Where?_____	To Whom?_____
What is it? (Product) Specify features, benefits, form, size, etc. and why		
How much will consumers pay for it? (Price) Specify cost and why		
How will consumers find out about it? (Promotion) Specify methods to inform and generate trial and why		
Where will consumers buy it? (Place) Specify types of retailers and why		
How is it different from others? (Points of Difference) Specify why it is superior to the competition		

CHAPTER 1: CREATING CUSTOMER RELATIONSHIPS AND VALUE THROUGH MARKETING

ICA 1-2: IN-CLASS ACTIVITY

What is Marketing?[1]

Learning Objective. To have students engage in the activities that comprise marketing.

Definitions. The following marketing terms are referred to in this in-class activity (ICA):

- Marketing: An organizational function and a set of processes for creating, communicating, and delivering value to customers and for managing customer relationships in ways that benefit the organization and its stakeholders.

- Marketing Mix: The marketing manager's controllable factors—product, price, promotion, and place—that can be used to solve a marketing problem.

- Marketing Program: A plan that integrates the marketing mix to provide a good, service, or idea to prospective buyers.

- Target Market: One or more specific groups of potential consumers toward which an organization directs its marketing program.

Nature of the Activity. To facilitate a class discussion of students' perceptions of marketing and to have them develop a simple marketing program to reach those market segments Rollerblade® has chosen to target within the inline skating industry.

Estimated Class Time. 20 minutes; 30 minutes if using optional material.

Materials Needed.

- The ICA01-1.doc Word, ICA01-1.ppt PowerPoint 2005RBBro.pdf Acrobat files contained in the ICA01-1 folder of the Instructor's CD #1 from the *Instructor's Survival Kit* box.

- Copies of the:
    a. 2005RBBro.pdf file (2005 Rollerblade Collection consumer brochure). See the enclosed Adobe Acrobat Portable Document Files (.pdf) in the 'pdf' folder within the ICA19-6 folder. [NOTE: You will need the Adobe Acrobat Reader to view and print the PDF documents. To download the latest version, go to www.adobe.com/products/acrobat.]
    b. Blank 2005 Rollerblade Collection: Segments, Benefits, Trends, and Marketing Program Handout (A): "Fitness/Recreation" and "Kids."
    c. Completed 2005 Rollerblade Collection: Segments, Benefits, Trends, and Marketing Program Answers Handout (A): "Fitness/Recreation" and "Kids."

---

[1] The authors wish to Nicholas Skally, Marketing and Public Relations Manager at Rollerblade, Inc., who assisted in the development of this ICA.

d.   OPTIONAL: Blank 2005 Rollerblade Collection: Segments, Benefits, Trends, and Marketing Program Handout (B): "Aggressive" and "Speed."

e.   OPTIONAL: Completed 2005 Rollerblade Collection: Segments, Benefits, Trends, and Marketing Program Answers Handout (B): "Aggressive" and "Speed."

- NOTE: Transparencies can be made of the handouts instead of making copies and using the PowerPoint presentation for those instructors who prefer this option.

Preparation Before Class. Follow the steps below:

1.   Read pp. 4-8, 16-19 of Chapter 1.

2.   Print, read, and if necessary, edit the ICA01-2.doc Word file.

3.   Print and/or review the PowerPoint slides from the ICA01-2.ppt PowerPoint file.

4.   Make copies of the:

a.   OPTIONAL: Selected pages from the 2005 Rollerblade Collection consumer brochure (see 2005RBBro.pdf file).

b.   Blank 2005 Rollerblade Collection: Segments, Benefits, Trends, and Marketing Program Handout (A) for each student. [(B) is OPTIONAL.]

c.   Completed 2005 Rollerblade Collection: Segments, Benefits, Trends, and Marketing Program Answers Handout (A) for each student. [(B) is OPTIONAL.]

5.   Skim the Rollerblade Video Case 1 on pp. 26-27 of *Marketing, 8th Edition*.

6.   OPTIONAL: Bookmark the Rollerblade (www.rollerblade.com) website on your classroom computer.

Instructions. Follow the steps below to conduct this ICA:

1.   Give the following mini-lecture about one's personal experiences with marketing:

"Each of you participates in the marketing process every day. Your experiences shopping for products gives you great insights into the world of marketing. As a result, you may already know many marketing terms, concepts, and principles."

2.   **Spend 2 minutes** and ask students what comes to their minds when they hear the term "marketing." If they have not yet read Chapter 1, they are likely to mention "advertising" or "selling." If they have read Chapter 1, they should mention the "four P's" or "marketing mix," "target markets," and/or "marketing program," etc.

3.   OPTIONAL: List the terms that students mention as a starting point for discussing the many activities that make up marketing. Write these on the board or a transparency.

4.   Form students into 4-person teams.

5. **Spend 1 minute** and give the following mini-lecture on inline skates and the marketing activities of Rollerblade:

"We will now turn our attention to the inline skate market and the activities that Rollerblade could use to reach its market segments. Rollerblade invented the inline skate in the early 1980s and has encouraged the 'fitness & fun' lifestyle ever since. In 2003, Rollerblade was purchased by Tecnica SPA, an Italian sporting goods firm and makers of Nordica ski equipment. According to Nicholas Skally, Rollerblade's Marketing & Public Relations Manager, 'Tecnica's sporting goods expertise will be an incredible asset to Rollerblade as it continues to lead the inline skating industry.'

Rollerblade develops several lines of inline skates to target specific customer groups. What I'd like to do now is ask about your experiences or perceptions of inline skating."

6. **Spend 2 minutes** and have students discuss their inline skating behavior and perceptions among team members. Then, have 3 to 5 students cite examples of marketing activities used by firms like Rollerblade or others in the inline skating industry (Salomon, UltraWheels, etc.) based on their personal inline skating experiences, advertisements seen, or visits to sporting goods stores.

7. Begin the ICA with the following statement:

"We will now discuss the inline skate market and the marketing programs that Rollerblade could use to reach its chosen target market segments."

2005 Rollerblade Consumer brochure

Slide 2

8. **Show Slide 2**: 2005 Rollerblade Consumer Brochure. [OPTIONAL: Open the 2005RBBro.pdf Acrobat file that contains this brochure and briefly go over the 12 pages.] This brochure describes the consumer market segments Rollerblade has targeted for 2005 and the products it has developed to meet the needs of these segments.

9. Pass out copies of the blank 2005 Rollerblade Collection: Segments, Benefits, Trends, and Marketing Program Handout (A) for the "Fitness/Recreation" and "Kids" segments.

10a. **Show Slide 3**: The Fitness/Recreation Segment. This segment consists of consumers who want an aerobic workout similar to running, cycling, etc. while enjoying the social aspect of inline skating.

10b. **Show Slide 4**: Aero 90 (Fitness) and Zetrablade (Recreation) Skates. Rollerblade designed the Aero 90 to meet the performance, fit, and lightweight needs of "Fitness" consumers and developed the Zetrablade to meet the fit, comfort, and price needs of "Recreation" consumers.

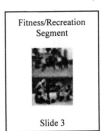

Fitness/Recreation Segment

Slide 3

Aero 90 & Zetrablade inline skates

Slide 4

11. Have student teams **spend 5 minutes** to complete the "Fitness/Recreation" column of the 2005 Rollerblade Collection: Segments, Benefits, Trends, and Marketing Program Handout (A). Inline skates for women (designated by a "W") are very similar to those made for men except that there are different color schemes, the sizes are a bit smaller, and there is more cushioning material. Therefore, Rollerblade does NOT segment nor develop a specific marketing program to target women inline skaters.

Based on their marketing and personal experiences, have the student teams develop a simple marketing program that targets the "Fitness/Recreation" market segment by identifying the:

- "Benefits" and "Trends" that impact this segment.
- "Product" features important to this segment.
- "Prices" this segment might be willing to pay.
- "Promotions" used to communicate to this segment.
- "Places" where this segment is likely to purchase inline skates.

12a. **Show Slide 5**: The Kids Segment. Inline skates designed for the "Kids" segment must be different than those created for adults. Kids feet need support. Also, parents don't want to spend too much for kids inline skates because they will quickly outgrow them.

12b. **Show Slide 6**: Microblade II Inline Skate (Kids Segment). Rollerblade has designed the Microblade II inline skate to meet the support, growth, price, and other needs of the "Kids" market segment. The Microblade is extendible up to four sizes to match the growth in their feet.

Kids Segment

Slide 5

Microblade II
inline skate

Slide 6

13. Have student teams **spend 5 minutes** to complete the "Kids" column of the 2005 Rollerblade Collection: Segments, Benefits, Trends, and Marketing Program Handout (A).

Ask student teams to develop a simple marketing program that targets the "Kids" market segment by identifying the:

- "Benefits" and "Trends" that impact this segment.
- "Product" features important to this segment.
- "Prices" this segment might be willing to pay.
- "Promotions" used to communicate to this segment.
- "Places" where this segment is likely to purchase inline skates.

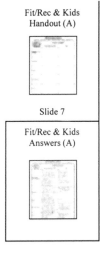

Fit/Rec & Kids
Handout (A)

Slide 7

Fit/Rec & Kids
Answers (A)

14. **Show Slide 7**: 2005 Rollerblade Collection: Segments, Benefits, Trends, and Marketing Program Handout (A). **Spend 5 minutes** discussing the benefits, trends, and marketing programs the student teams developed to reach the "Fitness/Recreation" and "Kids" target market segments.

15. Pass out copies of the completed 2005 Rollerblade Collection: Segments, Benefits, Trends, and Marketing Program Answers Handout (A). **Spend 5 minutes** and discuss the marketing programs that Rollerblade has developed to reach the "Fitness/Recreation" and "Kids" market segments. Compare Rollerblade's marketing programs with those of the student teams.

OPTIONAL:

Aggressive/Speed
Handout (B)

16. Pass out copies of the blank 2005 Rollerblade Collection: Segments, Benefits, Trends, and Marketing Program Handout (B) for the "Aggressive" and "Speed" segments.

17a. **Show Slide 8**: The Aggressive (Street/Vert) Segment. Inline skates designed for the "Aggressive" segment are usually endorsed by athletes. Consumers in this segment want high performance, durability, and style. Price is not a significant issue.

17b. **Show Slide 9**: TRS Treseder Inline Skate (Aggressive Segment). Rollerblade designed the TRS line to meet the performance, style, price, and other needs of the "Aggressive" market segment. The TRS Treseder is endorsed by one of the top professionals (Tony Treseder) in this inline skating genre who has competed in ESPN's X-Games.

Aggressive
Segment

Slide 8

TRS Treseder
inline skate

Slide 9

Aggressive/Speed
Handout (B)

18. Have student teams **spend 2 minutes** to complete the "Aggressive" column of the 2005 Rollerblade Collection: Segments, Benefits, Trends, and Marketing Program Handout (B).

Ask student teams to develop a simple marketing program that targets the "Aggressive" market segment by identifying the:

- "Benefits" and "Trends" that impact this segment.
- "Product" features important to this segment.
- "Prices" this segment might be willing to pay.
- "Promotions" used to communicate to this segment.
- "Places" where this segment is likely to purchase inline skates.

19a. **Show Slide 10**: The Speed Segment. Inline skates designed for the "Speed" segment must incorporate the latest technology for performance and fit. Price is of little concern for this segment.

19b. **Show Slide 11**: The Rollerblade Problade 100 Inline Skate (Speed Segment). Rollerblade has designed the Roadrunner inline skate to meet the technological needs for performance and fit of the "Speed" market segment.

Speed Segment

Slide 10

Problade 100 inline skate

Slide 11

Aggressive/Speed Handout (B)

20. Have student teams **spend 2 minutes** to complete the "Speed" column of the 2005 Rollerblade Collection: Segments, Benefits, Trends, and Marketing Program Handout (B).

Ask student teams to develop a simple marketing program that targets the "Speed" market segment by identifying the:

- "Benefits" and "Trends" that impact this segment.
- "Product" features important to this segment.
- "Prices" this segment might be willing to pay.
- "Promotions" used to communicate to this segment.
- "Places" where this segment is likely to purchase inline skates.

21. **Show Slide 12**: 2005 Rollerblade Collection: Segments, Benefits, Trends, and Marketing Program Handout (B): "Aggressive" and "Speed" Segments. **Spend 3 minutes** discussing the benefits, trends, and marketing programs the student teams developed to reach these two target market segments.

Aggressive/Speed Answers (B)

22. Pass out copies of the completed 2005 Rollerblade Collection: Segments, Benefits, Trends, and Marketing Program Answers Handout (B). **Spend 2 minutes** and discuss the marketing programs that Rollerblade has developed to reach the "Aggressive" and "Speed" market segments. Compare Rollerblade's marketing programs with those of the student teams.

Marketing Lessons. This ICA introduces students to the marketing mix. Students should conclude that: (a) marketing is much more than their initial perceptions; (b) they already know about marketing from their experiences as consumers; (c) most firms develop unique marketing programs to meet the specific needs of each targeted market segment; and (d) firms select specific segments to target due to resource and marketing considerations.

Website. Rollerblade's website is www.rollerblade.com.

BENEFITS, TRENDS, AND MARKETING PROGRAM	MARKET SEGMENT	
	FITNESS/RECREATION	KIDS
BENEFITS AND TRENDS		
PRODUCT		
PRICE		
PROMOTION		
PLACE		

ICA 1-2

OPTIONAL: 2005 Rollerblade Collection
Segments, Benefits, Trends, and Marketing Program Handout (B)

BENEFITS, TRENDS, AND MARKETING PROGRAM	MARKET SEGMENT	
	AGGRESSIVE (STREET/VERT)	SPEED
BENEFITS AND TRENDS		
PRODUCT		
PRICE		
PROMOTION		
PLACE		

2005 Rollerblade Collection
Segments, Benefits, Trends, and Marketing Program Answers Handout (A)

BENEFITS, TRENDS, AND MARKETING PROGRAM	MARKET SEGMENT	
	FITNESS/RECREATION	KIDS
BENEFITS AND TRENDS	• Fun • Get a serious workout (Fit) • Cross-train for hockey, ice skating, & figure skating (Fit) • Large and growing segment • Focus on technology for greater comfort and movement in ankles and legs (Rec) • Ultra-light weight (Fit) • Premium components (Fit) • Customizable frames (Fit) • Value-oriented (Rec) • ABT Lite braking (Rec)	• Fun • Fitness/coordination • Sports conditioning • Self-confidence • Growing segment • No ice skating in summer • Durability • Value-conscious • Protective gear bought in conjunction with skates • Skates adjust as kid grows
PRODUCT	[NOTE: W = also in women's] • RB Models (Fit): Lightning—10, 08/W, 06/W, 04/W; Aero—90/W, 10/W, 8/W, 6/W • RB Models (Rec): Zetrablade/W • Most firms have several skates in its product line • Other marketers: Chicago; Hypno; K2; Nike; Roces; Salomon; UltraWheels	• RB Model: Microblade XT II • Other marketers: Chicago; Corr, K2; Nike; Razors; Roces; Salomon; UltraWheels; private label
PRICE	• MSRPs (Fit): $150 - $400 • MSRPs (Rec): $50 - $200	• MSRPs: $20 - $150
PROMOTION	• 10-week Workout Plan and Calorie Usage Chart on website • Target health & fitness mags • E-marketing thru website • Point-of-purchase display • Sponsor inline skating marathons (Fit) and Free Skate Lesson (Rec) • Skating for Fitness (Fit/Rec)	• Show kids inline skating and having fun • Developed over 750 Skate in School program to boost youth fitness and self-esteem • Developed 18 Blade Schools™ to teach kids how to skate
PLACE	• Specialty inline skate shops • Sporting goods stores • Mass-merchandisers (Rec) • The Internet	• Specialty inline skate shops • Sporting goods stores • Mass-merchandisers • The Internet

BENEFITS, TRENDS, AND MARKETING PROGRAM	MARKET SEGMENT	
	AGGRESSIVE (STREET/VERT)	SPEED
BENEFITS AND TRENDS	• Comfort • High tech features • Performance • Image • Style similar to skateboard shoes • New skate parks opening • Now a sport: Gravity Games & ESPN X Games	• A small segment • Excitement • More product knowledge required • Probably started as a "fitness" inline or ice speed skater • Spends much more on equipment • Focus on technology that allows both power transmission and control
PRODUCT	• RB Models: TRS Treseder; TRS Broskow; TRS Alpha; TRS Downtown; TRS Jr. • Most firms have 1 to 3 skates in its product line • Other marketers: Corr; K2; Razors; Remz; Roces; Salomon; UltraWheels; USD	• RB Models: Problade 100; 84; Lightning 10 • "Speed" inline skates have 5 or 4 wheels • Other marketers: Bont; Hyper; K2; Riedell; Salomon; Simmons Racing; Tour; Verducci
PRICE	• MSRPs: $80 - $350	• MSRPs: $350 - $1,200
PROMOTION	• Inline skating events (skate ramps, street skating, etc.) • Sponsored athletes • Ads in local publications • E-mail customers about new products • Point-of-purchase display • Sponsor X- Games • Ads/signs in video games • www.teamtrs.com website	• Sponsor national & international team competitions/events • Sponsor athletes • www.teamrollerblade.com website
PLACE	• Specialty inline skate shops • Sporting goods stores • The Internet	• Specialty inline skate shops—sales reps require more product knowledge • The Internet

CHAPTER 1: CREATING CUSTOMER RELATIONSHIPS AND VALUE THROUGH MARKETING

ICA 1-3: IN-CLASS ACTIVITY

What Makes A Better Mousetrap? (Part 1)[1]

Learning Objectives. To have students (1) discover the importance of "points of difference" in meeting consumer wants and needs and (2) see how they vary by market segment.

Definitions. The following marketing terms are referred to in this in-class activity (ICA):

- Customer Value: The unique combination of benefits received by targeted buyers that includes quality, price, convenience, on-time delivery, and both before-sale and after-sale service.

- Market Segments: The relatively homogeneous groups of prospective buyers that result from the market segmentation process.

- Points of Difference: Those characteristics of a product that make it superior to competitive substitutes.

Nature of the Activity. To have students do in-class "marketing research" on why a better mousetrap failed more than two decades ago.

Estimated Class Time. 20 minutes.

Materials Needed.

- The original wooden Victor® Metal Bait Pedal and Live Catch mousetraps from the *Instructor's Survival Kit* box.

- The ICA01-3.doc Word and ICA01-3.ppt PowerPoint files contained in the ICA01-3 folder of the Instructor's CD#1 from the *Instructor's Survival Kit* box.

Preparation Before Class. Follow the steps below:

1. Read pp. 12-15 of Chapter 1 and pp. 234-241 of Chapter 9.

2. Print, read, and if necessary, edit the ICA1-3.doc Word file.

3. Print and/or review the slides from ICA1-3.ppt PowerPoint file.

4. OPTIONAL: Bookmark the Victor® Pest (www.victorpest.com) website on your classroom computer.

---

[1] The authors wish to thank Karolyn Warfel and Betsy Boyer of the Woodstream Corp. who assisted in the development of this ICA.

Instructions. Follow the steps below to conduct this ICA:

Slide 2

1. **Show Slide 2**: Ralph Waldo Emerson Quote and give the following mini-lecture:

   "If a man...makes a better mousetrap, the world will beat a path to his door."—Ralph Waldo Emerson

   Let's excuse Mr. Emerson for his sexist statement, written over a century ago! But let's see if he was right!"

Slide 3

2. **Show Slide 3** and continue with the following mini-lecture:

   "Over 25 years ago, Dick Woolworth, president of the Woodstream Corp., decided to take Emerson's adage to heart. Woodstream Corp.'s product was a 100 year-old wooden mousetrap that sold under the Victor® brand name in which peanut butter or cheese was placed on the metal bait pedal connected to the spring-loaded snap trap bar."

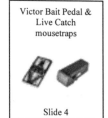

Slide 4

3. **Show Slide 4** and pass around the Victor® Metal Bait Pedal and Live Catch mousetraps obtained from the *Instructor's Survival Kit* box.

4. Continue with the following mini-lecture:

   "Woolworth decided that what the company needed to do was to build 'a better mousetrap and wait for the world to beat a path to its door.' He asked his engineers and scientists to study the eating, sleeping, and crawling habits of mice. They did and came up with a better mousetrap—one made of plastic. [NOTE: The Live Catch mousetrap being passed around was NOT this plastic trap but is being used here FOR EDUCATIONAL PURPOSES ONLY.]

   If we compare the new versus the old, the original Victor® Metal Bait Pedal trap sold in a package of 2 for 15 cents and was moderately efficient. The plastic trap sold individually for 25 cents and was very efficient. Thus, if 100 mice stepped on the old wooden trap, assume that 50 got caught (50% efficiency) while with the new plastic trap, assume that 90 got caught (90% efficiency). Woodstream Corp. introduced the new plastic trap in stores across the country. Suppose that the following problem emerged: Sales of the new better, plastic mousetrap did not meet sales expectations! Why do you suppose that happened?"

5. Form students into 4-person teams.

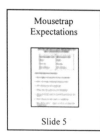

Slide 5

6. **Show Slide 5**: Why Did the New Plastic Mousetrap Not Meet Sales Expectations?

7. **Spend 10 minutes** and have students to answer the following questions:

- **Question 1: What triggers the decision to buy a mousetrap?**

  Answer: Seeing nibbled boxes of cereal or mouse droppings on the floor triggers the "buy" decision.

- **Question 2: Who in the family makes the decision to buy?**

  Answer: The decision maker is the person most bothered by the mouse, often the "Mom" of 25 years ago, when this case occurs.

- **Question 3: Who actually buys the mousetrap?**

  Answer: The purchaser is the person asked to "get rid of the problem," often the "Dad" of 25 years ago, when the case occurred.

- **Question 4: Where does the person buy the mousetrap?**

  Answers: Mousetraps might be purchased in hardware stores (Ace), supermarkets (Safeway), mass-merchandisers (Wal-Mart, Target), home improvement stores (Home Depot), or the Internet (BE Atlas). This points out the need for different outlets for different buyers in the family, or different market segments.

- **Question 5: Who in the family uses the mousetrap and how do they use it?**

  Answers: This is the key question and should turn up two distinct market segments: (1) the "disposers," who dispose of the dead mouse and the trap by throwing both of them into the trash, and (2) the "reusers," who throw the dead mouse into the trash but reuse the trap.

- **Question 6: What features do users want in a mousetrap?**

  Answers: The "disposer" market segment wants a cheap and relatively efficient way to handle its mouse problem. So the important "points of difference" in its buying decision are low-cost and disposability. The "reuser" segment wants greater efficiency in resolving its persistent mouse problem and may be willing to pay more for a trap as a result.

  The key message: What potential buyers see as "better" is more important than what the scientists and engineers designing the product see as "better."

- **Question 7: Why did sales of the "better" plastic mousetrap not meet sales expectations?** [Again, the Live Catch mousetrap is used here for educational purposes only.]

  Answers: Let the students suggest their answers and write them down on the board.

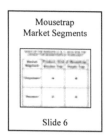

8. **Show Slide 6**: Mousetrap Market Segments and discuss the answers to Question 7:

"Twenty years ago, "efficiency" (the key 'point of difference' or benefit) of the plastic trap was not an important feature to most buyers. The "disposer" segment was especially reluctant to throw the dead mouse and the 25-cent plastic trap into the trash, but not at all hesitant to throw away the 7.5-cent wooden trap. If the wooden trap missed the mouse, these users just reset it. So the wooden trap provided greater **customer value** for most buyers. And because the largest market segments were 'A' and 'C' in the table above, the new 'better' plastic traps gathered dust on retail shelves across the country. The plastic traps also had a very practical problem: disposing of a live mouse can be tricky (if the lid opened, the mouse may jump out) or time consuming (need to find a place far away from home to release the mouse)."

[NOTE: Slide 6 is really a "market-product grid" that will be introduced in Chapter 9. However, this tool can help in this ICA since it allows students to answer the question: "What do we sell to whom?"]

Marketing Lessons. Customers define what a "better" product is and not the seller or its engineers! So, in a sense, Mr. Emerson was wrong! Key features or "points of difference" in the product provide customer value to users or market segments. These "points of difference" must be important to consumers and communicated to them in terms of: (1) benefits to customers, (2) advantages relative to substitute products from competitors, and (3) features, which are given to the firm's R&D engineers. Different market segments of buyers exist with different needs, but sometimes it is not possible to reach tiny market segments profitably.

Website. To view Woodstream Corp.'s current product line of Victor® Brand Mousetraps, go to www.victorpest.com.

WHY DID THE NEW PLASTIC MOUSETRAP NOT MEET SALES EXPECTATIONS?

OLD WOODEN TRAP	NEW PLASTIC TRAP
Wood	Plastic
2 for 15¢	25¢ each
50% efficiency	90% efficiency

Some Key Marketing Questions

1. What triggers the decision to buy a mousetrap?

2. Who in the family makes the decision to buy?

3. Who actually buys the mousetrap?

4. Where does the person buy the mousetrap?

5. Who in the family uses the mousetrap and how do they use it?

6. What features do users want in a mousetrap?

7. Why did the "better" plastic mousetrap not meet sales expectations?

ICA 1-3

WHICH OF THE MARKETS (A, B, C, OR D) WAS THE LARGEST FOR MOUSETRAPS 25 YEARS AGO?

Market Segment	Product: Kind of Mousetrap	
	Wooden Trap	Plastic Trap
"Disposers"	A	B
"Reusers"	C	D

CHAPTER 1: CREATING CUSTOMER RELATIONSHIPS AND VALUE THROUGH MARKETING

ICA 1-4: IN-CLASS ACTIVITY

The Five Hats of a Marketing or Product Manager[1]

Learning Objective. To illustrate the roles and responsibilities of a marketing or product manager that are necessary to develop successful marketing plans.

Definitions. The following marketing terms are referred to in this in-class activity (ICA):

- Marketing/Product Manager: A person who plans, implements, and controls the annual and long-range plans for the markets and products for which he or she is responsible.

- Marketing Plan: A road map for the marketing activities of an organization for a specified future period of time, such as one year or five years.

- Situation Analysis: Taking stock of where a firm or product has been recently, where it is now, and where it is headed in terms of the organization's plans and the external factors and trends affecting it.

- SWOT Analysis: An acronym describing an organization's appraisal of its internal **S**trengths and **W**eaknesses and its external **O**pportunities and **T**hreats.

Nature of the Activity. To have students discuss five roles and responsibilities of a marketing or product manager that are necessary to develop successful marketing plans.

Estimated Class Time. 15 minutes.

Materials Needed.

- The ICA01-4.doc Word and ICA01-4.ppt PowerPoint files contained in the ICA01-4 folder of the Instructor's CD #1 from the *Instructor's Survival Kit* box.

Preparation Before Class. Follow the steps below:

1. Read pp. 41-49 of Chapter 2 and p. 602 of Chapter 22.

2. Print, read, and if necessary, edit ICA01-4.doc Word file.

3. Print and/or review the PowerPoint slides from ICA01-4.ppt PowerPoint file.

---

[1] The authors wish to thank Mr. James Spiers, Senior Lecturer in the Department of Marketing of the W. P. Carey School of Business at Arizona State University, for developing this ICA.

Instructions. Follow the steps below to conduct this ICA:

1. Divide the class into five sets of teams and assign each student to a team based on the following types of "Hats."

   - **Team 1**: The Explorer's Hat.
   - **Team 2**: The Court Jester Hat.
   - **Team 3**: The Artist's Beret.
   - **Team 4**: The Judicial Wig.
   - **Team 5**: The Warrior Helmet.

2. Give students the following mini-lecture that describes a marketing and/or product manager in an organization:

   "The function of a marketing or product manager is to plan, implement, and control the annual and long-range plans for which he or she is responsible. As a result, they 'wear' at least five 'hats' that correspond to the roles they play in an organization. Each role has its own set of responsibilities that must be fulfilled to develop successful marketing plans. We will now discuss the role that is depicted by each of these five "hats" and the responsibilities that are associated with them."

   [NOTE: These "hats" are worn by James Spiers, Senior Lecturer in the Department of Marketing of the W. P. Carey School of Business at Arizona State University. During the Fall and Spring semesters, he teaches Principles of Marketing to sections of 350 students! To engage them, he has developed several creative strategies, such as this one, to stimulate student interest in marketing as a career.]

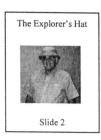

The Explorer's Hat

Slide 2

3. **Show Slide 2**: Team 1—The Explorer's Hat. Ask Team 1 the following questions:

   - Question 1: As one of the roles of a marketing or product manager, what do you think the Explorer's Hat symbolizes?

     Answer: This is a symbol that represents brave explorers going into the uncharted, dangerous areas of a marketplace.

   - Question 2: What are some of the responsibilities of the market or product manager that are described by The Explorer's Hat?

     Answers: Marketing or product managers must find out what is going on in the marketplace within which they operate. They must ask the tough questions, like:

     - Why do we do what we do the way we do it?
     - Are there other ways that might be better?
     - What are the trends?
     - What is the competition doing and how successful are they?
     - Do we understand what the opportunities and problems are?

These are some of the questions that are asked and answered in a situation (SWOT) analysis. Some businesses don't like to change. In the Army, it was only done the Army Way! It is vitally important to gather information that will give a good picture of the marketplace as it stands now. To be good at this, you will need a good staff to help in the research process. They need to be trained and motivated to get you that kind of information. This is the one "hat" that you will wear most of the time because you are always looking to identify both opportunities and problems to keep ahead of the competition.

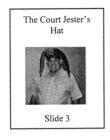

The Court Jester's Hat

Slide 3

4. **Show Slide 3**: Team 2—The Court Jester's Hat. Ask Team 2 the following questions:

- Question 1: As one of the roles of a marketing or product manager, what does The Court Jester's Hat symbolize?

  Answer: This is a symbol of the type of atmosphere that is needed to have creative and productive juices flow. It is not about telling jokes and laughing but creating a work place environment where people want to come to each day.

- Question 2: What are some of the responsibilities of the market or product manager that are described by The Court Jester's Hat?

  Answers: Increased morale means more creativity and greater productivity. Employees of the Seattle Fish Company "play around" but get the job done. As a marketing or product manager, what can you do to make the work place fun?

  "Brainstorm" this in the class as well as illustrate this through your own knowledge and experience.

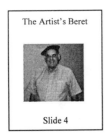

The Artist's Beret

Slide 4

5. **Show Slide 4**: Team 3—The Artist's Beret. Ask Team 3 the following questions:

- Question 1: As one of the roles of a marketing or product manager, what does The Artist's Beret symbolize?

  Answer: This is a symbol of the creative ideas that you as a marketing or product come up with yourself or in a team.

- Question 2: What are some of the responsibilities of the market or product manager that are described by The Artist's Beret?

  Answers: As a manger, you need to brainstorm with your staff to come up with the "ideas" that would help you solve a problem or take advantage of an opportunity. To start, take the information collected while wearing The Explorer's Hat. Then, you put on the Artist's Beret to generate all the possible ideas. At the end of the process, you will need to reduce the list of "ideas" down to 2-3-4 main "ideas" by combining ideas or expanding on some of the original thoughts. It is a creative and iterative process.

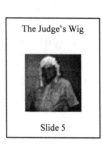

The Judge's Wig

Slide 5

6. **Show Slide 5**: Team 4—The Judge's Wig. Ask Team 4 the following questions:

• Question 1: As one of the roles of a marketing or product manager, what does The Judge's Wig symbolize?

Answer: You are like a judge sitting in judgment of all the marketing facts related to your market or product as you understand them.

• Question 2: What are some of the responsibilities of the market or product manager that are described by The Judge's Wig?

Answers: As the marketing or product manager, you are required to choose the best "idea" and develop it into a marketing plan. You need to understand all of the strategic marketing issues of your organization. Not all firms can use the same strategy successfully because of your firm's resource situation and your staff's ability to plan.

The Warrior's Helmet

Slide 6

7. **Show Slide 6**: Team 5—The Warrior's Helmet. Ask Team 5 the following questions:

• Question 1: As one of the roles of a marketing or product manager, what does The Warrior's Helmet symbolize?

Answer: A marketing or product manager is the leader of the team that develops, implements, and evaluates the marketing plans for its products. Once a proposed marketing plan has been developed, a marketing or product manager must be ready to defend it to the "decision makers," consisting of the senior management within the organization.

• Question 2: What are some of the responsibilities of the market or product manager that are described by The Warrior's Helmet?

Answers: To provide a vigorous defense to senior management, a marketing or product manager needs to understand the marketing plan inside and out and believe in it. One of the first areas of discussion with senior management concerns the budget: How much will the marketing plan for a product cost to develop, implement, and evaluate (and why so much!)? Then, once implemented, you essentially start the entire process over by putting The Explorer's Hat back on to monitor and control the execution of the marketing plan.

Marketing Lessons. This activity identifies the critical roles and responsibilities a marketing or product manager has within an organization. He or she must wear these "hats" to successfully develop a marketing plan and engage in the strategic marketing process.

THE EXPLORER'S HAT

THE COURT JESTER HAT

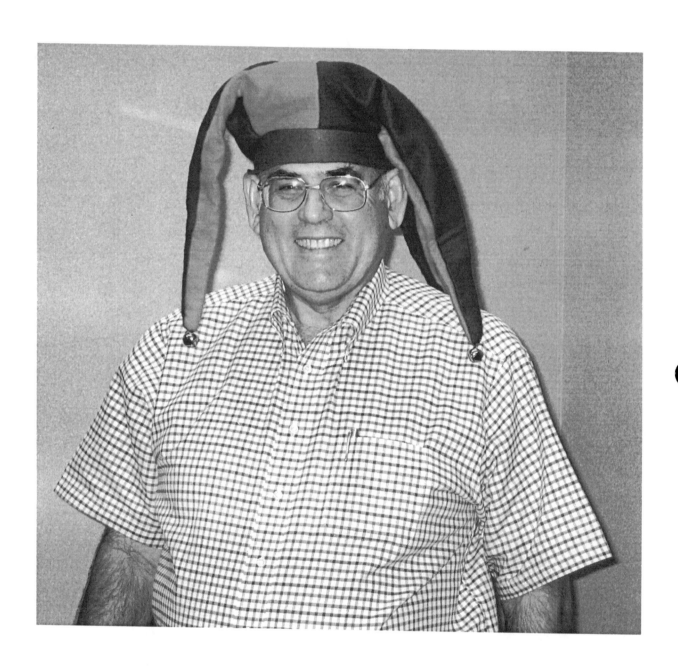

THE ARTIST'S BERET

THE JUDICIAL WIG

THE WARRIOR HAT

ICA 1-4

CHAPTER 1: CREATING CUSTOMER RELATIONSHIPS AND VALUE THROUGH MARKETING

ICA 1-5: IN-CLASS ACTIVITY

The Card Game: Letting Students "Do" Marketing[1]

Learning Objectives. To (1) illustrate the marketplace and the idea of exchange and (2) discuss how the marketing mix elements (the "4 P's") relate to the requirements of the marketing process.

Definitions. The following marketing terms are referred to in this in-class activity (ICA):

- Exchange: The trade of things of value between buyer and seller so that each is better off after the trade.

- Market: People with both the desire and the ability to buy a specific product.

- Marketing: An organizational function and a set of processes for creating, communicating, and delivering value to customers and for managing customer relationships in ways that benefit the organization and its stakeholders.

- Marketing Mix: The marketing manager's controllable factors—product, price, promotion, and place—that can be used to solve a marketing problem.

Nature of the Activity. To have students experience the dynamics that characterize a market and identify the marketing mix elements used to attract prospective buyers so that they will engage in exchange relationships that are mutually beneficial to each.

Estimated Class Time. 30 minutes, which consists of:

- 15 minutes for the activity.

- 15 minutes for the class discussion.

Materials Needed.

- The ICA01-5.doc Word and ICA01-5.ppt PowerPoint files contained in the ICA01-5 folder of the Instructor's CD #1 from the *Instructor's Survival Kit* box.

- Decks of playing cards, which is based on the number of student teams created for this ICA, which in turn is based on the number of students in the class. As a rule, **one (1) deck of playing cards is required for every 4 student teams**, assuming each team consists of 6 students. Thus, depending on the class size, the instructor may have to obtain or purchase several decks of playing cards to conduct this ICA. These decks can be purchased at toy stores like Toys 'Я' Us or game retailers like Games by James.

---

[1] The authors wish to thank Mr. James Spiers, Senior Lecturer in the Department of Marketing of the W. P. Carey School of Business at Arizona State University, for developing this ICA.

To calculate the number of decks needed, use the following formula:

$$\text{\# of decks} = \frac{\text{\# of students teams}}{4}$$

$$\text{\# of decks} = \frac{(\text{class size} \div \text{\# of students per team})}{4}$$

Example: Based on the requirement of 6 students per team, if the class size is 48 students, the number of decks of playing cards needed is 2:

# of decks = [(48 ÷ 6) ÷ 4] = 8 ÷ 4 = 2

[NOTE: For small class sizes, the instructor may want to have 3 students per team.]

If the number of student teams calculated has a remainder, round the number of student teams **DOWN** to the nearest whole number (e.g. if there are 50 students in the class and you want 6 students per team, the calculated number of student teams is 8.3. Round down to 8 student teams and assign the 2 remaining students to a team.

If the number of decks calculated has a remainder, round **UP** to the nearest whole number (e.g. if 3.5 decks is calculated, 4 decks are actually needed).

- The class roster to determine the class size and calculate the number of student teams.

- Slips of paper (such as those made from Sheet #1 and Sheet #2 below) equal to the number of students listed in the class roster.

- Blank placards (see below) equal to the number of student teams that will participate in the ICA.

- Tape (masking or duct) to affix the placards or easel paper to the classroom walls.

- OPTIONAL: Copies of The Card Game Objectives.

- OPTIONAL: A black marker or set of colored markers.

- OPTIONAL: A "prize" for the winner of The Card Game (such as a candy bar).

Preparation Before Class. Follow the steps below:

1. Read pp. 9-10, 14 of Chapter 1.

2. Print, read, and if necessary, edit ICA01-5.doc Word file.

3. Print and/or review the PowerPoint slides from ICA01-5.ppt PowerPoint file.

4. Determine the number of students that will participate in the ICA based on the latest class roster available. Then, decide whether you want each team to have either 3 or 6 students. Finally, calculate the number of student teams needed and round **down** if a remainder exists (see the formula above)..

5. Calculate the number of decks of playing cards that will be required based on the formula specified above and round **up** if a remainder exists. To obtain the required number of decks of playing cards, go to your local toy store or games retailer. If uncertain, ask for the "poker" size of either the Bee®, Bicycle®, or Hoyle® brand from The U. S. Playing Card Co. A deck of cards typically costs $2.00 to $3.50 per deck, depending on the quality.

6. Revise the "Teams" column in The Card Game Objectives (see below) or the PowerPoint presentation (see ICA01-5.ppt) that you want to use in the classroom to show the students what their objective will be for The Card Game. **Only this column can be edited!** The assignment of teams to obtain a given suit is based on the number of decks needed.

Recall that one (1) deck of playing cards is needed for every four (4) teams, with 2 decks as the minimum. Therefore, if 2 decks are needed, then 8 student teams are required. Thus, as the following table shows, The Card Game Objective for Teams 1-2 will be to obtain a straight flush of hearts (♥); Teams 3-4 will obtain spades (♠), Teams 5-6 will obtain diamonds (♦), and Teams 7-8 will obtain clubs (♣). However, if 5 decks are needed, then The Card Game Objective for Teams 1-5 will be to obtain a straight flush of hearts; Teams 6-10 will obtain spades, etc.

The Card Game Objective by Suit for Selected Teams

Number of Decks Needed	♥	♠	♦	♣
2	Teams 1-2	Teams 3-4	Teams 5-6	Teams 7-8
3	Teams 1-3	Teams 4-6	Teams 7-9	Teams 10-12
4	Teams 1-4	Teams 5-8	Teams 9-12	Teams 13-16
5	Teams 1-5	Teams 6-10	Teams 11-15	Teams 16-20
6	Teams 1-6	Teams 7-12	Teams 13-18	Teams 19-24
7	Teams 1-7	Teams 8-14	Teams 15-21	Teams 22-28
8	Teams 1-8	Teams 9-16	Teams 17-24	Teams 25-32
9	Teams 1-9	Teams 10-18	Teams 19-27	Teams 28-36
10	Teams 1-10	Teams 11-20	Teams 21-30	Teams 31-40

Once you have identified the number of decks needed, type in the appropriate range of team numbers in each row of the "Teams" column in The Card Game Objectives or the PowerPoint presentation (see ICA01-5.ppt).

7. Go to the Slips of Paper Template (see below) and print out six (6) copies (based on 6 students per team or 3 copies if you have only 3 students per team) of Sheet #1 if you have up to 20 student teams for this ICA or print 6 copies of both Sheet #1 and Sheet #2 if you have up to 40 student teams. Next, use a paper cutter or scissors and cut the Sheet #1 (and Sheet #2 if needed) print outs into individual square slips of paper with a number. The total number of slips of paper will equal the total number of students reported in the class roster (e.g. 50 students will require 50 slips of paper).

   OPTIONAL: Take blank pieces of copy paper and cut them up into slips of paper that will total the number of students reported in the class roster (e.g. 50 students will require 50 slips of paper). On these slips of paper, take a marker and write down team numbers in sequential order based on the total number of students teams calculated for the ICA (e.g. if there are 8 teams, write a '1' on the first slip of paper, a '2' on the next slip,…and an '8' on the 8th slip. Repeat the process another 5 times if there are 6 students per team (or 2 times if 3 students per team) until all the slips of paper have a team number on them.

8. Go to the Placards Template (see below) and print a copy of the placard with the #1 on it. Next, using the mouse, select (or highlight) the '1' and change it to a '2'. Then, print a copy of this placard. Repeat the process until you have created and printed a set of placards that total the number of student teams needed for this ICA.

   OPTIONAL: On sheets of easel paper, take a marker and write down team numbers in sequential order based on the total number of student teams calculated for the ICA.

9. When you get to the classroom, affix each placard/paper to the classroom wall equidistant (or some distance) from one another using masking or duct tape.

10. Take the decks of playing cards and remove the "Jokers" from ALL the decks.

Instructions. Follow the steps below to conduct this ICA:

1. Prior to the beginning of class, select one or two students to shuffle the decks of cards and then deal them out into plies based on the number of student teams. [NOTE: Each pile should have 13 cards.]

2. As students enter the classroom, hand each one the slip of paper that represents an assigned team number. These slips of paper MUST be handed out sequentially based on the number of teams calculated prior to the beginning of class.

3. Have students get out of their seats and stand by the placard on the classroom wall that has their team number.

4. Have a representative from each team come to the table where the piles of cards are located to pick up one pile and verify that it has 13 cards in it.

The Card Game
Objectives

Slide 2

5. **Show Slide 2** (as revised) that shows each student team what its objective will be when playing The Card Game. Essentially, ¼ of the teams will obtain a straight flush of hearts (♥), ¼ will obtain a straight flush of spades (♠), ¼ will obtain a straight flush of diamonds (♦), and the last ¼ will obtain a straight flush of clubs (♣).

6. Give students the following instructions on how to play The Card Game:

"Each pile of cards your team has just received represents the resources a company or organization has to offer the marketplace within which it chooses to operate. As these firms engage in the marketing process, they must continually upgrade their competitive position. For example, they might need to train staff, add parking, or change the hours of operation to achieve their objectives.

The objective of The Card Game is to obtain a 13 card 'straight flush' that consists of cards of the same suit—hearts, spades, diamonds, or clubs—in sequential order— Ace, King, Queen, Jack, 10, 9, 8, 7, 6, 5, 4, 3, and 2. As shown on the screen, teams [specify numbers] will obtain a straight flush of **hearts** (♥), teams [specify numbers] will obtain a straight flush of **spades** (♠), teams [specify numbers] will obtain a straight flush of **diamonds** (♦), and teams [specify numbers] will obtain a straight flush of **clubs** (♣).

There are 2 rules that must be followed as you accomplish your objective:

Rule #1: While obtaining your straight flush, you must engage in the activity of exchange, which is trading for something of value so that each party is better off. In this classroom 'marketplace', **no money can be exchanged; only barter can be used**. [NOTE: Some of you may have traded baseball cards, 'Pogs' or other things when you were younger, which is a form of barter.]

Rule #2: No unethical (deception) or illegal (theft) means can be used to obtain a desired card from another team. Any violations should be reported to me."

7. **Spend 2 minutes** and have students discuss with their fellow teammates the strategy their team may use to accomplish its objective.

8. Continue with the instructions of The Card Game:

"We will now begin The Card Game. The first team that turns in their straight flush to me will receive a prize." [NOTE: The 'prize' is up to the instructor. It may consist of extra credit point, candy bars, etc.]

9. **Spend 5-10 minutes** to play The Card Game. When the first student team turns in its straight flush, say:

"We have a winner and it's Team [specify]! Please stop now and return to your seats. Team [specify] has just won the prize, which is [specify]. We will now discuss some of the marketing aspects of the activity you just completed."

10. Give students the following mini-lecture regarding The Card Game:

"The purposes of this activity were to: (1) illustrate what a market is and for you to experience some of its dynamics; (2) understand the idea of exchange and how barter can be used instead of money as a means to value an idea, product, or service; and (3) discuss how the marketing mix elements (the "4 P's") relate to the requirements of the marketing process."

11. Ask students about the four factors required for marketing to occur relative to the activity just completed:

- Question 1: For marketing to occur, the first factor requires that two or more parties have unmet needs. For this activity, who were these parties and what was the unmet need?

   Answer: Teams of students (the parties) lacked the required cards to obtain a straight flush (the unmet need).

- Question 2: The second factor for marketing to occur requires that each of the parties have the desire and ability to satisfy these needs. For this activity, describe the desire and ability aspects of this factor?

   Answer: A prize motivated teams (the desire) if they were first to realize its objective to get a straight flush. The ability to satisfy its needs consisted of the unneeded cards it had that could be traded or bartered to other teams.

- Question 3: The third factor for marketing to occur requires a way for the parties to communicate. How did your teams communicate your needs?

   Answer: Teams probably used several communication means, such as verbal (talking, yelling?), writing (keeping track of cards obtained or needed), nonverbal (hand signals), etc.

- Question 4: The last factor for marketing to occur requires something to exchange. What was exchanged?

   Answer: The obvious answer is the cards. However, some teams may have exchanged other things of value (other than money) to obtain the cards they needed to achieve the objective of The Card Game, such as a share of the prize (depending on what it was).

ICA 1-5

12. Ask students about some of the aspects of the marketing process:

- Question 1: What is a "market" and describe the marketplace within which your teams operated?

  Answer: A market consists of people (who may represent companies or organizations) with the desire and with the ability to buy a specific idea, product, or service. The marketplace of this activity consisted of students (the 'people') with the desire (a motivation to achieve an objective) and with the ability (non-monetary resources, such as cards needed by other teams, creativity of the strategies used to barter for the cards needed, etc. used in a barter economy as the medium of exchange) to buy (trade) a product (cards).

- Question 2: What are some objectives that companies or organizations want to achieve?

  Answer: The objective of The Card Game was to obtain a straight flush. For profit-oriented firms, objectives include sales, profit, market share, being first-to-market, etc. For nonprofit organizations, objectives may be the number of clients served, efficiency in delivering services, etc.

- Question 3: What was exchanged in your marketplace? What is 'value' and how did you determine the value of the cards exchanged when you engaged in this barter economy? What was the value at the beginning and why was it harder to trade as the Game progressed?

  Answer: In this marketplace, playing cards were exchanged or traded. "Value" is the estimated worth of something exchanged. The value of a given trade was determined by the card(s) that was/were needed to achieve the objective. The closer a team was to realizing its objective, the value of the card(s) exchanged probably increased since the desire to satisfy the unmet need became greater.

- Question 4: Marketers develop the "marketing mix" to achieve their objectives. What are the elements of the marketing mix? For each element, give an example based on The Card Game activity.

  Answer: The marketing mix, also known as the 4 P's, consists of the following elements:

  Product: This was the playing card. Its features consisted of its suit (hearts, spades, diamonds, and clubs) and type (Ace, King, Queen, Jack, 10, 9, 8, 7, 6, 5, 4, 3, and 2).

  Price: In a barter economy, this was a (set of) card(s) that two or more teams were willing to trade.

  Promotion: This was the communication by a team to make other teams aware of its own unmet needs or how it can satisfy their unmet needs.

  Place (or distribution): This was the classroom where the exchanges occurred.

- Question 5: What strategies and tactics did your team try to implement? Were any successful?

  Answer: One strategy that may have been used by student teams is "Merger and Acquisition," in which two teams join forces to trade/swap cards. If the instructor does not want this strategy implemented, a third rule should be presented before the start of the game or obtain permission to determine if it was legal in this marketplace. Most likely, other strategies were used to obtain the cards needed.

Marketing Lessons. This activity has many lessons: (1) It is important to have a strategy to succeed in the marketplace. However, a strategy may need to be changed if marketplace conditions changed. (2) For people to satisfy unmet needs, there must be an exchange of value so that each partner of the transaction is better off. Otherwise, no exchange takes place.

SHEET #1
TEMPLATE TO CREATE SLIPS OF PAPER BASED ON THE NUMBER OF STUDENT TEAMS

1	2	3	4
5	6	7	8
9	10	11	12
13	14	15	16
17	18	19	20

SHEET #2
TEMPLATE TO CREATE SLIPS OF PAPER BASED ON
THE NUMBER OF STUDENT TEAMS

21 22 23 24

25 26 27 28

29 30 31 32

33 34 35 36

37 38 39 40

ICA 1-5

TEMPLATE TO CREATE PLACARDS
BASED ON THE NUMBER OF STUDENT TEAMS

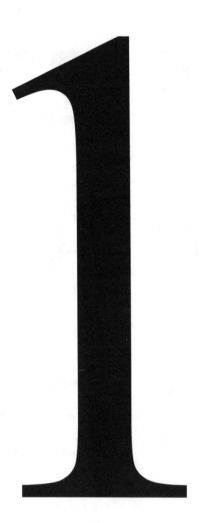

THE CARD GAME OBJECTIVES

TEAMS	♥	♠	♦	♣
1 - 2	X			
3 - 4		X		
5 - 6			X	
7 - 8				X

CHAPTER 2: DEVELOPING SUCCESSFUL MARKETING AND CORPORATE STRATEGIES

ICA 2-1: IN-CLASS ACTIVITY

What Makes A Better Mousetrap? (Part 2):
The Role of Cross-Functional Teams in New-Product Development[1]

Learning Objectives. To have students (1) see the role cross-functional or multi-disciplinary teams play in new product development and (2) experience the importance of linking customer value and "points of difference" to features of a new product.

Definitions. The following marketing terms are referred to in this in-class activity (ICA):

- Cross-Functional Teams: A small number of people from different departments in an organization who are mutually accountable to a common set of performance goals.

- Points of Difference: Those characteristics of a product that make it superior to competitive substitutes.

Nature of the Activity. To have students (1) role-play four different business functions that are represented on a cross-functional new product development team and (2) evaluate the product introduction of a new mousetrap design. This activity is the second part of an ICA introduced in Chapter 1 (ICA 1-3).

Estimated Class Time. 30 minutes.

Materials Needed.

- The Victor® Metal Bait Pedal, Live Catch, Easy Set, and Quick Kill mousetraps from the *Instructor's Survival Kit* box.

- The ICA02-1.doc Word and ICA02-1.ppt PowerPoint files contained in the ICA02-1 folder of the Instructor's CD#1 from the *Instructor's Survival Kit* box.

Preparation Before Class. Follow the steps below:

1. Review the material from ICA1-3: What Makes a Better Mousetrap? (Part 1).

2. Read pp. 31-32, 40-41, 45 of Chapter 2 and pp. 234-241 of Chapter 9.

3. Print, read, and if necessary, edit the ICA2-1.doc Word file.

4. Print and/or review the slides from ICA2-1.ppt PowerPoint file.

5. OPTIONAL: Bookmark the Victor® Pest (www.victorpest.com) website on your classroom computer.

---

[1] The authors wish to thank Karolyn Warfel and Betsy Boyer of the Woodstream Corp. who assisted in the development of this ICA.

Instructions. Follow the steps below to conduct this ICA:

1. Pass around the Victor® Metal Bait Pedal and Live Catch mousetraps obtained from the *Instructor's Survival Kit* box.

Victor Bait Pedal mousetrap

Slide 2

2. **Show Slide 2** and refresh students' memories of ICA 1-3: What Makes a Better Mousetrap? (Part 1) by giving the following mini-lecture:

   Over 100 years ago, Woodstream Corp. developed the original wooden Victor® Metal Bait Pedal mousetrap. This spring-loaded trap has a metal bait pedal to place peanut butter or cheese to kill a mouse. Today, the original wooden Victor® Metal Bait Pedal mousetrap sells for about $1.25 for a package of two. Consumers who buy this trap are part of the "disposer" market segment because they want a cheap and relatively efficient way to handle their mouse problem. So the important "points of difference" in this segment's buying decision are low-cost and disposability (convenience).

3. **Show Slide 3** and discuss the new Victor® Live Catch plastic mousetrap:

Victor Live Catch plastic mousetrap

Slide 3

   "Over 25 years ago, Dick Woolworth, president of the Woodstream Corp., decided to invent a better mousetrap. However, that plastic trap did not fair well in the marketplace. But that didn't stop Woodstream from innovating. In recent years, Woodstream launched a new plastic mousetrap because research shows that some people do not want to see or touch a captured mouse while others prefer to humanely release a live, but captured mouse. This newer plastic trap is the Victor Live Catch mousetrap and is different from the one discussed in ICA 1-3.

The newer Victor® Live-Catch mousetrap allows a user to place some cheese or peanut butter at the back end of the trap, which then is placed on the floor with the open end touching the ground. When the mouse enters, it tips the trap, which then slams the door and traps the mouse. The user then picks up the plastic trap, transports the live mouse outside, opens the door to the trap, and lets the mouse out.

The new Victor® Live Catch plastic mousetrap is even more efficient than the old plastic trap of 25 years ago. Now, almost 100 percent of mice are caught when they enter the plastic trap to eat the bait compared to 90 percent previously. The new Victor® Live Catch plastic mousetrap is priced at $2.50 for a package of two at retail (hardware, home improvement, mass-merchandisers, etc.) stores. Consumers who buy this trap are part of the 'reuser' market segment because they want greater efficiency and a more cost-effective means to resolve a persistent mouse problem. So the important 'points of difference' in this segment's buying decision are efficiency and humaneness."

4. Form students into 4-person teams.

5. **Show Slide 4** and introduce this ICA:

"Now, we're going to discuss this recently introduced Victor® Live Catch mousetrap as a new product idea. To do that, we are going to ask you to play four different roles in a cross-functional new product development team."

- **Person #1 is the group leader**. This person is responsible for keeping the group on task, ensuring all questions are answered and all points of view are aired. This person will also report the results to the whole class at the end of the exercise.

- **Person #2 is the research and development or technical representative**. This person should evaluate the Victor® Live-Catch mousetrap from a design perspective. How does the technology compare with the original wooden Victor® Metal Bait Pedal mousetrap? Is its performance better or worse? What new design ideas can be developed, consistent with past technological capabilities?

- **Person #3 is the marketing representative**. This person should think about customer reactions to the Victor® Live-Catch mousetrap. Who are the customers? How do they use traps? What needs does this trap satisfy? What weaknesses or problems exist with both the plastic and wooden traps and what solutions or improvements can we find? What are the pricing and promotion strategies that can be used to sell the plastic trap? Where should these plastic traps be sold?

- **Person #4 is the manufacturing representative**. This person is concerned about the durability and reliability of the product, and the ease with which it can be manufactured and assembled in the factory.

Tasks of the Cross-
Functional Teams

Slide 5

6. **Show Slide 5**: The Two Tasks of the "Better Mousetrap" Cross-Functional Teams and give the following instructions:

- **Task #1: Evaluate the new mousetrap. Spend 5 minutes** and have student identify the target segment(s) and the needs that this trap satisfies. What are the pros and cons of the trap? Should the trap be aggressively marketed or withdrawn? Why?

- **Task #2. Spend 5 minutes** and have student teams search for benefits and corresponding features to design a better mousetrap. Remember which function or department you are representing, and be sure to get your concerns addressed in this discussion. The team leader will report to the class.

7. Have each group report their conclusions. Record these on the board or a blank transparency. Points to raise or emphasize include:

Task #1: Evaluate the Victor® Live Catch mousetrap.

- Question 1: Who are the customers? How do they use traps? What needs does this trap satisfy?

Answers: Target market segment is mousetrap "reusers." They are: environmentally-conscious, humane (don't want to kill the mice), and concerned about potential health or injury risks.

- Question 2: How does the technology of the Victor® Live Catch mousetrap compare with the Victor® Metal Bait Pedal mousetrap? Is its performance (efficiency) better or worse? Would you recommend introducing this new trap?

  Answers: There are "Pros" and "Cons" to the Victor® Live Catch mousetrap:

  a. Pro's: Easy to set; no risk of injuring fingers from accidentally tripping the spring; more efficient at capture (weight shift of mouse inside trap closes door); simple, inexpensive design (1 moving part; 3 parts total); user protected from contamination from dead mouse; easy to remove (mouse slides out live).

  b. Con's: Live mouse to relocate (time consuming); higher unit price ($1.17 vs. $0.32); potential for mouse bite during removal.

- Question 3: What are some reasons for or against offering the new plastic trap?

  Answers: There are reasons to and not to introduce the new plastic trap:

  a. Reasons to introduce: Reach environmentally-conscious segment which does not want to touch or kill mouse; can reuse trap; easy disposal; relatively manufacturing and assembly due to few parts.

  b. Reasons not to introduce: Difficulties in switching manufacturing to this design, which uses different materials than wood.

Task #2: Search for benefits and corresponding features to design a better mousetrap!

- Question 1: What are some of the benefits and corresponding features in mousetraps that satisfy the needs of various markets?

  Answers: Benefits and features include:
  - Cheap
  - Not too messy
  - Kills mouse/doesn't kill mouse
  - Innovative design
  - Convenience
  - Reuse/dispose
  - Convenient
  - Value (price/performance)

- Question 2: What are some of the features to add to or improve upon existing mousetraps?

  Answers: Features to add to or improve upon existing mousetraps include:
  - Avoid need to replace peanut butter or cheese bait
  - Low kill rate (inefficient mousetrap)
  - What to do with the dead/live mouse
  - Trapping/catching more than one mouse before disposal
  - Using technologies that scare away mice from the dwelling

Victor EasySet
cheese mousetrap

Slide 6

8. OPTIONAL: **Show Slide 6**, pass around, and discuss the Victor®
    EasySet cheese mousetrap:

    "As you can see, the Victor® EasySet® mousetrap was designed as an
    improvement to the original wooden Victor® Metal Bait Petal trap. It
    comes with a clever yellow plastic 'Swiss cheese' pedal that requires no
    baiting because it has been infused with a scent mice find irresistible!
    When the mouse sniffs and touches the cheese, it triggers the spring-
    loaded bar, killing the mouse. This trap is priced at $0.37 per unit,
    slightly higher than the original wooden Victor® Metal Bait Petal trap
    ($0.32). It is sold in packages of two and can be found at home
    improvement, hardware, and mass-merchandiser stores."

- Question 1: Who are the customers of the Victor® EasySet® mousetrap with the
  infused cheese? How do they use traps? What needs does this trap satisfy?

  Answers: Target market segment is mousetrap "disposers." They want to use a
  trap that is very easy to operate (don't even want to bait the trap with cheese or
  peanut butter). They also are price-conscious, concerned about efficiency (hopes
  the mouse is dead), and unconcerned about potential health or injury risks.

- Question 2: What are the advantages and disadvantages of this trap?

  Answers: There are "Advantages" and "Disadvantages" to this trap:

  - Advantages of the Victor® EasySet® Cheese Mousetrap:
    - The permanent bait feature; they don't like the mess or risk of baiting a
      wooden, spring-loaded trap by hand for fear of accidental injury.
    - Modest 5¢ price increase per unit over the original wooden trap for the
      added feature of infused cheese smell.
    - Longer lever arm—the cheese gives a longer lever arm, thereby making
      the trap more sensitive and more efficient at killing mice.

  - Disadvantages of the Victor® EasySet® Cheese Mousetrap:
    - Must buy the trap in a package of two.
    - Unsure as to whether the "plastic cheese" infused with a mouse attractant
      is more effective at luring mice than real bait.
    - Danger of contamination when disposing of mouse.

Victor Quick Kill mousetrap

Slide 7

9. OPTIONAL: **Show Slide 7,** pass around, and discuss the Victor® Quick Kill mousetrap:

"Recently, Woodstream invented the Victor® Quick-Kill mousetrap (with the 'guillotine-like' killing bar), which is a completely new innovation. The black cover is lifted from the bait trough to place the bait. Next, the 'killing bar' is lifted and locked into place. To get at the bait, the mouse must poke its head between the cover and the trough. As it lifts the cover with its head, the mouse then activates the killing bar, causing it to forcefully snap down on the mouse's head/neck and killing it instantly. This trap is priced at $1.56 per unit, comes in a package of two, and can be found at home improvement, hardware, and mass-merchandiser stores."

[NOTE: When demonstrating this trap, be careful! The killing bar snaps down forcefully and could cause injury to fingers! After setting the killing bar, stick a pencil or pen in the hole created by the cover and trough to activate the mechanism. It will make a loud "SNAP!" To manually reset the trap, hold the bar while lifting up the bait cover. Lower the bar very slowly.]

•   Question 1: Who are the customers of the Victor® Quick Kill mousetrap? How do they use traps? What needs does this trap satisfy?

Answers: Target market segment is mousetrap "reusers." They want to use a trap that is very efficient (wants the mouse to be very dead)! Therefore, price is not as great a consideration and unconcerned about potential health or injury risks.

•   Question 2: What are the advantages and disadvantages of this trap?

Answers: There are "Advantages" and "Disadvantages" to this trap:

–   Advantages of the Victor® Quick Kill Mousetrap:
    •   The trap is extremely effective in killing mice.
    •   Innovative design.
    •   Durable design (tough plastic & metal; spring is of a higher gauge metal than wooden trap).

–   Disadvantages of the Victor® Quick Kill Mousetrap:
    •   Unit cost is $1.56 per trap (package of two required).
    •   Danger of contamination when disposing of mouse.
    •   "Killing bar" creates the perception of the least humane method for solving the mouse problem.
    •   Must be careful since the "killing bar" could injure fingers.

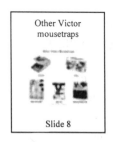

Other Victor mousetraps

Slide 8

10. OPTIONAL: **Show Slide 8** and discuss which segment the following Victor® mousetrap targets:

"Woodstream markets several other types of mousetraps. [Read description.] Which segment does this trap target?

- **Victor® Quick Set mousetrap**. Very easy to set this trap and to bait. It sets and releases with one click. [Target Segment: Reusers]
- **Victor® No See mousetrap**. This trap has a unique covered design. No need to touch or see the mouse. Trapping mechanism tells you when a mouse is caught. [Target Segment: Reusers]
- **Victor® Sonic PestChasers mousetrap**. Emits high frequency sound waves to create an acoustically hostile environment that effectively repels rodents from protected areas. Sound is inaudible to people and non-rodent pets. [Target Segment: Reusers]
- **Victor® Mouse Glue Trap**. There's no setting required; just place and catch. Glue traps are a great alternative to rodenticides. The tray design and glue surface catches mice and holds them securely. Trays can be used around food, water, children and pets. [Target Segment: Disposers]
- **Victor® Electronic mousetrap**. Delivers an electrical shock to exterminate the mouse in seconds. Has a unique tunnel design to prevent mouse from escaping. Built-in safety feature deactivates unit if door is accidentally opened. [Target Segment: Reusers]

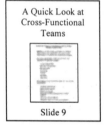

A Quick Look at Cross-Functional Teams

Slide 9

Epilogue. Show Slide 9 and conclude this ICA with the following mini-lecture on cross-functional teams:

"Every study that has examined new product development shows that collaboration among design, manufacturing, marketing, and other functional areas of an organization contributes to the success of a new product or service. Collaboration: (1) enhances the product design by linking the technology with the needs of the market; (2) improves the execution of the entire process from development to deployment; (3) makes assessment of the product's commercial viability easier, and (4) allows for the discovery of optimal design characteristics. This optimization occurs because each department has a unique perspective that is important to the overall process, and when it communicates with and challenges each other, the insights from each can be integrated to develop the best product possible.

One of the primary ways in which companies encourage this collaboration is the use of cross-functional new product development teams discussed throughout text. A cross-functional new product development team is a small group of people (8 to 10) representing a firm's various business functions or departments. The team is responsible for coordinating the design, engineering, and subsequent manufacture of components, subassemblies, or total systems that are part of the final product. The functions represented vary, but representatives from R&D, marketing, manufacturing, and finance are usually key players.

Firms do this in order to encourage parallel rather than sequential new product development. When all functions come on board at the beginning of a project, everyone can understand how decisions are arrived at and where ideas come from. It is then much easier to get commitment at a later stage. Being involved from the beginning also often leads to a greater sense of ownership of the project and a higher level of involvement. Development is also faster when done in parallel. All team members are working on their tasks at the same time, rather than waiting for something to be handed off to them, as in a serial process. Groups are generally felt to generate better solutions to complex problems than individuals. Group decisions are more creative because they integrate multiple viewpoints, and sharing ideas with others encourages comprehensive analysis of potential solutions to problems encountered."

Marketing Lessons. Customers define what a "better" product is and not the seller or its engineers! Key features or "points of difference" in the product provide customer value to users or market segments. These "points of difference" must be important to consumers and communicated to them in terms of: (1) benefits to customers, (2) advantages relative to substitute products from competitors, and (3) features, which are given to the firm's R&D engineers. Different market segments of buyers exist with different needs.

Website. To view Woodstream Corp.'s current product line of Victor® Brand Mousetraps, go to www.victorpest.com.

ROLES AND RESPONSIBILITIES OF FOUR MEMBERS OF THE "BETTER MOUSETRAP" CROSS-FUNCTIONAL TEAMS

In your group of four, count off: 1, 2, 3, & 4

❏ Person #1: Team Leader Responsibilities:

- Keep group on task; ensure that all views are aired.

- Report conclusions to class at end.

❏ Person #2: Technical/R&D Responsibilities:

- Focus on product design, technology, and performance.

- Make sure proposed ideas are consistent with past technological capabilities.

❏ Person #3: Marketing Responsibilities:

- Focus on the customer: Who are they? How do they use the trap? What needs are fulfilled?

- Identify weaknesses and problems with present mousetraps and try to suggest solutions.

- Suggest pricing, promotion, and place strategies.

❏ Person #4: Manufacturing Responsibilities:

- Focus on durability, quality, and reliability.

- Consider ease of manufacture and assembly.

THE TWO TASKS OF THE "BETTER MOUSETRAP" CROSS-FUNCTIONAL TEAMS

- Task #1: Evaluate the new mousetrap

  a. What is the target market segment and the needs this trap satisfies?

  b. What are the mousetrap's pros and cons? How does it compare with the wooden trap?

  c. Should we aggressively market this plastic mousetrap? Or withdraw it? Why?

- Task #2: Search for benefits and corresponding features to design a better mousetrap

  a. What features (customer benefits) of the wooden and plastic traps you have seen that are good and should be retained or enhanced?

  b. What features (customer benefits) should be added or improved?

  c. Recommend a mousetrap with the features you identified in "a" and "b" above.

CROSS-FUNCTIONAL NEW PRODUCT DEVELOPMENT TEAMS: A QUICK LOOK

- <u>Definition</u>: A small number of people from different departments in an organization who are mutually accountable to a common set of performance goals.

- <u>Functions represented</u>: Varies across firms and industries, but typically includes:

  - Product design/R&D

  - Materials management

  - Manufacturing

  - Accounting

  - Finance

  - Marketing

  - Operations

- Advantages of cross-functional teams for new product development:

  - Increases commitment

  - Eases implementation

  - Speeds up process

  - Integrates multiple perspectives for better solutions

  - Improves communications

  - Delegates tasks and fixes responsibilities

CHAPTER 2: DEVELOPING SUCCESSFUL MARKETING AND CORPORATE STRATEGIES

ICA 2-2: IN-CLASS ACTIVITY

Marketing Yourself[1]

Learning Objective. To show students, especially non-marketing majors, that marketing is applicable to their future by using the strategic marketing process and marketing mix when looking for a job.

Definitions. The following marketing terms are referred to in this in-class activity (ICA):

- Marketing Mix: The marketing manager's controllable factors—product, price, promotion, and place—that can be used to solve a marketing problem.

- Points of Difference: Those characteristics of a product that make it superior to competitive substitutes.

- Product Positioning: The place an offering occupies in consumers' minds on important attributes relative to competitive products.

- Situation Analysis: Taking stock of where a firm or product has been recently, where it is now, and where it is headed in terms of the organization's plans and the external factors and trends affecting it.

- Strategic Marketing Process: The approach whereby an organization allocates its marketing mix resources to reach its target markets.

- SWOT Analysis: An acronym describing an organization's appraisal of its internal **S**trengths and **W**eaknesses and its external **O**pportunities and **T**hreats.

Nature of the Activity. To have students apply the strategic marketing process to themselves as they seek employment.

Estimated Class Time. 25 minutes.

Materials Needed.

- The ICA02-2.doc Word and ICA02-2.ppt PowerPoint files contained in the ICA02-2 folder of the Instructor's CD #1 from the *Instructor's Survival Kit* box.

- Copies of the:
  a. Marketing Yourself Handout.
  b. The Do-It-Myself Marketing Plan Worksheet.

---

[1] The authors wish to thank Traci Moscowitz, Marketing Coordinator of Yahoo! HotJobs who assisted in the development of this ICA.

- NOTE: Transparencies can be made of the handouts instead of making copies and using the PowerPoint presentation for those instructors who prefer this option.

Preparation Before Class. Follow the steps below:

1. Read pp. 33, 36, 41-49 of Chapter 2.

2. Print, read, and if necessary, edit the ICA02-2.doc Word file.

3. Print and/or review the PowerPoint slides from the ICA02-2.ppt PowerPoint file.

4. Make copies of the:

    a. Marketing Yourself Handout.

    b. The Do-It-Myself Marketing Plan Worksheet.

5. OPTIONAL: Bookmark the Yahoo! HotJobs (www.hotjobs.com) website on your classroom computer.

Instructions. Follow the steps below to conduct this ICA:

1. Pass out copies of the Marketing Yourself Handout and the Do-It-Myself Marketing Plan Worksheet to each student.

2. **Show Slide 2**: HotJobs.com TV ad. [TRT = 0:30] This humorous ad shows how being both qualified and prepared for the job interview can lead to a job that fits both the applicant and the employer.

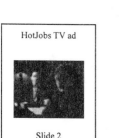

Slide 2

3. Ask students about the type of jobs they hope to land after graduation and how they intend to find these jobs. Most students will describe a "shotgun approach" of aiming at any job without any focused or targeted effort at specific careers (product management, marketing research, advertising, sales, etc.) or positions (assistant product manager, marketing research analyst, etc.).

4. Contrast the difference between a shotgun approach and a targeted marketing effort. This is a good opportunity to explain how research can help students develop information to identify alternative "target markets." For example, students can learn about potential opportunities through networking, internships, informational interviewing, and many secondary sources.

5. Using the Marketing Yourself Handout and the Do-It-Myself Marketing Plan Worksheet, **spend 10 minutes** and have students conduct:

    a. A situation analysis, which involves taking stock of what they have done regarding their career search, where they are now, and where they are headed in terms of their existing plans and the external factors and trends affecting their employment prospects.

    b. A SWOT analysis should be used to appraise students' personal strengths and weaknesses as well as their opportunities for and threats (or barriers) to successful employment.

        *   To conduct an **<u>internal</u>** analysis, ask students what some of their strengths and weaknesses are in terms of the courses taken and grades received, work experience, extra-curricular activities involvement, honors received, etc.

        *   To conduct an **<u>external</u>** analysis, ask students:
            –   Which industries or types of jobs are growing or in demand that may be opportunities?
            –   What advantages or "points of difference" do they have relative to other "competitors" (other students) seeking the same job opportunities, such as taking this marketing course, this educational institution's reputation, etc.?
            –   What other external forces can impact their job search, for example a downturn in the economy, the need to be computer literate, etc.?

        *   This type of focused approach helps to define potential market segments that can be targeted.

6. **<u>Spend 5 minutes</u>** and have students identify elements of their marketing mix.

    a. What type of "product" do you have to offer? What skill sets do you possess?

    b. What sort of "pricing" is appropriate? What salary and benefits do you want?

    c. What "promotion" will be utilized? How will inform prospective employers about yourself?

    d. What type of "place" or channel will be used? These include intermediaries such as on-campus career services, networking, employment agencies, and even the Internet, with firms such as Yahoo! HotJobs providing valuable services.

7. Call on several students and ask them to share portions of their personal marketing plan with the class. If students have few ideas about their marketing mix, ask about how information could be developed to help formulate an appropriate marketing mix.

Marketing Lesson. The strategic marketing process can be applied to products, services, ideas, and even to marketing yourself!

Website. To investigate some job possibilities, obtain information on writing résumés, etc., go to the Yahoo! HotJobs website, which is www.hotjobs.com.

MARKETING YOURSELF (1)

Planning Phase

Situation Analysis

- Internal Assessment: What are your strengths and weaknesses? What can you do to enhance your strengths and minimize your weaknesses? What points of difference or competitive advantage do YOU have? If you don't have one, can you develop one?

- External Analysis: What are the trends in the environmental factors that could impact your job search and career development? These consist of: sociocultural, economic, technological, competitive, and regulatory factors.

- Competitive Analysis: What type of background, experiences, strengths, and weaknesses do your competitors have?

- Market Analysis: What market segments (job opportunities) have you identified as having the best potential? How do you fit into these markets? [NOTE: This means doing some research!]

Focus and Goal Setting

- What are your objectives? Make them specific and measurable!

- What is your target market? Examples might be large public accounting firms, business-to-business sales, and marketing research for a consulting firm in Chicago, etc.

Marketing Program

- Product: YOU. Know yourself well. Continually improve yourself. Understand how you can meet the needs of your target market—prospective employers!

- Pricing: What salary and compensation package do you want? What are you willing to settle for? What's the average salary received by competitors in your target market?

- Promotion: Very important. Think about the buying process. How will you create awareness for yourself? What can you do to "break through the clutter" and get the opportunity for an interview? Your personal selling skills will be important for telephone contacts and face-to-face interviews. Probe to find out about the needs of the organization before that "sales call" and during the interview. Have your questions prepared.

- Place: What channels have you developed to access your target market, such as associations, personal contacts, professors, etc? Do some careful research on these. Don't assume that intensive distribution is necessarily the way to go. Focus your efforts to those target markets that hold promise.

MARKETING YOURSELF (2)

Implementation Phase

Develop a timetable and budget for research, wardrobe, résumés, and travel. Carry out your program. Contact your target market opportunities. Follow-up consistently. Remember that looking for a job requires a significant commitment of your time and effort.

Control Phase

Follow-up on all leads. Find out why you did or didn't make the cut. Ask at an interview what it was about your résumé that interested them. Even if you don't get the job, you have more insight. Similarly, when you call to follow-up on those cover letters and résumés that you sent out, ask when decisions will be made, when it would be appropriate to call back (and then do it). If you are rejected, call back and ask why. If you exhaust all of the possibilities in a given target market, go back to your situation analysis and identify new segments. Always send a "Thank You" note.

Resources:

• Your college placement office.

• Informational interviewing (a great opportunity to learn more about careers you are considering while you are still in school and can make some adjustments to your program).

• Internships. Good experience to build your résumé and potential contacts for positions. Even if you don't want to work there, they can possibly open doors for you elsewhere.

• Richard N. Bolles, *What Color is Your Parachute?: A Practical Manual for Job-Hunters and Career-Changers*, (Berkeley, CA: Ten Speed Press). A companion workbook is also available. See www.jobhuntersbible.com (Bolles' website) and www.tenspeedpress.com.

• Martin Yate, *Knock'em Dead; Cover Letters That Knock 'Em Dead; and Resumes That Knock 'Em Dead*, (Holbrook, MA: Adams Media Corporation). See www. adamsmedia.com.

Websites. The following contain resources on job searches, résumé writing, interviewing, job postings, etc.

www.careerbuilder.com   www.hotjobs.com
www.jonhuntersbible.com   www.monster.com

THE DO-IT-MYSELF MARKETING PLAN (1)

STRATEGIC MARKETING PROCESS		MY OWN MARKETING PLAN		
P L A N N I N G P H A S E	**Situation Analysis (SWOT)**	Location of Factor	Kind of Factor	
			Favorable	Unfavorable
		Internal: Me • Personality • Formal Education • Job Experience • Motivation • Other:_____	My Strengths:	My Weaknesses:
		External: • Economic • Technical • Legal • Other:_____	Opportunities For Me:	Threats Affecting Me:
	Focus and Goal Setting	My Goals Upon Graduation	Personal Goals:	
		My Desired Position	Job Description:	
		My Target Industries, Organizations, and Locations	Industries:	
			Organizations:	
			Geographical Areas:	
		My Uniqueness (Points of Difference)	Personality:	
			Education & Experience:	
			Other:	
		My "Positioning"	How You Compare to Other Job Applicants:	

THE DO-IT-MYSELF MARKETING PLAN (2)

MARKETING PROGRAM		MY OWN MARKETING PLAN	
P L A N N I N G P H A S E	**• Product Strategy** (Actions to Improve My "Marketability")	Formal Education/Courses:	
		Job Experiences/Projects Completed:	
		Extra-Curricular/Volunteer Activities:	
		Obstacles To Overcome:	
	• Price Strategy	Compensation Sought:	
	• Promotion Strategy	Résumé, Personal Interviews, and Letters/Telephone Calls:	
	• Place Strategy	Networking for Contacts and References:	
I M P L E M E N T A T I O N P H A S E	**• Schedule/Budget**	Actions to Take/Budget	Deadlines
	• Marketing Actions (Courses to take, summer jobs to get, résumés to write, clothes to buy, travel arrangements to make, etc.)	1. 2. 3. 4. 5.	1. 2. 3. 4. 5.
C O N T R O L P H A S E	**• Evaluation**	What Did and Didn't Work:	
	• Control	How to Modify Strategy:	

ICA 2-2

CHAPTER 3: SCANNING THE MARKETING ENVIRONMENT

ICA 3-1: IN-CLASS ACTIVITY

Competitive Intelligence: Fuld & Company[1]

Learning Objectives. To have students (1) learn about what competitive intelligence is and is not in order to benefit from this practice and (2) identify possible sources of information to use when gathering, analyzing, and acting on competitive intelligence.

Definitions. The following marketing terms are referred to in this in-class activity (ICA):

- Competitive Intelligence: According to Fuld & Company, "this phrase refers to legally and ethically collected information on a rival that has been analyzed to the point where you can make a decision."[2]

- Environmental Scanning: The process of continually acquiring information on events occurring outside the organization to identify and interpret potential trends.

Nature of the Activity. To have student teams (1) compare and contrast what competitive intelligence is and is not in order to benefit from this practice and (2) assess two scenarios to determine what competitive intelligence should be gathered.

Estimated Class Time. 20 minutes, which consists of:

- 5 minutes to explain the nature of this ICA and distribute the Fuld & Company Handout to student teams.

- 15 minutes to present summaries by student teams during the subsequent class period.

Materials Needed.

- The ICA03-1.doc Word and ICA03-1.ppt PowerPoint files contained in the ICA03-1 folder of the Instructor's CD #1 from the *Instructor's Survival Kit* box.

- The Fuld & Company brochure from the *Instructor's Survival Kit* box.

- Copies of the Competitive Intelligence Handout for each student.

- NOTE: Transparencies can be made of the handouts instead of making copies and using the PowerPoint presentation for those instructors who prefer this option.

Preparation Before Class. Follow the steps below:

1. Read pp. 85-87 of Chapter 3.

2. Print, read, and if necessary, edit the ICA03-1.doc Word file.

---

[1] The authors wish to thank Leonard Fuld, President of Fuld & Co. who assisted in the development of this ICA.
[2] See http://www.fuld.com/Tindex/IntelDict/record007.html.

3. Print and/or review the PowerPoint slides from the ICA03-1.ppt PowerPoint file.

4. Make copies of the Competitive Intelligence Handout for each student.

5. OPTIONAL: Bookmark the Fuld & Company website (www.fuld.com) on your classroom computer.

Instructions. Follow the steps below to conduct this ICA:

1. Pass around the Fuld & Company brochure from the *Instructor's Survival Kit* box.

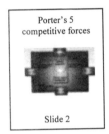
Porter's 5
competitive forces

Slide 2

1. **Show Slide 2** and give the following mini-lecture about competitive intelligence.

   "Competitive intelligence involves the legal and ethical collection of information about an organization's competitors. This activity is a critical part of an environmental scan that an organization performs when developing or evaluating its corporate and marketing strategies. After this information has been collected, marketers analyze it so that they can make decisions to improve the effectiveness of these strategies. It is this analysis that leads to 'intelligence.' While market research focuses on the customer, competitive intelligence analyzes Porter's five competitive forces (bargaining power of suppliers, threat of new entrants, bargaining power of buyers, threat of substitute products or services, and the competitive rivalry among firms in the industry)."

Fuld & Company
brochure

Slide 3

2. **Show Slide 3** and give the following mini-lecture about Fuld & Co.

   "Fuld & Company is the global leader in business and competitive intelligence. Fuld provides research and analysis, strategic and business intelligence consulting, and training to help its clients understand the competitive environment and make better decisions through the application of solid intelligence on their markets and competitors."

ICA 3-1
Comp. Intelligence
Handout

3. Form students into 4-person teams.

4. Pass out copies of the Competitive Intelligence Handout to each student.

5. Assign each student team **two** descriptions and **two** misconceptions of competitive intelligence.

6. **Spend 10 minutes** and have the student teams perform the following tasks:

   a. Read the Competitive Intelligence Handout regarding the 10 descriptions and misconceptions of intelligence.

   b. Write a 1-page brief that summarizes **two** descriptions and **two** misconceptions of competitive intelligence and analyzes its benefits and concerns to an organization's marketing strategy.

   c. Have the student teams hand in their briefs during the next class period.

7. **Spend 10 minutes** and select one student from 3 to 4 student teams to give a brief report on the competitive intelligence issues they summarized.

8. OPTIONAL: **Spend 10 minutes** and have students respond to the following competitive intelligence gathering scenarios. For each situation, read the description, ask 2 to 3 students what competitive intelligence they would need, and then read the answer developed by Fuld & Company.[3]

    a. **Situation 1: New product rumor.** Your best sources have heard a new product is under development by a competitor. To protect your market share, you need to be proactive. You need to gather competitive intelligence quickly and act upon it.

    Answer: The kinds of competitive intelligence you will need to gather include:

    - Rumor verification
    - Timing/availability of the new product
    - Test markets
    - Product Design (features/benefits)
    - Packaging
    - Price points
    - Target markets
    - Advertising/promotion plans
    - Distribution channels

    b. **Situation 2: New competitor in your market.** A new player has entered your turf. It could be an entrepreneurial start-up firm, a joint venture between companies in other industries, or a newly created division of a large conglomerate. Whatever form this new competitor takes, your must learn how its presence in the market will affect your organization.

    Answer: The kinds of competitive intelligence you will need to gather include:

    - Products/services—How do they compare to your own (features, value, etc.)?
    - Short- and long-range goals
    - Staying Power/Financial Resources
    - Technological Capabilities
    - Sales & Marketing Plans (positioning, target markets, strengths/weaknesses)
    - Management (profiles, level of control, culture/values)

Marketing Lessons. While some people may object to competitive intelligence gathering as the ethical equivalent of spying (the latter being both unethical and illegal), organizations can and should use ethical means to gather, analyze, and act on information about their competition. Who is responsible for the environmental scanning of competitive forces? Usually mid-level managers, particularly those in the market research area. However, all line and staff personnel should value its importance if not directly involved in its application.

Website. The Fuld & Company website is www.fuld.com.

---

[3] Excerpted from Fuld & Company Intelligence Organizer. See http://www.fuld.com/Tindex/IntelOrg.html.

COMPETITIVE INTELLIGENCE HANDOUT (1)[4]

Business people misunderstand what competitive intelligence is and what it is not. Below are ten descriptions and ten misconceptions of what intelligence is.

Competitive Intelligence Is...	Competitive Intelligence Is Not...
Information that has been analyzed to the point where you can make a decision. The purpose of competitive intelligence is to make decisions; the process of collecting and analyzing data is the means to the end.	**Spying.** Spying implies illegal or unethical activities. While spying does occur, it is rare. Think about it: corporations do not want to find themselves in court for this illegal activity.
A tool to alert management to early warning of both threats and opportunities. Given that major industry changes can appear overnight, marketers must create scenarios of possible futures and then rigorously monitor the competitive environment to compare the forecasts with reality.	**A crystal ball.** While intelligence does give corporations good approximations of reality, both near- and long-term, it does not predict the future.
A means to deliver reasonable assessments. Competitive intelligence offers approximations and best views of the market and the competition available at the time.	**Database search.** Databases do not massage or analyze the data. Humans do by examining the data and applying their common sense, experience, analytical tools, and intuition to make decisions.
Comes in many flavors. Competitive intelligence can mean many things to many people. A research scientist sees it as a heads-up on a competitor's new R&D initiatives. A salesperson considers it when bidding against another firm in order to win a contract. A senior manager believes intelligence to be a long-term view on a marketplace and its rivals.	**The Internet or rumor chasing.** The Internet is primarily a communications vehicle, not a deliverer of intelligence. You can find hints at competitive strategy, but you will also uncover rumors disguised as fact or speculation dressed up as reality. Be wary. Its reach is great, but you need to sift, sort, and be selective on its content.
A way for companies to improve their bottom line. Many firms have increased their revenues and profits as a result of the decisions made possible by the effective use of competitive intelligence.	**Paper.** Paper is the death of good intelligence. Think face-to-face discussion or a quick phone call rather than paper delivery. Never equate paper with competitive intelligence. Many managers think that by spending countless hours on PowerPoint slides, charts, graphs, and footnoted reports, they have delivered intelligence. In the process, they have likely hidden the intelligence by over-analyzing it.

---

[4] Leonard Fuld, "What Competitive Intelligence Is and Is Not!" Fuld & Company white paper.
See http://www.fuld.com/Company/CI.html.

ICA 3-1

COMPETITIVE INTELLIGENCE HANDOUT (2)

Competitive Intelligence Is...	Competitive Intelligence Is Not...
A way of life, a process. If a company uses CI correctly, it becomes a way of life for everyone in the corporation—not just the strategic planning or marketing staff.	**A job for one, smart person.** One person cannot do it all. At best, a CI coordinator keeps management informed and ensures that others in the organization become trained in ways to apply this tool.
Part of all best-in-class companies. Quality-focused firms apply competitive intelligence consistently. The Malcolm Baldridge Quality Award, the most prestigious total quality award for American corporations, includes the gathering and use of CI as a criterion.	**An invention of the 20th century.** CI has been around as long as business itself. It may have operated under a different name, or under no name at all, but it was always present.
Directed from the executive suite. The best-in-class intelligence efforts receive their direction and impetus from the CEO. While the CEO may not run the program, he/she dedicates budget and personnel. More importantly, the CEO promotes its use.	**Software.** Software does not in and of itself yield intelligence. Data warehousing and data mining software packages can, in some cases, analyze data. However, true analysis is a process that involves people reviewing the information and making strategic decisions.
Seeing outside the organization. Companies that successfully apply competitive intelligence gain an ability to see outside themselves. CI pushes the not-invented-here syndrome out the window.	**A news story.** Newspaper or television reports are very broad and not timely enough for managers concerned with specific competitors and competitive issues. If a manager first learns of an industry event from a newspaper or magazine report, chances are others in the industry have already learned of the news through other channels. While media reports may yield interesting sources for the CI analyst to interview, they are not always timely or specific enough for critical business decisions.
Both short- and long-term. A company can use intelligence for many immediate decisions, such as how to price a product or place an advertisement. At the same time, you can use the same set of data to decide on long-term product development or market positioning.	**A spreadsheet.** "If it's not a number, it's not intelligence." This is an unspoken, but often thought of, refrain among managers. Intelligence comes in many forms, only one of which is a spreadsheet or some quantifiable result. Management thinking, marketing strategy, and ability to innovate are only three among a host of issues that rely on a wide range of subjective, non-numeric intelligence.

CHAPTER 3: SCANNING THE MARKETING ENVIRONMENT

ICA 3-2: IN-CLASS ACTIVITY

Questions That Cannot Be Asked Outright in a Pre-Employment Interview[1]

Learning Objective. To sensitize students to the kinds of questions they can or cannot ask in pre-employment interviews, thereby avoiding possible allegations of discrimination in hiring practices, a growing area in the legal/regulatory environment.

Definitions. The following marketing terms are referred to in this in-class activity (ICA):

- Laws: Society's values and standards that are enforceable in the courts.

- Regulation: Restrictions state and federal laws place on business with regard to the conduct of its activities.

Nature of the Activity. To have students indicate whether or not they believe an interviewer can ask them certain questions in a pre-employment interview.

Estimated Class Time. 30 minutes, which consists of:

- 10 minutes for distribution, completion, and return of the Pre-employment Interview Questionnaire (PIQ) during one class period.

- 20 minutes to discuss student responses during the subsequent class period.

Materials Needed.

- The ICA03-2.doc Word and ICA03-2.ppt PowerPoint files contained in the ICA03-2 folder of the Instructor's CD #1 from the *Instructor's Survival Kit* box.

- Copies of the Pre-Employment Interview Questionnaire.

- NOTE: Transparencies can be made of the handouts instead of making copies and using the PowerPoint presentation for those instructors who prefer this option.

Preparation Before Class. Follow the steps below:

1. Read p. 87 of Chapter 3 and the material below.

2. Print, read, and if necessary, edit the ICA03-2.doc Word file.

3. Print and/or review the PowerPoint slides from the ICA03-2.ppt PowerPoint file.

4. Make copies of the Pre-Employment Interview Questionnaire (PIQ) for each student.

---

[1] The authors wish to thank Sharon Gibson of the University of St. Thomas who assisted in the development of this ICA.

Instructions. Follow the steps below to conduct this ICA:

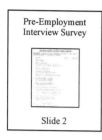

Pre-Employment
Interview Survey

Slide 2

1. Pass out copies of the Pre-Employment Interview Questionnaire (PIQ) to each student.

2. **Show Slide 2**: Pre-Employment Interview Questionnaire.

3. Ask students to check whether or not they believe it is appropriate to ask an interviewee each of the 16 questions listed on the PIQ.

4. Collect the PIQ and tabulate the responses for each question. Make a transparency of the PIQ to summarize the results during the following class period. Some time might be spent highlighting those questions that most students think can or cannot be asked.

5. Know that U.S. federal legislation, such as civil rights legislation and amendments (*Title VII of the Civil Rights Act of 1964*; *Age Discrimination in Employment Act of 1967*; *Americans with Disabilities Act (ADA) of 1990*; etc.), indicates that an interviewer **cannot ask any of the 16 questions posed on the PIQ in most situations**.

   a. Marital Status or Family Composition (Questions 1, 2, and 5).

   b. Creed or Religion (Question 10). You can ask if the applicant is available to work Saturday or Sunday.

   c. Organizations to which a person belongs (Question 7), where the name or character of the organization indicates race, creed, religion, national origin, sex, or ancestry of its member.

   d. Citizenship, National Origin, Ancestry, or Birthplace (Questions 12, 13 and 15), except to ask whether the applicant is legally entitled to work in the U.S.

   e. Relatives (Question 9).

   f. Physical Limitations (Question 8), except as they affect a person's ability to perform job-related functions. Violation of the ADA of 1990.

   g. Arrest Record and Convictions (Question 3), except felony convictions that reasonably relates to performing the job. The application must include a disclaimer that indicates a conviction does not automatically exclude an applicant.

   h. Financial Status (Questions 6 and 14).

   i. Photograph (Question 11).

j. Educational Attainment (Question 4), unless there is a valid reason for having a certain educational background that is necessary to perform the job or position.

k. Age (Question 16). Violation of the Age Discrimination in Employment Act of 1967. An employer can ask if the applicant is at least 18 years old (not a minor).

6. Tell students that the general rule for any question in an employment interview is: "Is this question job-related?" If it isn't, the question has a high probability of being discriminatory. Federal regulations now make it almost mandatory for employees to have well-defined job descriptions.

Marketing Lessons. While personal interviews are commonly used in hiring salespeople, interviewers cannot ask certain questions about interviewees. Knowledge of what cannot be asked is important for both the interviewer and interviewee. Also, federal and state laws and regulations are constantly evolving. The U. S. Equal Employment Opportunity Commission (EEOC) has issued guidelines that explain laws and regulations pertaining to employment discrimination.

Website. For more information about appropriate interview guidelines, sexual harassment, and other discrimination issues, contact the EEOC website at www.eeoc.gov.

PRE-EMPLOYMENT INTERVIEW QUESTIONNAIRE

ASSIGNMENT: Please check whether you believe an interviewer can ask you each of the following questions in a pre-employment interview.

Interviewer:	Can Ask	Cannot Ask
1. Are you married?	_____	_____
2. Whom do you live with?	_____	_____
3. Have you ever been arrested or spent time in jail?	_____	_____
4. Are you a college graduate?	_____	_____
5. Do you plan to have children?	_____	_____
6. Do you own your home or do you rent?	_____	_____
7. Which clubs or social fraternities do you belong?	_____	_____
8. Are you handicapped in any way (e.g., poor hearing, poor eyesight)?	_____	_____
9. What are the names and addresses of your brothers and/or sisters?	_____	_____
10. Which religious holidays do you observe?	_____	_____
11. Do you have a photograph to place on your resume?	_____	_____
12. Are you a citizen of a country other than the U.S.?	_____	_____
13. What is the ethnic origin of your last name?	_____	_____
14. Are you currently receiving alimony from your former spouse?	_____	_____
15. In what city and state were you born?	_____	_____
16. How old are you/What is your birth date?	_____	_____

CHAPTER 4: ETHICS AND SOCIAL RESPONSIBILITY IN MARKETING

ICA 4-1: IN-CLASS ACTIVITY

What Is Ethical and What Is Not: A Survey of Your Opinions

Learning Objectives. To have students (1) move from an abstract understanding of ethical dimensions of marketing to actual situations they may experience as working professionals and (2) demonstrate the differences in opinions regarding what is and is not ethical.

Definitions. The following marketing terms are referred to in this in-class activity (ICA):

- Ethics: The moral principles and values that govern the actions and decisions of an individual or group.

- Moral Idealism: A personal moral philosophy that considers certain individual rights or duties as universal, regardless of the outcome.

- Utilitarianism: A personal moral philosophy that focuses on the "greatest good for the greatest number," by assessing the costs and benefits of the consequences of ethical behavior.

Nature of the Activity. To have students complete a survey in which they are asked to indicate their opinion about whether particular business and marketing practices are unethical. The comparison of student responses generates enthusiastic discussion and provides a vehicle for linking Chapter 4 to familiar business practices.

Estimated Class Time. 30 minutes.

Materials Needed.

- The ICA04-1.doc Word and ICA04-1.ppt PowerPoint files contained in the ICA04-1 folder of the Instructor's CD #1 from the *Instructor's Survival Kit* box.

- Copies of the "What is Ethical and What is Not Survey" for each student.

- A calculator to calculate the percentages from the survey.

- NOTE: Transparencies can be made of the handouts instead of making copies and using the PowerPoint presentation for those instructors who prefer this option.

Preparation Before Class. Follow the steps below:

1. Read pp. 105-106 of Chapter 4.

2. Print, read, and if necessary, edit the ICA04-1.doc Word file.

3. Print and/or review the PowerPoint slides from the ICA04-1.ppt PowerPoint file.

4. Make copies of the What is Ethical and What is Not Survey for each student.

Instructions. Follow the steps below to conduct this ICA:

What is Ethical Survey

Slide 2

1. Pass out copies of the "What is Ethical and What is Not Survey" to each student.

2. **Show Slide 2**: What is Ethical and What is Not Survey. Ask students to complete the survey by circling the number that corresponds to how they feel about whether each sales situation or practice listed represents an ethical dilemma.

3. Collect the "What is Ethical and What is Not Survey" and tabulate the responses for each question using one of the following methods.

    a. **Method 1**: Collect the questionnaires from the students and have a student or a teaching assistant calculate the percentage of students answering "definitely yes" and "probably yes" to each of the questions.

    b. **Method 2**: Ask the students to self-report their responses in class.

4. Make a transparency of the Comparison of Answers on Ethics Questionnaire Given by Sales Representatives and Students to summarize the results during the current or subsequent class period. Some time might be spent highlighting those questions that most students think can or cannot be asked.

5. Discuss the results with students. There will be a broad range of student opinions regarding what is unethical. In addition, the summary form allows comparison of the students' opinions with those from a survey of sales representatives.

Marketing Lessons. Key lessons include:

1. Students view situations and practices from different perspectives, leading to differences in opinions about whether they are unethical.

2. **If Question B was unanswered**: Many companies lack corporate policies about many of these situations and practices.

3. The more general the situation, the greater the percentage of salespeople (and usually students) who felt it posed an ethical question. For example, more respondents view allowing personality differences to influence the terms of a sale as being unethical than asking purchasers for information about competitors.

WHAT IS ETHICAL AND WHAT IS NOT SURVEY: HOW DO YOU FEEL ABOUT THE FOLLOWING SALES SITUATIONS OR PRACTICES?

Instructions: Assume you are a field sales representative for a large corporation. For each situation or practice listed below, circle the number corresponding to whether you feel it presents an ethical question.

Situation or Practice	Does the situation/practice present an ethical question?				
	Definitely Yes	Probably Yes	Maybe Yes Maybe No	Probably No	Definitely No
1. Allowing personalities—liking for one purchaser and disliking for another—to affect price, delivery, and other decisions regarding the terms of sale.	1	2	3	4	5
2. Having less competitive prices or other terms for buyers who use your firm as the sole source of supply than for firms for which you are one of two or more suppliers.	1	2	3	4	5
3. Making statements to an existing purchaser that exaggerates the seriousness of his problem in order to obtain a bigger order or other concessions.	1	2	3	4	5
4. Soliciting low priority or low volume business that the salesperson's firm will not deliver or service in an economic slowdown or periods of resource shortages.	1	2	3	4	5
5. Giving preferential treatment to purchasers who higher levels of the firm's own management prefer or recommend.	1	2	3	4	5
6. Giving physical gifts, such as free sales promotion prizes or "purchase-volume incentive bonuses" to a purchaser.	1	2	3	4	5
7. Using the firm's economic power to obtain premium prices or other concessions from buyers.	1	2	3	4	5
8. Giving preferential treatment to customers who are also good suppliers.	1	2	3	4	5
9. Seeking information from purchasers on competitors' quotations for the purpose of submitting another quotation.	1	2	3	4	5
10. Providing free trips meals, or other entertainment to a purchaser.	1	2	3	4	5
11. Attempting to reach and influence other departments (such as engineering) directly rather than go through the purchasing dept. when such avoidance increases the likelihood of a sale.	1	2	3	4	5
12. Gaining information about competitors by asking purchasers.	1	2	3	4	5

Source: Adapted from Alan J. Dubinsky, Eric N. Berkowitz, William Rudelius, "Ethical Problems of Field Sales Personnel," *MSU Business Topics* (Summer, 1980), p. 14.

COMPARISON OF ANSWERS ON ETHICS QUESTIONNAIRE GIVEN BY SALES REPRESENTATIVES AND STUDENTS

Respondents Replying "Definitely Yes" (1) or "Probably Yes" (2)

Situation or Practice	An Ethical Question?			
	Sales Reps		Students	
	Rank	Percent-age	Rank	Percent-age
1. Allowing personalities to affect decisions	1	52%	_____	_____
2. Having less competitive prices for firms for which you are the sole source of supply.	2	50%	_____	_____
3. Making statements to a purchaser that exaggerates the seriousness of his/her problem.	3	49%	_____	_____
4. Soliciting low-priority business that won't be serviced in an economic slowdown or periods of resource shortages.	4	42%	_____	_____
5. Giving preferential treatment to purchasers recommended by firm's own management.	5	41%	_____	_____
6. Giving physical gifts to a purchaser.	6	39%	_____	_____
7. Using the firm's economic power to obtain concessions from buyers.	7	37%	_____	_____
8. Giving preferential treatment to customers who are also good suppliers.	8	36%	_____	_____
9. Seeking information from purchasers on competitor's quotations to submit a new quotation.	9	34%	_____	_____
10. Providing free trips, luncheons or dinners to a purchaser.	10	34%	_____	_____
11. Attempting to reach and influence other departments directly rather than go through the purchasing department.	11	29%	_____	_____
12. Gaining information about competitors by asking purchasers.	12	27%	_____	_____

Source: Adapted from Alan J. Dubinsky, Eric N. Berkowitz, William Rudelius, "Ethical Problems of Field Sales Personnel," *MSU Business Topics* (Summer, 1980), p. 14.

CHAPTER 4: ETHICS AND SOCIAL RESPONSIBILITY IN MARKETING

ICA 4-2: IN-CLASS ACTIVITY

The Ethics of Competitive Intelligence [1]

Learning Objectives. To enable students to collect vital information about competitors in a legal and ethical way and to demonstrate the opportunities and threats that information may present so that organizations can take pre-emptive or responsive marketing actions.

Definitions. The following marketing terms are referred to in this in-class activity (ICA):

- Competitive Intelligence: According to Fuld & Company, "this phrase refers to legally and ethically collected information on a rival that has been analyzed to the point where you can make a decision."[2]

- Environmental Scanning: The process of continually acquiring information on events occurring outside the organization to identify and interpret potential trends.

- Ethics: The moral principles and values that govern the actions and decisions of an individual or group.

Nature of the Activity. To students determines what competitive intelligence behavior scenarios described are ethical, legal, unethical, and/or illegal.

Estimated Class Time. 15 minutes.

- 5 minutes to explain the nature of this ICA and distribute the Fuld & Company Handout to student teams.

- 15 minutes to present summaries by student teams during the subsequent class period.

Materials Needed.

- The ICA04-2.doc Word and ICA04-2.ppt PowerPoint files contained in the ICA04-2 folder of the Instructor's CD #1 from the *Instructor's Survival Kit* box.

- The Fuld & Company brochure from the *Instructor's Survival Kit* box.

- NOTE: Transparencies can be made of the handouts instead of making copies and using the PowerPoint presentation for those instructors who prefer this option.

Preparation Before Class. Follow the steps below:

1. Read pp. 98-100, 102-103 of Chapter 4.

2. Print, read, and if necessary, edit the ICA04-2.doc Word file.

---

[1] The authors wish to thank Leonard Fuld, President of Fuld & Co. who assisted in the development of this ICA.
[2] See http://www.fuld.com/Tindex/IntelDict/record007.html.

3. Print and/or review the PowerPoint slides from the ICA04-2.ppt PowerPoint file.

4. Familiarize yourself with the Fuld & Company competitive intelligence behavior scenarios, which are found on the Fuld website (www.fuld.com).

5. Bookmark the Fuld & Company website (www.fuld.com) on your classroom computer.

Instructions. Follow the steps below to conduct this ICA:

1. Pass around the Fuld & Company brochure from the *Instructor's Survival Kit* box.

Fuld & Company brochure

Slide 2

2. **Show Slide 2** and give the following mini-lecture about competitive intelligence and Fuld & Company.

    "Before competitive intelligence is gathered, an organization must identify the legal restrictions based on the countries within which it operates and establish ethical guidelines based on industry norms and its organizational policies. According to Fuld & Company, the leader in business and competitive intelligence, many people responsible for competitive intelligence within their organizations were not aware of the *Economic Espionage Act* (1996) or other laws related to trade secret or information collection as well as their own organizations' policies on the subject. Recently, Fuld & Company and The Academy of Competitive Intelligence surveyed over 100 competitive intelligence professionals regarding four hypothetical intelligence-gathering scenarios to assess whether the behavior described was normal, aggressive, unethical, or illegal."[3]

3. <u>**Spend 15 minutes**</u> and have students respond to the following competitive intelligence gathering scenarios. For each scenario, read the description, ask 3 to 4 students whether this behavior is normal, aggressive, unethical, or illegal and their rationales, and then read the conclusion developed by Fuld & Company.

    *   **Scenario 1: Documents left behind at a hotel.** *You become aware that your competitor has its board meeting at a certain hotel, so you drop by that hotel towards the end of the day to see what documents someone had left behind.*

        Conclusion: The scenario is probably aggressive but not explicitly unethical or illegal behavior. Were the documents left in a relatively public space in the hotel, or were they left in the meeting room? Students who stated it was an unethical could have been reacting more to the discomfort level of the action rather than the ethicality of the practice itself.

---

[3] "Intelligence Gathering on Gut Instinct Rather Than on Knowledge," Fuld & Company white paper, May 15, 2001, pp. 1-4. See http://www.fuld.com/Tindex/WhitePapers/EthicalandLegalIntelligenceGathering.html.

- **Scenario 2: Airplane conversation.** *You are sitting in an airplane and overhear a competitor state to his friend information that appears to be confidential. Neither individual knows whom you are or that you can overhear them.*

  Conclusion: The scenario is legal and ethical.

- **Scenario 3: Trade show and badge removal.** *You are attending a trade show. You take off your badge that identifies you as a competitor, and you then approach a booth at the exhibition. You tell the representative you have an interest in the product.*

  Conclusion: Cultural norms, more than legality, should be the appropriate response of students. People from North America are generally more up front and identify who they are before asking questions at a trade show.

- **Scenario 4: Entering a private suite.** *You are attending a trade show. You take off your badge that identifies you as a competitor, and you then enter a private suite that is labeled "For Clients of Company X Only."*

  Conclusion: This scenario is certainly unethical and appears illegal because the suite holder warned potential entrants that it has applied some measures to protect its information. The competitor could argue that any unauthorized person taking information from that hotel suite is doing so illegally.

- **Scenario 5: Dumpster diving.** A contractor hired by Procter & Gamble went through the trash outside Unilever's Chicago office and obtained classified information on a Unilever hair care product. When P&G found out about the "competitive intelligence gathering" incident conducted on its behalf, it informed Unilever.

  Conclusion: The behavior by the contractor was both unethical and illegal (*Economic Espionage Act*). Competitive intelligence analysts regularly have to predict the nature and direction of a rival's products. However, instead of "dumpster diving," the contractor could have obtained information that is available in the public domain and draw actionable decisions based on it. P&G settled its corporate espionage case involving the theft of corporate secrets from Unilever in 2001.[4]

Marketing Lesson. According the Leonard Fuld, President of Fuld & Company, "Competition is not war in the pure sense. We cannot throw civilization to the dogs. We can't steal or kill for the information. Competitive intelligence, when done right, allows companies to fiercely compete, yet do so honestly with hard-won bits and pieces of information."[5]

Website. The Fuld & Company website is www.fuld.com.

---

[4] See http://www.fuld.com/News/PressReleases/pr010906.html.
[5] Ibid.

CHAPTER 4: ETHICS AND SOCIAL RESPONSIBILITY IN MARKETING

ICA 4-3: IN-CLASS ACTIVITY

Sustainable Development

Learning Objective. To have students learn how companies proactively balance shareholder value though environmental stewardship and corporate social responsibility in the markets they serve.

Definitions. The following marketing terms are referred to in this in-class activity (ICA):

- Social Responsibility: The idea that organizations are part of a larger society and are accountable to that society for their actions.

- Sustainable Development: Conducting business in a way that protects the natural environment while making economic progress.

Nature of the Activity. To have students identify and analyze how members of the World Business Council for Sustainable Development (WBCSD), a coalition of 165 international companies from over 30 countries, are committed to sustainable development.

Estimated Class Time. 20 minutes, which consists of:

- 10 minutes to explain the nature of this ICA and distribute the World Business Council for Sustainable Development Handout to student teams.

- 10 minutes to present summaries by student teams during the subsequent class period.

- [NOTE: Students will spend 30 minutes outside class to complete their assignment.]

Materials Needed.

- The ICA04-3.doc Word and ICA04-3.ppt PowerPoint files contained in the ICA04-3 folder of the Instructor's CD #1 from the *Instructor's Survival Kit* box.

- Copies of the World Business Council for Sustainable Development Handout.

- Student access to the Internet.

Preparation Before Class. Follow the steps below:

1. Read pp. 109-110 of Chapter 4.

2. Print, read, and if necessary, edit the ICA04-3.doc Word file.

3. Print and/or review the PowerPoint slides from the ICA04-3.ppt PowerPoint file.

4. Make copies of the World Business Council for Sustainable Development Handout.

5. Familiarize yourself with the World Business Council for Sustainable Development website, which is www.wbcsd.ch.

6. OPTIONAL: Bookmark the World Business Council for Sustainable Development website (www.wbcsd.ch) on your classroom computer.

Instructions. Follow the steps below to conduct this ICA:

1. Give students the following background mini-lecture on sustainable development:

   "According to the Dow Chemical Company, "The manifold interests of all Dow stakeholders converge under the Triple Bottom Line of Sustainable Development. The Triple Bottom Line is the ultimate balance sheet, calling attention to the three fundamental areas—economics, environment, and society—where companies impact the quality of life."[1] As part of this commitment, Dow is a member of the World Business Council for Sustainable Development (WBCSD), which is a coalition of 175 international companies from over 35 countries that are committed to the three pillars of sustainable development: economic growth, ecological balance, and social progress.

   The World Business Council for Sustainable Development believes that there are significant opportunities for companies to use sustainable development practices to both manufacture and market profitable products and services to developing countries because such practices can reward firms with both growth opportunities and cost savings. The WBCSD's mission is 'to provide business leadership as a catalyst for change toward sustainable development, and to promote the role of eco-efficiency, innovation and corporate social responsibility.' To accomplish its mission, the WBCSD has identified seven keys to implementing sustainable business practices:[2]

   a. **Innovate**: Technological and social innovation can do much to improve people's quality of life and tackle the depletion of resources and pollution.

   b. **Practice eco-efficiency**. This means creating more value with less impact. It can open up significant business opportunities and help economies grow.

   c. **Move from stakeholder dialogues to partnerships for progress**. This consists of alliances between business, government, and civil society to offer new solutions to common concerns.

   d. **Provide and inform consumer choice**. Individuals will change their consumption practices when they realize that they can gain financial benefits and better quality of life from sustainable behavior.

---

[1] Dow: Committed to Sustainable Development. See http://www.dow.com/commitments/intro/index.htm.
[2] World Business Council for Sustainable Development: *Sustainability Through the Market*.
See http://www.wbcsd.ch/web/publications/sustainability_through_the_market.pdf.

91   ICA 4-3

e. **Improve market framework conditions**. Sustainability is hindered by monopolies, corruption, perverse subsidies, and prices that do not reflect real economic, social, and environmental costs. Legislation and regulations should promote competition, intellectual and physical property rights, reliable contractual terms, fair and transparent accounting standards, freedom and democracy, and full-cost pricing of goods and services.

f. **Establish the worth of the Earth**. The market system needs to reflect the true environmental and social costs of goods and services. Proper valuation will help maintain the diversity of ecosystems, conserve natural resources, and prevent the build-up of toxic substances in the environment.

g. **Make the market work for everyone**. Poverty and protectionism are the largest barriers to achieving sustainability through the market. Protectionism makes it harder for firms to seize profitable business opportunities and therefore increase consumer purchasing power."

2. Pass out copies of the World Business Council for Sustainable Development Handout to each student.

3. Have the students go to the World Business Council for Sustainable Development (WBCSD) website, which is www.wbcsd.ch. Give them the following assignment:

   a. Click on the "Case studies" link, which showcases some of the best global business practices for sustainable development.

   b. Click on the "Sort by: company or date" link to select one case study on sustainable development.

   c. ASSIGNMENT: Have students write a ¾-page brief that summarizes the sustainable business practice implemented by the firm analyzed and the benefits to economic growth, ecological balance, and social progress plus a ¼-page commentary on the benefits of sustainable development to an organization's marketing strategy.

   d. Hand in their summaries during the subsequent class period.

4. At the beginning of the next class period, select one student from 2 to 3 student teams to give a brief report on the sustainable business practices they wrote about.

Marketing Lessons. Many firms view sustainable development as an opportunity, not a threat. As these case studies show, organizations that invest in such practices can have a positive effect on economic growth, ecological balance, and social progress as well as their bottom line.

Website. The World Business Council for Sustainable Development website is www.wbcsd.ch.

World Business Council For Sustainable Development Handout

❑ **Go to the World Business Council for Sustainable Development website (www.wbcsd.ch) and perform the following tasks...**

1. Click on the "Case studies" link, which showcases some of the best global business practices for sustainable development.

2. Click on the "Sort by: company or date" link to select one case study on sustainable development.

3. <u>ASSIGNMENT</u>: Write a ¾-page brief that summarizes the sustainable business practice implemented by the firm analyzed and the benefits to economic growth, ecological balance, and social progress plus a ¼-page commentary on the benefits of sustainable development to an organization's marketing strategy.

❑ **Hand in your briefs and be prepared to present and discuss the issues of sustainable development during the next class period.**

CHAPTER 5: CONSUMER BEHAVIOR

ICA 5-1: IN-CLASS ACTIVITY

Buying Process for Starbucks Coffee[1]

Learning Objective. To illustrate the consumer purchase decision process for coffee.

Definitions. The following marketing terms are referred to in this in-class activity (ICA):

- Consideration Set: The group of brands that a consumer would consider acceptable from among all the brands in the product class of which he or she is aware.

- Evaluative Criteria: Factors that represent both the objective attributes of a brand and the subjective ones a consumer uses to compare different products and brands.

- Purchase Decision Process: The stages a buyer passes through in making choices about which products and services to buy.

Nature of the Activity. To relate the consumer buying process to purchasing a cup of Starbucks coffee.

Estimated Class Time. 20 minutes.

Materials Needed.

- The ICA05-1.doc Word and ICA05-1.ppt PowerPoint files contained in the ICA05-1 folder of the Instructor's CD #1 from the *Instructor's Survival Kit* box.

- The bag of Starbucks House Blend Coffee from the *Instructor's Survival Kit* box.

Preparation Before Class. Follow the steps below:

1. Read pp. 120-123 of Chapter 5.

2. Print, read, and if necessary, edit the ICA05-1.doc Word file.

3. Print and/or review the PowerPoint slides from the ICA05-1.ppt PowerPoint file.

4. OPTIONAL: Bookmark the Starbucks website (www.starbucks.com) on your classroom computer.

---

[1] The authors wish to thank Chris Gorley, Product Placement—National Promotions of Starbucks, who assisted in the development of this ICA.

Instructions. Follow the steps below to conduct this ICA:

Starbucks
Serving House
Blend Coffee

Slide 2

1. Pass around the Starbucks House Blend Coffee bag from the *Instructor's Survival Kit* box.

2. **Show Slide 2**. Give the following mini-lecture about Starbucks:

   "Starbucks Coffee Company is the leading retailer, roaster, and brand of specialty coffee in the world. For 2004, Starbucks had sales of $5.3 billion. As of mid-2005, Starbucks had over 9,000 company-owned and franchised stores in 35 countries within North America, Latin America, Europe, the Pacific Rim, and the Middle East. The firm plans to open over 1,500 more stores in the near future, both in existing and new markets.[2]

   Coffee is a commodity. People can buy a cup of coffee almost anywhere in the world or make it themselves. With most commodities, firms cannot charge a premium price. However, Starbucks does charge a higher price for its cup of coffee because it has created and delivered a brand promise to serve only the finest coffee.

   Further, Starbucks is known for its corporate responsibility, including paying coffee farmers premium prices for their coffee and developing environmental and other programs for the sustainability and success of theese farmers. Starbucks "Cafe Practices" is being looked at as a model of how to do business in the coffee market.

   An example is the Starbucks House Blend, which is a straightforward blend of Latin American coffees. It can be purchased as regular or decaffeinated by the cup in three sizes for $1.60 to $1.80 or in one-pound bags (whole bean or ground) for a MSRP of $9.99 at Starbucks retail stores, restaurants that serve Starbucks, grocery store kiosks that sell Starbucks coffees, and via the Internet at www.starbucks.com."

2. Form students into 4-person teams.

3. **Spend 5 minutes** and have the student teams write down their ideas on the purchase decision process they use to buy a cup of coffee and then rank the top three factors that influence their coffee decision-making.

4. **Spend 5 minutes** and have 3 or 4 student teams share their ideas regarding the factors they use during the purchase decision process to buy a cup of coffee. Discuss these with the entire class.

---

[2] Starbucks press release (February 9, 2005).

Figure 5-1
Purchase decision
process

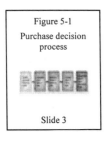

Slide 3

5. **Show Slide 3**, which is Figure 5-1: The Purchase Decision Process. Call on one or two student teams to answer each of the following questions about the purchase decision process for a cup of coffee:

- Question 1: What triggers the decision to buy a cup of coffee? Is it a need? A want?

  Answer: Thirsty, saw an ad, part of a routine, etc.

- Question 2: How do you seek information about the purchase of a cup of coffee, knowing that coffee is a commodity?

  Answer: Use past experiences recalled from memory (internal search; ask family and friends; consult a product-rating organization (*Consumer Reports*, local newspaper review, etc.), and/or ads or store signage (external search).

- Question 3: What evaluative criteria do you use when deciding to purchase a particular coffee brand?

  Answer: Taste, price, location, convenience (wait time), atmospherics (comfortable), service, etc.

- Question 4: What is your consideration set of coffee brands?

  Answer: Make at home: Folgers, etc. Buy at retailer: Starbucks, Caribou Coffee, etc.

- Question 5: When and where do you buy a cup of coffee?

  Answer: Multiple responses and use situations possible.

- Question 6: With respect to the purchase of your last cup of coffee, did you experience any cognitive dissonance? If dissatisfied, what was deficient? Did you tell anyone? Will you go back? What marketing activities could be undertaken to reduce this?

  Answer: Marketers have several options regarding the kinds of activities they can do, such as redesigning the product, reworking the advertising message or retraining salespeople if the product is being oversold, improving customer service, offering refunds, etc.

Marketing Lesson. Marketers must understand each step in the consumer purchase decision process as it applies to their products or services. By doing so, they can develop better marketing programs with which to target their customers more effectively.

Website. To view the current product line of coffees and other products and services at Starbucks, go to www.starbucks.com.

CHAPTER 5: CONSUMER BEHAVIOR

ICA 5-2: IN-CLASS ACTIVITY

What's the Bzz? Word of Mouth and BzzAgent[1]

Learning Objectives. To have students: (1) distinguish between buzz, viral, and word-of-mouth marketing; (2) develop a word-of mouth-campaign; and (3) participate in a word-of-mouth activity for a product or service.

Definitions. The following marketing terms are referred to in this in-class activity (ICA):

- Buzz: Popularity created by consumer word of mouth or an event or activity that generates publicity, excitement, and information to the consumer.

- Opinion Leaders: Individuals who exert direct or indirect social influence over others and are considered to be knowledgeable about or users of particular products and services.

- Viral Marketing: An Internet-enabled promotional strategy that encourages individuals to forward marketer-initiated messages to others via e-mail or an attempt to deliver a marketing message that spreads quickly and exponentially among consumers in the form of an e-mail or video.

- Word-of-Mouth: The influencing of people during conversations or the actual sharing of a natural and honest opinion about a product or service between two or more consumers.[2]

Nature of the Activity. To have students (1) develop a BzzCampaign for BzzAgent and (2) engage in word-of-mouth marketing by acting as a BzzAgent for a product or service (optional).

Estimated Class Time. 30 minutes, which consists of:

- 10 minutes to explain a BzzAgent BzzCampaign and the nature of this ICA.

- 20 minutes to conduct this ICA.

- OPTIONAL: Students will spend 30 minutes outside class to become a BzzAgent.

Materials Needed.

- The ICA05-2.doc Word and ICA05-2.ppt PowerPoint files contained in the ICA05-2 folder of the Instructor's CD #1 from the *Instructor's Survival Kit* box.

---

[1] The authors wish to thank Kelly Hulme, Media Relations Manager of BzzAgent and Bruce Palmer, Marketing Director of the National Outdoor Leadership Schools (NOLS), who assisted in the development of this ICA.
[2] David Balter, "The Word on Word of Mouth," p. 3.

- Copies of the:

  a. BzzGuide Background for the NOLS BzzCampaign Handout.

  b. Developing the BzzGuide for the NOLS BzzCampaign Handout.

  c. Answers to the BzzGuide Handout for the NOLS BzzCampaign.

- NOTE: Transparencies can be made of the handouts instead of making copies and using the PowerPoint presentation for those instructors who prefer this option.

Preparation Before Class. Follow the steps below:

1. Read pp. 135-136 of Chapter 5.

2. Print, read, and if necessary, edit the ICA05-2.doc Word file.

3. Print and/or review the PowerPoint slides from the ICA05-2.ppt PowerPoint file.

4. Make copies of the:

   a. BzzGuide Background for the NOLS BzzCampaign Handout.

   b. Developing the BzzGuide for the NOLS BzzCampaign Handout.

   c. Answers to the BzzGuide for the NOLS BzzCampaign Handout.

5. OPTIONAL: Bookmark the BzzAgent website (www.bzzagent.com) on your classroom computer.

Instructions. Follow the steps below to conduct this ICA:

1. Give the following mini-lecture about buzz, viral, and word-of-mouth marketing:

   "Many marketers use "buzz," "viral," and "word-of-mouth" marketing to influence consumer behavior. However, they use these terms without really knowing the distinctions between them. According to BzzAgent, the leading word-of-mouth marketing experts:

   - Buzz marketing is an event or activity that generates publicity, excitement, and information to the consumer. An example is Brandmarketer's T-Shirt-TV (www.t-shirttv.com).

   - Viral marketing is an attempt to deliver a marketing message that spreads quickly and exponentially among consumers in the form of an e-mail or video. An example is Burger King's 'Subservient Chicken' (www.subservientchicken.com).

   - Word-of-mouth marketing is the actual sharing of a natural and honest opinion about a product or service between two or more consumers. Segway used this prior to the launch of its Human Transporter (www.segway.com).

   BzzAgent believes that buzz and viral marketing are the 'manufactured marketing initiatives that are intended to capture people's attention and get them talking' while word-of-mouth requires 'actual brand advocacy…people must be willing to go out of their way to share an opinion, an experience, or their passion about a product.'

BzzAgent believes that everyone creates word-of-mouth. People who are passionate about products talk about them with their family, friends, co-workers, and other acquaintances. While some of these people may be opinion leaders, most are just passionate consumers wiling to share their honest opinions.[3]

Word-of-mouth must be used within the context of specific marketing objectives and conducted in an ethical manner. According to the Word of Mouth Marketing Association, ethical marketers who use word-of-mouth 'reject all tactics related to manipulation, shilling (paying people to talk about a product without disclosure), deception, or dishonesty. If it is faked or invented, it 'can create a consumer backlash, damage the brand, and tarnish the marketer's reputation.'"[4]

2. Give the following mini-lecture about BzzAgent:[5]

"BzzAgent was founded by David Balter in 2001. As of May of 2005, BzzAgent had a network of 85,000 volunteer (non paid) brand evangelists or BzzAgents who participate in 8-, 12-, or 16-week word-of-mouth BzzCampaigns. These help 'support and lend credibility to the messages clients convey using other media outlets, such as TV, radio, print, public relations, direct mail, and the Internet. The result of BzzCampaigns lead to increased awareness, trail, purchase, and brand loyalty of the clients' products or services.' According to BzzAgent's Kelly Hulme, a BZZCampaign provides "real-world feedback to companies as a result of this word-of-mouth campaign. Not only are people spreading the word about a product or service to people they know, they're also having conversations about how they use the product, what they like and dislike about it, etc. Companies have not historically engaged their customers in a real dialogue—instead, they have relied on more inauthentic methods, such as focus groups."

BzzCampaigns are conducted by BzzAgents who are networked to other people and are often familiar with the latest trends and express their opinions. They like access to new products and services and want to have fun spreading the 'Bzz' about them in creative ways. However, they are NOT salespeople or dishonest.

Becoming a BzzAgent involves the following:[6]

*   BzzAgents are recruited via www.bzzagent.com (see the 'Become a BzzAgent' link on the BzzAgent website) or the client's customer list. Prospective BzzAgents must answer a series of demographic, psychographic, and brand preference questions to determine which campaigns they might be interested in joining.

*   BzzAgents are offered and then can choose to opt-in to a BzzCampaign.

*   BzzAgents receive a package in the mail, which consists of a product sample and BzzGuide for the campaign they selected.

---

[3] Ibid., pp. 4, 10.
[4] "Word of Mouth 101: An Introduction to Word of Mouth Marketing," Word of Mouth Marketing Association White Paper (© 2005), pp. 3, 8. See www.womma.org.
[5] Information obtained from the BzzAgent website and other proprietary documents from BzzAgent.
[6] Rob Toof, "Experiential Word-of-Mouth Marketing and Customer Feedback Programs," BzzAgent.

- BzzAgents learn about the product or service, form honest opinions about it, and then, if interested, perform word-of-mouth activities on behalf of the product or service featured in the BzzCampaign. All BzzAgents abide by a Code of Conduct to ensure that their activities are honest, transparent, and ethical.

- BzzAgents file BzzReports online that discusses their activities and feedback regarding the BzzCampaign product/brand experience.

- BzzAgents are awarded points, which can be redeemed for rewards.

- When the BzzCampaign is closed, clients receive a final report from BzzAgent."

About This
Bzz Guide
Handout

Slide 2

3. **Show Slide 2** and give the following mini-lecture about a BzzGuide that is developed by BzzAgent for a BzzCampaign on behalf of a client:

"BzzAgent has developed BzzCampaigns for many clients, including Penguin Publishing, Kayem Foods, The March of Dimes, Ralph Lauren, among others. BzzAgent creates a BzzGuide, a custom guide created to help BzzAgents create real, honest word-of-mouth Bzz about a client's product or service. A BzzGuide consists of the following elements:[7]

- **What We're Bzzing**: A description of the client's product or service or "What makes the product worth talking about?"

- **The Bzz**: A positioning statement or the essential core benefit of the product or service that BzzAgents can use to begin spreading Bzz.

- **BzzStories**: Background information or interesting "folklore" on the client and its product or service that enable BzzAgents to spread more interesting Bzz.

- **BzzFacts**: Information on the features and benefits of the product or service, where to buy it, what it costs, how to use it, who makes, it, etc.

- **BzzTriggers**: Suggested contexts or use situations where it might be appropriate to bring up the client's product or service.

- **BzzTargets**: A list of potential users that may be interested in the client's product or service.

- **BzzActivities**: A list of suggested word-of-mouth marketing actions that a BzzAgent could take to Bzz the client's product or service."

NOLS BzzGuide
Background
Handout

4. Form students into 4-person teams.

5. Pass out copies of the BzzGuide Background Handout for the NOLS™ BzzCampaign to each student.

---

[7] Ibid.

6. Begin the ICA with the following statement:

"During the next 15 minutes, you will complete a BzzGuide for the National Outdoor Leadership School (NOLS), a world-famous outdoor adventure school that was recently 'Bzzed' by BzzAgent and its BzzAgents. The BzzCampaign for NOLS was conducted during the Winter of 2005. Over 3,000 BzzAgents generated word-of-mouth for the service. BzzAgent created the following BzzGuide to assist BzzAgents in creating word-of-mouth for NOLS.

7. If necessary, review the BzzGuide Background Handout for the NOLS™ BzzCampaign and then ask students if they have any questions.

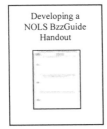

8. Give students the Developing a BzzGuide for the NOLS BzzCampaign Handout.

9. **Show Slides 3-7** and briefly review the following aspects of the Developing a BzzGuide Handout for the NOLS BzzCampaign.

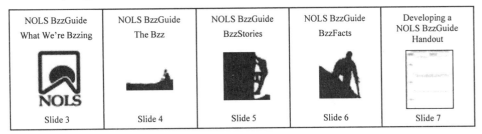

NOLS BzzGuide What We're Bzzing	NOLS BzzGuide The Bzz	NOLS BzzGuide BzzStories	NOLS BzzGuide BzzFacts	Developing a NOLS BzzGuide Handout
Slide 3	Slide 4	Slide 5	Slide 6	Slide 7

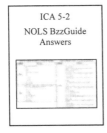

10. **Spend 15 minutes** and have student teams complete the Developing a BzzGuide for the NOLS BzzCampaign Handout. Each team should spend 5 minutes each on identifying the BzzTriggers, BzzTargets, and BzzActivities they would use for NOLS.

11. Give students the Answers to the BzzGuide for the NOLS™ BzzCampaign Handout.

12. Randomly select 3 teams to present the BzzTriggers (Team 1), BzzTargets (Team 2), and BzzActivities (Team 3) for the BzzGuide for the NOLS BzzCampaign.

13. **Spend 5 minutes** and have one student from each of these teams share their answers, discuss them with the rest of the class, and compare them to those suggested by BzzAgent.

14. Conclude this ICA with the following statement:

"After each word-of-mouth experience, BzzAgents file an online BzzReport that describes their activities and the resulting Bzz. BzzAgent then compiles these results and submits a final report to the client that provides feedback on the word-of-mouth Bzz generated and any positive or negative insights regarding the product or service."

15. OPTIONAL: Have students go to the BzzAgent website (www.bzzagent.com) and complete the online form to become a BzzAgent.

Marketing Lessons. This ICA introduces students to the essential concepts of buzz, viral, and word-of-mouth marketing that marketing and product managers could use to promote their products or services. To develop an effective word-of-mouth marketing campaign for a product or service, students need to be able to (1) communicate its features and benefits, (2) identify its target consumers and use situations that trigger its consumption, and (3) develop marketing activities that generate awareness, interest, trial, and adoption.

Websites. The BzzAgent website is www.bzzagent.com. The Word of Mouth Marketing Association website is www.womma.org. The National Outdoor Leadership School website is www.nols.edu.

BzzGuide Background Handout for the
National Outdoor Leadership School (NOLS) BzzCampaign

BZZGUIDE SECTION	DESCRIPTION
WHAT WE'RE BZZING	Founded in 1965, NOLS is one of the world's finest outdoor education programs. The purpose of NOLS is to nurture and train the next generation of leaders and outdoor enthusiasts. Over the past 40 years, NOLS has provided tens of thousands of people with a solid foundation in leadership skills, wilderness know-how, and environmental awareness. NOLS offers a wide range of programs and wilderness locations, such as: • Backpacking in the Yukon Territory. • Mountaineering in Patagonia. • Sea kayaking in the Pacific Northwest. • Coastal sailing in New Zealand. With NOLS, people learn important wilderness skills, such as first aid, nutrition, and environmental preservation. NOLS has been instrumental in developing and promoting the "Leave No Trace" philosophy of respect for the outdoors.
THE BZZ	NOLS is synonymous with wilderness leadership education. It has been educating people about thriving in and enjoying the wild—not just surviving the experience—for 40 years!

BZZ STORIES	• WHAT'S THE DIFFERENCE: NOLS stands out in the world of outdoor education.
	
	  – **Focus:** It's the only school that focuses exclusively on teaching outdoor skills, leadership, and environmental studies to highly motivated individuals.
	
	  – **Organization:** NOLS is centrally administered at the NOLS headquarters in Lander, Wyoming, so you get the same high quality experience wherever you take your course.
	
	  – **Expertise:** NOLS has the most experienced, well-rounded instructional staff in outdoor education. NOLS instructors have completed special training and on-course apprenticeships with NOLS before being certified to teach.
	
	  – **Satisfaction:** More than 97% of NOLS graduates report being satisfied with their experience, and 97% would recommend NOLS to a friend.
	
	• FLEXIBLE COURSE OFFERINGS: Courses range in length from 10 days to three months, so you can choose the course that's right for you. Many companies arrange customized NOLS programs for their employees; high school students sign up before they head off to college; people between jobs take a course to improve their leadership skills; college students opt for a change of scenery. In fact NOLS has formed relationships with 20 colleges and more than 400 colleges have accepted credits from students who took a NOLS course. All kinds of people can benefit from NOLS!
	
	• NOLS GRADS ARE LEADERS: What's the best way to become a leader? Lead! Every day at NOLS is physically, mentally, and emotionally challenging, and every NOLS student actively leads a part of each course. Graduates leave with the knowledge to face adversity, take decisive action, and implement plans effectively. Each is trained to enjoy the outdoors and practice responsible leadership in daily life.
	
	• TRAVEL THE WORLD WITH NOLS: There are five sites in North America, including the original NOLS site in the Rocky Mountains. NOLS also maintains residence at six international locations, including the newly opened NOLS New Zealand. Honoring the distinct ecosystems and recruiting highly skilled instructors from each region, NOLS provides a learning experience unmatched anywhere else.

BZZ FACTS	• *Outside Magazine* ranked NOLS the #1 school for learning wilderness skills. • Cable television's OLN (Outdoor Life Network) named NOLS the #1 Adventure Camp in the country. • NOLS has partnerships with a number of environmentally conscious companies, including Patagonia, Orvis, Silk, and Spenco. • The Wilderness Medicine Institute (WMI) of NOLS teaches wilderness medical skills using realistic wilderness scenarios on college campuses nationwide. • NOLS offers customizable courses tailored to meet your specific needs and interests or those of a group. • NOLS was a founding partner in the "*Leave No Trace*" program, which trains people to enjoy the wilderness without damaging it. Today's "Leave No Trace" curriculum for land managers, outdoor leaders, and other activists is developed by NOLS. • Famous NOLS graduates include: Sebastian Junger, author of *The Perfect Storm*; David Breashears, Director of the IMAX film *Everest*; Tom Scott, Co-founder of Nantucket Nectars; Candace Carpenter Olson, Founder of iVillage; J.F.K. Jr., and 22 year-old Britton Keeshan, the youngest person to achieve the highest summits on all seven continents.

Developing a BzzGuide for the NOLS BzzCampaign Handout

BZZGUIDE SECTION	DESCRIPTION
BZZ TRIGGERS	Check out the following list for some ideas about situations and topics where it's natural to share the Bzz about NOLS: • • • • • • • •
BZZ TARGETS	Who do you know that might be interested in learning about NOLS? Believe it or not, 85% of NOLS students heard about the school from a friend! Think about everyone you know and share the Bzz with someone who: • • • • • • •
BZZ ACTIVITIES	These are some recommendations for how to spread the word about NOLS: • • • • • • •

Answers to the BzzGuide Handout for the NOLS BzzCampaign (1)

BZZGUIDE SECTION	DESCRIPTION
BZZ TRIGGERS	Check out the following list for some ideas about situations and topics where it's natural to share the Bzz about NOLS: • Education • Leadership • Wilderness • Outdoor-related organizations and/or clubs • Outdoor sports (skiing, kayaking, etc.) • Travel • Adventure • The environment • Life-changing events • Studying abroad • Time off between high school and college • Hands-on learning • Summer opportunities or camps • Others as identified
BZZ TARGETS	Who do you know that might be interested in learning about NOLS? Believe it or not, 85% of NOLS students heard about the school from a friend! Think about everyone you know and share the Bzz with someone who: • Educates or wants to educate – a teacher, guidance counselor, scout leader, etc. • Works outdoors • Has children • Plays outdoors • Loves a challenge • Has participated in an outdoor program • Provides consulting services • Manages a company • Wants to gain new leadership skills • College student • Others as identified

BZZGUIDE SECTION	DESCRIPTION
BZZ ACTIVITIES	These are some recommendations for how to spread the word about NOLS: • **Create A NOLS Wish** Open the NOLS catalog and dare to dream. Let your imagination and sense of exploration run wild as you plan your ultimate NOLS experience, then tell someone else about your dream course. • **Refer Someone to NOLS** Maybe you know someone who just came back from a backpacking trip and seems antsy for the 'Next Big Thing'. Or, maybe there's someone who is bored with office life. Refer tomorrow's leaders and wilderness adventurers to NOLS! • **Show Off the Materials** From the lavish catalog to the *Wilderness Wisdom* book, share your NOLS literature and inspire your friends and colleagues. No bulletin board is complete without a NOLS poster! • **Get Outside** It's called the Great Outdoors for a reason. Next time you're outside with someone, make sure they know about NOLS. You could even join an outdoor club in order to share adventures and swap recommendations with others. • **Bzz Online** Let people know that **NOLS.edu** is the perfect place to learn more about one of the world's most respected outdoors school. Don't forget to spread the word about NOLS if you belong to an online community where people talk about education or the outdoors. • **Shop for the Outdoors** Next time you are shopping for outdoor equipment with a friend or family member, spread the Bzz about NOLS! • **Get Your Friends Talking** Keep a copy of the course catalogue/book on your desk or coffee table and let your friends and family imagine the possibilities of the ultimate life experience they can find at NOLS. You could even plan a trip together! • **Inspire a Leader** Who doesn't want to learn to thrive in the wilderness or gain valuable life and leadership skills? Tell an ambitious person about NOLS and make the world a better place. • **Create Your Own Bzz** Being the independent spirit that you are, we know that you will be Bzzing about NOLS in your own unique way. Just be sure to stick to the BzzAgent Code of Conduct and have fun!

CHAPTER 6: ORGANIZATIONAL MARKETS AND BUYER BEHAVIOR

ICA 6-1: IN-CLASS ACTIVITY

Buying Center Role-Play[1]

Learning Objectives. To have students (1) understand the cross-functional nature of the organizational buying process and (2) identify the key roles within the buying center.

Definitions. The following marketing terms are referred to in this in-class activity (ICA):

- Buying Center: The group of people in an organization who participate in the buying process and share common goals, risks, and knowledge important to a purchase decision.

- New Buy: The first-time purchase of a product or service, involving greater potential risk.

- Organizational Buying Behavior: The decision-making process that organizations use to establish the need for products and services and identify, evaluate, and choose among alternative brands and suppliers.

Nature of the Activity. To have several students conduct a role-play by assuming different characters to discuss an organizational purchase of Sprint's FonPromotions program.

Estimated Class Time. 20 minutes.

Materials Needed.

- The ICA06-1.doc Word and ICA06-1.ppt PowerPoint files contained in the ICA06-1 folder of the Instructor's CD #1 from the *Instructor's Survival Kit* box.

- Seven (7) copies of the Buying Center Role-Play Script.

- Seven (7) name cards, one for each of the student participants in the role-play.

- NOTE: Transparencies can be made of the handouts instead of making copies and using the PowerPoint presentation for those instructors who prefer this option.

Preparation Before Class. Follow the steps below:

1. Read pp. 156-258 of Chapter 6.

2. Print, read, and if necessary, edit the ICA06-1.doc Word file.

3. Print and/or review the PowerPoint slides from the ICA06-1.ppt PowerPoint file.

---

[1] The authors wish to thank Glenn Cheshire, Prepaid Marketing and Graphic Design of Sprint, who assisted in the development of this ICA.

4. Prepare name cards for each of the characters.

5. Make seven (7) copies of the Buying Center Role-Play Script, one for each of the participants, and highlight the particular parts for each character's script.

6. Set up a table and chairs in front of the classroom for the "meeting."

7. OPTIONAL: Bookmark the Sprint website (www.sprint.com) on your classroom computer.

Instructions. Follow the steps below to conduct this ICA:

1. Recruit students to play the seven characters in the role-play. Seat the characters at a table in front of the class and give each the corresponding "script."

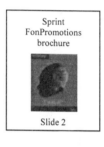

Sprint
FonPromotions
brochure

Slide 2

2. **Show Slide 2.** While the role-playing students are reviewing the scripts, give the following background and then introduce the characters:

    "You are about to see a glimpse inside FarNorth, Inc., a successful manufacturer of golf accessories (bags, apparel, gloves, etc.) for men and women that are sold to golf pro shops, golf superstores, and sporting goods stores in the U.S. FarNorth's management has asked Lisa Ludwig, the sales representative for Sprint FonPromotions, to present a proposal for a marketing program to stimulate sales and motivate the firm's sales people. However, Sprint FonPromotions, which costs $100,000, is more than what was budgeted for advertising and sales promotion for the current fiscal year. Before we listen in to the conversation between Lisa and the co-workers that constitute FarNorth's buying center for marketing programs, let me introduce you to our cast:

Character	Job Title	Role in FarNorth's Buying Center
Lisa Ludwig	Sales Representative, Sprint	SUPPLIER: Sprint FonPromotions
Carol Woods	President and CEO, FarNorth	INFLUENCER
Lynn Tan	VP - Marketing, FarNorth	DECIDER/INFLUENCER
Sam Hawthorne	Purchasing Manager, FarNorth	GATEKEEPER/BUYER/INFLUENCER
Neil Vanathan	Sales Manager, FarNorth	USER/INFLUENCER
Thor Sandholm	Advertising Manager, FarNorth	USER/INFLUENCER
Basil Winters	Finance Manager, FarNorth	INFLUENCER

3. Introduce the cast and his/her job title and role in the FarNorth buying center.

4. **Show Slides 3-4** during the presentation. Have the students read the buying center role-play script in front of the class.

Sprint Pre-Paid Business Card

Slide 3

Sprint Pre-Paid Phone Card

Slide 4

5. When finished with the role-play, say: "So we now leave FarNorth's marketing promotions buying center. Let's discuss what we've observed by answering some questions."

6. Ask students the questions below to facilitate the buying center discussion:

- Question 1: What buying center roles did each of the participants play? Which characters were Influencers? Gatekeepers? Deciders? Buyers? Users?

  Answers: See above.

- Question 2: Who do you feel is the key buying influence for this decision? Why?

  Answers: Lynn Tan (VP – Marketing) and Thor Sandholm (Advertising Manager) are probably the key buying center constituents for this decision. They raise the most questions that require answers before a decision can be made. Neil Vanathan (Sales Manager) is also a key player since he is directly responsible for implementing the program. The CEO, Carol Woods, appears to seek Lynn's approval for going ahead with the program.

- Question 3: What are the marketing challenges that face Lisa Ludwig or any business-to-business sales person with a buying center such as this?

  Answer: One of the biggest challenges for a business-to-business sales person is to determine the people who constitute the organization's buying center and what roles they play. Different roles are concerned about different issues. It is a challenge to attempt to address all of these different needs at the same time. Salespeople need to prepare, research, and learn about a potential customer's buying center participants in order to effectively meet their needs and generate the sales they desire.

Marketing Lesson. Organizational buying decisions can be more complex than those for consumers because of the number of individuals involved and their differing needs and perspectives within the buying center. This complexity is particularly evident in a "new buy" situation, such as the one illustrated.

Website. To learn more about Sprint's FonPromotions program, go to its website, which is www.sprint.com/fonpromotions.

BUYING CENTER ROLE-PLAY SCRIPT

Lisa: In summary, the Sprint FonPromotions program, with its Sprint Prepaid Business Card and Prepaid Phone Card, would accomplish the following marketing objectives for FarNorth:

- First, to build brand awareness among customers and prospects, the Sprint Prepaid Business Card looks like your regular business card but offers 20-minutes of free domestic long-distance calls. On the front of the card is your sales person's contact information. On the back are the telephone and ID numbers that allows your customers and prospects to make their free calls. The Sprint Prepaid Business Card encourages these customers and prospects to think you and the free long distance minutes they received every time they view your unique business card.

- Second, to generate excitement and motivate sales people and other FarNorth employees, the Sprint Prepaid Phone Card can be used to create an interactive sweepstakes. Each would receive a free, 30-minute Sprint Prepaid Phone Card. On the card would be a toll-free number that employees would use to enter the contest. Participants then enter a six-digit number of their choice, and if it matched the winning numbers, they instantly win a prize ranging from a weekend get-a-way to a free Sprint Prepaid Phone Card.

Sam: Thank you for your presentation, Lisa. I'm sure that there are a few questions.

Lynn: Yes, Sam. Lisa, have those sales improvement figures been verified by an independent agency? I can't believe that we would see those increases in our situation.

Lisa: Yes, they have Lynn. That information is in Appendix II of the sales proposal, which you each have in front of you. However, according to a recent study from one of our clients that you may contact, sales increased by 10 percent over the six-month promotional period.

Neil: What about procedures? Our sales people haven't had any experience with this type of promotional program and we're very busy at the moment. What level of support or training does Sprint provide?

Lynn: We can't afford time for training. This is the prime selling season for our golf accessories.

Thor: We have already made our media buys for the season. We're going to have to increase our budget to…

Basil: Wait a minute! You want more money for advertising? Can't you just reallocate from one budget category to another?

BUYING CENTER ROLE-PLAY SCRIPT

Thor: Not really. We have signed contracts with our advertising agency so our budget is basically spent for this selling season. Increasing our budget for this Spring FonPromotions program could sufficiently increase sales to cover any increase we need if Lisa's projections are on target.

Basil: But that's a lot of money. Can't you defer some advertising until the next fiscal year?

Lynn: That could be difficult given our marketing plan, Basil.

Thor: Marketing has very ambitious goals for this year, Basil. Not spending the already allocated funds on advertising could have very serious implications on this year's sales.

Neil: Well, if we did implement Lisa's program, it could increase sales from new and existing customers since they and our employees would be even more motivated.

Sam: Excuse me, but are there more questions for Lisa concerning the specifics of the Sprint FonPromotions program?

Lisa: I'd like to answer Neil's question about procedures. I would work closely with Lynn, Neil, and Thor to customize the design of the program. We have 2 customer service reps (one for marketing that would train your sales people and one for data processing that would interface with your data processing people) that would help you implement the program. We would manage the reporting of all sales activity. You would receive daily sales updates by region, channel member, etc. via our link to FarNorth's Intranet.

Basil: Do you have any "canned" or turnkey programs? Any programs that have already been developed for other clients that we could reuse with only minor modifications?

Thor: [Thor gives Basil a dirty look.]

Lisa: I think that you would be interested in the financial projections that I've prepared. At your current sales rates, the Sprint FonPromotions program would pay for itself in less than 9 months.

Carol: I find these projections in Appendix II very compelling, Lisa. What do you think about the program, Lynn? Given our current sales figures, we could project the impact of the purchase. Sam, could you develop a cost-benefit analysis of the program based on Lisa's projections?

[**End of the Role-play**]

CHAPTER 6: ORGANIZATIONAL MARKETS AND BUYER BEHAVIOR

ICA 6-2: IN-CLASS ACTIVITY

Daktronics Brochure to Reach Organizations Buying Video Displays[1]

Learning Objective. To have students identify what kinds of buying information should be in a Daktronics brochure selling video displays that will satisfy initial evaluative criteria of an organizational buyer making a "new buy."

Definitions. The following marketing terms are referred to in this in-class activity (ICA):

- Buying Center: The group of people in an organization who participate in the buying process and share common goals, risks, and knowledge important to a purchase decision.

- Consideration Set: The group of brands that a consumer would consider acceptable from among all the brands in the product class of which he or she is aware.

- Evaluative Criteria: Factors that represent both the objective attributes of a brand and the subjective ones a consumer uses to compare different products and brands.

- New Buy: The buying situation in which the organization is a first-time buyer of the product or service.

- Organizational Buyers: Those manufacturers, wholesalers, retailers, and government agencies that buy goods and services for their own use or for resale.

Nature of the Activity. To have students suggest what information would be most useful in an 8-page Daktronics sales brochure.

Estimated Class Time. 15 minutes.

Materials Needed.

- The ICA06-2.doc Word and ICA06-2.ppt PowerPoint files contained in the ICA06-2 folder of the Instructor's CD #1 from the *Instructor's Survival Kit* box.

- The Daktronics 8-page "Communication Solutions through Technology" brochure contained in the *Instructor's Survival Kit* box.

- Copies of the Buying a College Football Scoreboard Handout.

- NOTE: Transparencies can be made of the handouts instead of making copies and using the PowerPoint presentation for those instructors who prefer this option.

---

[1] The authors wish to thank Dr. Aelred (Al) J. Kurtenbach, co-founder and Chairman, LaVetta Foster, Assistant to Dr. Kurtenbach, and Nichole Bjerke of Daktronics, Inc., who assisted in the development of this ICA.

Preparation Before Class. Follow the steps below:

1. Read pp. 121-122 of Chapter 5 and pp. 148-149, 156-157 of Chapter 6.

2. Print, read, and if necessary, edit the ICA06-2.doc Word file.

3. Print and/or review the PowerPoint slides from the ICA06-2.ppt PowerPoint file.

4. Review the Daktronics 8-page brochure from the *Instructor's Survival Kit* box.

5. Skim the Daktronics Appendix D Case D-6 on pp. 629-631 of *Marketing, 8ᵗʰ Edition.*

6. Make copies of the Buying a College Football Scoreboard Answers Handout.

7. OPTIONAL: Bookmark the Daktronics website (www.daktronics.com) on your classroom computer.

Instructions. Follow the steps below to conduct this ICA:

Daktronics Brochure (Cover)

Slide 2

Daktronics Brochure (Sports)

Slide 3

Daktronics Brochure (Business)

Slide 4

Daktronics Brochure (Government)

Slide 5

1. **Show Slide 2.** Pass around the Daktronics 8-page "Communication Solutions through Technology" brochure obtained from the *Instructor's Survival Kit* box.

2. **Show Slides 3-5** and give students this background mini-lecture on Daktronics:

"Daktronics is the world leader in providing electronic scoreboards and displays for three segments: sports (70 percent of Daktronics' sales), business (20 percent), and government (10 percent).

Like many other small manufacturers, Daktronics attends several dozen trade shows annually where it has a booth and hands out brochures to interest perspective organizational customers in its scoreboards and displays. However, the goal of this Daktronics sales brochure is not to make an immediate sale of its really complex product but to provide enough information so that Daktronics' products will meet the initial evaluative criteria of an organization's buying center to make it into the 'consideration set' of alternative suppliers.

In designing its 8-page brochure, Daktronics has a special problem: It must include enough information to interest prospective customers in all three of its market segments—sports, business, and government— because it cannot afford to have separate 'introductory' brochures for each segment. If this brochure whets the interest of prospective customers, then more detailed, specialized brochures are sent to prospects and Daktronics sales representatives will call on them.

For this activity, let's assume a small college is thinking about buying a new scoreboard for its varsity football stadium."

3. On the board in the front of the class or an overhead transparency, draw the table shown below, without listing either (a) the individuals in the buying center or (b) the initial information they might seek in looking at a Daktronics brochure.

4. Then ask the class the following question: "Who might be members of the buying center for the college football scoreboard and why might they be in it?" Some possible **answers for the rows in the table** and reasons include:

   a. **Athletic department representatives** (football coach, athletic director). A scoreboard is a big part of student experiences at a home football game.

   b. **College president**. Wants the scoreboard to look "respectable" for alumni at home football games.

   c. **College vice-president of finance**. Is concerned about paying for the scoreboard

   d. **College alumni relations/development director**. Might get an alumnus to contribute/pay for scoreboard as a gift to the college.

   e. **College director of buildings and grounds**. Must be able to maintain the scoreboard (replace lighting, etc.).

   f. **College director of purchasing**. Perhaps needs to get competitive bids and secure a formal contract with the supplier, such as Daktronics.

   g. **Potential sponsor**. Organization/alumnus that/who might be willing to pay a "naming rights" fee to cover some or all of the scoreboard's cost.

   h. Others as identified.

5. Now ask the class, "What information might be desirable in the initial Daktronics brochure that members of the buying center might look at?" Some possible **answers for the columns** in the table include:

   a. Supplier's past experience in building scoreboards.

   b. Attractiveness of the scoreboard.

   c. Ease of installation and operation.

   d. Technical support/service.

   e. Price.

   f. Others as identified.

Daktronics
Scoreboard
Handout

6. Pass out copies of the Buying a College Football Scoreboard Handout to each student.

7. Now ask the class to put checks "√'s" in the boxes that indicate the information that might be important to each member of the buying center.

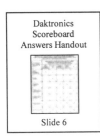
8. **Show Slide 6**: Buying a College Football Scoreboard Answers Handout. The "√'s" on the handout should lead to student discussion on these points.

9. Finally, obtain the Daktronics brochure from the students and show it to the class or **show Slides 2-5 again**. Discuss which of the criteria in the **columns** in the table the Daktronics brochure addresses. [NOTE: It is impossible for a small brochure to cover **all** market segments. Stress to the class that the goal of the brochure is to have the college contact Daktronics to request more information.

Marketing Lesson. In trying to reach complex buying centers in organizations in different market segments, a simple sales brochure, such as the one developed by Daktronics, can encourage interested potential customers to contact the supplier so that it in turn can follow-up by responding to questions, setting up a demonstration, etc.

Website. To view the latest Daktronics lines of displays, go to www.daktronics.com.

BUYING A COLLEGE FOOTBALL SCOREBOARD HANDOUT:
(1) WHO IS IN THE "BUYING CENTER" AND (2) WHAT INITIAL INFORMATION DO THEY SEEK IN A DAKTRONICS BROCHURE?

Individual in the "Buying Center"	Information in Daktronics Brochure in Initial "Screening" Value for Buying Criteria				
	Past Experience in College Scoreboards	Attractive-ness	Ease of Installation/ Operation	Technical Support/ Service	Price
Athletic department representatives					
College President					
College vice-president of finance					
College alumni relations/development director					
College director of buildings and grounds					
College director of purchasing					
Potential sponsor					

BUYING A COLLEGE FOOTBALL SCOREBOARD ANSWERS HANDOUT:
(1) WHO IS IN THE "BUYING CENTER" AND (2) WHAT INITIAL INFORMATION DO THEY SEEK IN A DAKTRONICS BROCHURE?

Individual in the "Buying Center"	Information in Daktronics Brochure in Initial "Screening" Value for Buying Criteria				
	Past Experience in College Scoreboards	Attractive-ness	Ease of Installation/ Operation	Technical Support/ Service	Price
Athletic department representatives	√	√			
College President		√			√
College vice-president of finance			√	√	√
College alumni relations/development director					√
College director of buildings and grounds			√	√	
College director of purchasing	√		√	√	√
Potential sponsor	√	√	√		√

ICA 6-2

CHAPTER 7: REACHING GLOBAL MARKETS

ICA 7-1: IN-CLASS ACTIVITY

Marketing Across Borders: Reintroducing the MINI® Brand to the U.S.[1]

Learning Objectives. To have students (1) determine whether the MINI brand, which is owned by the BMW Group, is an international firm (extends its domestic marketing strategy), a multinational firm (uses a multi-domestic marketing strategy), or a transnational firm (employs a global marketing strategy), (2) identify the problems global marketers face when selling a product—in this case a well-known British car—to American consumers, and (3) discuss any marketing mix modifications that MINI might need to make to appeal to American consumers.

Definitions. The following marketing terms are referred to in this in-class activity (ICA):

- Global Marketing Strategy: Transnational firms that employ the practice of standardizing marketing activities when there are cultural similarities and adapting them when cultures differ.

- Multidomestic Marketing Strategy: Multinational firms that have as many different product variations, brand names, and advertising programs as countries in which they do business.

Nature of the Activity. To have students assess selected elements of the MINI brand's marketing mix contained in (1) a PowerPoint presentation and (2) background information provided by the instructor to discuss the typical problems that global marketers face when targeting American consumers.

Estimated Class Time. 20 minutes.

Materials Needed.

- The ICA07-1.doc Word and ICA07-1.ppt PowerPoint files contained in the ICA07-1 folder of the Instructor's CD #1 from the *Instructor's Survival Kit* box.

- The MINI Encyclopedia of Open Motoring brochure contained in the *Instructor's Survival Kit* box.

- Copies of the Marketing Actions to Improve the MINI Brand's Chances of Successfully Targeting the U.S. Market Handout.

- NOTE: Transparencies can be made of the handouts instead of making copies and using the PowerPoint presentation for those instructors who prefer this option.

---

[1] The authors wish to thank Kerri L. Martin, Guardian of Brand Soul for MINI, who assisted in the development of this ICA.

Preparation Before Class. Follow the steps below:

1. Read p. 178 of Chapter 7.

2. Print, read, and if necessary, edit the ICA07-1.doc Word file.

3. Print and/or review the PowerPoint slides from the ICA07-1.ppt PowerPoint file.

4. Make copies of the Marketing Actions to Improve the MINI Brand's Chances of Successfully Targeting the U.S. Market Handout.

5. OPTIONAL: Bookmark the MINI websites (www.miniusa.com) and (www.mini.com) on your classroom computer.

Instructions. Follow the steps below to conduct this ICA:

1. Give students this background mini-lecture on global marketing strategy alternatives:

   "While many U. S. companies engage in global marketing and trade with consumers in foreign countries, the reverse is also true. The U. S. can be a fertile place to expand sales and profits for foreign companies. Companies engaged in global commerce may be characterized as either:

   a. An **international firm**, which engages in trade and marketing in different countries as an extension of the marketing strategy it uses in its home country.

   b. A **multinational firm**, which uses a **multidomestic marketing strategy** that creates as many different product variations, brand names, and advertising programs as countries in which they do business.

   c. A **transnational firm**, which uses a **global marketing strategy** that standardizes its marketing practices across all countries to the extent possible, modifying it only when there are cultural differences.

   When a firm looks for new markets for its products in foreign countries, it often encounters unexpected problems—often because of a lack of understanding of the language, culture, and habits of consumers in the new country. Let's assume you are marketing consultants to MINI's International Marketing Team (a division of the BMW Group) that wants to export its MINI Cooper, MINI Cooper S, MINI Cooper Convertible, and MINI Cooper S Convertible automobiles to U.S. consumers."

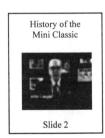

History of the Mini Classic

Slide 2

2. OPTIONAL: **Show Slide 2**: History of the MINI brand, which is narrated by John Cooper, the creator of the Mini Cooper. [TRT = 2:52] Then, give the following background mini-lecture on the history of the Mini Classic:

   "In the late 1950's, there was a fuel crisis caused by tensions in the Middle East. Therefore, to compete with the growing number of small fuel-efficient cars, Sir Leonard Lord challenged Alec Issigonis to design and engineer a fuel efficient car capable of carrying four adults within the economic reach of just about anyone.

The first Classic Mini was first sold in 1959 for approximately $800 (USD) and became Britain's most popular car, selling over 5.3 million units during its 40+ years. In 1999, an international panel of judges ranked the Classic Mini the #2 global car of the 20th century. Ford's Model T was ranked #1.

Mini Cooper got its name in 1961 when racecar driver John Cooper modified the Classic Mini and developed a high performance model. In 1964, 1965, and 1967, the Mini Cooper won the prestigious Monte Carlo race over other European sports cars. From 1960 to 1967, about 10,000 Classic Mini Coopers were sold in the U.S. In 1968, the U.S. government issued more restrictive safety and emissions regulations, and the Mini was withdrawn from the market. In September 2000, the all new MINI premiered at the Mondial De L'Automobile Show in Paris. Days later, the last Classic Mini rolled off the line in Longbridge, UK. The Classic Mini became MINI when it made its European debut in September 2001."

MINI Brand launch to the U.S. in 2002

Slide 3

3. OPTIONAL: **Show Slide 3**: Launch of the MINI brand in the U.S. in 2002. [TRT = 1:49]

4. **Show Slides 4-5** and give the following background mini-lecture on the four MINI models exported to the **U.S.** market:

"Currently, there are four MINI models that are exported from England to the U.S.:

   a. Slide 4: The MINI Cooper ($17,500), which was reintroduced to the U.S. in March 2002.

   b. Slide 4: The MINI Cooper S ($20,950), which was introduced in 2003.

   c. Slide 5: The MINI Cooper Convertible ($22,000), which was introduced in 2004.

   d. Slide 5: The MINI Cooper S Convertible ($25,450), which also was introduced in 2004."

MINI Cooper & MINI Cooper S

Slide 4

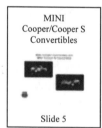

MINI Cooper/Cooper S Convertibles

Slide 5

5. Pass around the MINI Encyclopedia of Open Motoring brochure obtained from the *Instructor's Survival Kit* box.

MINI Cooper
Convertible

Slide 6

6. **Show Slide 6**. Discuss the following "product" attributes of the MINI Cooper Convertible (see www.MINIUSA.com):

   a. Is 143.1" long (bumper-to-bumper) by 66.5" wide (wheel-to-wheel), or 1/3 larger than the Classic Mini. Has go-kart like handling with the wheels at each corner.

   b. The MINI Cooper Convertible has a 1.6 liter, transverse 4-cylinder, 115 horsepower engine. The MINI Cooper S Convertible has a 1.6 liter, supercharged and intercooled, 4-cylinder, 168 horsepower engine.

   c. "Sips" gas: fuel economy is 27 mpg city and 35 mpg highway.

   d. Has 4 standard airbags with Smart Technology that is able to sense which airbags need to inflate and when they need to inflate.

   e. Can "Build-to-Order" via the MINIUSA.com website with 40+ paint combinations, MINI Motoring Gear, Genuine MINI Motoring Accessories, and other options are available online.

   f. Incorporates the latest generation 4-sensor, Anti-Lock Braking System (ABS).

   g. Has front wheel drive.

   h. Has the only fully automatic convertible top with a sunroof function.

   i. Has park distance control, which is standard.

   j. Has a heated glass rear window.

   k. Has 50/50 split folding rear seats for extra storage and loading ease.

7. Discuss the following "price" attributes of the MINI Cooper Convertible (see www.MINIUSA.com):

   a. MINI Cooper Convertible MSRP is $22,000, **including** destination and handling charges.

   b. Options and accessories are extra.

   c. Financing is available from MINI Financial Services.

8. Discuss the following "promotion" attributes of the MINI brand:

   a. Demographics are insignificant since people from 16 to 60 find themselves attracted to the MINI. Instead, it's about the mindset.

   b. **Show Slide 7**. Created the innovative "Encyclopedia of Open Motoring" brochure, which relies on a combination of "cheeky" humor, the motoring philosophy, and product substance highlights to communicate the marketing message.

   c. Does NOT use TV advertising. Instead, MINI use other traditional media in non-traditional ways:

MINI Motoring
brochure

Slide 7

121   ICA 7-1

- **Show Slide 8**. Billboards with the following messages "The SUV Backlash Officially Starts Now," "Let's Sip Not Guzzle," or "Topless…Always Open."

- **Show Slide 9**. Magazine ads, such as buying the margin around a news story in *Rolling Stone* and *Motor Trend*.

MINI Cooper Convertible Billboard

Slide 8

MINI Cooper Convertible Magazine ad

Slide 9

- Guerilla marketing (mounting MINIs atop SUVs and driving around major metropolitan cities).

- Video ads on the MINIUSA.com United States website (see http://www.miniusa.com/link/motoron/miniproductions/movie1) and the MINI.com international website (see http://www.mini.com/com/en/mini_cabrio_film_clips/).

    d. "Starred" in the Austin Powers, Italian Job, and other movies.

9. Discuss the following "place" (or distribution) attributes of the MINI Cooper Convertible:

    a. Sold through a network of approximately 80 MINI dealers located primarily in major metropolitan areas in the U.S.

    b. MINI dealership showrooms are architecturally separate from BMW dealership showrooms. One dealer located its MINI dealership in a regional shopping center (Minneapolis, MN: Southdale Mall).

    c. Can "Build Your Own" MINI using the MINIUSA.com website.

10. Form students into 4-person teams.

MINI Brand Handout

Slide 10

11. **Show Slide 10**. Pass out copies of the Marketing Actions to Improve the MINI Brand's Chances of Successfully Targeting the U.S. Market Handout to each student.

12. Give the students the following instructions:

"In your teams, take 5 to 10 minutes to (1) identify the issues or problems in global marketing and (2) recommend an action for each of four marketing mix elements that your team thinks will improve the MINI brand's chances of successfully targeting the U.S. market:

    a. Product modifications.

    b. Price modifications.

    c. Promotion modifications.

    d. Place (distribution or dealer network) modifications.

13. Ask student teams to share their ideas and discuss them. See below for some points that may emerge in the discussion.

14. **Question**: Ask students to classify MINI, the firm that sells the MINI Cooper Convertible automobiles in the U.S., either as an international firm, a multinational firm, or a transnational firm.

    Answer: The MINI Brand should be classified as a **transnational firm** because it uses a **global marketing strategy**. The BMW Group and the MINI International Marketing Team have standardized the marketing practices for its MINI Cooper automobiles in the U.S. to the extent possible, modifying them only when there are cultural or legal differences to those employed in England (its home country) and the other European countries it targets.

    For example, the MINI Cooper Convertible has the same overall body style and technologies regardless of where the cars are sold. However, one significant product modification is the position of the driver and location of the steering wheel (in England, it's on the right and in America, it's on the left). Also, the humor is culturally determined; therefore, what may be humorous in England may not be in America due to the cultural context within which it is presented.

Marketing Lessons. It is difficult to take a product from one country to another without making changes in the marketing mix. Because of the potential pitfalls inherent in executing any kind of marketing program across borders, marketing, brand, and product managers should conduct marketing research when seeking to enter new global markets.

Websites. To obtain a price quote for a new MINI Cooper/Cooper S Convertible or build one online, visit MINIUSA.com. To see some interesting international videos, go to MINI.com.

Marketing Mix Element	Issue/Problem	Action/Solution
Product Improvements	• In England, car is small • In England, steering wheel on the right (wrong!) side • U.S. fuel economy standards • U.S. safety standards • Comfort • Ability to customize	• Make car larger • Design MINI with steering wheel on left side • Design a fuel-efficient engine • Conform to U.S. safety standards • Focus on technology that allows for greater comfort and movement in upper body and legs • Offer "Build-to-Order" via website that offers features & accessories that American prefer (CD players)
Pricing Improvements	• Currency exchange risks since cars are produced in England (£) and exported to the U.S. ($) • Price of options higher to keep base price under $25,000	• Price guarantees for a fixed period of time • Show comparison prices of similar options for selected competitor cars
Promotion Improvements	• No TV ads; Americans like TV • Movie product placement may not be seen by target market • Non traditional use of traditional media may not appeal to target customers • British humor, if used, may not be fully appreciated by Americans	• Must use very creative alternative media to inform potential target customers, such as magazine ads, billboards, public relations, etc. • Use multiple product placement situations that are consistent with brand image • Use humor that is culturally accepted
Place (Distribution) Improvements	• Dealers in only 56 major U.S. cities • MINI dealer showrooms separate from BMW dealer showrooms	• Ability to configure a car via the Internet • MINI is a unique brand personality that needs to be separate from BMW

MARKETING ACTIONS TO IMPROVE THE MINI® BRAND'S CHANCES OF SUCCESSFULLY TARGETING THE U.S. MARKET

MARKETING STRATEGY AREA	ISSUE/PROBLEM	ACTION/SOLUTION
Product Improvements		
Pricing Improvements		
Promotion Improvements		
Place (Dealer) Improvements		

CHAPTER 7: REACHING GLOBAL MARKETS

ICA 7-2: IN-CLASS ACTIVITY

Are You an Ethnocentric Consumer?

Learning Objectives. To have students (1) discover their personal orientation toward foreign-made products and (2) consider the implication of consumer ethnocentrism for global marketing.

Definitions. The following marketing terms are referred to in this in-class activity (ICA):

- <u>Consumer Ethnocentrism</u>: The tendency to believe that it is inappropriate, indeed immoral, to purchase foreign-made products.

- <u>Sustainable Development</u>: Conducting business in a way that protects the natural environment while making economic progress.

Nature of the Activity. To expose students to the dimensions of consumer ethnocentrism and generate discussion about consumer attitudes toward foreign-made products.

Estimated Class Time. 30 minutes, which consists of:

- 20 minutes to distribute, complete, score, and return the Consumer Sentiment Questionnaire (CSQ) during one class period.

- 10 minutes to discuss the results of the CSQ during the subsequent class period.

Materials Needed.

- The ICA07-2.doc Word and ICA07-2.ppt PowerPoint files contained in the ICA07-2 folder of the Instructor's CD #1 from the *Instructor's Survival Kit* box.

- Copies of the Consumer Sentiment Questionnaire.

- A calculator to calculate the percentages and means from the survey.

- [OPTIONAL: A computer with a statistical program (SPSS, StatPac, or Excel) to calculate the percentages, means, and any differences in the responses for men and women in the survey. A T-test could be performed between the means.]

Preparation Before Class. Follow the steps below:

1. Read p. 184 of Chapter 7.

2. Print, read, and if necessary, edit the ICA07-2.doc Word file.

3. Print and/or review the PowerPoint slides from the ICA07-2.ppt PowerPoint file.

4. Make copies of the Consumer Sentiment Questionnaire.

Instructions. Follow the steps below to conduct this ICA:

1. Distribute the Consumer Sentiment Questionnaire to the class.

2. Inform students that they should respond to all 17 items plus the gender question.

3. **Spend 5 minutes** and have the students complete the Consumer Sentiment Questionnaire. Once done, ask students to pass their completed forms to the instructor. [OPTIONAL: Hand out the surveys at the beginning of the class period. After students have completed the survey, collect them. Then, during the time between classes, input the data into a statistical program and calculate the percentages, means, and t-tests for the survey. Make overheads and discuss the results.]

4. Tally the scores and create a frequency distribution and calculate the means. The numerical range of scores is from 17 to 102.

5. When presenting the final results, instructors might note that there is positive relationship between scores on the Consumer Sentiment Questionnaire and the following variables: patriotism, political-economic conservatism, dogmatism, domestic car ownership, intention to buy a domestic car, and country-of-origin importance. There is a negative relationship between scores on the CSQ and education, income, and consumer attitudes toward foreign-made products.

6. For additional reading on consumer ethnocentrism, see Subhash Sharma, Terence A. Shimp, and Jeongshin Shin, "Consumer Ethnocentrism: A Test of Antecedents and Moderators," *Journal of the Academy of Marketing Science* (Winter, 1995), pp. 26-37.

Marketing Lessons. Consumer ethnocentrism can be measured. Attitudes toward domestic and foreign-made products are often related to attitudes toward a country's world trade policies. Moreover, attitudes toward domestic and foreign-made products are often linked to actual purchase behavior.

CONSUMER SENTIMENT QUESTIONNAIRE

Please indicate the extent to which you agree with the following 17 statements:

	Statement	Strongly Agree	Agree	Neither Agree nor Disagree	Disagree	Strongly Disagree
1.	American people should always buy American-made products instead of imports.	☐	☐	☐	☐	☐
2.	Only those products that are unavailable in the U.S. should be imported.	☐	☐	☐	☐	☐
3.	Buying U.S. -made products keeps us working.	☐	☐	☐	☐	☐
4.	American products, first, last, and foremost.	☐	☐	☐	☐	☐
5.	Purchasing foreign-made products is un-American.	☐	☐	☐	☐	☐
6.	It is not right to purchase foreign products, because it puts Americans out of jobs.	☐	☐	☐	☐	☐
7.	A real American should always buy American-made products.	☐	☐	☐	☐	☐
8.	We should purchase products manufactured in America instead of letting other countries get rich off us.	☐	☐	☐	☐	☐
9.	It is always best to purchase American products.	☐	☐	☐	☐	☐
10.	There should be very little trading or purchasing of goods from other countries unless out of necessity.	☐	☐	☐	☐	☐
11.	Americans should not buy foreign products, because this hurts American businesses and causes unemployment.	☐	☐	☐	☐	☐
12.	Curbs should be put on all imports.	☐	☐	☐	☐	☐
13.	It may cost me in the long run but I prefer to support American products.	☐	☐	☐	☐	☐
14.	Foreigners should not be allowed to put their products on our markets.	☐	☐	☐	☐	☐
15.	Foreign products should be taxed heavily to reduce their entry into the U.S.	☐	☐	☐	☐	☐
16.	We should buy from foreign countries only those products that we can't obtain in our own country.	☐	☐	☐	☐	☐
17.	American consumers who purchase products made in other countries are responsible for putting their fellow Americans out of work.	☐	☐	☐	☐	☐

Gender: Male ☐   Female ☐

CHAPTER 8: MARKETING RESEARCH: FROM INFORMATION TO ACTION

ICA 8-1: IN-CLASS ACTIVITY

Websites of Interest to Marketing Students

Learning Objective. To have students experience the wide variety of marketing information that is available on the Internet.

Definition. The following marketing term is referred to in this in-class activity (ICA):

- Internet: An integrated global network of computers that gives users access to information and documents.

Nature of the Activity. To have students visit three websites that have been discussed in the text or are likely to be of interest to marketing students and then select one website they find interesting and summarize the kinds of information that this website offers.

Estimated Class Time.

- If Internet access is available in the classroom, 20 minutes of "surfing" and discussion should be adequate.

- If Internet access is not available, two class sessions—one for assigning websites to visit and one for discussion—will be necessary.

Materials Needed.

- The ICA08-1.doc Word and ICA08-1.ppt PowerPoint files contained in the ICA08-1 folder of the Instructor's CD #1 from the *Instructor's Survival Kit* box.

- Copies of the Websites of Interest to Marketing Students Handout.

- Internet access and projection equipment the classroom that will allow the websites to be shown on an overhead screen.

- NOTE: Transparencies can be made of the handouts instead of making copies and using the PowerPoint presentation for those instructors who prefer this option.

Preparation Before Class. Follow the steps below:

1. Read p. 212 of Chapter 8.

2. Print, read, and if necessary, edit the ICA08-1.doc Word file.

3. Print and/or review the PowerPoint slides from the ICA08-1.ppt PowerPoint file.

4. Make copies of the Websites of Interest to Marketing Students Handout.

5. Familiarize yourself with each of the websites identified in the Websites of Interest to Marketing Students Handout.

6. OPTIONAL: Bookmark the websites referred to in this ICA on your classroom computer.

Instructions. Follow the steps below to conduct this ICA:

1. Ask students about their experience "surfing" the Internet. Solicit examples of what Internet websites interest them.

2. Pass out the Websites of Interest to Marketing Students Handout.

Slide 2

3. **Show Slide 2**: Websites of Interest to Marketing Students Handout.

4. If the classroom has Internet access, select 2 to 3 websites to visit, such as the American Marketing Association's www.marketingpower.com and the U.S. government's portal, www.firstgov.gov. If the classroom does not have Internet access, assign 3 to 4 websites to (teams of) students and ask them to visit these websites before the next class.

5. Discuss the marketing implications of the websites.

Marketing Lessons. The websites listed on Websites of Interest to Marketing Students Handout demonstrate the wide variety of marketing information and activities available on the Internet. The American Marketing Association and American Advertising Federation websites are resources for marketing students and professionals. Firstgov.gov and the *Wall Street Journal Interactive Edition* websites demonstrate the growing access to marketing information. Finally, the McGraw-Hill Higher Education website provides information about this marketing book!

Websites. See those listed on the Websites of Interest to Marketing Students Handout.

Websites of Interest to Marketing Students Handout

[NOTE: "http://" is assumed before "www"]

1. The American Marketing Association   www.marketingpower.com

2. The American Advertising Federation   www.aaf.org

3. Ad Forum.com (15,000 print/TV ads)   www.adforum.com

4. eBay (on-line auction)   www.ebay.com

5. McGraw-Hill Higher Education   www.mhhe.com/kerin

6. Career Builder (careers)   www.careerbuilder.com

7. iVillage.com (portal for women)   www.ivillage.com

8. Pollstar (concert locator)   www.pollstar.com

9. The Drudge Report (political news)   www.drudgereport.com

10. Amazon.com (purchase books, CDs)   www.amazon.com

11. Business Week (business news)   www.businessweek.com

12. Wall Street Journal Interactive Edition   www.wsj.com

13. Yahoo! (portal)   www.yahoo.com

14. Google (search engine)   www.google.com

15. Firstgov.gov (U.S. government portal)   www.firstgov.gov

CHAPTER 8: MARKETING RESEARCH: FROM INFORMATION TO ACTION

ICA 8-2: IN-CLASS ACTIVITY

Designing a Taste Test Questionnaire for Howlin' Coyote Chili

Learning Objectives. To have students (1) design three questions for a taste test questionnaire of a possible new Howlin' Coyote® chili and (2) compare their questions with those actually used in the taste test.

Definitions. The following marketing terms are referred to in this in-class activity (ICA):

- Questionnaire Data: Facts and figures obtained by asking people about their attitudes, awareness, intentions, and behaviors.

- Scale: A fixed alternative question with three or more choices that measures the variation or intensity in a respondent's attitude, opinion, and/or behavior.

Nature of the Activity. To have students design questions for a survey, each using a scale to measure the attitudes and behaviors and appreciate the difficulty in developing questions that assess consumer attitudes, opinions, and/or behaviors.

Estimated Class Time. 20 minutes.

Materials Needed.

- The ICA08-2.doc Word and ICA08-2.ppt PowerPoint files contained in the ICA08-2 folder of the Instructor's CD #1 from the *Instructor's Survival Kit* box.

- The Howlin' Coyote Chili Challenge Taste Test Questionnaire from the *Instructor's Survival Kit* box.

- Copies of the:
  a. Try Your Hand at Designing a Chili Taste-Test Questionnaire Handout.
  b. Howlin' Coyote Chili Challenge Taste Test Questionnaire.

- NOTE: Transparencies can be made of the handouts instead of making copies and using the PowerPoint presentation for those instructors who prefer this option.

Preparation Before Class. Follow the steps below:

1. Read pp. 55-69 of Appendix A that give some background on Howlin' Coyote Chili and pp. 217-219 of Chapter 8 on questionnaire design.

2. Print, read, and if necessary, edit the ICA08-2.doc Word file.

3. Print and/or review the PowerPoint slides from the ICA08-2.ppt PowerPoint file.

4. Make copies of:

   a. Try Your Hand at Designing a Chili Taste-Test Questionnaire Handout.

   b. Howlin' Coyote Chili Challenge Taste Test Questionnaire.

5. Review the Howlin' Coyote Chili Challenge Taste Test Questionnaire.

Instructions. Follow the steps below to conduct this ICA:

Slide 2

1. **Show Slide 2** and pass out copies of the Try Your Hand at Designing a Chili Taste-Test Questionnaire Handout.

2. Give the following background mini-lecture:

   Paradise Kitchens (see Appendix A) often does taste tests to evaluate a new chili that might be added to its Howlin' Coyote line. As a part of the taste test, participants are asked to complete a short questionnaire that summarizes their feelings. This questionnaire must be simple and worded very carefully so that participants are able to provide the information requested.

3. **Spend 5 minutes** and have students design each of the three scales or questions shown on the Try Your Hand at Designing a Chili Taste-Test Questionnaire Handout.

4. Have several students suggest their proposed scales for each of the three questions from the Try Your Hand at Designing a Chili Taste-Test Questionnaire Handout, and perhaps have them write them on the board.

Slide 3

5. **Show Slide 3** and pass out copies of the Howlin' Coyote Chili Challenge Taste Test Questionnaire.

6. Make these points about the three questions posed on the Howlin' Coyote Chili Challenge Taste Test Questionnaire:

- **Question #1.** As shown in Questions 1 and 2 in the Howlin' Coyote Chili Challenge Taste Test Questionnaire, the six scale points are:

  - Dislike extremely
  - Dislike somewhat
  - Neutral
  - Like somewhat
  - Like very much
  - Like extremely

  Point out (1) the "neutral point" is **not** in the center of the scale, thereby giving more scale points and discrimination to the positive reactions; instead, a "5-point" scale should have been used if a neutral point is desired and (2) the "faces" on the scale are intended to make the question less threatening to respondents and serve as surrogates for verbal descriptors.

ICA 8-2

- **Question #2**. This should have been easy. The chili spiciness scale is:

    – Mild   – Medium   – Hot

- **Question #3**. See Question 8 in the Howlin' Coyote Chili Challenge Taste Test Questionnaire. Point out to the class that (1) the time period covered is the past **6 months** (not a year, which would be more difficult for participants to remember) and (2) the scale points are "none", "1 to 5 times", and "6 or more times." Clearly, the heavy users (6 or more times) are of greatest interest to Paradise Kitchens.

7. Ask students to comment on or critique other parts of the actual Howlin' Coyote Chili Challenge Taste Test Questionnaire. Also, ask them to develop marketing actions that could result from each question.

    - **Opening Statement**. Offering "valuable coupons" and a "raffle entry to win prizes" may entice some respondents to not only complete the survey (+) but also potentially provide more favorable responses to the questions asked than they normally would in hopes of receiving the coupons or winning the prize, thus skewing the survey results (–).

    - **Questions #1 & #2**. Adding the faces to the verbal adjectives for the scales in these questions is a good idea because some respondents process information visually and view these cues as helpful.

    - **Question #3**. "choose" should be capitalized.

    - **Question #5**. A comma should be placed after "chili."

    - **Question #7**. Seems out of sequence. Better survey design needed.

    - **Question #9**. Age ranges are not mutually exclusive (what if a respondent is 35 years old, which response option would be checked: 22 – 35 or 35 – 55?) or exhaustive (what if a respondent is 18 years old? or is 56 – 60 years old?).

    - **Overall Questionnaire Design**. Too many questions bunched at the bottom of the page. Either use two pages (front and back) or eliminate a question or two and use just one page.

    Marketing Lesson. It is critically important that marketing research questionnaires (1) be simple, (2) be precisely worded, (3) be visually appealing, and (4) most importantly, lead to tangible marketing actions.

TRY YOUR HAND AT DESIGNING
A CHILI TASTE-TEST QUESTIONNAIRE HANDOUT

1. You have a respondent taste a new Howlin' Coyote chili being considered for manufacture. Suggest names for the <u>six</u> scale points seeking the respondent's reaction, where one of the scale points is "neutral."

_____ _____ _____ _____ _____ _____

2. Suggest three names on a "spiciness scale" to evaluate the new chili.

_____ _____ _____

3. You are especially interested in reactions to consumers who frequently eat chili. Compose a question to measure a respondent's frequency of consuming chili.

ICA 8-2

CHAPTER 8: MARKETING RESEARCH: FROM INFORMATION TO ACTION

ICA 8-3: IN-CLASS ACTIVITY

Pepsi vs. Coke Taste Test[1]

Learning Objectives. To have students run an experiment, collect data, and interpret the results by replicating the "Pepsi Challenge" with Pepsi Cola and Coca-Cola.

Definitions. The following marketing terms are referred to in this in-class activity (ICA):

- Data: The facts and figures related to the problem divided into two main parts: secondary data and primary data.

- Experiment: Obtaining data by manipulating factors under tightly controlled conditions to test cause and effect.

Nature of the Activity. To have students conduct (and replicate a historic) an in-class taste test experiment by comparing Pepsi and Coke.

Estimated Class Time. 20 minutes.

Materials Needed.

- The ICA08-3.doc Word and ICA08-3.ppt PowerPoint files contained in the ICA08-3 folder of the Instructor's CD #1 from the *Instructor's Survival Kit* box.

- Copies of the Pepsi vs. Coke Taste Test Questionnaire.

- A sufficient number of 2-liter bottles of Pepsi Cola and Coca-Cola so that each student in the class can participate in the experiment.

- A sufficient number of 2-ounce Dixie® paper cups for each student in the class.

- 1 box of regular crackers (e.g. Nabisco's Original Premium® Saltines).

- A marker to write letters on the side or bottom of each cup.

- 1 large container of water.

- A calculator or computer in the classroom with Microsoft Excel to calculate the percentages for the survey.

- [OPTIONAL: Blindfolds (depending on the size of your class) so that students cannot see the color of the soft drink.]

---

[1] The authors wish to Lisa Castaldo of Pepsico who assisted in the development of this ICA.

- NOTE: Transparencies can be made of the handouts instead of making copies and using the PowerPoint presentation for those instructors who prefer this option.

Preparation Before Class. Follow the steps below:

1. Read pp. 220-221 of Chapter 8.

2. Print, read, and if necessary, edit the ICA08-3.doc Word file.

3. Print and/or review the PowerPoint slides from the ICA08-3.ppt PowerPoint file.

4. Purchase a sufficient number of 2-liter bottles of Pepsi Cola and Coca-Cola. To calculate the number of each soft drink needed, count the number of students, multiply by 2 ounces, and then divide by 88, the number of ounces in a 2-liter bottle.

5. Purchase a package of 2-ounce Dixie paper cups and 1-2 boxes of saltine crackers.

6. Write a "B" on ⅓ of the paper cups, an "N" on another ⅓ of the paper cups, and a "W" on the last ⅓ of the paper cups with a marker.

7. Refrigerate the bottles of Pepsi and Coke until just before class.

8. Arrange for a pitcher of cool water to be brought to class on the day of the taste test.

9. Make copies of the Pepsi vs. Coke Taste Test Questionnaire.

10. [OPTIONAL: Buy or make 1 to 3 blindfolds to create a true "blind" taste test.]

11. Before class starts, set up two taste test stations at the front of the classroom that consists of a shield (to prohibit taste-testers from identifying the soft drink brands being evaluated), labeled cups, water, saltines, surveys, and (optional) blindfolds.

12. At the start of class, select two teams of 1 to 2 students at random to manage each taste test stations. Recruit students who are responsible to perform this task. Have them randomly assign the letters "B" or "N" to either Pepsi or Coke.

13. OPTIONAL: Bookmark the Pepsi (www.pepsi.com) and Coca Cola (www.cocacola.com) websites on your classroom computer.

Instructions. Follow the steps below to conduct this ICA:

New Pepsi Challenge TV ad

Slide 2

1. **Show Slide 2**: Pepsi Challenge TV ad. [TRT = 0:30] and pass out copies of Pepsi vs. Coke Taste Test Questionnaire.

2. Give the following background mini-lecture:

"During the late 1970s and early 1980s, Pepsi Cola conducted a nationwide comparative taste test known as the "Pepsi Challenge." Pepsi set up stations on college campuses and at other public arenas to have consumers compare the taste of Pepsi to Coca-Cola (the original brand, now known as "Coca-Cola Classic"). This "blind" taste test was conducted in the following manner:

a. Two small cups were labeled "B" and "N." To prohibit taste-testers from identifying which cola was poured into which cup, one was filled with Pepsi and the other one with Coke behind a cardboard backdrop or shield.

b. Next, a taste-tester was asked to take a sip from cup "B." Then, the taste-tester was required to eat one saltine cracker and take a sip of water to remove any aftertaste in his/her mouth. Lastly, the taste-tester took a sip from cup "N." Since both colas were brown in color, no blindfold was necessary.

c. When finished, the taste-tester was asked to state (verbally and on a brief survey) which tasted better: cola "B" or cola "N." After recording the result, the taste-tester was informed of the identity of the cola in each cup and asked for her/his reaction. The presumption was that since Coca-Cola had a greater market share than Pepsi, more taste-testers would prefer Coke to Pepsi. According to Pepsi, the results of the taste test were just the opposite: more people preferred the taste of Pepsi because it was sweeter than Coke.

In 1985, Coca-Cola decided to conduct its own Coke Taste Test when it compared a reformulated, sweeter "New" Coke with the original Coca-Cola formula. Based on results obtained from blind taste tests run on almost 200,000 people:

- Consumers preferred New Coke (55%) to "Old" Coke (45%).
- Consumers preferred New Coke (52%) to Pepsi Cola (48%).
- However, after New Coke was introduced, new studies showed only 30% of consumers liked New Coke.

Thus, consumers preferred the taste of "new" Coke over "old" Coke, and more importantly, over Pepsi. As astute marketers, Coca-Cola made the decision to pull "old" Coke from the market and replace it with "new" Coke to reinvigorate the brand and gain market share.

However, the results of this strategy were disastrous for Coca-Cola! During the taste test, Coca-Cola had failed to assess the impact on the results if its customers/testers were told that "old" Coke would be pulled off the market if consumers in general preferred the "new" Coke to both "old" Coke and Pepsi. Brand-loyal consumers, who highly valued both the history and somewhat bitter taste of the old Coca Cola formula, rebelled when Coca-Cola pulled "old" Coke. They boycotted Coca-Cola products and generated a massive write-in campaign demanding that "old" Coke be reinstated. After a brief period, Coca-Cola reintroduced the old formulation as "Coca-Cola Classic" and ultimately removed New Coke from the market.

Pepsi vs. Coke
Taste Challenge

Slide 3

3. **Show Slide 3**. Inform students that we are going to replicate the Pepsi Challenge and Coke Taste Test experiments."[2]

4. Behind a shield, have Team 1 put Pepsi in cup "B and Coke in cup "N." Team 2 will put Coke in cup "B" and Pepsi in cup "N." All teams will fill the "W" cups with water.

5. To begin the taste test, have students come down by rows. Have students from odd numbered rows go to station 1 and those from even rows go to station 2. Then, place a blindfold on the student. Next, take one "B", "N", and "W" cup from behind the shield and place them in front of the student.

6. With a blindfold on, have each taste-tester take a sip from cup "B." Then, have him/her take a bite of a saltine cracker and a sip of water. Next, have her/him repeat the process for cup "N." When finished, place the used cups behind the shield before you tell the tester to remove his/her blindfold. Have the student give you his/her copy of the Pepsi vs. Coke Taste Test Questionnaire. **Write down the station number on the student's Pepsi vs. Coke Taste Test Questionnaire**.

7. When finished the taste test, have each student fill out and hand in the Pepsi vs. Coke Taste Test Questionnaire. When all students have completed the test and turned in their surveys, take a poll by station number as to which brand (cup "B" or cup "N") tasted the better and record the results on the blackboard or a blank overhead transparency. Finally, inform them which brand was in which cup for each station or wait until the end of (or next) class period when the survey results have been tabulated.

8. Have someone tabulate the results on a calculator or the classroom PC using Excel during the middle of class and discuss the results.

9. Conclude this ICA with the following mini-lecture:

"Experiments like the one we just completed are useful because it allows marketers to test one or more aspects of the marketing mix under strictly controlled conditions to determine which features, prices, promotions, etc. customers prefer. However, two drawbacks of experiments as a research tool are that (1) consumers' behavior may not match that shown when operating in the marketplace and (2) actions of competitors can distort the results or impact the marketing actions taken by the firm as a result of the experiment.

[2] Robert F. Hartley, "*Marketing Mistakes and Successes*," 8th ed. (New York: John Wiley & Sons, 2001), pp. 11-14.

ICA 8-3

Two controls were built into the Pepsi vs. Coke Taste Test experiment:

- **Randomly assigning letters to the brands**. This is done to eliminate students guessing which letter would be given a particular brand. However, this does not overcome the potential problem of a student preference for one letter in the alphabet over another.

- **Eating a saltine cracker and drinking water between tastes**. This is done to avoid a possible lingering "aftertaste" that might be caused from tasting the previous brand."

9. Tabulate the results of the Pepsi vs. Coke Taste Test experiment. The simplest analysis is based on tabulating the taste test results on a blank copy of the form and calculating the percentages for each question with a calculator or Excel.

   Tabulations of Questions 1 and 2 tell how the two brands compare with each other in paired-comparison tests. An in-class discussion led by the instructor might initially assume that the class test results were consistent with the shares reported in the surveys. Ask students how they might explain the discrepancy between their stated preferences and the results from the in-class taste test experiment.

   Marketing Lessons. Intentions expressed in an experiment do not always translate well into actual practice. The experimental condition itself can affect results (the Hawthorne effect: people know they're being evaluated). Measuring only one element of the marketing mix (the "product") does not provide the whole marketing mix context within which consumers may evaluate products and make purchase decisions of how consumers will react to the entire offering).

   Websites. Pepsi's website is www.pepsi.com. Coca-Cola's website is www.cocacola.com.

PEPSI VS. COKE TASTE TEST QUESTIONNAIRE

STATION NUMBER: _____

1. In comparing the tastes of brand "B" and brand "N":

   I prefer "B" ..... ☐   I am indifferent between "B" and "N" ..... ☐   I prefer "N" ..... ☐

2. Based on your station number, which soft drink brand is "B" and which is "N"?

   "B" is: _____   "N" is: _____

3. Are you a "Heavy", "Medium", "Light" or "Non" user or consumer of soft drinks?

   Heavy User ..... ☐   Medium User... ☐   Light User....... ☐   Non User......... ☐

4. Which is your preferred brand: "Pepsi," "Coca-Cola," or "None"?

   Pepsi .... ☐   Coca-Cola............. ☐   None.................... ☐

5. What is your gender: Male .... ☐   Female....... ☐

CHAPTER 8: MARKETING RESEARCH: FROM INFORMATION TO ACTION

ICA 8-4: IN-CLASS ACTIVITY

Arbitron Radio Ratings: What Do People Listen To?[1]

Learning Objectives. To have students: (1) engage in a simple marketing research activity, (2) interpret data in selected formats, and (3) suggest marketing actions.

Definitions. The following marketing terms are referred to in this in-class activity (ICA):

- Format: Describes the type of content that is broadcasted on a particular radio station based on the preference of a chosen target audience.

- Primary Data: Facts and figures that are newly collected for the project.

- Probability Sampling: Involves using precise rules to select the sample such that each element of the population has a specific known chance of being selected.

- Questionnaire Data: Facts and figures obtained by asking people about their attitudes, awareness, intentions, and behaviors.

- Rating: The radio listening audience expressed as a percentage of the total population. $\text{Rating}_{\text{population}}\ (\%) = (\text{Listeners} \div \text{Population}) \times 100$.[2]

- Share: The percentage of those listening to the radio in a market who are listening to a particular radio station. $\text{Share}_{\text{radio station}}\ (\%) = (\text{Rating}_{\text{radio station}} \div \text{Rating}_{\text{population}}) \times 100$.[2]

Nature of the Activity. To have students: (1) complete an abridged Arbitron Radio Ratings Diary; (2) interpret data in tabular and graphical form concerning the demographics and behaviors of radio listeners; and (3) recommend marketing actions.

Estimated Class Time. 30 minutes.

Materials Needed.

- The ICA08-4.doc Word and ICA08-4.ppt PowerPoint files contained in the ICA08-4 folder of the Instructor's CD #1 from the *Instructor's Survival Kit* box.

- Copies of the Arbitron Radio Ratings Diary Handout for each student.

- OPTIONAL: A calculator to calculate the percentage responses to the behaviors and demographic questions asked in the Arbitron Radio Ratings Diary.

---

[1] The authors wish to thank Jessica Benbow, Press Assistant at Arbitron, who assisted in the development of this ICA. All Arbitron images and materials are copyrighted to Arbitron Inc. and are for demonstration purposes only. Arbitron materials may not be used in any manner without the express written permission of Arbitron.

[2] "Terms of the Trade," Arbitron online glossary. See http://www.arbitron.com/radio_stations/reference_using.htm.

- NOTE: Transparencies can be made of the handouts instead of making copies and using the PowerPoint presentation for those instructors who prefer this option.

Preparation Before Class. Follow the steps below:

1. Read pp. 210, 215-217, 227 of Chapter 8.

2. Print, read, and if necessary, edit the ICA08-4.doc Word file.

3. Print and/or review the PowerPoint slides from the ICA08-4.ppt PowerPoint file.

4. Make copies of the Arbitron Radio Ratings Diary Handout for each student.

5. OPTIONAL: Bookmark the Arbitron (www.arbitron.com) and Friday Morning Quarterback (www.fmqb.com) websites on your classroom computer.

Instructions. Follow the steps below to conduct this ICA:

1. Form students into 4-person teams.

2. Give the following mini-lecture about Arbitron:

   "Arbitron is a media and market research firm whose core business is to measure the behaviors and obtain demographic data of national and local market radio listeners. Radio stations use this information to: (1) determine their ratings; (2) identify the demographics and behaviors of those who listen during particular times of the day; (3) set advertising rates for organizations who want to reach these consumers; and (4) make any changes in programming format based on the results. Advertisers use this information to select and "buy" advertising time on those radio stations in a market that closely matches the target market profile for a product or service."

Arbitron Radio
Ratings Diary

Slide 2

3. **Show Slide 2**: Arbitron Radio Ratings Diary Kit and give the following mini-lecture about Arbitron's Radio Ratings Diary:

   "Arbitron sends its Radio Ratings Diary to a carefully selected probability sample of the population four times each year to obtain listener behavior. Arbitron places over 5 million telephone calls each year to potential respondents to request their participation. In 2004, about 60 percent of those contacted consent to participate and are mailed the Arbitron Radio Ratings Diary package, which consists of:

   - A seven-day radio listening diary, designed to be personally maintained by each member of the household 12 and older.
   - An easy-to-follow diary instructions.
   - A thank-you letter for participation.
   - A $5 cash premium for each participant.
   Of those that agreed to participate, about 60 percent actually complete the Arbitron Radio Ratings Diary and return it to Arbitron in 2004."

4. **Show Slide 3** and pass out the Arbitron Radio Ratings Diary Handout.

5. Continue with the mini-lecture about Arbitron's Radio Ratings Diary:

"In the Arbitron's Radio Ratings Diary, participants are asked to record:

- Start and stop times.

- Radio station information (call letters, whether AM or FM, etc.).

- Listening locations (home, car, work, etc.).

- Whether or not they listened at all to radio that particular day.

- Demographics, such as age, sex, residence, employment status, education, children under 12, and household income.

- Comments they have about specific radio stations, programs, etc.

Respondents are asked to return their diaries in a timely manner and encouraged to call a toll-free number if they have any questions."

6. **Spend 5 to 10 minutes** and have students complete their abridged Arbitron Radio Ratings Diary. Give them the following directions:

"Turn to the first page of the Arbitron Radio Ratings Diary Handout. You will now write down the time, stations, and places you listened to the radio yesterday. Be sure to read the instructions at the top before starting. When you are finished, turn over the handout and answer the questions about yourself. Note that a few of the questions do not have response options because for our purposes, they aren't relevant."

7. **Spend 5 to 10 minutes** and use the board or a transparency to tally the responses to the radio listening behavior of students from the Arbitron Radio Ratings Diary. [OPTIONAL: You may want to calculate the percentages using a calculator.]:

- **Start and stop times**. When did students listen to the radio? Was it during the early morning (5 AM to 10 AM), midday (10 AM to 3 PM), late afternoon (3 PM to 7 PM), or night (7 PM to 5 AM)? Calculate the frequencies and discuss. Ask students how many hours per week, on average, they listen to the radio.

  Answer: Most students probably listened to the radio during the early morning, late afternoon, or evening. Evening students might listen during midday. Most probably listen to the radio about 20 to 25 hours per week.

- **Radio stations**. What radio stations did listen to the radio? How would students classify the formats are these (adult contemporary, alternative, country, news/sports/talk, rock, Spanish, urban, etc.)? Are these AM or FM stations?

  Answer: Students probably listen to 3 or 4 different formats, depending on their mood, interests, etc. Typically, most news/sports/talk stations are AM while music stations are FM.

- **Place**. Where do students typically listen to the radio? At home, walking to/from class, car, work, other? Ask them if they listen to satellite radio or radio programs via the Internet. Calculate the frequencies and discuss.

    Answer: Due to the transient and innovative nature of students, they probably listen to the radio in a variety of places and means.

8. **Spend 3 minutes** and use the board or a transparency to tally the students' responses to the demographic questions from the Arbitron Radio Ratings Diary. <u>**Only questions 1 and 2 are assessed here**</u>. [OPTIONAL: You may want to (1) discuss student responses to Question 4 on employment status and (2) calculate the percentages using a calculator.]

    - **Age (Question 1)**. What form does Arbitron use to ask this question? What is the age distribution of students? [NOTE: You should develop age categories *a priori* (before the fact) before tabulating the results from students. These categories should be identical to those from the Census Bureau (18 – 24 yrs old; 25 – 34 yrs old; 35 yrs and older.]

        Answer: Arbitron asks this question in discrete (writing in their age in the space provided) rather than in categorical (checking a response option box that corresponds to an age range) form. With discrete questions, marketers obtain *ratio data*, which can be used to create averages or group data *post hoc* (or after the fact) to make more meaningful analyses. Arbitron uses Census age categories to report the ages of radio listeners in reports to its clients.

    - **Gender (Question 2)**. What form does Arbitron use to ask this question? What is the gender distribution of students?

        Answer: This question is in a *nominal* (non ordered) categorical form.

    9. **Spend 5 minutes** to make the following statement and ask different student teams the following questions:

        "Arbitron uses tables to present findings from the Arbitron Radio Ratings Diary to clients in its *Radio Today* reports."

Arbitron Radio
Ratings Formats
Table

Slide 4

        - Question 1: **Show Slide 4**: Arbitron Radio Ratings Formats Table and ask the following: What are the (*a*) strengths and (*b*) weaknesses of using tables in a report?

            Answers:

            a. **Strengths**. Allows quantities of data to be summarized succinctly, provided that good column heads and row stubs have been selected. Data can be presented in detail—to the nearest penny or percentage point.

            b. **Weaknesses**. Can overwhelm the reader with quantities of data, in which key points can be lost. Even an experienced interpreter may need time to see critical information from a table of data.

- Question 2: Continue to show Slide 4 and ask the following: (*a*) Which formats are most/least popular in 2004? (*b*) Which formats are growing/declining over the three-year period? (*c*) What marketing actions should radio stations or advertisers take as a result of your interpretation of this data?

  Answers:

  a. **Formats most/least popular.** In 2004, the most popular radio formats were news/talk/information (share = 15.9%), country (13.2%), and adult contemporary (12.8%). The least popular formats were classical (2.2%), new AC/smooth jazz (2.3%), and religious (2.8%).

  b. **Formats growing/declining.** Formats that significantly increased their growth over the three-year period were news/talk/information (+1.2 points), urban (+0.9), and Spanish (+0.7). Formats that declined in popularity were religious (-2.4) and adult contemporary (-0.8).

  c. **Marketing actions radio stations or advertisers should take.** Radio stations with small or declining shares must be concerned about the advertising rates they will be able to charge for the next year. Some may want to change programming or even formats to catch a rising trend in listener preferences. Advertisers must determine whether their target markets have changed their listening behavior before buying and placing ads with a radio station using a particular format.

  OPTIONAL: To see the most popular formats for your market, go to the "Friday Morning Quarterback" website and type in the following link http://www.fmqb.com/ratings.asp. Then, select the city and view the results. Are they similar to the responses of your students?

10. Give the following mini-lecture about radio listening behavior in the U.S.[3]

"There are about 175 million people 12 years and older who listen to the more than 13,800 radio stations in the U.S. Of these, about 5,000 are AM stations and 8,800 are FM stations. In 2005, listeners had almost 50 radio formats to choose from, with new ones added each year and others that fade in popularity. Radio content is delivered through a variety of systems today: standalone radios, mp3-type devices, cable TV digital channels, car-satellite systems, and the Internet. As a result, radio reaches about 95 percent of the U.S. population 12 years and older each week.

During the weekday, the majority of radio listeners tune in at home in the early morning or evening hours but listen at places outside the home (car, work, etc.) during midday and late afternoon hours. On average, listeners spend almost 20 hours listening to the radio each week. Heavy listeners are those 25 – 54 yrs old."

---

[3] "Radio Today: How America Listens to Radio (2005 Edition)," Arbitron, pp. 3-5, 8, 12, 23-25, 35-37, 59-61, 63-65. See http://www.arbitron.com/downloads/radiotoday05.pdf.

11. **Spend 5 minutes** to make the following statement and ask different student teams the following questions:

"Arbitron also uses charts and graphs to present findings from the Arbitron Radio Ratings Diary to clients in its *Radio Today* reports."

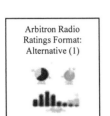

Slide 5

- Question 1: **Show Slide 5** and ask the following: What are the (*a*) strengths and (*b*) weaknesses of using charts/graphs in a report?

  Answers:

  a. **Strengths**. Allows high and low points to be seen at a glance. A line or bar graph or a pie chart will be the best choice in different circumstances. If data points are too close together, more space can be assigned to sharpen the picture.

  b. **Weaknesses**. Lack of precision and backup detail.

Slide 6

- Question 2: **Show Slide 5 and Slide 6** and ask the following: (*a*) Who listens to this format? (*b*) What marketing actions should radio stations or advertisers take as a result of your interpretation of this data?

  Answers: 'Alternative' includes 'New or Alternative Rock' music.

  a. **Who listens**. In 2004, Alternative format listeners were men (63%), 18 – 24 yrs old (22%) or 25 – 34 yrs old (28%), and who reside in the New England or Western U.S.

  b. **Marketing actions radio stations or advertisers should take**. Advertisers whose target markets include men and/or consumers 18 – 34 yrs old should consider buying and placing ads with radio stations located in markets in the Northeast or Western U.S. that use this particular format.

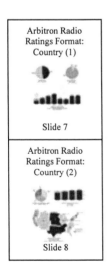

Slide 7

Slide 8

- Question 3: **Show Slide 7 and Slide 8** and ask the following: (*a*) Who listens to this format? (*b*) What marketing actions should radio stations or advertisers take as a result of your interpretation of this data?

  Answers: 'Country' includes traditional and modern country music.

  a. **Who listens**. In 2004, Country format listeners were tended to be women (53%), those 35 – 44 yrs old (19%), and who reside in the West North Central or South Central U.S.

  b. **Marketing actions radio stations or advertisers should take**. Advertisers whose target markets include both men and women and/or consumers 18 – 34 yrs old should consider buying and placing ads with radio stations located in markets in the West North Central or South Central U.S that use this particular format.

12. Conclude this ICA with a mini-lecture on using tables and graphics in a report:

   "As Arbitron has effectively shown in its *Radio Today* report, combining tables, charts, and graphs can overcome the weaknesses and benefit from the strengths of each format."

13. OPTIONAL: To view and interpret additional format examples, such as Rock, Spanish, and Urban, go to Arbitron's website (www.arbitron.com). Type in the following link (http://www.arbitron.com/downloads/radiotoday05.pdf) to download the 'pdf' of the *Radio Today* 2005 Edition report. Scroll through the document until you come to the formats desired. [NOTE: You will need the latest Adobe Acrobat Reader to view or print the document. See www.adobe.com/products/acrobat/ and click on the 'Get Adobe Reader' link.]

Marketing Lessons. Marketers conduct and purchase studies that use a variety of primary data collection methods. Data collection and analysis are important skills marketers must possess to fully understand the attitudes, behaviors, and characteristics of customers. However, to be truly effective, marketers must be able to take marketing actions based on the findings presented to them in reports and presentations. These data can be effectively presented in tables, graphs, and charts, although each has its strengths and weaknesses.

Websites. Arbitron's website is (www.arbitron.com) and Friday Morning Quarterback's website is (www.fmqb.com).

ARBITRON RADIO RATINGS DIARY HANDOUT[4]

● **No matter how much or how little you listen to the radio, you're responses are important!**
You're one of the few people picked in your area to have the chance to tell radio stations what you listen to. This is *your* ratings diary. Please make sure you fill it out yourself.

Here's what we mean by "listening": "Listening" is any time you can hear a radio—whether you choose the station or not. When you hear a radio, write it down—whether you're at home, in a car, at work, or someplace else.

Time: Write the time you start listening and the time you stop. If you start at one time of day and stop in another, draw a line from the time you start to the time you stop.

Station: Write the call letters, dial setting, or station name. Mark AM or FM. AM or FM stations can have the same call letters. Make sure you mark ⊠ the right box.

Place: Mark where you listen: at home; in a car; at work; or other place. **If you haven't listened to the radio all day, mark the box at the bottom of the page**.

YESTERDAY									
Time			**Station**			**Place**			
	Start	Stop	Call Letters, Dial Setting, or Station Name	Mark ⊠ One		Mark ⊠ One			
				AM	FM	At Home	In a Car	At Work	Other Place
Early Morning (from 5 AM)	:	:							
	:	:							
	:	:							
	:	:							
Midday	:	:							
	:	:							
	:	:							
	:	:							
Late Afternoon	:	:							
	:	:							
	:	:							
	:	:							
Night (to 5 AM)	:	:							
	:	:							
	:	:							
	:	:							

If you didn't listen to the radio today, please mark ⊠ here. ☐

---

[4] "Your Personal Radio Ratings Diary," (Abridged and edited due to space considerations), Arbitron Ratings.

ARBITRON RADIO RATINGS DIARY HANDOUT

Quick Questions...For You

The following questions apply to you yourself.

1. What is you age? _____

2. Are you male or female? ☐ Male ☐ Female

3. Where do you live? [NOTE: Response options omitted for this question.]

4. Are you employed full time or part time? ☐ Yes ☐ No

   If 'Yes': How many hours per week are you usually employed? ☐ < 35 ☐ 35 or more

   What is your zip code at your usual place of work? [NOTE: Response option omitted for this question.]

5. What was the last grade of school you completed? [NOTE: Response options omitted for this question.]

6. Thinking back 6 months ago, what radio station did you listen to most at that time? Write down the call letters, dial setting or station name. Mark AM or FM. [NOTE: Response options omitted for this question.]

7. How many children under age 12 live in this household? [NOTE: Response options omitted for this question.]

8. Which of the following categories best describes your household income from all sources (before taxes) for the past year? [NOTE: Response options omitted for this question.]

9. Your opinion counts. Use this space to make any comments you like about specific stations, announcers or programs.

   _____

   _____

   We appreciate the time you've taken to be a part of the radio ratings. Thank you for your help.

Average Share of People 12 and Older Listening to a Format Category in the U.S.

Format Category	2002	2003	2004
Adult Contemporary	13.6	13.0	12.8
Alternative	4.2	4.0	4.0
Contemporary Hits Radio	10.6	10.3	10.3
Classical	2.3	2.3	2.2
Country	12.9	13.0	13.2
New AC/Smooth Jazz	2.4	2.5	2.3
News/Talk/Information	14.7	15.8	15.9
Oldies	7.3	7.1	7.1
Religious	5.2	5.2	2.8
Rock	9.9	9.2	9.0
Spanish	5.7	5.8	6.4
Urban	6.7	7.4	7.6
All Other	4.5	4.4	6.4

Sources: Radio Today—How America Listens to Radio (2003, 2004, and 2005 Editions)

ICA 8-4

CHAPTER 9: IDENTIFYING MARKET SEGMENTS AND TARGETS

ICA 9-1: IN-CLASS ACTIVITY

Interpreting Census Data [1]

Learning Objectives. To have students: (1) learn how Census 2000 data were and the new American Community Survey are being collected and (2) identify the size of market segments for five hypothetical marketing problems by interpreting Census 2000 data tables.

Definitions. The following marketing terms are referred to in this in-class activity (ICA):

• Market Segments: The relatively homogeneous groups of prospective buyers that result from the market segmentation process.

• Secondary Data: Facts and figures that have already been recorded before the project at hand.

Nature of the Activity. To have students look at two data tables from the U.S. Census 2000 and find specific numbers that provide initial estimates of the size of the market segments in five hypothetical marketing situations.

Estimated Class Time. 15 minutes.

Materials Needed.

• The ICA09-1.doc Word and ICA09-1.ppt PowerPoint files contained in the ICA09-1 folder of the Instructor's CD #1 from the *Instructor's Survival Kit* box.

• The U.S. Census 2000 Short Form and the American Community Survey contained in the *Instructor's Survival Kit* box.

• Copies of the:

   a. U.S. Census 2000 Short Form (1 page). [OPTIONAL: U.S. Census Long Form (6 pages) or use the accompanying Census2000LongForm.pdf document.]

   b. U.S. Census 2000 DP-1: Profile of General Demographic Characteristics and DP-2: Profile of Selected Social Characteristics data tables (2 pages). [OPTIONAL: DP-3: Profile of Selected Economic Characteristics data table (1 page) or use the accompanying Census2000Data.pdf document–p. 3.]

   c. [NOTE: For the documents above, see the enclosed Adobe Acrobat Portable Document Files (.pdf) in the 'pdf' folder within the ICA19-1 folder. You will need the Adobe Acrobat Reader to view and print the PDF documents. To download the latest version, go to www.adobe.com/products/acrobat.].

   d. How Big is the Market? Handout (1 page).

---

[1] The authors wish to thank Kimberly Crews and Tom Webster, Public Information Office of the U.S. Census Bureau, who assisted in the development of this ICA.

- NOTE: Transparencies can be made of the handouts instead of making copies and using the PowerPoint presentation for those instructors who prefer this option.

Preparation Before Class. Follow the steps below:

1. Read p. 211 of Chapter 8 and pp. 238-242 of Chapter 9.

2. Print, read, and if necessary, edit the ICA09-1.doc Word file.

3. Print and/or review the PowerPoint slides from the ICA09-1.ppt PowerPoint file.

4. Make a one 4-page handout for each student from the:

    a. U.S. Census 2000 Short Form (1 page). [OPTIONAL: U.S. Census Long Form (+ 6 pages) or use the accompanying '.pdf' document.]

    b. U.S. Census 2000 DP-1 and DP-2 data tables (2 pages). [OPTIONAL: DP-3 (+ 1 page) or use the accompanying '.pdf' document.]

    c. How Big is the Market? Handout (1 page).

5. OPTIONAL: Bookmark the Census 2000 website (www.census.gov) on your classroom computer.

Instructions. Follow the steps below to conduct this ICA:

1. Pass around the U.S. Census 2000 Short Form from the *Instructor's Survival Kit* box.

2. Pass out the 4-page handout that contains the U.S. Census 2000 Short Form, the U.S. Census 2000 DP-1 and DP-2 data tables, and the How Big is the Market? Handout.

US Census promotional video

Slide 2

Census 2000 Short Form

Slide 3

Census 2000 Long Form 'pdf'

3. **Show Slide 2**: Census 2000 promotional B-roll [TRT = 1:30] and then give the following mini-lecture about the U.S. Census 2000:

    "Many of you are familiar with the 10-year census that reports statistics on U.S. population and housing. This census is required by the U.S. Constitution and results are used to apportion seats in the U.S. House of Representatives, redistrict state legislatures, allocate federal funds, etc."

4. **Show Slide 3**: Census 2000 Short Form. [**OPTIONAL: Also show the 6-page 'pdf' version of the Census 2000 Long Form.**] Continue with the mini-lecture:

    "In April 2000, most U.S. households received the Census 2000 "short form" that contained 8 basic questions, as shown on the slide and the first page of your handout. However, 1 in 6 households (or 20 million) received the Census 2000 "long form" that contained many additional questions regarding marital status, education, occupation, household income, etc. to obtain information on what a community looks like.

This information is useful to marketers and government planners because it can identify market opportunities or where is the greatest need for job training programs, how many persons speak a language other than English, how long it take to get to work, where in the community are veterans and elderly residents located, etc. to improve the quality of life in those communities."

5. **Show Slides 4-6**: U.S. Census 2000 DP-1, DP-2, and DP-3 data tables. **[OPTIONAL: Show the 3-page 'pdf' version of the Census 2000 DP-1, DP-2, and DP-3 data tables**, which must be viewed using Adobe Acrobat Reader in a separate window from the PowerPoint presentation.] Continue with the mini-lecture:

"Two data tables generated from the Census 2000 'long form' are DP-1: Profile of General Demographic Characteristics and DP-2: Profile of Selected Social Characteristics [OPTIONAL: DP-3: Profile of Selected Economic Characteristics] data tables, which are shown in these slides and are the second and third pages of your handout."

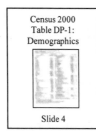

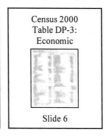

6. **Spend 1 minute** and go over the major demographic and social (and economic) categories based on the Census 2000 long form.

7. Give the students the following instructions to complete this activity:

"Now look at the five hypothetical marketing situations given on the last page of your handout. **Spend 5 minutes** and answer the questions using the data in Tables DP-1, DP-2, and DP-3."

8. After the five minutes are up, call on students to share their answers with the class. Stress that this would just be the first step in a marketing research study to identify potential market segments and that in an actual marketing situation, these data would probably be supplemented with other secondary and primary data.

9. Ask students the following questions:

• Question 1: What are the advantages of secondary data like those from U.S. Census 2000?

Answer: The tremendous time and cost savings over having the business collect this information on its own.

- Question 2: What are the disadvantages of the U.S. Census 2000 data?

  Answer: The categories may not be precise enough to apply to the specific problem a marketing manager faces and the information may be too out-of-date.

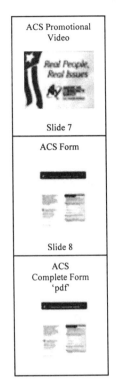

ACS Promotional Video

Slide 7

ACS Form

Slide 8

ACS Complete Form 'pdf'

10. **Show Slide 7**: American Community Survey promotional B-roll [TRT = 1:30] and **Slide 8**: ACS Form (page 1) and then conclude this activity with the flowing mini-lecture on the American Community Survey:[2]

"Between decennial censuses, businesses, nonprofit organizations, and local governments cannot rely on increasingly out-of-date Census data to identify market opportunities or assess and finance local needs, such as where to build new roads, schools or senior centers. Costly mistakes can result when planners do not have current data on which to base their decisions or when local communities do not get a fair share of the $200 billion in federal funding to help fund needed local projects. Target, a national retail chain, uses Census data 'to shape merchandising and marketing decisions and pick locations for new stores.'[3]

The American Community Survey (ACS) is part of the U.S. Census Bureau's effort to streamline and improve the census. It will replace the 'long form' and provide communities a vibrant, moving picture every year instead of once every 10 years. In 2005, the ACS, which has over 60 questions, will be sent to 250,000 households each month or 1 in 40 households per year. While responding to the ACS is mandatory under federal law (like the Census), no household will receive the survey more often that once every five years.

Starting in 2006, data will be available annually for all areas with populations of 65,000 or more. For smaller areas, it will take three to five years to accumulate a large enough sample to produce annual data. For example, areas of 20,000 to 65,000 can receive data averaged over three years. For rural areas, small urban neighborhoods or population groups of less than 20,000, it will take five years to accumulate a sample size comparable to the decennial census. These averages will be updated every succeeding year."

Marketing Lessons. Marketers need up-to-date information to use in identifying the size of potential market segments on which to base marketing strategies. The 10-year U.S. Census has traditionally been the foundation of much initial marketing research for marketing managers. It will now be supplemented by American Community Survey that will provide annual data for communities over 65,000 starting in 2006.

Websites. The Census 2000 website is www.census.gov/main/www/cen2000.html and the American Community Survey website is www.census.gov/acs/www.

---

[2] American Community Survey Fact Sheet, U.S. Census Bureau.
[3] Haya El Nasser, "Rolling Survey for 2010 Census Keeps Data Up To Date," *USA Today*, January 16, 2005. See http://www.usatoday.com/news/bythenumbers/2005-01-16-census-2010_x.htm.

INSTRUCTOR'S KEY: How Big is the Market? Handout

The U.S. Census provides business, nonprofit, and government organizations with valuable information upon which to make key decisions. Marketing managers find U.S. census data especially valuable in trying to quantify the size of key market segments they might try to target. Listed below are questions that marketing managers might ask about the size of a market segment in which they have special interest. Using data from the U.S. Census 2000, try to give them an initial answer about the size of the segment:

1. Assume Herff-Jones, a publisher, is considering producing a coloring book for pre-schoolers:

   A: What is the number of children under 5 years of age?

   Answer: 19,175,798 are under 5 years of age. (Table DP-1, column 1)

   B: Assuming nursery school and preschool children might use the coloring book, how big is that market segment?

   Answer: 4,957,582 children are in nursery school or preschool. (Table DP-2, column 2)

2. Assume an Hispanic American entrepreneur is considering developing a chain of U.S. fast-food restaurants. She assumes the initial "core customers" will be other Hispanic Americans:

   A: What is the size of this market?

   Answer: 35,305,818 people are shown as Hispanic or Latino. (Table DP-1, column 2)

   B: What is the largest sub-segment of Hispanic Americans and how big is it?

   Answer: The 20,640,711 Mexican Americans. (Table DP-1, column 2)

3. Assume Home Depot is planning a TV advertising campaign to target do-it yourselfers who do maintenance projects on the house, condo, or other dwelling unit they own and in which they live:

   A: How many housing units like this are there?

   Answer: 69,815,753 owner-occupied housing units. (Table DP-1, column 2)

   B: If Home Depot also targets renter-occupied housing units, how many of these are there?

   Answer: 35,664,348 renter-occupied housing units. (Table DP-1, column 2)

4. Assume that a task force from the U.S. Senate is studying likely health and special care needs among the U.S. population:

   A: What is the total number of working-age adults with a disability that are not in an institution?

   Answer: 30,553,796 adults from 21 to 64 years of age have a disability. (Table DP-2, column 1)

   B: Among working-age adults, what percentage of those with a disability is employed compared to those without a disability?

   Answer: Among those 21 to 64 years of age, 56.6% of those with a disability are working compared to 77.2% without a disability. (Table DP-2, column 1)

5. Assume Nordic Reach, a magazine targeting Americans of Scandinavian ancestry, wants an estimate of the number of these people in the U.S. from Census 2000 data:

   A: How many are there in the tabulation?

   In the table, three Scandinavian Americans segments are shown: Danish (1,430,897), Norwegian (4,477,725), and Swedish (3,998,310), which totals 9,906,932 people. (Table DP-2, column 2)

   B: The editor must make sure there are ones of interest to those with the largest segment of Scandinavian-Americans. What is it?

   Answer: Norwegians are the largest Scandinavian segment with 4,477,725 people. (Table DP-2, column 2)

6. Given the importance of services to the U.S. economy, what percentage of American households is employed in service occupations? [NOTE: A calculator is needed.]

   Answer: 19,276,947 people 16 and older work in service occupations out of a total of 128,279,228 or about 15%. (Table DP-3, column 1)

How Big is the Market? Handout

The U.S. Census provides business, nonprofit, and government organizations with valuable information upon which to make key decisions. Marketing managers find U.S. census data especially valuable in trying to quantify the size of key market segments they might try to target. Listed below are questions that marketing managers might ask about the size of a market segment in which they have special interest. Using data from the U.S. Census 2000, try to give them an initial answer about the size of the segment:

1. Assume Herff-Jones, a publisher, is considering producing a coloring book for pre-schoolers:

   A: What is the number of children under 5 years of age?

   B: Assuming nursery school and preschool children might use the coloring book, how big is that market segment?

2. Assume an Hispanic American entrepreneur is considering developing a chain of U.S. fast-food restaurants. She assumes the initial "core customers" will be other Hispanic Americans:

   A: What is the size of this market?

   B: What is the largest sub-segment of Hispanic Americans and how big is it?

3. Assume Home Depot is planning a TV advertising campaign to target do-it yourselfers who do maintenance projects on the house, condo, or other dwelling unit they own and in which they live:

   A: How many housing units like this are there?

   B: If Home Depot also targets renter-occupied housing units, how many of these are there?

4. Assume that a task force from the U.S. Senate is studying likely health and special care needs among the U.S. population:

   A: What is the total number of working-age adults with a disability that are not in an institution?

   B: Among working-age adults, what percentage of those with a disability is employed compared to those without a disability?

5. Assume Nordic Reach, a magazine targeting Americans of Scandinavian ancestry, wants an estimate of the number of these people in the U.S. from Census 2000 data:

   A: How many are there in the tabulation?

   B: The editor must make sure there are ones of interest to those with the largest segment of Scandinavian-Americans. What is it?

6. Given the importance of services to the U.S. economy, what percentage of American households is employed in service occupations? [NOTE: A calculator is needed.]

CHAPTER 9: IDENTIFYING MARKET SEGMENTS AND TARGETS

ICA 9-2: IN-CLASS ACTIVITY

Product Categorization to Identify Product Groups and Competitors[1]

Learning Objectives. To have students: (1) discover the process of categorization and how different people categorize the same objects in different ways; (2) explore some of the reasons for these differences; and (3) understand the importance of categorization in identifying both market segments and competitors.

Definitions. The following marketing terms are referred to in this in-class activity (ICA):

- Product Class: The entire product category or industry.

- Product Form: Variations of a product within the product class.

- Product Item: A specific product as noted by a unique brand, size, or price.

- Product Line: A group of products that are closely related because they satisfy a class of needs, are used together, are sold to the same customer group, are distributed through the same type of outlets, or fall within a given price range.

Nature of the Activity. To have two students independently group some snack and candy items into different categories. Students in the class are able to observe the differences in the ways different people group items and discuss some of the reasons for these differences.

Estimated Class Time. 15 minutes.

Materials Needed.

- The ICA09-2.doc Word and ICA09-2.ppt PowerPoint files contained in the ICA09-2 folder of the Instructor's CD #1 from the *Instructor's Survival Kit* box.

- The Honey Nut Cheerios® Milk 'n Cereal bar and the Starbucks Penza Caramel Dolce Nutrition bar from the *Instructor's Survival Kit* box.

- A variety of several candies and other food items purchased from a grocery, such as:

  – M&M's (Plain, Almond, Peanut, Peanut Butter, & Crispy)
  – Snickers
  – A package of Frito Lay sunflower seeds
  – A package of Planter's mixed nuts
  – A Quaker Oats Chewy granola bar
  – A package of Fruit Roll-ups® fruit snacks
  – An apple, banana, or orange

---

[1] The authors wish to thank Muffie Taggett and Denise Bosch of General Mills and Chris Gorley, Product Placement—National Promotions of Starbucks, who assisted in the development of this ICA. Honey Nut Cheerios® and Fruit Roll-ups® are registered trademarks of General Mills and used by permission.

Preparation Before Class. Follow the steps below:

1. Read p. 244 of Chapter 9.

2. Print, read, and if necessary, edit the ICA09-2.doc Word file.

3. Print and/or review the PowerPoint slides from the ICA09-2.ppt PowerPoint file.

4. Purchase the above-mentioned items.

5. OPTIONAL: Bookmark the General Mills website (www.generalmills.com) and the Starbucks website (www.starbucks.com) on your classroom computer.

Instructions. Follow the steps below to conduct this ICA:

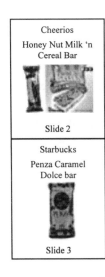

Cheerios Honey Nut Milk 'n Cereal Bar

Slide 2

Starbucks Penza Caramel Dolce bar

Slide 3

1. **Show Slides 2-3**. Lay the assortment of "snack items" (the Honey Nut Cheerios® Milk 'n Cereal bar and the Starbucks Penza Caramel Dolce Nutrition bar from the *Instructor's Survival Kit* box as well as those items purchased from the grocery store) out on a table in the front of the classroom.

2. Ask for two student volunteers. Have one student go out of the room. Then give the other student the following instruction:

   "Your task is to take these objects and group them together in any way that you wish. The only requirement is that there must be at least two objects in each group. You have 2 minutes to complete this task."

3. When finished, ask the student why he or she grouped items in the manner described. For example, there may be one group with items that contain chocolate or one with items that contain nuts...or perhaps the student has a "healthy snack group." Either the instructor or another student should write down on the board or transparency the way the items are categorized by the student and the rationale given for grouping these items.

4. Have that student sit down, bring in the other student, and repeat the grouping process. The student's explanation of the grouping should also, once again, be recorded. The groupings by the two students will more than likely be very different.

5. Use the following as discussion points:

   a. The way items are categorized by one person is usually very different than the way another person may group the items. Ask students what some of the factors are that may account for the differences. Common answers include:

      • Prior experience with the items (those with nuts vs. those that have caramel).

      • Knowledge (those items which are more nutritional).

- Appearance or packaging (some students may group all brown colored packages together).
- Personal preferences or attitudes towards different items (groups based on items the person likes or dislikes).
- Advertising or position the product has in the consumer's mind. With no personal experience with an item, a student may think that granola bars are healthy based on advertisements for the items.
- Brand name (even if a student has never seen or tasted the Honey Nut Cheerios Milk 'n Cereal bar or the Starbucks Penza Caramel Dolce Nutrition bar, the student may assign a positive value to the product based on the Cheerios® and/or Starbucks brand name).
- Others as identified.

b. Ask students the following questions:

- <u>Question 1</u>: What are the product items?

    <u>Answer</u>: The Honey Nut Cheerios Milk 'n Cereal bar, Starbucks Penza Caramel Dolce Nutrition bar, M&M's (Plain, Almond, Peanut, Peanut Butter, & Crispy), Snickers, Frito Lay sunflower seeds, Planter's mixed nuts, a Quaker Oats granola bar, Fruit Roll-ups fruit snacks, and an apple, banana or orange.

- <u>Question 2</u>: What are the product forms?

    <u>Answer</u>: "Candy," "fruit," and "granola/nuts/seeds." Others as identified.

- <u>Question 3</u>: What are the product lines?

    <u>Answer</u>: M&M's (Plain, Almond, Peanut, Peanut Butter, & Crispy).

- <u>Question 4</u>: What is/are the product class(es)?

    <u>Answer</u>: "Snacks."

- <u>Question 5</u>: Why product categorization is important in marketing?

    <u>Answer</u>: An individual may group items together that are considered substitutes for each other by that individual. This helps define the class of products, the market segments, and the competitors to these segments.

    For example, if a student groups a granola bar, Fruit Roll-ups fruit snacks, and a piece of fruit together as "healthy" snacks, this student probably would accept a granola bar in place of a piece of fruit. However, another student may group the granola bar with "candy" items and consider them all junk food. When this student craves a "healthy" snack (the "market segment"), a granola bar will not substitute for a piece of fruit since it is outside the "product grouping" for acceptable substitutes.

- Question 6: What products do the Honey Nut Cheerios Milk 'n Cereal bar and Starbucks Penza Caramel Dolce Nutrition bar most directly compete with?

  Answers:

  a. For the Honey Nut Cheerios Milk 'n Cereal bar:

     – Starbucks Penza Caramel Dolce Nutrition bar
     – A Quaker Oats Chewy granola bar
     – An apple, banana, or orange (because of their nutritional value and "one-handed" convenience)

  b. For the Starbucks Penza Caramel Dolce Nutrition bar:

     – Honey Nut Cheerios Milk 'n Cereal bar
     – Snickers (because the Starbucks Penza Caramel Dolce Nutrition bar has chocolate, caramel, and sugar for energy)
     – A Quaker Oats Chewy granola bar
     – An apple, banana, or orange (because of their nutritional value and "one-handed" convenience)

- Question 7: What special promotional strategies suggested by this competitive set?

  Answer: Multiple responses possible. Some students may have seen an ad for the Honey Nut Cheerios Milk 'n Cereal bar.

Marketing Lessons. Marketers need to understand how consumers categorize objects because it helps define both the market segments, acceptable substitutes in the product grouping, and the competitors to these segments. Marketers, through advertising, packaging, and branding, can influence the way consumers categorize products. This influence is especially critical for new products that consumers may be unfamiliar with.

Websites. The Honey Nut Cheerios Milk 'n Cereal bar and Fruit Roll-ups fruit snacks do not have websites; see the General Mills website, which is www.generalmills.com. To view the current product line of coffees and other products and services at Starbucks, go to www.starbucks.com. Websites for products referred to in this ICA are: M&M's (www.m-ms.com); Snickers (www.snickers.com); Frito Lay (www.fritolay.com); Planters (www.planters.com); and Quaker Oats (www.quakerchewy.com).

ICA 9-3: IN-CLASS ACTIVITY

Product Positioning for Consumers and Retailers[1]

Learning Objectives. To have students study a product and its packaging to identify the benefits to both consumers and retailers and (2) suggest a positioning statement for the product.

Definitions. The following marketing terms are referred to in this in-class activity (ICA):

- Branding: A basic decision in marketing products in which an organization uses a name, phrase, design, or symbols, or combination of these to identify its products and distinguish them from those of competitors.

- Label: An integral part of the package that typically identifies the product or brand, who made it, where and when it was made, how it is to be used, and package contents and ingredients.

- Packaging: A component of a product that refers to any container in which it is offered for sale and on which label information is conveyed.

- Product Positioning: The place an offering occupies in consumers' minds on important attributes relative to competitive products.

Nature of the Activity. To have students study a 1-pack "blister card" that contains a Post-it® Flag Highlighter sample from 3M. Students will (1) suggest consumer benefits and retailer benefits and (2) compose a product positioning statement that links it to 3M's product branding and packaging strategies for the product.

Estimated Class Time. 30 minutes.

Materials Needed.

- The ICA09-3.doc Word and ICA09-3.ppt PowerPoint files contained in the ICA09-3 folder of the Instructor's CD #1 from the *Instructor's Survival Kit* box.

- The 3M Post-it® Flag Highlighter from the *Instructor's Survival Kit* box.

- Copies of the:

  a. 3M Post-it® Flag Highlighter Product and Branding Strategies Handout.

  b. 3M Post-it® Flag Highlighter Packaging Strategies Handout.

  c. 3M Post-it® Flag Highlighter Product and Branding Strategies Answers Handout.

  d. 3M Post-it® Flag Highlighter Packaging Strategies Answers Handout.

---

[1] The authors wish to thank David Windorski, New Product Development Senior Specialist of the 3M Company, who assisted in the development of this ICA.

- OPTIONAL: A second 3M Post-it® Flag Highlighter to (1) demonstrate its use as a highlighter and page marker and (2) make copies of the **front** and **back** of the 1-pack blister card. You can purchase a 3M Post-it® Flag Highlighter 1-pack blister card in your college bookstore or office supply store for $3.99 to $4.29. [NOTE: Gently remove the product from the plastic package without tearing the printed material.]

- NOTE: Transparencies can be made of the handouts instead of making copies and using the PowerPoint presentation for those instructors who prefer this option.

Preparation Before Class. Follow the steps below:

1. Read pp. 249-252 of Chapter 9 on positioning and p. 276 of Chapter 10 to familiarize yourself with the 3M Post-it® Flag Highlighter developed by David Windorski of 3M. You may also want to ask students to read this page as well.

2. Print, read, and if necessary, edit the ICA09-3.doc Word file.

3. Print and/or review the slides from ICA09-3.ppt PowerPoint file.

4. Make copies of the:

   a. 3M Post-it® Flag Highlighter Product and Branding Strategies Handout for the "product and brand" teams.

   b. 3M Post-it® Flag Highlighter Packaging Strategies Handout for the "packaging" teams.

   c. 3M Post-it® Flag Highlighter Product and Branding Strategies Answers Handout for the "product and brand" teams.

   d. 3M Post-it® Flag Highlighter Packaging Strategies Answers Handout for the "packaging" teams.

5. OPTIONAL: Bring the second, opened 3M Post-it® Flag Highlighter to class to demonstrate its use to as a highlighter and page marker.

6. OPTIONAL: Make copies from **Slide 6** of the **front** and **back** of Post-it® Flag Highlighter 1-pack blister card for each student.

7. OPTIONAL: Bookmark the 3M Post-it® Flag Highlighter website (www.3m.com/us/office/postit/products_flags_pen.jhtml) on your classroom computer.

Instructions. Follow the steps below to conduct this ICA:

1. **Spend 2 minutes** and ask students the following questions about their study habits:

   - Question 1: How many of you have ever used a highlighter as you read a textbook? Why?

     Answer: Students use a highlighter for a variety of reasons (indicate an important sentence or passage, etc.).

- <u>Question 2</u>: How many of you have ever used Post-it® Notes or Flags? Why?

  <u>Answer</u>: Students use Post-it® Notes and Flags for a variety of reasons (make notes, reminder of something important, correct a typo on a draft of their paper, etc.).

2. Give the following mini-lecture about 3M Post-it® Notes.

   "3M Post-it® Notes began in 1968 when a 3M scientist discovered a 'sticky but not too sticky' adhesive. However, it wasn't until 1974 when another 3M scientist, Art Fry, came up with a solution to a dream: a light adhesive that could be applied to a bookmark so that it wouldn't keep falling out of his hymnal while singing in a church choir. After 3 years of development, 3M introduced Post-it® Notes. By 1980, they were sold throughout the U.S. Today, there are over 600 Post-it® products that are sold worldwide!"

3. **Show Slide 2**: 3M Post-it® Notes TV ad. [TRT = 0:30]

4. OPTIONAL: **Show Slide 3**: David Windorski and the development of the 3M Post-it® Flag Highlighter. [TRT = 6:00]

5. Give the following mini-lecture about the 3M Post-it® Flag Highlighter.

   "Fast forward to 2002. David Windorski, a researcher at 3M, had observed and interviewed students concerning their study habits. Many students like to use a felt-tip highlighter to indicate important material in a textbook. However, some students also used Post-it® Notes and Flags to mark the pages in the textbook they wanted to study further."

6. Pass around the 3M Post-it® Flag Highlighter obtained from the *Instructor's Survival Kit* box.

7. **Show Slide 4**: 3M Post-it® Flag Highlighter and continue with the following mini-lecture: [NOTE: Click the mouse while giving the mini-lecture to show the effect of marrying the 3M Post-it® Flags plus a highlighter equals the 3M Post-it® Flag Highlighter.]

   "As the video and TV ad demonstrated, Windorski's breakthrough idea was to marry the two products by putting Post-it® Flags inside a highlighter!"

8. **Show Slide 5**: 3M Post-it® Flag Highlighter colors and packaging options (1-pack and 3-pack) and **Show Slide 6**: 3M Post-it® Flag Highlighter front and back of 1-pack blister card packaging and continue with the following mini-lecture:

"The 3M Post-it® Flag Highlighter comes in either yellow, blue, or pink ink and barrel colors and two packaging options: (1) a 1-pack blister card and (2) a 3-pack blister card. Each highlighter is loaded with 50 red flags and is packaged with 2 refills. It also comes as a pen with black ink."

3M Post-it®
Flag Highlighter
Colors & Packaging

Slide 5

Flag Highlighter
1-pack Blister Card
Packaging

Slide 6

9. **Spend 1 minute** and ask students the following question:

   - Question 3: How many of you have used the 3M Post-it® Flag Highlighter? Why?

     Answer: Students may have used the 3M Post-it® Flag Highlighter for a variety of reasons (combination of a highlighter and page marker when indicating important material in a textbook, etc.).

10. Form students into 4-person teams. Designate half the teams as the "product and brand team" and the other half as the "packaging team."

11. Pass out copies of the:

    a. 3M Post-it® Flag Highlighter Product and Branding Strategies Handout to the "product and brand" teams.

    b. 3M Post-it® Flag Highlighter Packaging Strategies Handout to the "packaging" teams.

    c. OPTIONAL: **Front** and **back** of the 3M Post-it® Flag Highlighter 1-pack blister card to all students made from **Slide 6**.

Product & Brand
Teams Handout

Packaging Teams
Handout

Post-it® Flag
Highlighter
Handout

Product & Brand
Team Handout

Slide 7

12. **Show Slide 7** and briefly explain the nature of this ICA to the "product and brand" teams.

    a. Identify the perceived benefits and their importance to both consumers and retailers based on brand name, product concept, features, and design of the 3M Post-it® Flag Highlighter. You may need to define "branding."

b. Compose a 15 to 20 word positioning statement for the 3M Post-it® Flag Highlighter to both consumers and retailers. You may need to define "product positioning."

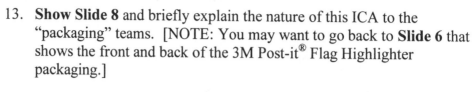

13. **Show Slide 8** and briefly explain the nature of this ICA to the "packaging" teams. [NOTE: You may want to go back to **Slide 6** that shows the front and back of the 3M Post-it® Flag Highlighter packaging.]

a. Identify the perceived benefits and their importance to both consumers and retailers based on the blister card packaging, label information, and graphics of the 3M Post-it® Flag Highlighter. You may need to define "packaging" and "label."

b. Compose a 15 to 20 word positioning statement for the 3M Post-it® Flag Highlighter to both consumers and retailers. You may need to define "product positioning."

14. **Spend 10 minutes** and have the "product and brand" and "packaging" teams complete the "benefit/importance" and "positioning statement" sections of their respective handouts. Mention the following:

"Reasonably priced writing instruments such as highlighters are often seen by both consumers and retailers as commodities. 3M has used its creativity and marketing expertise to add value to its 3M Post-it® Flag Highlighter for both consumers and retailers.

15. **Spend 3 minutes** and have 2 to 3 students from both the "product and brand" and "packaging" teams share their answers regarding:

a. The benefits and importance of the selected product and branding or packaging strategies for both consumers and retailers.

b. The 15 to 20 word positioning statements suggested by the benefits and importance for both consumers and retailers of the selected product and branding or packaging strategies.

18. Pass out copies of the 3M Post-it® Flag Highlighter Product and Branding Strategies Answers Handout to the "product and brand" teams and copies of the 3M Post-it® Flag Highlighter Packaging Strategies Answers Handout to the "packaging" teams.
[OPTIONAL: **Show Slides 9-10** or use transparencies made from these "completed" handouts.]

19. **Spend 3 minutes** and have 2 to 3 students from each team compare their answers with those contained in the handouts. Conclude this ICA with the following mini-lecture:

"Two short product positioning statements might be:

- For consumers: "A combination Post-it® Flag and highlighter package that enables users to have the convenience of both for many applications."
- For retailers: "A combination Post-it® Flag and highlighter product line with a recognized brand name and logo, attention-getting packaging, and high potential volume."

These positioning statements help 3M distinguish its products in the minds of consumers and retailers from competitive products, as discussed at the end of Chapter 9."

Marketing Lesson. Firms selling convenience products that are traditionally seen as "commodities" can break through the clutter by using creative product, branding, and packaging strategies to achieve a strong position in the minds of consumers and retailers.

Website. The 3M Post-it® Flag Highlighter website is: www.3m.com/us/office/postit/products_flags_pen.jhtml.

3M POST-IT® FLAG HIGHLIGHTER
PRODUCT & BRANDING STRATEGIES HANDOUT

(A) Identify the benefits and importance to consumers and retailers

(B) Compose a positioning strategy

Product and Branding Strategy	(A) Benefits/Importance to Consumers	(A) Benefits/Importance to Retailers
1. Post-it® brand name and logo.		
2. Post-it® Flag Highlighter concept: A product that combines Post-it® Flags with a highlighter.		
3. Design: Highlighter style and size of pen barrel, Post-it® Flags dispenser in pen, colors of highlighter ink, flags, and barrel, clip on cap.	⇩	⇩
B. A 15 to 20 word product positioning statement suggested by above the strategies.		

3M POST-IT® FLAG HIGHLIGHTER
PACKAGING STRATEGIES HANDOUT

(A) Identify benefits and importance to consumers and retailers

(B) Compose a positioning strategy

Packaging Strategy	(A) Benefits/Importance to Consumers	(A) Benefits/Importance to Retailers
1. "Blister card" package design: 1 to 3 Post-it® Flag Highlighters; thicker, stronger blister card stock and plastic shell.		
2. Label information and graphics on front (example photo, logo, number, etc.) and back ("how to" photos, refill diagram, etc.) on back of package.		
3. Can package products in blister cards or in bulk (boxes).	⇩	⇩
B. A 15 to 20 word product positioning statement suggested by above the strategies.		

ICA 9-3

3M POST-IT® FLAG HIGHLIGHTER
PRODUCT AND BRANDING STRATEGIES ANSWERS HANDOUT

Product and Branding Strategy	(A) Benefits/Importance to Consumers	(A) Benefits/Importance to Retailers
1. Post-it® brand name and logo.	• Provided immediate credibility for potential buyers because of recognition of 3M name and Post-it® brand. • Aids future consumer recognition and recall of company and brand.	• 3M and Post-it® brand names provide immediate credibility for potential retailers considering stocking the items because of their recognition by consumers. • Post-it® logo conveys the theme of the product line.
2. Post-it® Flag Highlighter concept: A product that combines Post-it® Flags with a highlighter.	• Provides 2-in-1 benefits of both: (a) Post-it® Flags and (b) highlighting. • Provides Post-it® Flag refills in blister card.	• Provides a complete product line: Post-it® Flag Highlighters, Post-it® Flag Pens, and refills.
3. Design: Highlighter style and size of pen barrel, Post-it® Flags dispenser in pen, colors of highlighter ink, flags, and barrel, clip on cap.	• Similar to highlighters that consumers may be familiar with. • Convenient, easy-to-use dispenser of small flags. • 3 colors available to meet consumer preferences; typical colors used in other highlighters. • Adequate supply of flags: 50 in highlighter plus 2 refill packs; good value for the piece paid ($3.99 to $4.29).	• Helps convince retail buyer of product's marketability. • Helps retailer see opportunity for follow-on sales of more Post-it® Flag Highlighters and refills.
B. A 15 to 20 word product positioning statement suggested by above the strategies.	"A combination Post-it® Flags and highlighter package that enables users to have the convenience of both for many applications."	"A combination Post-it® Flags and highlighter product line with a recognized brand name and logo, attention-getting packaging, and high potential volume."

3M POST-IT® FLAG HIGHLIGHTER
PACKAGING STRATEGIES ANSWERS HANDOUT

Packaging Strategy	(A) Benefits/Importance to Consumers	(A) Benefits/Importance to Retailers
1. "Blister card" package design: 1 to 3 Post-it® Flag Highlighters; thicker, stronger blister card stock and plastic shell.	• Provides economic purchase quantity for consumers. • Looks more substantial to consumers. • Enhances consumers' perceptions of quality. • Protects instruments.	• Uses common blister card sizes to make display easier, more convenient. • Strong blister pack and card stock: (a) reduces spoilage and theft (b) avoids highlighter and refills breaking out of blister cards during shipment and display. • Makes blister cards look neat and hang properly on display hook.
2. Label information and graphics on front (example photo, logo, number, etc.) and back ("how to" photos, refill diagram, etc.) on back of package.	• Provides aesthetically pleasing, attention-getting package. • Enhances consumers' perceptions of quality. • Provides instructions on use.	• Helps establish greater credibility with retail buyers. • Reduces need for sales personnel to instruct consumers on how to use the product.
3. Can package products in blister cards or in bulk (boxes).	• Customers can obtain quantity discounts, if desired (particularly small business and corporate customers).	• Permits sellers to obtain Post-it® Flag Highlighters in quantities and packaging they desire. • Reduces chances of pilferage with bulk quantity option.
B. A 15 to 20 word product positioning statement suggested by above the strategies.	"A combination Post-it® Flags and highlighter package that enables users to have the convenience of both for many applications."	"A combination Post-it® Flags and highlighter product line with a recognized brand name and logo, attention-getting packaging, and high potential volume."

ICA 9-3

CHAPTER 10: DEVELOPING NEW PRODUCTS AND SERVICES

ICA 10-1: IN-CLASS ACTIVITY

Focus Group for Convergent Digital Devices[1]

Learning Objective. To have students demonstrate the use of focus groups as a marketing research method to test new product ideas and concepts.

Definitions. The following marketing terms are referred to in this in-class activity (ICA):

- <u>3G</u>: Third generation mobile telecommunications services that may include voice, high-speed data transfer, such as messaging, wireless Internet access and web browsing, paging, etc., pictures, video, music, e-commerce, personal organizer applications, such as contact lists, date book, memos, etc., and business productivity software, such as word processing, spreadsheet, etc.

- <u>Focus Group</u>: An informal session of 6 to 10 past, present, or prospective customers in which a discussion leader, or moderator, asks their opinions about the firm's and its competitors' products, how they use these products, and special needs they have that these products don't address.

- <u>Idea Generation</u>: The stage of the new-product process that involves developing a pool of concepts as candidates for new products.

- <u>Screening and Evaluation</u>: The stage of the new-product process that involves internal and external evaluations of the new-product ideas to eliminate those that warrant no further effort.

Nature of the Activity. To have the instructor moderate a focus group with 6 to 8 students to explore reactions to a new convergent handheld device from Nokia.

Estimated Class Time. 30 minutes.

Materials Needed.

- The ICA10-1.doc Word and ICA10-1.ppt PowerPoint files contained in the ICA10-1 folder of the Instructor's CD #1 from the *Instructor's Survival Kit* box.

- The Nokia 7610 mobile phone brochure contained in the *Instructor's Survival Kit* box.

- Blank name cards and markers for making nametags for focus group participants.

- A table and enough chairs for the moderator, recorder, and focus group members.

- OPTIONAL: A blank transparency (ies).

---

[1] The authors wish to thank Keith Nowak, Media Relations Manager of Nokia, who assisted in the development of this ICA.

- Copies of the Nokia 7610 Mobile Phone Handout made from the he Nokia 7610 mobile phone brochure. See the enclosed Adobe Acrobat Portable Document Files (.pdf) in the 'pdf' folder within the ICA10-1 folder. [NOTE: You will need the Adobe Acrobat Reader to view and print the PDF documents. To download the latest version, go to www.adobe.com/products/acrobat.]

Preparation Before Class. Follow the steps below:

1. Read p. 216 of Chapter 8 and pp. 273-277 of Chapter 10.

2. Print, read, and if necessary, edit the ICA10-1.doc Word file.

3. Print and/or review the PowerPoint slides from the ICA10-1.ppt PowerPoint file.

4. Make copies of the Nokia 7610 Mobile Phone Handout (from the .pdf of the brochure).

5. OPTIONAL: Bookmark the Nokia website (www.nokiausa.com/phones/7610) on your classroom computer.

Instructions. Follow the steps below to conduct this ICA:

1. Give students this background mini-lecture on Nokia and how it uses focus groups to generate, screen, and evaluate ideas for new products:

   "Nokia is the world leader in mobile communications, with global sales of about $40 billion. Nokia's mission is "Connecting People," which is accomplished by identifying consumer needs and providing offerings that meet those needs in the rapidly changing mobile phone market. Marketers like Nokia use a variety of primary research methods (experiments, interviews, surveys, etc.; see Chapter 8) to help them generate, screen, and evaluate ideas for new or existing products and services. One such method is the focus group.

   Today, we will conduct a brief focus group to evaluate a new product—the Nokia 7610 mobile phone. Recall that focus groups: (1) start with general background questions and then focus more specifically on the main topic of interest; (2) cost less than personal depth interviews or mail surveys; (3) can stimulate new ideas through group interaction; and (4) usually involve 6 to 10 participants."

2. Recruit 6 to 8 students for the focus group on convergent digital devices. Seat them in the front of the room and have them write their names on the cards. Recruit another student to record the focus group participants' responses to the questions asked by the moderator on the board or a blank transparency.

3. When all have been seated, welcome the focus group by thanking them for agreeing to participate in this activity. Tell the participants that they will be asked to give their opinions on a new digital device. You will act as the moderator, the person who facilitates the focus group discussion.

4. Tell the focus group that the only rules are (1) no opinion or idea is to be thought of as foolish and (2) everyone in the group must have a chance to share his/her opinions.

5. As the moderator, have the focus group participants answer the following questions:

- Question 1: Do any of you use a mobile phone? Why or why not?

  Answer: If yes: the need to communicate with anyone anywhere, safety, need for work, talk with a lot of friends, etc. If no: no need or can wait, device too expensive, fear of losing it, don't want to be bothered, want all-in-one device, etc.

- Question 2: Do any of you use any type of method to keep track of your assignments, appointments, activities, and other personal information? Explain?

  Answer: Methods may include: memory, notebook, calendar, personal digital assistant (PDA) computer, DayTimer, etc.

- Question 3: Do any of you own/use a digital camera? Why or why not?

  Answer: If yes: the ability to download pictures to a computer; send e-mails of them to family/friends, etc. If no: no need, cost, want all-in-one device, etc.

- Question 4: What kinds of features do you think people want in a mobile phone?

  Answer: Features may include large memory for phone numbers or voice messages, speed dial, call waiting, three-way calling, receive messages or e-mail, have the unit and services reasonably priced, small enough to fit into pocket or purse, take pictures, send video, play mp3/iTunes, play games, etc.

- Question 5: If you were to design an integrated or 3G (third generation) personal information and communications device, what kinds of information, functions, or applications would you want or need, regardless of how feasible it may be? Remember, no idea is "off the wall" and ignore what the cost might be.

  Answer: **Have the student recorder write down the group's ideas on the board or a blank transparency**.

Nokia 7610 mobile phone

Slide 2

6. **Show Slide 2** and pass around the Nokia 7610 mobile phone brochure from the *Instructor's Survival Kit* box. [OPTIONAL: And copies of the brochure made from the .pdf to students.]

7. **Spend 1 minute** and have the group read the Nokia 7610 mobile phone brochure.

8. Ask focus group members what they like and dislike about the Nokia 7610 mobile phone.

9. Have the student recorder write down these likes and dislikes on the board or a blank transparency.

10. Ask the focus group participants whether they would buy the Nokia 7610 mobile phone for $449.99 for just the unit itself or $199.99 with a service plan/contract and rebates. Probe for their reasons.

11. OPTIONAL: **Show Slides 3-5** and have the group evaluate the following features that Nokia may include in future mobile phones:

   a. **Show Slide 3**: Future music. [TRT = 0:40]

   b. **Show Slide 4**: Future shopping. [TRT = 0:30]

   c. **Show Slide 5**: Future video. [TRT = 0:30]

Slide 3

Slide 4

Slide 5

   e. Ask the members if they like or dislike these features any why.

12. Thank the focus group participants for evaluating the new convergent digital device and excuse them from the focus group.

13. Acting as the instructor, have the entire class answer the following questions:

   • Question 1: How was the interaction among the focus group participants? Did you think everyone had a chance to share his/her opinions?

   Answer: If interaction is good, many diverse opinions can lead to ideas to develop new or improve existing products. If interaction is poor, it diminishes the value of this marketing research technique and perhaps conducting personal depth interviews or administering a survey would have had better results.

   • Question 2: What do you think about the convergence of digital devices? Would you buy one of these 3G devices today? Why or why not?

   Answer: Many possible responses exist.

Marketing Lessons. Methods such as focus groups are useful in generating new product ideas or evaluating of new product concepts in very early stages of development before a great deal of time, effort, and resources are expended. They are also used to evaluate existing products to assess quality, whether all the features are necessary or if others ones are needed, etc. However, focus groups are based on small, nonprobability samples that can limit the ability to generalize the results to an entire target market.

Website. Go to www.nokiausa.com for the current line of Nokia mobile phones.

CHAPTER 10: DEVELOPING NEW PRODUCTS AND SERVICES

ICA 10-2: IN-CLASS ACTIVITY

What *Were* They Thinking? Analyzing Some New Product Disasters[1]

Learning Objectives. To have students study six new product failures and in each case assess: (1) who the target market was, (2) some likely reasons it failed, and (3) what simple marketing research might have been done to identify and avert these problems early.

Definitions. Although many of the marketing terms below are not formally listed as "key terms" in the textbook, they are central to the successful completion of this ICA. These are the seven marketing reasons for new product failures shown in *Marketing, 8th Edition*. Note that all have significant areas of subjectivity:

- Insignificant "Point of Difference": Characteristics of a product that make it superior to substitutes.

- Incomplete Market and Product Definition Before Product Development Starts: A new product needs to precisely define the target market, its needs, wants, and preferences, and what it will be and do.

- Too Little Market Attractiveness: The market is too small and/or has too many competitors to warrant the expense to reach it.

- Poor Execution of the Marketing Mix: The critical elements, such as the name, package, price, promotion, and/or distribution are deficient, leading to lackluster sales.

- Poor Product Quality or Sensitivity to Customer Needs on Critical Factors: The product is defective or fails to meet customer expectations on 1 or 2 key features.

- Bad Timing: The product is introduced too soon, too late, or at a time when consumer tastes had shifted dramatically.

- No Economical Access to Buyers: The costs of advertising, creating a distribution network, or other necessary costs of reaching prospective customers are prohibitive.

Nature of the Activity. To have students work in teams to identify key reasons for the failure of six—sometimes outrageous—consumer products. These examples, and the accompanying photos, are adapted from Robert M. McMath's book "What *Were* They Thinking?" and his website (www.newproductworks.com).[2]

Estimated Class Time. 15 minutes.

---

[1] The authors wish to thank Robert M. McMath of New Product Works who assisted in the development of this ICA.
[2] Robert M. McMath and Thom Forbes, "*What* Were *They Thinking*?" (New York: Times Business, 1998). See also NewProductWorks at www.newproductworks.com.

Materials Needed.

- The ICA10-2.doc Word and ICA10-2.ppt PowerPoint files contained in the ICA10-2 folder of the Instructor's CD #1 from the *Instructor's Survival Kit* box.

- Copies of the:

    a. Six Consumer Products With Problems Handout.

    b. Worksheet to Analyze Why Six Consumer Products Failed.

- OPTIONAL: A transparency made from Answers to Worksheet to Analyze Why Six Consumer Products Failed.

Preparation Before Class. Follow the steps below:

1. Read pp. 268-272 of Chapter 10.

2. Print, read, and if necessary, edit the ICA10-2.doc Word file.

3. Print and/or review the PowerPoint slides from the ICA10-2.ppt PowerPoint file.

4. Make copies of the:

    a. Six Consumer Products With Problems Handout.

    b. Worksheet to Analyze Why Six Consumer Products Failed.

5. OPTIONAL: Bookmark the NewProductWorks (www.newproductworks.com) website on your classroom computer.

Instructions. Follow the steps below to conduct this ICA:

1. Review with students the 7 critical marketing factors that often separate new product successes and failures discussed on pp. 268-272 of Chapter 10.

2. Form students into 4-person teams.

Six Products
w/Problems

Slide 2

3. **Show Slide 2**: Six Consumer Products With Problems Handout and pass out copies of the handout to students.

4. **Show Slides 3-8**: Problem Products A – F. Provide a brief overview of each of the six products, describing what the product was and what it was intended to do.

Problem Product A

Adam's Body
Smarts

Slide 3

Problem Product B

Coca Cola's
Surge

Slide 4

Problem Product C

Wheaties
Dunk-A-Balls

Slide 5

Problem Product D

Garlic
Cake

Slide 6

Problem Product E

Kellogg's
Special K Plus

Slide 7

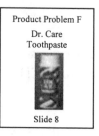

Product Problem F

Dr. Care
Toothpaste

Slide 8

Worksheet for Six
Product Failures

Slide 9

5. **Show Slide 9**: Worksheet to Analyze Why Six Consumer Products Failed and pass out copies of the handout to students.

6. Assign half of the student teams to analyze products A, B, and C and the other half to analyze products D, E, and F.

7. **Spend 5 minutes** and have the student teams complete the Worksheet to Analyze Why Six Consumer Products Failed handout. Before they begin, give them the following instructions:

   a. Under the "Target Market" column, have students identify to whom they think each product was targeted.

   b. Under columns 1–7 for each product, have the respective teams (A–C or D–F) check the one or more reason (s) why the product failed.

   c. Suggest some possible marketing research activities that the firm could have done to avoid the failure.

   d. [NOTE: If a team finishes its analysis early, it can work on the other products.]

8. For each product listed on the Worksheet to Analyze Why Six Consumer Products Failed handout, have 1 or 2 teams share its analysis for a given product (row) and obtain comments from other students about the analysis (agree/disagree; why?).

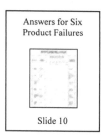

Answers for Six
Product Failures

Slide 10

9. **Show Slide 10**: Answers to Worksheet to Analyze Why Six Consumer Products Failed (or a transparency made from it; see below).

10. Discuss the following comments made by Robert M. McMath and the subjective assessments of the co-authors of *Marketing, 8ᵗʰ Edition*:

   a. **Body Smarts**. Show Slide 3 if needed. In early 2002, Adams pulled the product off retailer shelves despite a $70 million market-introduction campaign that involves advertising, in-store promotions, and national sampling. The problem was: The taste was not good enough to satisfy nutrition-conscious consumers!

   b. **Surge**. Show Slide 4 if needed. Starting with a $50 million promotional launch in 1995, Surge faced difficulties in beating out Pepsi Cola's strongly entrenched Mountain Dew in the citrus drink category, both in terms of gaining consumer preference and space on retailers' shelves.

c. **Wheaties Dunk-A-Balls Cereal**. Show Slide 5 if needed. C'mon! A cereal that encourages kids to "shoot baskets" with it around the kitchen? Introduced in 1994, Mom (and Dad!) didn't want their kids playing with their cereal.

d. **Garlic Cake**. Show Slide 6 if needed. Introduced in 1989, the product was supposed to be served as an hors d'oeuvre with sweet breads, spreads, and meats. But the company never adequately explained this to prospective customers, who spent their time wondering what garlic cake was and when to eat it.

e. **Special K Plus cereal**. Show Slide 7 if needed. Launched in the fall of 1999 with a $15 million campaign, the product's extra calcium may have been an important point of difference for a significant number of consumers. But the resealable milk carton-like package was a big part of the problem. While it contained the same number of servings as a regular cereal box, consumers thought it contained less. And the smaller shelf facings were not very attention-getting on grocery shelves.

f. **Dr. Care Toothpaste**. Show Slide 8 if needed. Think about this for three seconds: Turning a six-year old loose in the bathroom with a toothpaste-filled aerosol can? The vanilla-mint flavor may have been OK, but parents saw the aerosol can as a "show-stopper."

11. Conclude this ICA with the following mini-lecture:

"As Robert M. McMath asks, "What *Were* They Thinking?" Or, how could these (and other) product disasters have happened, especially since many of the problems are so obvious afterwards? Listed below are a few partial explanations:

a. **Pressure to increase revenues**. Product managers face extreme pressures to generate increased revenues, often turning to new products for the quick answer.

b. **Short deadlines**. Pressures to increase revenues often force product managers to "go to market" with products they know have not received adequate marketing research.

c. **'Groupthink.'** New product teams—like all teams—are under pressure to develop cohesiveness. So when a team member asks embarrassing questions about a new product concept, he or she can get ostracized from the group and not be seen as a 'team player.' So knowledgeable team members 'bite their tongues' and don't ask the tough questions so that they can remain a respected member of 'the team,' or what has sometimes been labeled as 'groupthink.'"

Marketing Lessons. Introducing successful new products is difficult, but (1) having a clear product concept and definite point of difference, (2) knowing traditional marketing reasons for failure, and (3) conducting simple marketing research can reduce the new product risks.

Website. To view more examples of new product failures (and successes), go to Robert M. McMath's NewProductWorks website, which is www.newproductworks.com.

SIX CONSUMER PRODUCTS WITH PROBLEMS HANDOUT

A. <u>**Body Smarts**</u>:

Produced by Adams
(a division of Pfizer).
Nutritional crunch bars and
fruit chews.

B. <u>**Surge**</u>:

Produced by Coca-Cola.
High caffeine, citrus-flavored
soft drink.

C. <u>**Wheaties Dunk-A-Balls**</u>:

Produced by General Mills.
Basketball-shaped sweetened
corn and wheat puffs
breakfast cereal.

D. <u>**Garlic Cake**</u>:

Produced by Gunderson &
Rosario. A hors d' oeuvre for
cocktail parties.

E. <u>**Special K Plus**</u>:

Produced by Kellogg's.
An extension of Special K
cereal with more calcium,
packaged in a recloseable
milk carton-like container.

F. <u>**Dr. Care**</u>:

Produced by Dairimetrics, Ltd.
A vanilla mint-flavored
toothpaste in an aerosol
container.

WORKSHEET TO ANALYZE WHY
SIX CONSUMER PRODUCTS FAILED

PRODUCT	TARGET MARKET	REASON (S) FOR FAILURE							POSSIBLE MARKETING RESEARCH
		1 Bad Pt. of Diff.	2 Bad Prod/ Mkt Def.	3 Too Small Mkt	4 Bad Mkt Mix Exec	5 Poor Prod Qual	6 Bad Time	7 Poor Access to Buyers	
A. Body Smarts	Nutrition-conscious adults								Consumer taste tests
B. Surge	18 – 34 year old males								Paired-comparison taste test with Mountain Dew
C. Wheaties Dunk-A-Balls	Kids								Ask moms about product concept
D. Garlic Cake	Adults								Consumer education & taste tests
E. Kellogg's Special K Plus	Health-conscious adults								Package tests on consumers and retailers
F. Dr. Care Tooth-paste	Families								Ask moms and dads about product concept

ICA 10-2

ANSWERS TO WORKSHEET TO ANALYZE
WHY SIX CONSUMER PRODUCTS FAILED

PRODUCT	TARGET MARKET	REASON (S) FOR FAILURE							POSSIBLE MARKETING RESEARCH
		1 Bad Pt. of Diff.	2 Bad Prod/ Mkt Def.	3 Too Small Mkt	4 Bad Mkt Mix Exec	5 Poor Prod Qual	6 Bad Time	7 Poor Access to Buyers	
A. Body Smarts	Nutrition-conscious adults	√				√			Consumer taste tests
B. Surge	18 – 34 year old males	√					√	√	Paired-comparison taste test with Mountain Dew
C. Wheaties Dunk-A-Balls	Kids	√	√		√				Ask moms about product concept
D. Garlic Cake	Adults	√	√	√	√				Consumer education & taste tests
E. Kellogg's Special K Plus	Health-conscious adults				√			√	Package tests on consumers and retailers
F. Dr. Care Toothpaste	Families	√	√		√				Ask moms and dads about product concept

CHAPTER 10: DEVELOPING NEW PRODUCTS AND SERVICES

ICA 10-3: IN-CLASS ACTIVITY

Communicating Important Points of Difference to Skeptical Design Engineers[1]

Learning Objectives. To have students study a 3M marketing program for its innovative 3M® VHB™ (Very High Bonding) Tape to discover: (1) how skeptical students and design engineers might respond to 3M's VHB Tape, (2) what key points of difference 3M stresses in brochures and advertisements, and (3) how 3M can effectively communicate these points of difference to its target markets.

Definitions. The following marketing terms are referred to in this in-class activity (ICA):

- Consideration Set: The group of brands that a consumer would consider acceptable from among all the brands in the product class of which he or she is aware.

- Evaluative Criteria: Factors that represent both the objective attributes of a brand and the subjective ones a consumer uses to compare different products and brands.

- Points of Difference: Those characteristics of a product that make it superior to competitive substitutes.

Nature of the Activity. To demonstrate to students a key point of difference of 3M's VHB Tape (its incredibly effective ability to hold two smooth surfaces together) in a very creative way by challenging students to pull apart the two thin materials of 3M's VHB Tape and how this point of difference should be communicated to skeptical design engineers.

Estimated Class Time. 20 minutes.

Materials Needed.

- The ICA10-3.doc Word and ICA10-3.ppt PowerPoint files contained in the ICA10-3 folder of the Instructor's CD #1 from the *Instructor's Survival Kit* box.

- The packet of 3M VHB Tapes contained in the *Instructor's Survival Kit* box.

- Copies of the "Fasteners in the Skull" and "Screw on the Psychiatrist's Couch" ads. See the enclosed Adobe Acrobat Portable Document Files (.pdf) in the 'pdf' folder within the ICA10-3 folder. [NOTE: You will need the Adobe Acrobat Reader to view and print the PDF documents. To download the latest version, go to www.adobe.com/products/acrobat.]

Preparation Before Class. Follow the steps below:

1. Read pp. 121-122 of Chapter 5 and pp. 269-270 of Chapter 10.

---

[1] The authors wish to thank Chad Carney, Business Development Manager for 3M, who assisted in the development of this ICA.

2. Print, read, and if necessary, edit the ICA10-3.doc Word file.

3. Print and/or review the PowerPoint slides from the ICA10-3.ppt PowerPoint file.

4. OPTIONAL: Bookmark the 3M VHB Tape website (www.3m.com/us/mfg_industrial/adhesives/vhb/) on your classroom computer.

Instructions. Follow the steps below to conduct this ICA:

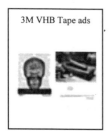

3M VHB Tape ads

1. Pass out copies of the "Fasteners in the Skull" and "Screw on the Psychiatrist's Couch" ads to each student. Have students read these ads while giving the mini-lecture below.

2. Pass around a few of the 3M's VHB Tapes from the packet contained in the *Instructor's Survival Kit* box.

3M VHB Tape

Slide 2

3. **Show Slide 2**. Give students this background mini-lecture on 3M's VHB Tape:

   "For 20 years, 3M has asked skeptical engineers to 'Imagine your world without rivets, screws, and welding!' when it developed very high bonding, double-sided foam VHB Tape."

4. **Show Slides 3-6**. Continue the background mini-lecture on 3M's VHB Tape:

   "Sound like an exaggeration? This is exactly the problem 3M faces. 3M's VHB Tape is meant to replace mechanical fasteners, such as screws, rivets, etc. for a variety of applications. These include applying steel strips to aluminum airplane wings, joining truck cab frames to the body, bonding metal and plastic in electronic components, etc. The marketing challenge 3M has is to convince design engineers, who for years have specified more traditional fasteners in their designs, that its VHB Tape is not just as good but better than the consideration set currently used. Typically, these design engineers viewed foam tapes useful only in non-critical, lightweight attachment applications, such as for mounting posters or soap dispensers. 3M has countered this perception by developing creative advertising, such as the 'Fasteners in the Skull,' 'In Emergency Break Glass,' or the 'Screw on the Psychiatrist's Couch' brochures and ads."

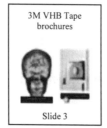

3M VHB Tape brochures

Slide 3

3M VHB Tape Applications (1)

Slide 4

3m VHB Tape Applications (2)

Slide 5

3M VHB Tape ad

Slide 6

5. Conduct a quick "Yes" or "No" market research survey by asking the class whether they believe 3M's claims about its VHB Tape. [NOTE: If there are engineers in the class, the instructor might tabulate their answers separately!]

   a. Write the results of the survey on the board.

   b. Ask students to explain their answers.

6. Ask the students the following questions about 3M's VHB Tape:

   • Question 1: What special concerns might design engineers have in specifying 3M's VHB Tape in their new designs?

     Answer: Students may suggest strength, durability, test results under various use conditions, etc.

   • Question 2: What kinds of applications might design engineers consider using 3M's VHB Tape?

     Answer: Students may suggest small appliances or other applications where stress forces aren't that great and/or safety is not an issue if the VHB Tape fails.

   • Question 3: What kinds of applications might design engineers be very hesitant to use 3M's VHB Tape?

     Answer: Students may suggest applications with a lot of stress and where failure of the adhesive might be life threatening.

7. 3M's VHB Tape brochure and ads, which are placed in several technical magazines targeted at design engineers, identify and describe several "points of difference" for the 3M's VHB Tape. The key points of difference are:

   a. Provides strong, reliable, durable adhesive bonding.
   b. Reduces corrosion.
   c. Absorbs impact.
   d. Lessens metal fatigue.
   e. Eliminates weight.
   f. Dampens sound.
   g. Reduces parts inventory.
   h. Simplifies manufacturing processes/eliminates labor-intensive processes.
   i. Increases design freedom.

8. Ask students what is the single most critical point of difference for most design engineers. The answer: "**a**" in the list above, which is "strong, reliable durable adhesive bonding." This is the **necessary condition**—the essential requirement—for many design engineers to allow 3M's VHB Tape into their "consideration set" of fastening alternatives and to be genuinely considered for use in an engineering design. Unless 3M's VHB Tape has this attribute, all other attributes are secondary.

9. Give two students a 3M VHB Tape sample from the *Instructor's Survival Kit*. Ask them to try to pull or tear the two strips apart. Then ask the class two final questions:

- Question 1: Why did 3M include actual "tear-apart" strips in its brochure?

   Answer: To gain attention for and directly address the skepticism that design engineers may have about the adhesive power of 3M's VHB Tape.

   [NOTE: Some students may be able to pull the strips apart and conclude the 3M VHB Tape doesn't work. The tear-apart strips are an attention-getter, not a formal test! In real applications, the VHB Tape is subjected to **tension** and **compression** forces that it handles very well and **NOT** the **shear** forces to which the students may be subjecting the 3M VHB Tape.]

- Question 2: What does 3M have in its "Screw on the Psychiatrist's Couch" ad to trigger immediate action by design engineers?

   Answer: Having grabbed an engineer's attention, the brochure provides the opportunity for two immediate actions: To (1) call 3M using the 800 number at the bottom of the ad and (2) visit its website.

Marketing Lessons. It often takes creative marketing and advertising programs to overcome the tradition-bound inertia among both ultimate consumers and business-to-business customers for these potential buyers to genuinely consider innovative products that can satisfy their wants and needs. This usually involves focusing on the product's points of difference, important evaluative criteria customers use when determining the consideration set of brands they will assess while making purchase decisions.

Website. To obtain the latest information on 3M's VHB Tape, go to 3M's website at www.3M.com/vhb.

Marketing Mix Element	Issue/Problem	Action/Solution
Product Improvements	• In England, car is small • In England, steering wheel on the right (wrong!) side • U.S. fuel economy standards • U.S. safety standards • Comfort • Ability to customize	• Make car larger • Design MINI with steering wheel on left side • Design a fuel-efficient engine • Conform to U.S. safety standards • Focus on technology that allows for greater comfort and movement in upper body and legs • Offer "Build-to-Order" via website that offers features & accessories that American prefer (CD players)
Pricing Improvements	• Currency exchange risks since cars are produced in England (£) and exported to the U.S. ($) • Price of options higher to keep base price under $25,000	• Price guarantees for a fixed period of time • Show comparison prices of similar options for selected competitor cars
Promotion Improvements	• No TV ads; Americans like TV • Movie product placement may not be seen by target market • Non traditional use of traditional media may not appeal to target customers • British humor, if used, may not be fully appreciated by Americans	• Must use very creative alternative media to inform potential target customers, such as magazine ads, billboards, public relations, etc. • Use multiple product placement situations that are consistent with brand image • Use humor that is culturally accepted
Place (Distribution) Improvements	• Dealers in only 56 major U.S. cities • MINI dealer showrooms separate from BMW dealer showrooms	• Ability to configure a car via the Internet • MINI is a unique brand personality that needs to be separate from BMW

MARKETING ACTIONS TO IMPROVE THE MINI® BRAND'S CHANCES OF SUCCESSFULLY TARGETING THE U.S. MARKET

MARKETING STRATEGY AREA	ISSUE/PROBLEM	ACTION/SOLUTION
Product Improvements		
Pricing Improvements		
Promotion Improvements		
Place (Dealer) Improvements		

CHAPTER 10: DEVELOPING NEW PRODUCTS AND SERVICES

ICA 10-4: IN-CLASS ACTIVITY

Using Method 6–3–5 to Find New Product Ideas for Magnetic Poetry[®1]

Learning Objectives. To have students (1) participate in Method 6–3–5,[2] an idea generation technique and as a result (2) develop new product ideas for Magnetic Poetry.

Definitions. The following marketing terms are referred to in this in-class activity (ICA):

- Brand Extension: A branding strategy of using a current brand name to enter a completely different product class.

- Idea Generation: The stage of the new-product process that involves developing a pool of concepts as candidates for new products.

- Line Extension: A branding strategy of using a current brand name to enter a new market segment in its product class.

Nature of the Activity. To have students participate in small groups to generate ideas for line and brand extensions for Magnetic Poetry.

Estimated Class Time. 20 minutes.

Materials Needed.

- The ICA10-4.doc Word and ICA10-4.ppt PowerPoint files contained in the ICA10-4 folder of the Instructor's CD #1 from the *Instructor's Survival Kit* box.

- The Original or Sequel Magnetic Poetry kit contained in the *Instructor's Survival Kit* box.[3]

- Copies of the:
    a. Ground Rules for Method 6–3–5 Handout.
    b. Using Method 6–3–5 to Find New Product Ideas for Magnetic Poetry Handout.

Preparation Before Class. Follow the steps below:

1. Read pp. 273-275 of Chapter 10 and pp. 299-304 of Chapter 11.

2. Print, read, and if necessary, edit the ICA10-4.doc Word file.

3. Print and/or review the PowerPoint slides from the ICA10-4.ppt PowerPoint file.

---

[1] The authors wish to thank Greg Lee, Marketing Director of Magnetic Poetry, who assisted in the development of this ICA.

[2] Bryan Mattimore, "Eureka: How to Invent a New Product," *The Futurist* (March-April 1995), pp. 34-38.

[3] NOTE: Some *Instructor's Survival Kit* boxes will have the Original Magnetic Poetry kit while others will have the Sequel Magnetic Poetry kit.

4. Make copies of the:

   a. Ground Rules for Method 6–3–5 Handout.

   b. Using Method 6–3–5 to Find New Product Ideas for Magnetic Poetry Handout.

5. OPTIONAL: Bookmark the Magnetic Poetry website (www.magneticpoetry.com) on your classroom computer.

Instructions. Follow the steps below to conduct this ICA:

Magnetic Poetry
(Original or Sequel)

Slide 2

1. **Show Slide 2** and pass around the Pass around the Original or Sequel Magnetic Poetry Kit obtained from the *Instructor's Survival Kit* box.

2. Give students this background mini-lecture on Magnetic Poetry.

   "The story behind the creation of Magnetic Poetry has taken on the quality of urban legend, but this one is true, and the man who sneezed it into being is Dave Kapell.

   Yes, Dave (at the time a cash-poor songwriter and ex-cab driver) was cutting up things, like old letters and newspaper articles in ransom-note style, as a lyric writing experiment. When Dave sneezed, it sent all of his carefully arranged words and letters flying. They spawned the idea of gluing a piece of magnet to the back of each tiny slip and sticking the newly 'magnetized' words to a cookie sheet. From there, the first Magnetic Poetry Kit was born.

   Since that day in 1993, Magnetic Poetry has grown into a multi-million dollar business with dozens of different products. Magnetic Poetry has been sighted on the fridge in Hugh Grant's apartment in *Notting Hill*, *Conspiracy Theory*, and Seinfeld. And as reported in *Newsweek*, all but 4 words from Madonna's hit single "Candy Perfume Girl" are contained in Magnetic Poetry's Sequel Kit. Coincidence? A linguistic expert and professional mathematician figured out the odds. A conservative estimate put the odds at 1 in 4.2 trillion that she didn't use the kit."

3. Form students into 6-person teams and have them sit in a circle, if possible. [NOTE: This is the '**6**' in Method 6–3–5.]

4. Pass out copies of the Ground Rules for Method 6–3–5 Handout and the Using Method 6–3–5 to Find New Product Ideas for Magnetic Poetry Handout to each student to each student.

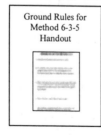

Ground Rules for
Method 6-3-5
Handout

Using Method
6-3-5 Handout

5. Introduce the Method 6–3–5 activity as follows:

Ground Rules for
Method 6-3-5

Slide 3

"We've all heard of brainstorming as a technique for generating ideas. Organizations use these techniques to develop or improve products or advertising campaigns. Like brainstorming, Method 6–3–5 encourages creative thinking."

6. **Show Slide 3**: Ground Rules for Methods 6-3-5 and briefly go over the instructions for this activity.

Using Method
6-3-5

Slide 4

7. **Show Slide 4**: Using Method 6–3–5 to Find New Product Ideas for Magnetic Poetry. Tell the student teams they will have **3 minutes** (the '**3**' in Method 6–3–5) to come up with 5 (the '**5**' in Method 6–3–5) new line and brand extensions of the Original Magnetic Poetry Kit that the company might bring to market. [NOTE: The goal is to come up with good new product ideas. Students can debate later whether a product idea is really a line or brand extension. HINT: The Sequel Magnetic Poetry Kit shown in Slide 2 is a line extension.]

8. After 3 minutes, have each team member pass their ideas on to the team member to the left, who **spends 3 minutes** elaborating and improving on the 5 ideas on the paper in front of them. After 3 minutes, have each team member again pass their ideas on to the team member to the left, who **spends 3 minutes** elaborating and improving on the 5 ideas on the paper in front of them. [NOTE: This process could be repeated so that all team members had a chance to review each member's ideas. However, due to time constraints, only 2 iterations will be done.]

9. Ask each team to share 3 of their better ideas with the class and discuss what they thought of Method 6–3–5 for generating ideas. Did the opportunity to elaborate on other team members' ideas help to refine those ideas or generate more new ideas?

10. Compare the line and brand extensions offered by Magnetic Poetry with those ideas that students generated as a result of Method 6–3–5.

Magnetic Poetry
Line Extensions

Slide 5

a. **Show Slide 5**: Magnetic Poetry Line Extensions.

- **Foreign language kits**. Spanish, French, German, Sign, etc.
- **Specialized kits**. For cooks, artists, dog lovers, etc.
- **Face kits**. To transform photos of faces.
- **Souvenir kits**. For cities such as New York or London.
- **StoryMaker**™. A colorful collection of over 150 words and phrases to let young children learn to compose sentences.
- **Custom kits**. For colleges and universities, corporations, etc.
- **Magnetic Poetry Online**. Click on one of several online Magnetic Poetry Kits to create and submit poetry.

Magnetic Poetry
Brand Extensions

Slide 6

b. **Show Slide 6**: Magnetic Poetry Brand Extensions.

- **Poetry Stones**™. A kit for making tinted, word-bearing concrete cobblestones to border gardens or walkways.
- **Magnetic Poetry: The Game**. A fast-paced board game where teams earn points creating poetry.
- **Poetry Beads**. A kit for making necklaces with personalized messages.
- **Magnetic Poetry Society**. For $14.95, members receive a Magnetic Poetry T-shirt, newsletter, and discounts on products.
- **Creativity Journal**. Engaging writing activities with word magnets to get started.
- **Mind Over Magnets**. A fun way to keep great ideas hanging around. Kits include Pointless Knowledge 1-4, Seven Sins & Virtues, Hierarchy of Needs, etc.
- **Backpack Games**. Backgammon, Tic-Tac-Toe, Dominoes, Chess, Checkers, etc. to be played anytime and anywhere.

Marketing Lesson. Method 6–3–5 demonstrates one of many techniques used to develop new or improve existing products and services. Other techniques include brainstorming (see ICA 10-1), IDEO Method Cards (see ICA 10-5), etc.

Website. To view Magnetic Poetry's product line, go to www.magneticpoetry.com.

GROUND RULES FOR METHOD 6–3–5

1. Use teams of <u>6</u> people each and sit in a circle.

2. In <u>3</u> minutes, have each team member come up with <u>5</u> ideas (written down on the Using Method 6-3-5 to Find New Product Ideas for Magnetic Poetry Handout).

3. After 3 minutes, have each team member pass their ideas on to the team member to the left who spends 3 minutes elaborating and improving on the 5 ideas on the paper in front of them.

4. After 3 minutes, repeat Step 3 (above) again.*

* This could be repeated all around the circle, but to save time only 2 improvement iterations are done here.

USING METHOD 6–3–5 TO FIND NEW PRODUCT IDEAS FOR MAGNETIC POETRY®

IDEA	ORIGINAL IDEA	FIRST REWORK	SECOND REWORK
#1			
#2			
#3			
#4			
#5			

CHAPTER 10: DEVELOPING NEW PRODUCTS AND SERVICES

ICA 10-5: IN-CLASS ACTIVITY

Idea Generation: The IDEO Way[1]

Learning Objective. To have students apply unique methods used to generate ideas for new products, services, and processes.

Definitions. The following marketing terms are referred to in this in-class activity (ICA):

- Idea Generation: The stage of the new-product process that involves developing a pool of concepts as candidates for new products.

- New-Product Process: The stages a firm goes through to identify business opportunities and convert them to a salable good or service.

- Product: A good, service, or idea consisting of a bundle of tangible and intangible attributes that satisfies consumers and is received in exchange for money or some other unit of value.

Nature of the Activity. To have students discover opportunities and generate ideas for a new product, service or process by using one of four IDEO's Method Cards, a design tool to explore a critical stage of the new-product process.

Estimated Class Time. 45 minutes, which consists of:

- 15 minutes to discuss IDEO and its perspective on generating new ideas.

- 30 minutes to conduct this ICA. [NOTE: The instructor may want to have students do this ICA outside of class and discuss the results during the next class period.]

Materials Needed.

- The four IDEO Method Cards from the *Instructor's Survival Kit* box.

- The ICA10-5.doc Word and ICA10-5.ppt PowerPoint files contained in the ICA10-5 folder of the Instructor's CD #1 from the *Instructor's Survival Kit* box.

- Copies of the:
    a. IDEO Method Cards Look, Ask, Learn, and Try Team Handouts.
    b. IDEO Method Cards: Ask "Card Sort" Template Handout.
    c. IDEO Method Cards "Suggestions" Handout.

---

[1] The authors wish to thank Lynn Winter, Marketing Manager, Jane Fulton Suri, Director of Human Factors Design and Research, Scott Underwood, Marketing, Whitney Mortimer, Media Relations, and Kelly Robinson, Marketing Assistant of IDEO, who assisted in the development of this ICA.

- NOTE: Transparencies can be made of the handouts instead of making copies and using the PowerPoint presentation for those instructors who prefer this option.

Preparation Before Class. Follow the steps below:

1. Read pp. 273-275 in Chapter 10 about the idea generation stage of the new-product process.

2. Print, read, and if necessary, edit the ICA10-5.doc Word file.

3. Print and/or review the slides from the ICA10-5.ppt PowerPoint file.

4. Make copies of the:

   a. IDEO Method Cards Look, Ask, Learn, and Try Team Handouts.

   b. IDEO Method Cards: Ask "Card Sort" Template Handout.

   c. IDEO Method Cards "Suggestions" Handout.

5. OPTIONAL: Bookmark the IDEO website (www.ideo.com) on your classroom computer.

Steps in the New-Product Process

Slide 2

Instructions. Follow the steps below to conduct this ICA:

1. **Show Slide 2**: Steps in the New-Product Process and give the following mini-lecture about idea generation and IDEO:

   "Organizations go through several steps to identify salable new products and services. One of the most critical involves generating a set of ideas or concepts that leads to new products or services to satisfy a consumer need. This is the second step of the new-product process.

   Many organizations use design firms like IDEO to generate ideas for new or to refine existing products. IDEO has designed hundreds of new products and won numerous awards for their efforts on behalf of clients."

2. **Show Slides 3-6**: IDEO's New Product Innovations.[2]

   [Click the mouse while describing a few of the new-product innovations generated by IDEO.]

   a. *Steelcase Leap Chair* (2000). An office chair with superior support.

   b. *Evenflo Car Seats* (2001). Car seats with improved harnesses, buckles, and shells that offer better safety and security for children.

   c. *ApproTec MoneyMaker Deep Lift Pump* (2003). A stair-stepping machine-like water pump for farmers and entrepreneurs in Africa.

   d. *Zyliss Kitchen Tools* (2004). Kitchen tools for cutting, slicing, etc.

IDEO: Steelcase
Leap Chair

Slide 3

IDEO: Evenflo
Car Seats

Slide 4

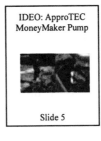
IDEO: ApproTEC
MoneyMaker Pump

Slide 5

IDEO: Zyliss
Kitchen Tools

Slide 6

3. Continue the mini-lecture about IDEO's perspective on new-product design:

"IDEO has a unique perspective to generate new product ideas:

a. At IDEO, new product design is a team effort. 'There are no solo efforts anymore.'[3] Its innovations are due to this culture.[4]

b. IDEO believes that new product design must involve the study of human behavior[5] by looking at consumers 'through the eyes of anthropologists, graphics designers, engineers, and psychologists.'[6]

c. IDEO 'requires its clients to participate in virtually all the consumer research, analysis, and decisions that go into developing solutions.'[7]

IDEO's new-product design approach uses a four-step process.[8]

a. *Observation and Synthesis.* First, members of the IDEO and client team go out and observe consumers to understand both what they are trying to accomplish and the circumstances (physical and social) in which they are doing this. This involves:

– Watching, photographing or videotaping them shop and use products or perform activities.
– Interviewing people who know—or know nothing—about the product or activity and asking them to tell there personal stories about their problems or experiences.
– Exploring ideas on how to solve problems.

Then, the team synthesizes their observations to develop a perspective on what are the key issues and opportunity areas.

b. *Idea Generation.* Next, using these issues and opportunity areas as a starting point, the team uses brainstorming to come up with a broad range of ideas. There are several rules for team members to ensure productive brainstorming sessions:

– Defer judgment and don't dismiss any idea.
– Build on the ideas of others.
– Encourage wild ideas.
– Go for quantity.
– Stay focused on the topic.
– Have one conversation at a time.

c. *Rapid Prototyping*. Third, after selecting, and sometimes combining the best of several, ideas from brainstorming the team develops mock-ups to visualize possible solutions. This must be done fast, not sweating over the details, but just enough to let the team get a sense of the solution and learn what really works.

d. *Implementation*. Last, reduce the choices to a few realistic possibilities and create a prototype of the new product, service or process. The team may feel the pressure to add features. Design is a funneling process, always asking: What is appropriate? What can be stripped away?[9] Thus, in good design, 'less is more.'"

4. Divide students into 4-person teams based on the four IDEO Method Cards: Look, Ask, Learn, and Try.

5. Pass out copies of the following to each student:

a. IDEO Method Cards "Look, Ask, Learn, and Try" Team Handouts.

b. IDEO Method Cards: Ask "Card Sort" Template Handout.

c. IDEO Method Cards "Suggestions" Handout.

IDEO Method Card Look, Ask, Learn, & Try Team Handouts | IDEO Method Card Ask 'Card Sort' Template Handout | IDEO Method Card Suggestions Handout

IDEO
Method Cards

Slide 7

6. **Show Slide 7**: IDEO's Method Cards and continue the mini-lecture:

"In 2003, IDEO offered IDEO's Method Cards to help companies innovate by writing down the strategies it uses to understand consumers and their experiences, behaviors, perceptions, and needs. IDEO Method Cards consist of 51 cards that represent diverse ways new-product designers can generate and analyze new ideas for products and services. Each card explains how and when the method is best used and how IDEO applied it to a real project. According to Jane Fulton Suri, Director of Human Factors Design and Research at IDEO, 'The reason we made 51 (not a full-deck of 52) cards was because the point is that this is not a complete set of methods for generating ideas. The deck was designed to be *inspirational* about the many ways we might explore context and behavior, not *prescriptive* of a specific process.'"

7. **Show Slides 8-11**: IDEO's Method Cards (Look, Ask, Learn, Try).

"The cards are classified into four "suits," like playing cards, that represent ways to empathize with people. Each suit (Look, Ask, Learn, and Try) defines the types of activities involved in using each method.

a. The '*Look*' set of IDEO Method Cards. Observe people to discover what they do rather than what they say they do.

b. The '*Ask*' set of IDEO Method Cards. Enlist people's participation to elicit information relevant to your project.

c. The '*Learn*' set of IDEO Method Cards. Analyze information you've collected to identify patterns and insights.

d. The '*Try*' set of IDEO Method Cards. Create simulations to help empathize with people and to evaluate designs."

IDEO Method Cards: Look	IDEO Method Cards: Ask	IDEO Method Cards: Learn	IDEO Method Cards: Try

Slide 8	Slide 9	Slide 10	Slide 11

8. Explain the purpose of this ICA to all students.

"Each team represents a "suit" and has one card from this set of IDEO Method Cards. For the purpose of this activity, each team consists of people from IDEO and the 'client,' who is interested in generating new product, service, or process ideas regarding studying—a behavior you are all familiar with. Therefore, during the next several minutes, each 'Look,' 'Ask,' 'Learn,' and 'Try' team will use its IDEO Method Card and apply it to studying. This activity will allow you to empathize with "customers" so that you can generate and evaluate ideas that lead to new study-related products, services or processes. Look at your handouts as I describe the activity for each team. You will have 15 minutes to complete this activity:

a. *Marketing Task.* The goal is to generate new product, service or process ideas aimed at students to enhance their studying experience. Team members will assume their target market is collegiate students and the task limited to a specific studying behavior: **completing a textbook reading assignment**. Due to time constraints, use the following studying elements. You are free to add or modify them based on your team's collective analysis and the time allotted.

b. *Context.* The textbook reading assignment is from the syllabus, a handout, or instructor comment made during class.

c. *Setting.* Students typically study at three locations: residence (dorm, apartment), eating establishment (cafeteria, restaurant), or library.

d. *Process.* The studying sequence for accomplishing the textbook reading assignment typically involves reading, underlining, marking, note-taking, etc. the important points of the text.

e. *Study Aids.* The aids typically used by students to facilitate their study of the textbook material include something to write with and on or to type or record into the important points of the text."

199   ICA 10-5

IDEO Method
Cards: Look
Handout

Slide 12

9. **Show Slide 12** and explain this ICA to the "Look—Shadowing" teams.

   a. Describe the routines and interactions each of your team members would use to study and complete the assigned textbook reading.

   b. Identify opportunities that affect or complement your studying behavior.

   c. Suggest any new product, service or process that may be developed as a result of your analysis.

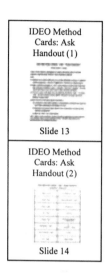

IDEO Method
Cards: Ask
Handout (1)

Slide 13

IDEO Method
Cards: Ask
Handout (2)

Slide 14

10. **Show Slides 13-14** and explain this ICA to the "Ask—Card Sort" teams.

   a. Identify 6 to 8 possible study aids and 2 to 3 of their attributes (type, size, color, etc.) involved in studying a textbook reading assignment.

   b. Carefully cut the 1" by 3" cards (see template) based on the study aids and their attributes your team identifies. Print the names of any new study aid and/or associated attribute (2 or 3 maximum) on the blank cards provided. Do not exceed 32 cards.

   c. Rank order the study aids and the associated 2 to 3 attributes to indicate their importance to each team member. Record these rankings on a separate sheet of paper.

   d. Suggest any new product, service or process that may be developed as a result of your analysis.

IDEO Method
Cards: Learn
Handout

Slide 15

11. **Show Slide 15** and explain this ICA to the "Learn—Affinity Diagram" teams.

   a. Create a spatial representation of the elements used (context, setting, process, study aids) when studying a textbook reading assignment. .

   b. Write down the study elements, cluster or group common elements, and draw links between them to show the relationships that exist.

   c. Identify connections between elements.

   d. Suggest any new product, service or process that may be developed as a result of your analysis.

IDEO Method
Cards: Try Handout

Slide 16

12. **Show Slide 16** and explain this ICA to the "Try—Bodystorming" teams.

   a. Create a scenario or role-play, with or without props, that describes how students' study relative to the textbook reading assignment. Stop and take stock of whatever you are thinking and feeling at different points through the process of studying.

   b. Suggest any new product, service or process that may be developed as a result of your analysis.

13. **Spend 15 minutes** and have 3 to 5 students from each set of teams share their behaviors and ideas for new study products or services.

Marketing Lessons. Generating and evaluating ideas for new products and services starts with empathizing with customers. Tools like IDEO's Method Cards assist marketers in understanding behaviors and providing insights into this crucial step of the new-product process.

Websites. IDEO's website is www.ideo.com. IDEO Method Cards are available exclusively at William Stout Architectural Books for $49. Call 415-391-6757 or purchase online at www.stoutbooks.com and type 'IDEO' in the 'Search' field to locate the webpage. You can also purchase IDEO co-founder Thomas Kelley's book, *The Art of Innovations: Lessons in Creativity from IDEO*.

IDEO METHOD CARDS: "LOOK" TEAM HANDOUT
"SHADOWING" CARD

TASK: Identify students' actual behavior when studying a textbook.

HOW: Describe the routines and interactions on how students' study.

WHY: Identify opportunities that affect or complement students' study behavior.

STUDYING ELEMENT	DESCRIBE ROUTINES AND INTERACTIONS
1. Context: Textbook reading assignment from syllabus, handout, or instructor.	
2. Setting: Dorm room, apartment, cafeteria, library, restaurant, etc.	
3. Process: Read text; underline text, flag text; write, type, dictate notes onto paper/into a PC/voice recorder, etc.	
4. Study Aids: Paper, pencil, pen, Internet, telephone, highlighter, Post-it® Notes/Flags, PC, voice recorder, iPod/mp3 player & headphones, etc.	
5. Suggest any new product, service or process that may be developed as a result of this analysis.	

IDEO METHOD CARDS: "ASK" TEAM HANDOUT
"CARD SORT" CARD

TASK: Enlist students' participation to obtain information about important attributes regarding their behavior when studying a textbook.

HOW:

(1) Identify 6 to 8 STUDY AIDS and 2 to 3 of their attributes involved in a textbook reading assignment. [Use the "Suggestions" handout as a starting point.]

(2) Make a sufficient number of 1" by 3" cards based on all the STUDY AIDS and their attributes identified in step '1' using the "Card Sort" template. You have some blank ones in you want to add a study aid and/or attributes.

(3) Print the names of all study aids and attributes identified in step '1' on these cards. DO NOT exceed 32 cards. [NOTE: Only print one study aid and an attribute on each card.]

(4) Each person on the team spend 5 minutes to:

(a) Arrange the cards either spatially or sequentially to indicate how important each study aid/attribute combination is to you.

(b) Generate new product ideas based on the combination of study aid and attribute combinations.

(c) Rank the "best" new product ideas.

WHY: Helps to show students' mental processes regarding their study behavior and indicates what is most important to them. Reveals expectations and priorities about the intended functions.

ICA 10-5

IDEO METHOD CARDS: "ASK" TEAM HANDOUT
"CARD SORT" TEMPLATE

Paper: Color	PC Software: Type
Paper: Size	Voice Recorder: Type
Paper: Type	Telephone
Pen: Type	Internet
Pencil: Type	iPod/mp3 player & headphones
Highlighter: Type	PC: Software—Word
Post-it® Notes: Type	Eating
PC: Type	Other Books

IDEO METHOD CARDS: "ASK" TEAM HANDOUT
"CARD SORT" CARD TEMPLATE

IDEO METHOD CARDS: "LEARN" TEAM HANDOUT

"AFFINITY DIAGRAM" CARD

TASK: Create a spatial representation of the elements used (context, setting, process, study aids) when studying a textbook reading assignment.

HOW: Write down the study elements, cluster or group common elements, and draw links between them to show the relationships that exist.

WHY: Identify connections between elements to generate new ideas.

STUDYING ELEMENT	DRAW A DIAGRAM THAT DEPICTS THE RELATIONSHIPS AMONG THE STUDY ELEMENTS
1. Context: Textbook reading assignment from syllabus, handout, or instructor.	
2. Setting: Dorm room, apartment, cafeteria, library, restaurant, etc.	
3. Process: Read text; underline text, flag text; write, type, dictate notes onto paper/into a PC/voice recorder, etc.	
4. Study Aids: Paper, pencil, pen, Internet, telephone, highlighter, Post-it® Notes/Flags, PC, voice recorder, iPod/mp3 player & headphones, etc.	
5. Suggest any new product, service or process that may be developed as a result of this analysis.	

IDEO METHOD CARDS: "TRY" TEAM HANDOUT

"BODYSTORMING" CARD

TASK: Develop simulations to help empathize with students when studying a textbook to evaluate proposed designs.

HOW: Create a scenario or role-play, with or without props, describing how students' study.

WHY: Quickly generate and test several context- and behavior-based concepts related to students' study behavior.

STUDYING ELEMENT	DEVELOP SCENARIO OR ROLE-PLAY WITH PROPS
1. Context: Textbook reading assignment from syllabus, handout, or instructor.	
2. Setting: Dorm room, apartment, cafeteria, library, restaurant, etc.	
3. Process: Read text; underline text, flag text; write, type, dictate notes onto paper/into a PC/voice recorder, etc.	
4. Study Aids: Paper, pencil, pen, Internet, telephone, highlighter, Post-it® Notes/Flags, PC, voice recorder, iPod/mp3 player & headphones, etc.	
5. Suggest any new product, service or process that may be developed as a result of this analysis.	

ICA 10-5

IDEO METHOD CARDS: "SUGGESTIONS" HANDOUT

STUDYING ELEMENT	IDENTIFY ROUTINES, INTERACTIONS, & CONTEXTS
1. Context: Textbook reading assignment from syllabus, handout, or instructor.	• Check syllabus or handout, recall instructor's verbal textbook reading assignment. • Get textbook and other study items. • Place textbook/PC on a desk, bed, table, etc. • Open textbook to beginning page of assigned reading. [NOTE: If textbook is on a CD, get CD, insert into PC, and then find the assigned pages.] • Others as identified.
2. Setting: Dorm room, apartment, cafeteria, library, restaurant, etc.	• Dorm room/apartment: sit at desk; lie in bed; lay book on desk, table, bed; adjust lighting; turn on/off music; etc. • Cafeteria/restaurant: sit a table; get food/beverage; ignore distractions; etc. • Library: go to quiet location; sit at table; etc. • Note whether other people are around, the lighting, noise levels, and what is behind these choices. • Others as identified.
3. Process: Read text; underline text, flag text; write, type, dictate notes onto paper/into a PC/voice recorder, etc.	• Find the right textbook, chapter, and page. Begin reading. • Indicate important points: underline, mark, flag, write, type, dictate, etc. • Optional: Record important points (paper; PC/voice recorder). • Review important points. • Compare important points from textbook and class notes. • Organize important points for quiz, exam, paper, etc. • Note interruptions of any kind. Any multitasking (drinking/eating)? • Others as identified.
4. Study Aids: Paper, pencil, pen, highlighter, Post-it® Notes/Flags, PC, voice recorder, headphones, etc.	• Check to see if study aids are in adequate supply for the study session. • Obtain any needed study aids: make do as is, borrow, or buy at bookstore or office supply store. • Store study aids in desk, back pack, purse, etc. until needed. • Bring/retrieve study aids to study setting. • Use study aids during study session. • Others as identified.
5. Suggest any new product or service that may be developed as a result of this analysis.	• The 3M Post-it® Flag Highlighter. • Online summaries, Q & A exercises, etc. • 'Please Do Not Disturb' lights for dorm room doors. • Others as identified.

IDEO METHOD CARDS—LEARN: "AFFINITY DIAGRAM" HANDOUT

Learn   Look   Ask   Try

Affinity Diagrams

HOW: Cluster design elements according to intuitive relationships such as similarity, dependence, proximity, etc.

WHY: This method is a useful way to identify connections between issues and reveal innovation opportunities.

Clustering the elements related to transporting the family helped the IDEO team to discover some significant opportunities for stroller design.

IDEO
www.ideo.com

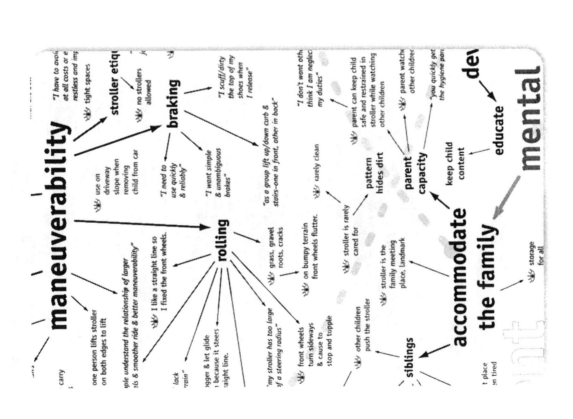

ICA 10-5

IDEO METHOD CARDS—LOOK: "SHADOWING" HANDOUT

Learn   Look   Ask   Try

Shadowing

HOW: Tag along with people to observe and understand their day-to-day routines, interactions, and contexts.

WHY: This is a valuable way to reveal design opportunities and show how a product might affect or complement users' behavior.

The IDEO team accompanied truckers on their routes in order to understand how they might be affected by a device capable of detecting their drowsiness.

www.ideo.com

IDEO

IDEO METHOD CARDS—ASK: "CARD SORT" HANDOUT

Learn   Look   Ask   Try

Card Sort

HOW: On separate cards, name possible features, functions, or design attributes. Ask people to organize the cards spatially, in ways that make sense to them.

WHY: This helps to expose people's mental models of a device or system. Their organization reveals expectations and priorities about the intended functions.

In a project to design a new digital phone service, a card-sorting exercise enabled potential users to influence the final menu structure and naming.

IDEO

www.ideo.com

IDEO METHOD CARDS—TRY: "BODYSTORMING" HANDOUT

Learn   Look   Ask   Try

Bodystorming

HOW: Set up a scenario and act out roles, with or without props, focusing on the intuitive responses prompted by the physical enactment.

WHY: This method helps to quickly generate and test many context- and behavior-based concepts.

Bodystorming various ways of sleeping in airplanes helped the IDEO design team to generate a wide variety of concepts for an airplane interior.

www.ideo.com

ICA 10-5

212

Endnotes:

[2] Information obtained from the IDEO website. Click on the 'Out Work' link at www.ideo.com.

[3] "Q&A with Tom Kelley," Opening Keynote Address, Product Development & Management Association (PDMA) 2001. See www.pdma.org/2001/q_and_a.jsp.

[4] GK VanPatter, "Innovation by Design: Understanding IDEO Now! An Interview with Tom Brown," *NextD Journal*, published by the NextDesign Leadership Institute, Issue FOUR, Conversation 4.2. See www.nextd.org.

[5] Herb Brody, "Master of Design," *Technology Review*, June 25, 2003. See www.technologyreview.com.

[6] Bruce Nussbaum, "The Power of Design," Business Week, May 17, 2004. See www.businessweek.com (subscription access required); Daniel Pink, "Out of the Box," *Fast Company*, Issue 75, October 2003, p. 104. See www.fastcompany.com/magazine/75/outofthebox.html.

[7] Ibid.

[8] Ibid.

[9] Master of Design.

CHAPTER 11: MANAGING PRODUCTS AND BRANDS

ICA 11-1: IN-CLASS ACTIVITY

Managing the Product Life Cycle[1]

Learning Objective. To have students learn about the strategies firms use in managing and extending the product life cycle (PLC) of their products and brands by having them suggest specific actions for Golden Valley Microwave Foods (GVMF) to use with its ACT II® Microwave Popcorn.

Definitions. The following marketing terms are referred to in this in-class activity (ICA):

- Market Modification: A strategy in which a company tries to find new customers, increase a product's use among existing customers, or create new use situations.

- Product Life Cycle: Describes the stages a new product goes through in the marketplace: introduction, growth, maturity, and decline.

- Product Modification: Altering a product's characteristic, such as its quality, performance, or appearance, to try to increase the product's sales.

- Product Repositioning: Changing the place an offering occupies in a consumer's mind relative to competitive products.

Nature of the Activity. To have student teams start with a single product of GVMF ACT II Microwave Popcorn and then address the challenging task of developing new PLC ideas for **microwave popcorn only**. [NOTE: Ideas outside the popcorn line are not within the scope of this ICA.]

Estimated Class Time. 30 minutes.

Materials Needed.

- The ICA11-1.doc Word and ICA11-1.ppt PowerPoint files contained in the ICA11-1 folder of the Instructor's CD #1 from the *Instructor's Survival Kit* box.

- The packages of ACT II Butter Lover's Microwave Popcorn and ACT II Light Butter Microwave Popcorn contained in the *Instructor's Survival Kit* box.

- Copies of the Managing and Extending the Product Life Cycle (PLC) for ACT II® Butter Lover's Microwave Popcorn Handout.

- OPTIONAL: The instructor may want to "pop" several bags of different flavors of ACT II microwave popcorn before class and serve it during this ICA.

- NOTE: Transparencies can be made of the handout instead of making copies and using the PowerPoint presentation for those instructors who prefer this option.

---

[1] The authors wish to thank Frank Lynch, President, and Patty Serie, Marketing Departmentof ConAgra Snack Foods, who assisted in the development of this ICA.

Preparation Before Class. Follow the steps below:

1. Read pp. 297-299 of Chapter 11.

2. Print, read, and if necessary, edit the ICA11-1.doc Word file.

3. Print and/or review the PowerPoint slides from the ICA11-1.ppt PowerPoint file.

4. Make copies of the Managing and Extending the Product Life Cycle (PLC) for ACT II® Butter Lover's Microwave Popcorn Handout.

5. Skim the ACT II Video Case 15 on pp. 417-419 of *Marketing, 8th Edition*.

6. OPTIONAL: "Popped" bags of several flavors of ACT II Microwave Popcorn.

7. OPTIONAL: Bookmark the ACT II website (www.actii.com) on your classroom computer.

Instructions. Follow the steps below to conduct this ICA:

1. OPTIONAL: As students come into the classroom, offer them the opportunity to grab a handful of one of the ACT II Microwave Popcorn flavors to snack on.

2. Pass around the packages of ACT II Butter Lover's Microwave Popcorn and ACT II Light Butter Microwave Popcorn obtained from the *Instructor's Survival Kit* box.

3. Form students into 4-person teams.

ACT II Butter
Lover's Microwave
Popcorn

Slide 2

4. **Show Slide 2** and give students this background mini-lecture on Golden Valley Microwave Foods and ACT II Microwave Popcorn:

"When a firm has a strong brand or product, it is critical that the firm find ways to exploit it—often through managing and extending its product life cycle. This is exactly the situation for Golden Valley Microwave Foods and its microwave popcorn. Now, let's assume you're a consulting team contracted to help GVMF come up with ideas for generating additional revenue from its microwave popcorn. To simplify your task, let's also make these assumptions.

a. The time is right after GVMF was founded and it has only one product—ACT II Butter Lover's Microwave Popcorn.

b. Because an agreement with General Mills precluded it from marketing its microwave popcorn through supermarkets for 10 years, GVMF chose to rely initially on the non-grocery channels, such as vending machines, convenience stores, mass-merchandisers, memberships warehouse clubs, and drug stores.

c. Consider **only** microwave popcorn and **not** other snack foods, such as chips, or other microwave foods, such as Hot Pockets."

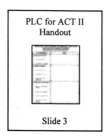
5. Pass out copies of the Managing and Extending the Product Life Cycle (PLC) for ACT II® Butter Lover's Microwave Popcorn Handout.

6. **Show Slide 3** and **spend 10 minutes** to have the student teams come up with ideas for GVMF to generate more revenues from its ACT II Butter Lover's Microwave Popcorn using the strategies shown on this slide.

7. Ask the student teams for their ideas and write them down on the board.

8. **Show Slides 4-6 after** the student teams have shared their ideas, tell the class what some of the actions of GVMF has taken, **as summarized in the table below**. Also note that there is some "overlap" among the strategies.

ACT II Microwave
Popcorn
Classic Lines

Slide 4

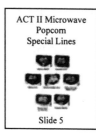

ACT II Microwave
Popcorn
Special Lines

Slide 5

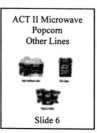

ACT II Microwave
Popcorn
Other Lines

Slide 6

Marketing Lesson. It is critical for organizations to use creative marketing strategies to manage and extend the product life cycle for their key brands, products, and services. Also, it is usually far less expensive and risky to do that, rather than try to come up with successful new-to-the-company or new-to-the-world products or services.

Websites. Golden Valley Microwave Foods was purchased by ConAgra Foods, which is a marketer of a variety of consumer packaged goods and snacks and whose website is www.conagra.com. The website for ACT II microwave popcorn is www.actii.com.

PLC STRATEGY	IDEA	GVMF USES?	
		YES	NO
Modify the Product			
Add New Features	• Add new flavors: **Show Slides 4-5**	✔	
	• Add new forms, such as popcorn balls: **Show Slide 6**	✔	
Change the Package	• Increase individual package size from normal to "jumbo" to reach heavy users.	✔	
	• Add a single-serve and 6-pack to reach light and heavy users respectively.	✔	
	• Increase package size to reach institutions. Not practical: they generally use either the regular packages or ready-to-eat popcorn.		✔
Modify the Market			
Find New Users	• Appeal to corn-lovers segment with "Corn-on-the-Cob" flavor.	✔	
Increase the Use	• Use co-operative advertising with video rental stores during winter months.	✔	
Create New Use Situations	• Market as snack to college students through vending machines on campus.	✔	
Reposition the Product			
React to Competitor's Position	• Enter supermarkets, video rental stores, etc. and offer retailers convenient point-of-purchase display.	✔	
Reach New Markets	• Enter global markets.	✔	
	• Target kids by promoting movie tie-ins.	✔	
	• Position as a more sophisticated cocktail snack. Not practical today.		✔
Catch a Rising	• Appeal to health-conscious segment with 94% Fat Free Butter and 94% Fat Free Kettle Corn.	✔	
Change the Value Offered	• Put more popcorn in the package. Not practical because of serving size.		✔

ICA 11-1

MANAGING AND EXTENDING THE PRODUCT LIFE CYCLE (PLC) FOR ACT II® BUTTER LOVER'S MICROWAVE POPCORN HANDOUT

PLC STRATEGY	IDEA
Modify the Product • Add New Flavors • Change the Package	
Modify the Market • Find New Users • Increase the Use • Create New Use Situations	
Reposition the Product • React to Competitor's Position • Reach New Markets • Catch a Rising Trend • Change the Value Offered	

CHAPTER 11: MANAGING PRODUCTS AND BRANDS

ICA 11-2: IN-CLASS ACTIVITY

Using Brainstorming and N/3 Techniques for Breathe Right® Nasal Strips[1]

Learning Objectives. To have students: (1) experience an actual brainstorming session with a fun and rather outrageous product and (2) evaluate the emerging ideas using an N/3 ("N over 3") rating process to assess some of the strengths and weaknesses of both techniques.

Definition. The following marketing term is referred to in this in-class activity (ICA):

- Brainstorming: To generate ideas about products, services, processes, or ideas.

Nature of the Activity. To have students engage in brainstorming and N/3 activities based on specific guidelines to generate advertising featuring the Breathe Right nasal strips.

Estimated Class Time. 20 minutes.

Materials Needed.

- The ICA11-2.doc Word and ICA11-2.ppt PowerPoint files contained in the ICA11-2 folder of the Instructor's CD #1 from the *Instructor's Survival Kit* box.

- The Breathe Right Nasal Strips "Back-in-the-Sack" Pack sample promotion contained in the *Instructor's Survival Kit* box.

- Copies of the:
  - a. Brainstorming Ground Rules Handout.
  - b. N/3 Ground Rules Handout.

- OPTIONAL: The instructor may want to purchase enough package(s) of tan and/or clear adult (small/medium) Breathe Right nasal strips for students and have them try them during this ICA. Breathe Right nasal strips are sold in grocery or drug stores, and are found in the cough/colds section. Retail price: $4.99 for a box of 12 strips.

- NOTE: Transparencies can be made of the handouts instead of making copies and using the PowerPoint presentation for those instructors who prefer this option.

Preparation Before Class. Follow the steps below:

1. Read pp. 173-274 of Chapter 10 and pp. 297-299 of Chapter 11.

2. Print, read, and if necessary, edit the ICA11-2.doc Word file.

3. Print and/or review the PowerPoint slides from the ICA11-2.ppt PowerPoint file.

---

[1] The authors wish to thank Carol Watzke, Vice President—Consumer Strategy and Jo Anne Harms, Marketing of CNS, Inc. as well as Mary Brown of Bolin Advertising who assisted in the development of this ICA.

4. Make copies of the:

    a. Brainstorming Ground Rules Handout.

    b. N/3 Ground Rules Handout.

5. Skim the CNS Video Case 7 on pp. 198-199 of *Marketing, 8th Edition*.

6. Go to the Breathe Right nasal strip website at www.breatheright.com to learn more about the product and its uses.

7. Practice placing a Breathe Right nasal strip on your nose to be able to demonstrate the procedure to students in class.

8. OPTIONAL: Enough tan and/or clear adult (small/medium) Breathe Right nasal strips for students.

9. OPTIONAL: Bookmark the CNS (www.cns.com) and Breathe Right (www.breatheright.com) websites on your classroom computer.

Instructions. Follow the steps below to conduct this ICA:

1. OPTIONAL: As students come into the classroom, offer them a Breathe Right nasal strip but DO NOT allow them to try it on until you begin this ICA.

2. Pass around the Breathe Right Nasal Strips "Back-in-the-Sack" Pack sample promotion obtained from the *Instructor's Survival Kit* box.

3. Form students into 4-person teams.

    4. Pass out copies of the Brainstorming Ground Rules Handout and the N/3 Ground Rules Handout to students.

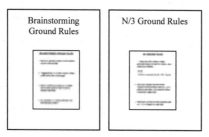

    5. **Show Slide 2** and give students this background mini-lecture on CNS and Breathe Right Nasal Strips:

    "Breathe Right nasal strips, made by CNS, Inc., became popular among both professional athletes and consumers to open their nasal passages and improve their breathing when San Francisco 49ers' Jerry Rice used one during an outstanding Super Bowl performance. In 1995, the U.S. Food and Drug Administration (FDA) allowed CNS to claim that use of its Breathe Right nasal strips reduced nighttime snoring.

Breathe Right nasal strips are sold 'over-the-counter' (OTC) in grocery, drug, and other stores where products like aspirin or cough syrup that customers can buy without a doctor's prescription are sold. Breathe Right nasal strips are innovative adhesive strips with patented dual flex bars inside. When attached to the nose, they gently lift and hold open nasal passages, making it easier to breathe. Breathe Right strips are used to help users breathe better through the nose, such as athletes, snorers, and allergy, sinusitis, and cold sufferers looking for drug-free relief from nasal congestion.

In fiscal 2005, CNS had its best year ever, with sales approaching $100 million. This was due to strong sales of Breathe Right Nasal Strips, both in the U.S. and internationally, and FiberChoice, a soluble dietary fiber supplement. Breathe Right sales exceeded $73 million, as CNS successfully relaunched its clear Breathe Right nasal strip in the U.S. and because there was a longer cold and flu season."

6. **Show Slides 3-4** and give students this background mini-lecture on the Breathe Right Nasal Strips Back-in-the-Sack sample promotion:

"Recently, CNS developed Breathe Right Nasal Strips Back-in-the-Sack sample promotion, which was designed to get potential target customers to try the strip for six nights to 'bring couples together by lifting their nostrils apart.' Included in the sample of six strips was a page of instructions on how to put on a Breathe Right nasal strip."

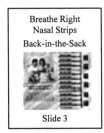

Breathe Right
Nasal Strips

Back-in-the-Sack

Slide 3

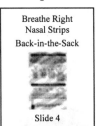

Breathe Right
Nasal Strips

Back-in-the-Sack

Slide 4

7. **Continue to show Slide 4** and have 2 to 3 student volunteers try on the Breathe Right nasal strip from Back-in-the-Sack promotion. OPTIONAL: Have **every** student try on a Breathe Right nasal strip from those purchased from the store and handed out earlier in class. Go over the instructions on how to put on the Breathe Right nasal strip.

8. Introduce the purpose of this ICA (or write on the board the sentence in single quotes below):

"Your goal is to 'Generate ideas of characters or situations for use in advertisements for a Breathe Right nasal strip could be highlighted to target the "snorers" market segment.' To do this, get into your teams."

Brainstorming
Instructions

Slide 5

9. **Show Slide 5**: Brainstorming Ground Rules. Explain that brainstorming is often used to come up with new product ideas as well as advertising ideas. Answer any questions students have concerning this technique

before proceeding with this part of the ICA.

10. **Spend 5 minutes** to have the student teams generate as many advertising ideas (characters or use situations) as possible. Ideas will be evaluated later, so encourage students to be as creative as they want and strive for at least 15 or 20 ideas.

11. List the advertising ideas on either the board or a transparency.

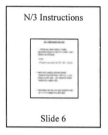

Slide 6

12. **Show Slide 6**: N/3 Ground Rules. Explain that the N/3 technique is often used to evaluate new product and advertising ideas. Answer any questions students have concerning this technique before proceeding.

13. **Spend 5 minutes** to have the student teams evaluate which of the 15 to 20 ideas are better. Have them identify their top ten advertising characters and use situations.

14. List the top ideas on either the board or a transparency.

15. **Show Slides 7-12 after** the student teams have shared their ideas, show the class what some of the examples of CNS' advertising characters and use situations. Do any match the characters or use situations the students came up with? Have students comment on the effectiveness of both the print and TV ads in communicating the benefits of a Breathe Right nasal strip.

- Slide 7: Brand personality magazine ads.
- Slide 8: NYC marathon specialty strip and magazine ad.
- Slide 9: Breathe Right nasal strip newspaper ad.

Breathe Right Magazine ad — Slide 7

Breathe Right Special strip & ad — Slide 8

Breathe Right Newspaper ad — Slide 9

- Slide 10: "Back-in-the-Sack" TV ad [TRT = 0:30].
- Slide 11: Breathe Right Snore Relief Throat Spray TV ad [TRT = 0:30].
- Slide 12: Breathe Right nasal strip for kids TV ad [TRT = 0:30].

Breathe Right Back-in-the-sack TV ad — Slide 10

Breathe Right Snore Relief Throat Spray TV ad — Slide 11

Breathe Right Back-in-the-sack TV ad — Slide 12

16. Summarize the advantages and disadvantages of the "Brainstorming" technique:

- Advantages:

    a. Helps focus a group of people on generating a list of alternative solutions to a defined problem.

    b. Enables "piggybacking," which often leads to more creative solutions among the group.

    c. Gives a time deadline to generate the creative solutions rather than it out over a longer period.

- Disadvantages:

    a. Limits the list of candidate solutions to those given by a specific group of people at one specific time.

    b. Possibly generates many trivial, impractical candidates.

    c. Does not provide for systematic screening of the generated ideas (which is one of the benefits of the N/3 technique).

17. Summarize the advantages and disadvantages of the "N/3" technique:

- Advantages:

    a. Provides a ranking that utilizes judgments from a knowledgeable cross-section of people.

    b. Allows, through the 3, 2, 1, 0 point system, peoples' judgments to be weighted to reflect their personal priorities.

- Disadvantages:

    a. May be biased by an individual's voting for his/her ideas submitted in the brainstorming session.

    b. Omits inclusion of other ideas not coming from the brainstorming session.

    c. Utilizes initial impressions for the evaluation judgments rather than greater in-depth business analysis.

Marketing Lesson. Marketers use brainstorming and N/3 techniques to develop and evaluate new or refine existing products and services in terms of their features, as well as price, promotion (advertising), and distribution strategies and tactics.

Websites. The CNS website is (www.cns.com) and the Breathe Right website is (www.breatheright.com). The latter will provide more information about: (1) the target markets for Breathe Right nasal strips (i.e. congestion, allergies, athletic and exercise performance enhancement, etc.; (2) a demo of what they are and how they work; and (3) a detailed discussion of the causes of snoring.

BRAINSTORMING GROUND RULES

1. Strive for quantity of ideas, without special concern about quality.

2. "Piggybacking" on another person's ideas is OK, and is even encouraged.

3. Stress creativity by looking at a problem from another point of view in order to develop new ideas.

4. No evaluation or criticism allowed in the brainstorming session.

N/3 GROUND RULES

1. Divide the total number of ideas generated (N) by 3 to get the "points" each student can allocate.

   Example:

   If 30 ideas are generated, then N/3 = 30/3 = 10 points.

2. Have each student allocate her/his 10 points to the 30 items, with 3, 2, 1, or 0 points to each item—the maximum being 3 points for a given item.

3. Read down the list and have students hold up 1, 2, or 3 fingers for each item.

ICA 11-2

CHAPTER 11: MANAGING PRODUCTS AND BRANDS

ICA 11-3: IN-CLASS ACTIVITY

Creating Customer Value Through Packaging and Labeling[1]

Learning Objectives. To have students assess the packaging and labeling of an exciting new consumer product from Frito-Lay™ in terms of (1) direct benefits to consumers and (2) global concerns.

Definitions. The following marketing terms are referred to in this in-class activity (ICA):

- Label: An integral part of the package that typically identifies the product or brand, who made it, where and when it was made, how it is to be used, and package contents and ingredients.

- Packaging: A component of a product that refers to any container in which it is offered for sale and on which label information is conveyed.

- Stock Keeping Unit (SKU): A unique identification number that defines an item for ordering or inventory purposes.

Nature of the Activity. To have students assess the effectiveness of Frito-Lay's new Lay's® Stax® canister packaging and labeling from both a consumer and societal point of view.

Estimated Class Time. 20 minutes.

Materials Needed.

- The ICA11-3.doc Word and ICA11-3.ppt PowerPoint files contained in the ICA11-3 folder of the Instructor's CD #1 from the *Instructor's Survival Kit* box.

- The Lay's Stax Original canister contained in the *Instructor's Survival Kit* box.

- Copies of the:

  a. Lay's Stax Package and Label Analysis Handout.

  b. An Analysis of the Lay's Stax Package and Label Handout.

- NOTE: Transparencies can be made of the handouts instead of making copies and using the PowerPoint presentation for those instructors who prefer this option.

Preparation Before Class. Follow the steps below:

1. Read pp. 306-309 of Chapter 11.

2. Print, read, and if necessary, edit the ICA11-3.doc Word file.

---

[1] The authors wish to thank Greg Rodriguez, Lay's Brand Marketing of Frito-Lay, who assisted in the development of this ICA.

3. Print and/or review the PowerPoint slides from the ICA11-3.ppt PowerPoint file.

4. Make copies of the:

   a. Lay's Stax Package and Label Analysis Handout.

   b. An Analysis of the Lay's Stax Package and Label Handout.

5. OPTIONAL: Bookmark the Frito-Lay website (www.fritolay.com) on your classroom computer.

Instructions. Follow the steps below to conduct this ICA:

1. Form students into 4-person teams.

2. Pass around the Lay's Stax Original potato crisps canister obtained from the *Instructor's Survival Kit* box.

Lay's Stax Original potato crisps

Slide 2

3. **Show Slide 2** and give students this background mini-lecture on Lay's Stax potato crisps:

   "In August 2003 and with a $50 million integrated marketing communications (IMC) program, Frito-Lay launched Lay's Stax potato 'crisps' (not chips). Lay's Stax comes in a colorful, resealable, 'proprietary' crush-resistant, and convenient canister designed to fit the fast-paced lifestyles of today's consumers. By doing so, Lay's was competing directly with Pringles (P&G), which at the time had created and dominated the $300 million pre-formed, stackable 'chips' market."[2]

4. **Show Slides 3-7** and give students this background mini-lecture on Lay's Stax potato crisps IMC program:

   a. **Show Slide 3**. "High-Rollers" TV ad. [TRT = 0:30] This ad features Dana Carvey demonstrating the 'stackability' of Lay's Stax.

   b. **Show Slide 4**. "Stock Boy" TV ad. [TRT = 0:30] This comparative ad positions Lay's Stax as tasting better than Pringles.

   c. **Show Slide 5**. Newspaper FSI ad/coupon.

Lay's Stax "High Roller" TV ad

Slide 3

Lay's Stax "Stockboy" TV ad

Slide 4

Lay's Stax FSI

Slide 5

   d. **Show Slide 6**. In-Store promotion.

---

[2] Theresa Howard, "Frito-Lay's New Stax to Take a Stand," *USA Today*, August 14, 2003. See http://www.usatoday.com/money/industries/food/2003-08-14-stax_x.htm.

ICA 11-3

e. **Show Slide 7**. Point-of-purchase displays.

f. **Show Slide 8**. Product line at launch: Original, Sour Cream & Onion, Cheddar, and Barbecue.

Lay's Stax in-store promotion

Slide 6

Lay's Stax POP displays

Slide 7

Lay's Stax product line

Slide 8

5. **Show Slide 2** again and conclude this mini-lecture:

"Lay's Stax potato crisps come in a compact, 9"-tall, hourglass design. The crush-proof plastic packaging is designed for easy portability and fits perfectly into a car's cup-holder. Its pop-off, resealable lid means you can close and reopen a Lay's Stax canister anytime. Today, Lay's Stax also comes in Dill Pickle, Hidden Valley Ranch, KC Masterpiece BBQ, Monterey Pepper Jack, Pizza, and Salt and Vinegar flavors. Lay's Stax is sold in supermarkets, mass merchandisers, convenience stores, and drug stores at a suggested retail price of $1.59 per canister."

6. Pass out the Lay's Stax Package and Label Analysis Handout.

7. **Show Slide 9**: Lay's Stax Package and Label Analysis Handout. **Spend 10 minutes** and have the student teams complete the handout by identifying and assessing the features of the Lay's Stax package and label that relate to: (1) direct consumer benefits and (2) global concerns.

8. Ask each student team to identify and assess a feature and let other class members comment. Write down their assessments on either the board or transparency made from the Lay's Stax Package and Label Analysis Handout.

9. Pass out the An Analysis of the Lay's Stax Package and Label Handout and use it as a short, closing wrap-up lecture note to the class discussion.

Marketing Lesson. Creative, consumer-beneficial, environmentally-sensitive packaging and labeling can give consumer product marketers like Frito-Lay a competitive edge in today's marketplace among both its channels of distribution (supermarkets, mass merchandisers, convenience stores, and drug stores) and its targeted consumers.

Website. The Frito-Lay website is www.fritolay.com. Unlike some of Frito-Lay's other products, Lay's Stax does not yet have a website.

LAY'S STAX PACKAGE & LABEL ANALYSIS HANDOUT

ASSESSMENT AREA	SPECIFIC ISSUE	FEATURE ASSESSMENT
DIRECT CONSUMER BENEFITS	Communication Benefits	
	Functional Benefits	
	Perceptual Benefits	
GLOBAL CONCERNS	Environmental Recycling	
	Health and Safety	

ICA 11-3

AN ANALYSIS OF THE LAY'S STAX PACKAGE & LABEL HANDOUT

ASSESSMENT AREA	SPECIFIC ISSUE	FEATURE ASSESSMENT
DIRECT CONSUMER BENEFITS	**Communication Benefits**	• Label's appeal: Attention-getting, colorful Stax graphic • Picture of product: Shows consumer what the snack is inside the package • Stand-up package: Gives clear shelf facing to prospective buyers • Nutritional label large and readable • Customer toll-free telephone contact number to elicit questions/comments
	Functional Benefits	• Rigid "crush-proof" package: Reduces breakage of the snack in transit, on retail shelf, in back pack, etc. • Reclosable package: Increases convenience; snack stays fresh if not fully consumed in one "snacking" period • Slender center canister design: Allows consumers to easily grip the package • Grooves on package bottom may help protect contents in transport
	Perceptual Benefits	• Product image: Colorful, modern label suggests innovative, contemporary, high-quality product in consumer's mind • Canister size: Large size connotes value for price paid • Canister shape: "Hour-glass-like" shape connotes "stacking" of contents
GLOBAL CONCERNS	**Environmental Recycling**	• Recycling: Plastic package can be recycled • Recycling: "Please Recycle" graphic on label encourages recycling
	Health and Safety	• Sealed package: Reduces likelihood of tampering in store compared to traditional snack or potato chip packages • Reclosable package: Reduces likelihood of bugs or dirt spoiling the snack after it is opened

CHAPTER 12: MANAGING SERVICES

ICA 12-1: IN-CLASS ACTIVITY

Airline Customer Service and Southwest Airlines[1]

Learning Objectives. To have students: (1) identify key measures of customer service that airlines might use; (2) understand the importance that Southwest Airlines places on customer service; and (3) discover how Southwest Airlines and other U.S. airlines compare on a U.S. Department of Transportation (DOT) measure of customer complaints.

Definitions. The following marketing terms are referred to in this in-class activity (ICA):

- Customer Service: The ability of logistics management to satisfy users in terms of time, dependability, communication, and convenience.

- Gap Analysis: A type of analysis that identifies the differences between a consumer's expectations about and experiences with a service based on dimensions of service quality.

Nature of the Activity. To have students: (1) identify candidate measures of customer service for airlines based on their own airline travel experiences; (2) compare the relative performance of major U.S. airlines from information obtained from the DOT website about customer complaints; and (3) discuss the importance Southwest Airlines places on customer service.

Estimated Class Time. 20 minutes.

Materials Needed.

- The ICA12-1.doc Word and ICA12-1.ppt PowerPoint files contained in the ICA12-1 folder of the Instructor's CD #2 from the *Instructor's Survival Kit* box.

- The Southwest Airline inflatable airplane from the *Instructor's Survival Kit* box.

- Copies of the:

    a. Airline Quality Rating Consumer Complaint Categories Handout.

    b. The annual press release (usually in April of each year; see (http://www.aqr.aero/press_releases.htm) and/or selected pages (**such as p. 55 of the 2005 report: 2004 Total Complaints to DOT by Month for U.S. Airlines**) of the most recent annual Airline Quality Rating (AQR) report co-published by Brent Bowen, director and professor, University of Nebraska at Omaha (UNO) Aviation Institute/School of Public Administration, and Dean Headley, associate professor of marketing at Wichita State University (WSU). You can access the AQR website to obtain this press release and the annual AQR report. [NOTE: You will need the Adobe Acrobat Reader to view and print the PDF documents. To download the latest version, go to www.adobe.com/products/acrobat.]

---

[1] The authors wish to thank Southwest Airlines who assisted in the development of this ICA.

Preparation Before Class. Follow the steps below:

1. Read pp. 324-326 of Chapter 12.

2. Print, read, and if necessary, edit the ICA12-1.doc Word file.

3. Print and/or review the PowerPoint slides from the ICA12-1.ppt PowerPoint file.

4. Make copies of:

   a. The Airline Quality Rating Consumer Complaint Categories Handout.

   b. The annual press release and/or selected pages (**such as p. 55 of the 2005 report: 2004 Total Complaints to DOT by Month for U.S. Airlines**) of the most recent annual Airline Quality Rating (AQR) report. The last two pages of the AQR report identify and describe the "Customer Complaint Categories" or service quality dimensions the co-authors use in their "gap analysis."

5. Familiarize yourself with the AQR website to learn more about the measures and rankings of airline service quality.

6. Familiarize yourself with the AQR website to learn more about the measures and rankings of airline service quality.

7. OPTIONAL: Bookmark the Airline Quality Rating (AQR) report (www.aqr.aero) and Southwest Airlines (www.southwest.com) websites on your classroom computer.

Instructions. Follow the steps below to conduct this ICA:

1. Pass around the Southwest Airline inflatable airplane from the *Instructor's Survival Kit* box obtained from the *Instructor's Survival Kit* box.

Southwest Airlines
& Service Quality

Slide 2

2. **Show Slide 2** and give students this background mini-lecture on service quality and Southwest Airlines:

   "This activity is about assessing customer service for airline flights. The process used to evaluate customer service is called 'gap analysis,' which involves asking consumers to compare the actual service delivered with what was expected relative to several service quality dimensions, such as time, dependability, convenience, etc.

Two researchers that follow the industry publish the annual Airline Quality Rating (AQR) report. The AQR report is based on data submitted to the U.S. Department of Transportation (DOT), which tracks the service quality for the airline industry. The AQR report provides consumers with information on the quality of airline services delivered and helps airlines identify and remedy any 'gaps' with respect to the service quality dimensions that are measured. Many airlines, such as Southwest Airlines, have used the favorable rankings they received to promote the quality of their service.

Southwest Airlines not only stresses its low fares for airline service but also emphasizes its commitment to delivering the highest-quality customer service possible. An average of the annual ratings from 1987 finds that Southwest is the #1 airline in terms of the fewest complaints per 100,000 passengers. In fact, Southwest's mission statement says,

> 'The mission of Southwest Airlines is dedication to the highest quality of Customer Service delivered with a sense of warmth, friendliness, individual pride, and Company Spirit.' [NOTE: Both "Customer Service" and "Company Spirit" are in capitals.]

In terms of overall service quality for 2004, it ranked third, behind two much smaller discount airlines Jet Blue and Air Tran. Improving or maintaining service quality is a challenge in today's environment due to the airport overcrowding and increased security measures imposed as a result of the Sept. 11, 2001 tragedy."

3. **Spend 5 minutes** and ask students the following two questions, writing only answers to the first question on the board or a blank transparency.

- Question 1: What are some key customer service factors you think of when flying on an airline?

  Answers: Flight leaving or arriving on time, fare was not changed between time of reservation and flight, flight not over-booked, baggage not damaged or lost, food quality, leg room, competent and courteous ticket agents and flight attendants, etc.

- Question 2: Can you describe a recent experience with an airline that illustrates an especially good or bad example of customer service on that factor?

  Answers: Multiple responses possible.

4. Ask students what measures of "airline customer service" the DOT/Air Quality Rating (AQR) report might use and what the best one might be. Class discussion will probably turn up measures like percentage of on-time departures, percentage of on-time arrivals, and percentage of flight cancellations. Perhaps the best, all-inclusive measure is "rate of complaints per 100,000 enplanements" (or passengers), which is the one the AQR uses. [NOTE: This data is in a table on **p. 55 of the 2005 report: 2004 Total Complaints to DOT by Month for U.S. Airlines**, which is shown as Slide 4 in the accompanying PowerPoint presentation. **DO NOT SHOW THIS SLIDE IF YOU WANT TO USE THE MOST RECENT AQR REPORT.**]

5. Pass out the Airline Quality Rating Consumer Complaint Categories Handout.

6. **Show Slide 3** and compare the customer service factors students identified with the "Complaint Categories" from the AQR report. Have students identify which of these categories are most important to them when engaging in air travel.

Slide 4

7. OPTIONAL: **Show Slide 4** and/or pass out the annual press release and/or selected pages (**such as p. 55 of the 2005 report: 2004 Total Complaints to DOT by Month for U.S. Airlines**) of the most recent annual Airline Quality Rating (AQR) report.

8. Give the following mini-lecture on Southwest Airline's commitment to service quality.

   "For 2004 (or the most recent data available), the Air Quality Rating (AQR) report stated that among U.S. airlines, Southwest Airlines ranked No. 1 in terms of the lowest number of complaints per 100,000 enplanements (0.18). This was ⅓ less than the second best airline Jet Blue (0.27)!

9. Briefly discus the press release and/or selected pages, noting the ranking of the airlines that students fly the most. Ask students to comment on the ranking of their preferred airline. Any "gaps" that need to be analyzed?

10. Briefly discus the press release and/or selected pages, noting the ranking of the airlines that students fly the most. Ask students to comment on the ranking of their preferred airline. Any "gaps" that need to be analyzed?

11. Briefly discuss the marketing implications for Southwest and other service providers, such as banks and hotels, that stress the delivery of high-quality services to their customers. Students should respond by saying that while costly, delivering services that meet or exceed customer expectations, both in the short- and long-term, can lead to increased sales and profits due to enhanced customer value.

   Marketing Lesson. Assessing the quality of customer service is becoming more important as airlines and other service providers face increasing competition. The Airline Quality Rating (AQR) report provides actual statistics regarding the key dimensions of customer service for airline passengers. Such reports can help airlines identify any service quality gaps, which then can be remedied to improve overall service and ultimately, enhance sales and profits.

   Websites. The Airline Quality Rating (AQR) report website is www.aqr.aero and the Southwest Airlines website is www.southwest.com.

AIRLINE QUALITY RATING CONSUMER COMPLAINT CATEGORIES HANDOUT

- **Flight Problems**: Cancellations, delays, or any other deviations from schedule.

- **Oversales**: Passengers who hold confirmed reservations and are denied boarding ("bumped") from a flight because it is oversold.

- **Reservations, Ticketing, and Boarding**: Airline or travel agent mistakes in reservations and ticketing, problems in making reservations and obtaining tickets due to busy phone lines, waiting in line, or delays in mailing tickets. Problems boarding the aircraft.

- **Fares**: Incorrect or incomplete information about fares, discount fare conditions or availability, overcharges, fare increases and levels.

- **Refunds**: Problems in obtaining refunds for unused or lost tickets or fare adjustments.

- **Baggage**: Claims for lost, damaged or delayed baggage, charges for excess baggage, and carry-on problems.

- **Customer Service**: Rude or unhelpful employees, inadequate meals or cabin service, treatment of delayed passengers.

- **Disability**: Civil rights complaints by air travelers with disabilities.

- **Advertising**: Advertising that is unfair, misleading or offensive.

- **Discrimination**: Civil rights complaints by air travelers based on race, national origin, religion, etc.

- **Animals**: Loss, injury or death of an animal during air transport provided by an air carrier.

- **Other**: Frequent flyer, smoking, credit, problems with scheduled or charter tour packages, cargo problems, security, airport facilities, claims for bodily injury, etc. not classified above.

ICA 12-1

CHAPTER 12: MANAGING SERVICES

ICA 12-2: IN-CLASS ACTIVITY

Customer Contact Audit for a Service

Learning Objective. To have students identify, describe, and assess the elements of a service to understand the activities that employees and customers perform during the service delivery process.

Definitions. The following marketing terms are referred to in this in-class activity (ICA):

- Customer Contact Audit: A flowchart of the points of interaction between a consumer and a service provider.

- Customer Service: The ability of logistics management to satisfy users in terms of time, dependability, communication, and convenience.

- Gap Analysis: A type of analysis that identifies the differences between a consumer's expectations about and experiences with a service based on dimensions of service quality.

- Service Encounter: The points in the service delivery process where the customer interacts with the service organization.

Nature of the Activity. To have students develop a simple customer contact audit for a service they are familiar with.

Estimated Class Time. 20 minutes.

Materials Needed.

- The ICA12-2.doc Word and ICA12-2.ppt PowerPoint files contained in the ICA12-2 folder of the Instructor's CD #2 from the *Instructor's Survival Kit* box.

- Copies of the Customer Contact Audit Handout.

- Chalk/markers for students to write their customer contact audits on the board. OPTIONAL: Self-stick 3M Post-It easel pad with enough sheets for students to write their customer contact audits on the paper and affix to the classroom wall.

Preparation Before Class. Follow the steps below:

1. Read pp. 324-326 of Chapter 12.

2. Print, read, and if necessary, edit the ICA12-2.doc Word file.

3. Print and/or review the PowerPoint slides from the ICA12-2.ppt PowerPoint file.

4. Make copies of the Customer Contact Audit Handout.

5. Bring the chalk/markers and/or easel pad to class.

Instructions. Follow the steps below to conduct this ICA:

1. Give students this background mini-lecture on services:

   "Most of you have used or are familiar with financial, hospitality, entertainment, and educational services. As a result, you have participated in the service delivery process, by opening a bank account, checking into a hotel, renting a video, or enrolling in this class!"

2. Ask students the following question:

   - Question 1: Why do organizations focus on services?

     Answers: Probe and discuss the responses below:

     a. Services are an increasingly important part of the U.S. economy, accounting for almost 40% of GDP.

     b. Services frequently provide higher profit margins than products and/or additional revenues.

     c. Customer satisfaction and loyalty are driven by service excellence.

     d. Services can be used as points of difference in competitive markets.

     e. Many graduates will work for a services organization.

3. Give students this background mini-lecture on the delivery of services and the use of a customer contact audit to improve service quality:

   "When developing a new or refining an existing service, marketers need to match its specifications with customer expectations. To do this, marketers use **gap analysis**, which identifies the differences between a consumer's expectations about and experiences with a service based on dimensions of service quality. The **customer contact audit**, which is a flowchart of the points of interaction between a consumer and a service provider, can help in this analysis.

   The customer contact audit graphically depicts the service delivery process and the points of customer contact, or **service encounters**, so that marketers and employees understand what the service is and their roles in its delivery. A customer contact audit breaks down a service into its components and depicts:

   a. **The logical steps or tasks in the process**. These include the activities and interactions that contact and support employees as well as customers engage in during the delivery of the service.

   b. **Service encounters**. The tangible aspects of the service delivery process as seen by the customer, such as reliability, empathy, courtesy, accuracy, timeliness, etc. These become the indicators of service quality from the customer's perspective.

   Any deviations between customers' expectations and the service that is delivered indicate a service failure or bottleneck that can be used to improve service quality."

ICA 12-2

4. Ask students the following questions:

Fig 12-7
Hertz Customer
Contact Audit

Slide 2

- Question 2: How many of you have ever rented a car? How would you describe the service delivery process?

  Answers: Create a simple customer contact audit on the board or a transparency based on the students' responses.

5. **Show Slide 2** and briefly go over Figure 12-7: Customer contact audit for Hertz Car Rental.

Customer Contact
Audit Handout

6. Form students into 4-person teams. Designate half the teams as the "banking" team and the other half as the "fast-food" team.

7. Pass out the Customer Contact Audit Handout.

8. OPTIONAL: Pass out one sheet of easel paper to each team.

9. Briefly explain the nature of this ICA to the "banking" and "fast-food" teams:

"In your teams, using the Customer Contact Audit Handout as a guide, create a customer contact audit for your service. After **about 10 minutes**, one of your team members may be selected to present your blueprint to the class."

a. **Banking teams**. Making a deposit into a checking account at a local bank. [NOTE: The deposit should be made to a teller inside the lobby and NOT via an ATM or drive-thru.]

b. **Fast-Food teams**. Ordering food at a local fast-food restaurant. [NOTE: Order food inside to dine in, NOT via a drive-thru or for take-out.]

10. **After 10 minutes**, have a representative from each team write/tape their customer contact audits for their "banking" or "fast-food" services on the board/classroom wall.

11. **Spend 5 minutes** and select 2 teams from each service type to discuss their customer contact audits. Have the rest of the students comment on their customer contact audits. Ask the class the following questions:

- Question 3: What, if any, significant service encounters or "behind-the-scenes" activities are missing from this audit?

  Answers: Probe and clarify the students' responses.

- Question 4: Where are service failures likely to occur and if a problem, how can they be corrected?

  Answers: Probe and clarify the students' responses.

SAMPLE ANSWERS FOR CUSTOMER CONTACT AUDIT
(THESE ARE NOT MEANT TO BE EXHAUSTIVE)

AUDIT ISSUE	(A) BANKING	(B) FAST-FOOD
1. How does "Customer" initiate service?	• Parks car in parking lot. • Walks into lobby. • Fills out deposit slip. • Walks to teller window. • Waits until teller is ready. • Gives deposit to teller.	• Parks car in parking lot. • Walks into restaurant to counter. • Waits until server is ready to take order. • Gives money to server.
2. What does the "Customer contact person" do?	• Greets customer and asks what he/she can do. • Takes deposit slip and ID. • Uses computer to verify the checking account info. • Takes check/money for deposit. • Processes deposit. • Gives customer a receipt. • Thanks customer.	• Greets customer and asks to take the order. • Suggests to customer optional menu items. • Verifies order. • Takes customer's money and makes change. • Assembles order. • Gives customer the order. • Thanks customer.
3. What does the "Support Personnel" do?	• Teller Supervisor: Makes sure there is enough money for change; handles problems. • Bank Operations: Makes sure computer and security systems operate; interacts with armored car personnel; ensures supplies are adequately stocked. • Maintenance: Cleans lobby, bathrooms, and parking lot.	• Line Cooks: Makes food; fulfills beverage orders. • Maintenance: Cleans dining area, bathrooms, and parking lot. • Manager. Orders food from suppliers; pays employees.
4. How to correct service failures?	• Clear communication of role in service delivery, job description, expectations. • Training. • Apologize and resolve the problem.	• Clear communication of role in service delivery, job description, expectations. • Training. • Apologize and resolve the problem.

Marketing Lesson. Marketers use customer contact audits to understand the service delivery process from the customer's perspective. It allows them to monitor the service encounter for customer satisfaction and quality at each point of customer contact.

ICA 12-2

CUSTOMER CONTACT AUDIT HANDOUT

1. Identify the service delivery process to be audited.

2. Analyze the service delivery process from the "customer's" point of view. Answer the questions:

   (a) How does the "Customer" initiate the service?

   (b) What steps, activities, etc. does the "Customer" perform during the delivery of the service?

3. Identify the "customer contact personnel" who actually deliver the service to the customer. Answer the questions:

   (a) Who are the "Customer Contact Employees" that deliver the service to customers?

   (b) What steps, activities, etc. does each "Customer Contact Employee" perform during the delivery of the service?

4. Identify the service "support personnel" who assist the customer contact personnel in delivering the service. Answer the questions:

   (a) Who are the "Support Personnel" that enable the customer contact personnel to deliver the service to customers?

   (b) What steps, 'behind-the-scene' activities, etc. does each of these "Support Personnel" perform during the delivery of the service?

5. Identify the service encounters and the potential contacts where service failure can occur.

6. If you have experienced a service failure for the service your team is analyzing, what could the organization do to recover from it?

CHAPTER 12: MANAGING SERVICES

ICA 12-3: IN-CLASS ACTIVITY

Marketing a Women's Team Sport

Learning Objective. To have students apply the concepts related to the marketing of products to sports marketing, a growing sector of the services economy.

Definitions. The following marketing terms are referred to in this in-class activity (ICA):

- Marketing Program: A plan that integrates the marketing mix to provide a good, service, or idea to prospective buyers.

- Product (Service) Positioning: The place an offering occupies in consumers' minds on important attributes relative to competitive products (services).

- Services: Intangible activities or benefits that an organization provides to consumers in exchange money or something else of value.

- Target Market: One or more specific groups of potential consumers toward which an organization directs its marketing program.

Nature of the Activity. To have students: (1) identify the target market(s); (2) compose a service positioning statement; and (3) develop a simple marketing program for a local collegiate or professional women's sports franchise.

Estimated Class Time. 30 minutes.

Materials Needed.

- The ICA12-3.doc Word and ICA12-3.ppt PowerPoint files contained in the ICA12-3 folder of the Instructor's CD #2 from the *Instructor's Survival Kit* box.

- Copies of the:
    a. Women's Sports Team Target Market and Positioning Handout.
    b. Women's Sports Team Marketing Program Handout.

- NOTE: Transparencies can be made of the handouts instead of making copies and using the PowerPoint presentation for those instructors who prefer this option.

Preparation Before Class. Follow the steps below:

1. Read pp. 321 of Chapter 12 and review Video Case 12 on the Philadelphia Phillies.

2. Print, read, and if necessary, edit the ICA12-3.doc Word file.

3. Print and/or review the slides from ICA12-3.ppt PowerPoint file.

4. Make copies of the:

   a. Women's Sports Team Target Market and Positioning Handout.

   b. Women's Sports Team Marketing Program Handout.

5. OPTIONAL: Bookmark the local collegiate and/or professional women's sports teams' websites on your classroom computer.

Instructions. Follow the steps below to conduct this ICA:

1. **Spend 2 minutes** and ask students the following question about their personal experiences with sports as a TV viewer, spectator, and participant:

   - Question 1: Sports is a huge part of the U.S. and global culture. How many of you view sports on TV? Which ones and why?

     Answers: Most students have viewed multiple sporting events on TV. Their reasons are numerous, such as entertainment, like to watch the athletes, participated in the sport in high school, etc.

   - Question 2: How many of you attend sporting events? Which ones and why?

     Answers: Most students have attended multiple sporting events. Their reasons are numerous, such as like to see sporting events in person (different from watching on TV or listening to on radio), entertainment, etc.

   - Question 3: How many of you participated in sports in high school or college (intramurals, recreational, etc.)?

     Answers: Most students have participated in some organized or recreational sport.

2. **Spend 1 minute** and give the following mini-lecture about the impact of sports.

   "Many of you are sports enthusiasts! This reflects both a U.S. and global trend. For example, the number of viewers of sporting events, such as the NFL's Super Bowl, the World Cup Soccer Finals, the World Series, the NBA Finals, NASCAR races, etc. is huge. ESPN, which broadcasts sports 'round-the-clock' on a number of cable and radio channels, just turned 25 years old, riding the wave of the popularity of sports.

   Attendance at professional sporting events has also risen. In 2004, 73 million fans attended Major League Baseball games, 21 million fans attended NBA games, and 17 million attended NFL games.[1] As a result, sports have become one of the largest and fastest growing service sectors in the U.S. economy. Moreover:

   a. Advertising on national/cable TV, radio, and stadium billboards was $27 billion.

   b. Merchandise licensing of professional, collegiate, and other sports was $11 billion.

   c. Sponsorships of leagues, teams, and TV/radio/Internet broadcasts were $6.4 billion.

   d. Spending by spectators exceeded $26 billion."[2]

---

[1] Attendance figures provided by ESPN.com. See sports.espn.go.com.

[2] "About Us: The Sports Industry," *Street & Smith's Sports Business Journal.* See www.sportsbusinessjournal.com.

3. **Spend 4 minutes** and give the following mini-lecture about women's sports.

"In 1972, Congress passed Title IX, a law designed to prevent discrimination based on gender in athletics and other extracurricular programs with respect to participation, scholarships, etc. at the high school and collegiate levels.[3] This and other factors contributed to a significant increase in participation by women in both organized and recreational sporting activities. According to the National Sporting Goods Association, females who are at least 7 years old participated in the following sports in 2003:

a. Basketball: Almost 9 million, or 31% of total participants.

b. Softball: Almost 6 million, or 46% of total participants.

c. Golf: Almost 6 million, or 23% of total participants.

d. Volleyball: Almost 6 million, or 56% of total participants.

e. Soccer: Over 4 million, or 37% of total participants.

f. Football (tackle + touch): Almost 3 million, or 14% of total participants.[4]

Since 1972, more schools now offer more sports for girls/women. Also, there are more women coaches, administrators, sports marketers, and owners of professional sports franchises.[5] With the growing trend of women in sports, there has been a rise (and fall) of women's professional sports leagues and franchises:

a. **Women's National Basketball Association** (WNBA). Launched in 1997 with 8 teams. The season runs from May to October with 34 regular season games plus playoffs. Today, there are 13 teams, but most of them are owned by an NBA franchise and given operating subsidies. A few franchises have been added and disbanded over the years. Attendance exceeded 1.9 million fans in 2004, a 10% decline from 2003. WNBA officials believe that the league will turn a profit by 2007. Currently, it has several large corporate sponsors (or 'marketing partners'), including Coca-Cola, GM, Nike, and Southwest Airlines.[6]

b. **National Pro Fastpitch Softball League**. Began with 6 teams in 2004. The season runs from June to August with 48 regular season games plus playoffs. Rosters include former Olympic and collegiate players. Games are 7 innings long. Sponsors include Mizuno and Major League Baseball.[7]

c. **Ladies Professional Golf Association** (LPGA). Founded in 1950, it is the longest women's professional sports organization. In 2004, the LPGA Tour season included 33 events totaling $42 million in prize money. Major sponsors include State Farm Insurance. Many events are shown on ESPN.[8]

---

[3] "Title IX Q & A," Women's Sports Foundation, April 19, 2002. See www.womenssportsfoundation.org.
[4] "2003 Sports Participation Ranked by Total Participation," National Sporting Goods Association.
See www.nsga.org.
[5] "27 Year Study Shows Progression of Women in College Athletics," Women's Sports Foundation, June 8, 2004.
[6] Information obtained from the WNBA website (www.wnba.com) and www.womensbasketballonline.com/wnba/wnbattendance.html.
[7] Information obtained from the National Pro Fastpitch website (www.profastpitch.com).
[8] Information obtained from the LPGA website (www.lpga.com).

d. **Women's United Soccer Association** (WUSA). Started in 2001 with 8 teams after the huge success of the 1999 USA women's World Cup soccer team. The WUSA lasted only 3 seasons before ceasing operations. In its inaugural 2001 season, attendance peaked at 680,000. By 2003, attendance fell to 560,000 due in part to the economic recession as a result of the September 11 attacks. There is currently a move to revive the WUSA.[9]

e. **Full contact tackle football**. There are three women's professional football leagues.[10]

   • **The Independent Women's Football League** (IWFL). Founded in 2000, the IWFL season runs from April to July and consists of 8 to 10 regular season games plus playoffs. It currently has 31 teams mainly on the east and west coasts. Sponsors include Nike and The Sports Authority.[11]

   • **The National Women's Football Association** (NWFA). Also founded in 2000, the NWFA season runs from April to July and consists of 8 regular season games plus playoffs. Currently, the league has 35 teams. Sponsors include Pepsi, the U.S. Army, and UPS.[12]

   • **The Women's Professional Football League** (WPFL). The WPFL was founded in 1999 and currently has 19 teams across the country. The WPFL season runs from July to November and consists of 10 regular season games plus playoffs. All the senior WPFL executives are women who are responsible for the league's marketing. Sponsors include Wilson.[13]"

Several marketing issues face both collegiate and professional women's teams. These include:

a. Obtaining national corporate sponsors. Many professional franchises rely on local sponsors (restaurants, hair salons, etc.).

b. Getting sporting goods manufacturers to design equipment (shoes, pads, helmets, uniforms, etc.) for a woman's anatomy.

4. Form students into 4-person teams. Designate half the teams as the "target market and positioning" team and the other half as the "marketing program" team. Have each team select a women's collegiate or professional sport (basketball, hockey, softball, football, or soccer, but NOT golf since this is an individual not a team sport).

5. Pass out copies of the:

a. Women's Sports Team Target Market and Positioning Handout to the "target market and positioning" teams.

b. Women's Sports Team Marketing Program Handout to the "marketing program" teams.

---

[9] Information obtained from the WUSA website (www.wusa.com).
[10] Ibid.
[11] Information obtained from the IWFL website (www.iwflsports.com).
[12] Information obtained from the NWFA website (www.womensfootballcentral.com).
[13] Information obtained from the WPFL website (www.womensprofootball.com).

6. Briefly explain the purpose of this ICA to both the "target market and positioning" and "marketing program" teams.

    "You have been hired by the local collegiate or professional women's sport team to provide marketing consulting services. Your objective is to develop a set of simple recommendations that will increase the number of fans who pay to see a game."

Target Market & Positioning Team Handout

Slide 2

7. **Show Slide 2**. Briefly explain the nature of this ICA to the "target market and positioning" teams.

    a. The "target market and positioning" teams will describe the target market and develop a positioning statement for their local collegiate or professional women's sports team. Have each person in the team take one or two aspects and then discuss them as a team. [NOTE: You may need to define "target market" and "product positioning."]

    b. Identify the target market(s).

        •   Who is/are the target market(s) consumers (fans)?

        •   What are the characteristics (geographic, demographic, lifestyle, and behavioral)?

            –   Geographic (region, city size, maximum radius from stadium in terms of miles/drive time)?

            –   Demographic (gender, age, generational cohort, family life cycle, income)?

            –   Lifestyle (attitudes, interests)?

            –   Behavioral (sports, media usage)?

            –   Benefits Sought (needs fulfilled)?

    c. Compose a 15 to 20 word positioning statement for the Women's sports team.

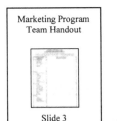

Marketing Program Team Handout

Slide 3

8. **Show Slide 3**. Briefly explain the nature of this ICA to the "marketing program" teams.

    a. The "marketing program" teams will develop a simple marketing program for their local collegiate or professional women's sports team. Have each person in the team take one aspect and then discuss them as a team. [NOTE: You may need to define "marketing program."]

    b. Define the product/service offering.

        •   What is the core benefit or 'experience' or service?

        •   What are the points of difference?

        •   What additional services (ticketing, concessions, parking, restrooms, etc.) are essential?

    c. Recommend a set of prices.

- Based on your experiences, how should the team price its service in terms of single games/season ticket prices? Merchandise? Concessions? Programs? Others?

- Should differential pricing be used based on seat location (higher for 50 yard line or lower row seats; lower prices for end zone or higher row seats)?

    d. Identify promotional strategies.

- What forms of advertising should the team use? Should it offer sales promotion (coupons, contests, game-day give-aways, etc.)? Should team officials and players personally sell tickets? How should public relations, such as publicity and news releases be used? Should the team use direct marketing? What should the website do to promote fan interest?

- What kinds of sponsors should the team seek?

    e. Describe the "place" of a game/match.

- How should the seating be arranged? Reserved or "first come, first served?

- What amenities should be offered?"

9. **Spend 10 minutes** to have both the "target market and positioning" and the "marketing program" teams complete their respective handouts for their local collegiate or professional women's sports team.

10. **Spend 5 minutes** and have 2 to 3 students from the "target market and positioning" teams share their answers regarding the target market and 15 to 20 word positioning statement for their local collegiate or professional women's sports team.

11. **Spend 5 minutes** and have 2 to 3 students from the "marketing program" teams share their answers regarding the marketing program for their local collegiate or professional women's sports team.

    Marketing Lesson. Service providers, including sports teams, regardless of gender, must develop offerings that are compelling experiences and have significant points of difference. Give scarce resources for women's sports team in particular, marketers must clearly identify the target markets served, position the service in the minds of these consumers, and then reach them with creative but cost effective marketing programs.

WOMENS SPORTS TEAM
TARGET MARKET AND POSITIONING HANDOUT

(A) Identify the target market for the women's professional football team

(B) Compose a positioning strategy for the women's professional football team

(A) Target Market Characteristics	Recommendations
1. Geographic • Region of the U.S. • City/market size. • Radius (miles/drive time).	
2. Demographic • Gender. • Age. • Generational Cohort • Family life cycle. • Income (social class).	
3. Lifestyle • Attitudes. • Interests.	
4. Behavioral • Sports. • Media usage.	
B. A 15 to 20 word positioning statement.	

ICA 12-3

WOMENS SPORTS TEAM
MARKETING PROGRAM HANDOUT

Specify a marketing program for the women's professional football team

Marketing Program Elements	Recommendations
1. Product/Service • Core benefit or experience. • Points of difference. • Other services provided.	
2. Price • Single game/season tickets. • Merchandise. • Concessions. • Programs. • Parking. • Differential seating.	
3. Promotion • Advertising. • Sales promotion. • Personal selling. • Public relations. • Direct marketing. • Website. • Sponsors.	
4. Place • Location. • When (day, time, time of year). • Seating arrangement.	

CHAPTER 13: BUILDING THE PRICE FOUNDATION

ICA 13-1: IN-CLASS ACTIVITY

Pricing a Panasonic DVD Recorder[1]

Learning Objective. To have students learn the concept of value as it pertains to the prices set for a DVD recorder.

Definitions. The following marketing terms are referred to in this in-class activity (ICA):

- Price: The money or other considerations (including other goods and services) exchanged for the ownership or use of a good or service.

- Value: The ratio of perceived benefits to price; or Value = (Perceived benefits divided by Price).

Nature of the Activity. To have students discuss the pricing of DVD video recorders from Panasonic and other consumer electronics manufacturers.

Estimated Class Time. 20 minutes.

Materials Needed.

- The ICA13-1.doc Word and ICA13-1.ppt PowerPoint files contained in the ICA13-1 folder of the Instructor's CD #2 from the *Instructor's Survival Kit* box.

- The Panasonic DVD video recorder brochure from the *Instructor's Survival Kit* box.

- Copies of the Prices for DVD Recorders Handout for each student.

Preparation Before Class. Follow the steps below:

1. Read pp. 336-339 of Chapter 13.

2. Print and read the ICA13-1.doc Word file.

3. Print and/or review the PowerPoint slides from the ICA13-1.ppt PowerPoint file.

4. OPTIONAL: Either edit the Prices for DVD Recorders Handout or create a transparency if the models and prices have changed from the manufacturers or retailers identified below. Write down the prices for only those DVD recorders models that have a hard drive, both high definition and regular models:

   a. Visit the Panasonic website, which is at www.panasonic.com.

---

[1] The authors wish to thank Karen McCall, Advertising/Promotion Manager, of Panasonic who assisted in the development of this ICA. Images used by permission of Panasonic Corporation of North America.

b. Visit the websites of other DVD recorder competitors, such as Sony, Panasonic's principal competitor (www.sonystyle.com), Humax, a low-cost manufacturer that has partnered with TiVo (www.humaxusa.com), JVC (www.jvc.com), Philips (www.philips.com), Pioneer (www.pioneerelectronics.com), and Toshiba, which has also partnered with TiVo (www.toshiba.com).

c. Next, visit the website of Best Buy, a value-based electronics retailer, whose web address is www.bestbuy.com. View its selection and prices of DVD recorders from several manufacturers, including Panasonic.

d. Then, visit an upscale electronics retailer, Ultimate Electronics, whose website is www.ultimateelectronics.com.

e. Visit the websites of Amazon.com (www.amazon.com), which carries multiple brands in its own warehouse or offers selected models from other retailers, Circuit City (www.circuitcity.com), another value-based electronics retailer and competitor to Best Buy, or other national and local retailers.

5. Make copies of the existing or edited Prices for DVD Recorders Handout.

6. OPTIONAL: Review the Panasonic 2004 DVD Recorder catalog to become more familiar with the various applications and features available for Panasonic and other DVD recorders. You may want to print and make copies of selected pages for students. See the enclosed DVDCatalog.pdf file in the 'pdf' folder within the ICA13-1 folder. [NOTE: You will need the Adobe Acrobat Reader to view and print the PDF documents. To download the latest version, go to www.adobe.com/products/acrobat.]

7. OPTIONAL: Bookmark the above mentioned websites on your classroom computer.

Instructions. Follow the steps below to conduct this ICA:

1. Pass around the Panasonic DVD video recorder brochure from the *Instructor's Survival Kit* box.

Panasonic DVD Recorder TV ad

Slide 2

Panasonic DVD Recorder print ads

Slide 3

2. **Show Slide 2**: Panasonic DVD Recorder TV ad. [TRT = 0:30]

3. **Show Slide 3**: Panasonic DVD Recorder print ads that were made into the brochure that is currently being passed around the classroom.

4. Give students this background mini-lecture on the Panasonic DVD Recorder and DVD recorders in general:

"These ads show the applications and features for the Panasonic DVD Recorder with a hard drive. DVD players and the DVD format have revolutionized the home entertainment industry during the past decade by offering image and sound quality significantly better than VHS tape. Recently, consumer electronics manufacturers like Panasonic have introduced DVD recorders, which allow users to record, store, and play back TV shows, home videos, photos, etc. for their personal enjoyment.

DVD recorders with a hard drive allow consumers to: (1) play DVDs and record, store, and play back their favorite television programming; (2) transfer, store, and play back home movies made by digital video cameras as well as record them on a DVD; (3) play music and mp3 CDs, including those made from iTunes; and (4) transfer and edit photos taken by digital cameras and then record them on DVDs. Several of the newer DVD recorders can create "high definition" DVDs. The amount of video, music, and photo storage on the DVD recorder is dependent upon the size of the hard drive. Typically, the larger the hard drive, which can store more video, the higher the price of the DVD recorder."

5. **Spend 5 minutes** and ask students if any of them own/rent a DVD recorder, what brand it is, where they bought/rented it, and how they like it.

6. Ask students to estimate a perceived minimum and maximum price for a DVD recorder with a hard drive. Write the lowest and highest on the board.

7. Ask students what they, personally, would be willing to pay for a DVD recorder with a hard drive. Write some of their responses on the board. Probe for their reasons.

Prices for DVD Recorders Handout

Slide 4

8. Pass out copies of the Prices for DVD Recorders Handout.

9. **Show Slide 4** and ask students to explain the wide range of prices for the Panasonic and other DVD recorders shown. Develop these points:

   a. Brand name, such as Panasonic.

   b. Features and functions of the DVD recorder.

   c. Compatibility of the DVD recorder with specific brands or models of TVs or home entertainment systems.

   d. Ease of use (recording TV programming, making a DVD, etc.).

   e. Brand loyalty and satisfaction with other Panasonic or manufacturers' products.

   f. Aesthetics of the DVD recorder.

   g. Price versus value received.

Marketing Lessons. Price is not simply cost plus a mark-up. Price is determined by the value received *in the eyes of the customer*. Customers who do not value or perceive any functional difference in DVD recorders are not willing to pay much for a DVD recorder. Conversely, certain customers and market segments are willing to pay significantly more for a DVD recorder based on the features and benefits offered, which increases the value received. Smart marketers recognize these differences in market segments and therefore influence perceptions of their target segments regarding the value received through the marketing mix.

Websites. Connect to the Panasonic website at www.panasonic.com to obtain more information on updated models of its DVD recorder. Also, check out the other websites to check out the latest Panasonic and other manufacturer's DVD recorders and their prices.

PRICES FOR DVD RECORDERS (WITH HARD DISKS) HANDOUT

BRAND	MODEL	HARD DISK SIZE	MSRP	BEST BUY	ULTIMATE ELECTRONICS
Panasonic	DMR-EH50S	100 GB	$449.95		
	DMR-E85HS	120 GB	$599.95		$499.95
	DMR-E95HS	160 GB	$799.95		$699.95
	DMR-E100HS	120 GB	$1,199.95		$697.95
	DMR-E500HS	400 GB	$1,499.95		
Sony	RDR-HX900	160 GB	$799.95	$799.99	
	DHG-HDD250 (High Definition)	250 GB	$799.99		
	DHG-HDD500 (High Definition)	500 GB	$999.99		
Humax	DRT-400	40 GB	$399.99		
	DRT-800 (w/ TiVo)	80 GB	$499.99	$499.99 (Rebates: $100)	
	DRT-2000	200 GB	$599.99		
	DRT-2500	250 GB	$599.99		
JVC	DR-MX1S (w/ VHS)	80 GB	$999.95		$699.95
	DR-MH30S	160 GB	$899.95		
Philips	DVDR520H/37	80 GB	$499.99		
	HDRW720/17	120 GB	$599.99		
Pioneer	DVR-520H-S	80 GB	$799.00		$597.95
Toshiba	RS-TX20	120 GB	$599.99	$599.99 (Rebates: $100)	
	RS-TX60 (w/ TiVo)	160 GB	$699.99	$699.99 (Rebates: $100)	
	RD-XS32 (High Definition)	80 GB	$499.99		
	RD-XS34 (High Definition)	160 GB	$499.99		
	RD-XS52 (High Definition)	160 GB	$599.99		

CHAPTER 14: ARRIVING AT THE FINAL PRICE

ICA 14-1: IN-CLASS ACTIVITY

Extra Value Meal Bundle Pricing at McDonald's

Learning Objectives. To have students: (1) analyze the bundle pricing practice of a fast food restaurant and (2) suggest the benefits of bundle pricing to customers and the company as well as the effects on other fast-food restaurant competitors.

Definitions. The following marketing terms are referred to in this in-class activity (ICA):

- Bundle Pricing: The marketing of two or more products in a single package price.

- Value: The ratio of perceived benefits to price; or Value = (Perceived benefits divided by Price).

Nature of the Activity. To have students discuss the reasons why McDonald's would adopt an "Extra Value Meals" (EVM) product bundle pricing strategy.

Estimated Class Time. 10 minutes.

Materials Needed.

- The ICA14-1.doc Word and ICA14-1.ppt PowerPoint files contained in the ICA14-1 folder of the Instructor's CD #2 from the *Instructor's Survival Kit* box.

- Copies of the:
    a. "Extra Value Meal" Bundle Pricing at McDonald's Handout.
    b. Why McDonald's Uses Bundle Pricing for "Extra Value Meals" Handout.

- NOTE: Transparencies can be made of the handouts instead of making copies and using the PowerPoint presentation for those instructors who prefer this option.

Preparation Before Class. Follow the steps below:

1. Read pp. 364-365 of Chapter 14.

2. Print, read, and if necessary, edit the ICA14-1.doc Word file.

3. Print and/or review the PowerPoint slides from the ICA14-1.ppt PowerPoint file.

4. Try an "Extra Value Meal" at your local McDonald's restaurant to add a personal example to the class discussion. Write down the prices this restaurant charges for the Big Mac®, the Quarter Pounder with Cheese™, and the Chicken McGrill™ to compare them with those listed on the "Extra Value Meal" Bundle Pricing at McDonald's Handout.

5. Make copies of:

    a. "Extra Value Meal" Bundle Pricing at McDonald's Handout.

    b. Why McDonald's Uses Bundle Pricing for "Extra Value Meals" Handout.

6. OPTIONAL: Bookmark the McDonald's website (www.mcdonalds.com) on your classroom computer.

Instructions. Follow the steps below to conduct this ICA:

1. Ask students if they are familiar with McDonald's Extra Value Meals. Briefly explain that they include a sandwich (either a burger, chicken, or fish), a large fries, and a medium soft drink—all for a single price that is lower than if the three items were purchased separately.

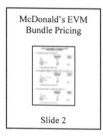

McDonald's EVM
Bundle Pricing

Slide 2

2. **Show Slide 2**: "Extra Value Meal" Bundle Pricing at McDonald's Handout, which identifies the bundled EVM prices for a Big Mac, a Quarter Pounder with Cheese, and a Chicken McGrill as well as the unbundled prices if each item was purchased separately.

3. Give the following background mini-lecture:

"The prices McDonald's charges may vary by type of sandwich. Popular sandwiches, or ones with more costly ingredients, may be priced higher (e.g. the Big Mac EVM: $3.59; the Quarter Pounder w/ Cheese EVM: $3.69; and Chicken McGrill EVM: $4.39). Prices may also be higher at a McDonald's restaurant located in airports, highway rest stops, or prime downtown locations in major cities. Furthermore, prices may vary according to whether the restaurant is owed by McDonald's or a franchisee. Finally, each restaurant may charge its own price based on competitive or promotional considerations (e.g. a Big Mac EVM is $3.59 at location 'A' vs. $3.39 at location 'B', which is two miles from 'A')."

Why use EVM
Bundle Pricing?

Slide 3

4. Ask students why McDonald's would use a bundle pricing strategy. Why not just sell the items separately and charge the higher prices?

5. **Show Slide 3**: Why McDonald's Uses Bundle Pricing for "Extra Value Meals" Handout.

6. Have students individually or in teams suggest reasons why McDonald's would use bundle pricing based on the three factors that influence price: customer, company, and competition. Write the reasons down on the board or a transparency made from the Why McDonald's Uses Bundle Pricing for "Extra Value Meals" Handout. Typical student answers include:

- Customer Factors:

    a. **To get customers to buy more**. This is done in two ways: (a) buys additional items, such as fries, even if they weren't intending to because the item is only a few cents more with the EVM or (b) buys the larger item, such as fries, because a customer who would normally buy a small fries finds it more profitable to buy an Extra Value Meal, thereby purchasing the large fries for slightly more on a per item cost basis, but receiving the entire meal at an aggregate cost savings. This is a form of "trade-up bundling" according to Eppen, et. al.[1]

    A recent strategy by McDonald's (and other fast food restaurants) is to "Super Size" the Extra Value Meal to increase the value to customers even further by upgrading the large fries to a super size fries and a medium soft drink to a large one for a modest price increase of $0.49.

    b. **To give customers a unique value from the product bundle**. This is to expedite the ordering process due to the myriad number of menu offerings at restaurants like McDonald's. For example, McDonald's segregates its EVMs on its menu boards both inside and at the drive-thru from the itemized listing of sandwiches, fries, and soft drinks. Moreover, it gives each EVM a number (e.g. the Big Mac EVM is a #1, the Quarter Pounder w/ Cheese EVM is a #3, and the Chicken McGrill EVM is a #10) to expedite customer orders, thereby increasing the time value of the purchase experience.

    With a sense of humor, this can also be related to the idea of "joint performance bundling," since with the salty food and fries, the meal is definitely enhanced with some form of beverage, making the bundle superior to a meal without a drink.[2]

    - Question 1: Why not just give customers lower prices on individual items if saving consumers money is the goal?

        Answer: The lower price of an Extra Value Meal gets people to try items they might not have normally tried and then they will value them in the future.

    c. **To reach the meal segment**. The bundle is actually the product aimed at a specific "meal" market segment, and the individual items are aimed at the "niche" customer segments (a form of "aggregation bundling").[3] Also, EVM's are designed to target particular sandwich preferences (beef, chicken, or fish) and time of day (breakfast and lunch/dinner).

---

[1] Gary D. Eppen, Ward A. Hanson and R. Kipp Martin, "Bundling—New Products, New Markets, Low Risk," *Sloan Management Review*, (Summer, 1991), pp. 7-14.

[2] Ibid.

[3] Ibid.

- Company Factors:

    a. **To get customers to buy higher margin items**. The highest-margin items at fast food restaurants are soft drinks. For a $0.99 soft drink, the cost to a restaurant is less than 10¢, with the cup costing the most. Fries are also one of the highest-margin food items. This is a form of "margin spread bundling."[4]

    b. **To reduce the time for transactions and order processing**. This has two benefits. First, it reduces the length of the queue, thereby reducing the time spent in the cashiers' line by customers, which generates more orders during peak traffic times. Second, it reduces the labor costs associated with processing orders, which a form of "production efficiency bundling."[5]

    c. **To obtain additional cost efficiencies**. There are additional production efficiencies in being better able to plan orders and buying items that will see increased volume because they are included in Extra Value Meals. This is another aspect of "production efficiency bundling."[6]

- Competition Factors:

    To compete better with other fast-food restaurants. Value meals were first introduced in the late 1980's when Taco Bell introduced its new "value pricing" strategy to the fast food industry. Taco Bell's strategy was to price all of its items under $1.00, with items such as tacos priced as low as $0.59. This shocked the fast food industry. McDonald's initial response to Taco Bell's strategy was to cut the price of its basic hamburger to $0.59.

    - Question 2: Which costs more to make: a taco or a burger?

        Answer: Some students will say that a taco is much less expensive to make than a burger (or chicken or fish) because it is made up of much less expensive ingredients. If so, McDonald's is at a competitive disadvantage on an item-for-item basis with Taco Bell. Yet, if McDonald's can compete on a *meal-for-meal* basis, it can lessen its relative competitive disadvantage.

        For example, to feel satisfied when eating a lunch or dinner meal, it may take 5 tacos from Taco Bell to feel satisfied compared to an EVM (a burger, large fries, and a medium soft drink) from McDonald's. Some students will say it is to match the competition, which is what happened with McDonald's and its competitors since the late 1980s.

Marketing Lesson. McDonald's Extra Value Meal bundle pricing strategy has been one of the most successful pricing strategies ever devised.

Websites. McDonald's website is www.mcdonalds.com. To obtain a reprint of the Eppen article on product bundle pricing, visit the *Sloan Management Review* website at www.mit-smr.com.

---

[4] Ibid.
[5] Ibid.
[6] Ibid.

"EXTRA VALUE MEALS" BUNDLE PRICING AT MCDONALD'S HANDOUT

■ **THE BIG MAC EXTRA VALUE MEAL (#1):**

ITEM	UNBUNDLED PRICE (ITEMS BOUGHT SEPARATELY)	BUNDLED PRICE (EXTRA VALUE MEAL)
• Big Mac	$2.59	✓
• Large Fries	$1.79	✓
• Medium Soft Drink	$1.59	✓
TOTAL	**$5.97**	**$4.29**

- **So the bundle price saves $1.68**

■ **THE QUARTER POUNDER W/ CHEESE EXTRA VALUE MEAL (#3):**

ITEM	UNBUNDLED PRICE (ITEMS BOUGHT SEPARATELY)	BUNDLED PRICE (EXTRA VALUE MEAL)
• Quarter Pounder w/ Cheese	$2.59	✓
• Large Fries	$1.79	✓
• Medium Soft Drink	$1.59	✓
TOTAL	**$5.97**	**$4.29**

- **So the bundle price saves $1.68**

■ **THE CHICKEN MCGRILL EXTRA VALUE MEAL (#10):**

ITEM	UNBUNDLED PRICE (ITEMS BOUGHT SEPARATELY)	BUNDLED PRICE (EXTRA VALUE MEAL)
• Chicken McGrill	$3.29	✓
• Large Fries	$1.79	✓
• Medium Soft Drink	$1.59	✓
TOTAL	**$6.67**	**$4.99**

- **So the bundle price saves $1.68**

ICA 14-1

WHY MCDONALD'S USES BUNDLE PRICING
FOR "EXTRA VALUE MEALS" HANDOUT

FACTOR	REASONS FOR BUNDLE PRICING
• Customer	
• Company	
• Competition	

CHAPTER 15: MANAGING MARKETING CHANNELS
AND WHOLESALING

ICA 15-1: IN-CLASS ACTIVITY

Marketing Channels for Apple Computer[1]

Learning Objective. To have students learn about the marketing channels currently used by Apple Computer to sell its computers, digital devices, and software products to consumers.

Definitions. The following marketing terms are referred to in this in-class activity (ICA):

- Direct Channel: A marketing channel where a producer and ultimate consumers deal directly with each other.

- Indirect Channel: A marketing channels where intermediaries are inserted between the producer and consumers and perform numerous channel functions.

- Marketing Channel: Individuals and firms involved in the process of making a product or service available for use or consumption by consumers or industrial users.

- Strategic Channel Alliance: A practice whereby one firm's marketing channel is used to sell another firm's products.

Nature of the Activity. To have students identify those channel members that sell Apple products and classify the channel strategies used by Apple, and in one case, Microsoft.

Estimated Class Time. 15 minutes.

Material Needed. The ICA15-1.doc Word and ICA15-1.ppt PowerPoint files contained in the ICA15-1 folder of the Instructor's CD #2 from the *Instructor's Survival Kit* box.

Preparation Before Class. Follow the steps below:

1. Read pp. 398-402 of Chapter 15.

2. Print, read, and if necessary, edit the ICA15-1.doc Word file.

3. Print and/or review the PowerPoint slides from the ICA15-1.ppt PowerPoint file.

4. OPTIONAL: Bookmark Apple Computer's website (www.apple.com) on your classroom computer.

---

[1] The authors wish to thank Bob Robinson of Apple Computer who assisted in the development of this ICA.

Instructions. Follow the steps below to conduct this ICA:

Apple Computer products

Slide 2

1. **Show Slide 2**: Apple Computer Products Distributed Through Marketing Channels. To determine how familiar students are with Apple's marketing channel structure, ask them the following question:

   • Question 1: Within the last year, have any of you purchased a product (computer, iPod, software, etc.) manufactured or sold by Apple Computer? If yes, where they purchased it?

   Answer: If yes, several channels exist that will be discussed below.

2. Ask students the following questions regarding Apple Computer's marketing channel structure:

   • Question 2: Since the late 1990s, Apple has allowed consumers to purchase its products online via its Apple Store. If you were to purchase an Apple product from the **Apple Store**, (a) identify the channels members as a producer, wholesaler, and/or retailer and (b) classify the channel strategy used by Apple and its channel members as direct, indirect, and/or strategic channel alliance.

   Answers:

   (a) Channel members are "Producer (Apple)→Consumer."

   (b) Channel strategy is "Direct Channel."

   Online Apple Store

   Slide 3

   Rationale: **Show Slide 3**: Apple Online Store. Apple and consumers interact directly with each other through its Internet website. There is no intermediary and therefore Apple must perform all channel functions.

   • Question 3: By mid-2005, Apple had opened over 100 Apple Stores, including England and Japan with plans to open 20 others in the near future. Apple also has opened several "mini" stores in strip malls. If you were to purchase an Apple product from an **Apple Retail Store**, (a) identify the channels members as a producer, wholesaler, and/or retailer and (b) classify the channel strategy used by Apple and its channel members as direct, indirect and/or strategic channel alliance.

   Answers:

   (a) Channel members are "Producer (Apple)→Consumer."

   (b) Channel strategy is "Direct Channel."

   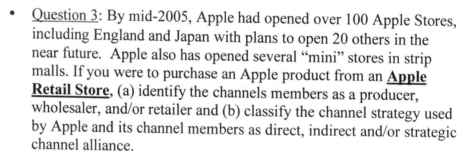

   Apple Retail Store

   Slide 4

   Rationale: **Show Slide 4**: Apple Retail Store. Again, Apple and consumers interact directly with each other through its retail stores so there is no intermediary. Therefore, Apple must perform all channel functions.

- Question 4: Under its Authorized Apple Reseller program, Apple has established relationships with many firms to sell Apple products. One such reseller is CompUSA, the nation's largest computer superstore reseller of personal computer-related products and services, with approximately 230 Superstores in over 90 major metropolitan markets. However, under a unique arrangement with Apple, CompUSA has established a "store-within-a-store" that is staffed by employees trained and paid solely by Apple. Presumably, CompUSA receives a sales commission or other compensation for allowing Apple to use some of its store space

  If you were to purchase an Apple product from **CompUSA**, (a) identify the channels members as a producer, wholesaler, and/or retailer and (b) classify the channel strategy used by Apple and its channel members as direct, indirect, and/or strategic channel alliance.

  Answers:
  (a) Channel members are "Producer (Apple)→Retailer (CompUSA)→Consumer."
  (b) Channel strategies are "Direct Channel" and "Strategic Channel Alliance."

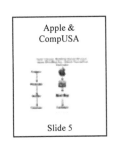

Apple & CompUSA

Slide 5

  Rationale: **Show Slide 5**: CompUSA. Apple and consumers interact directly with each other ("direct channel"), even though sales occur within an "Apple store-within-a-store," which is located within a specific area within a CompUSA retail store. Apple and CompUSA have entered into a "strategic channel alliance," whereby Apple performs some channel functions (provides inventory management, sales employees, financing, etc.) in exchange for space in additional retail outlets while CompUSA performs other channel functions (provides retail floor space, transactional services, etc.) in exchange for sales commissions and other considerations.

- Question 5: Under its Authorized Apple Reseller program, Apple has also established a relationship with Best Buy, the #1 retail electronics chain in the U.S., with over 780 stores across the U.S. Each store's layout is organized into departments. The computer department contains Apple computers and software products and is staffed by Best Buy employees. Assume that Best Buy obtains its entire inventory from **Ingram Micro**, the nation's largest technology product distributor.

  If you were to purchase an Apple product from **Best Buy**, (a) identify the channels members as a producer, wholesaler, and/or retailer and (b) classify the channel strategy used by Apple and its channel members as direct, indirect, and/or strategic channel alliance.

Answers:

(a) Channel members are "Producer (Apple)→Wholesaler (Ingram Micro)→Retailer (Best Buy)→Consumer."

(b) Channel strategy is "Indirect Channel."

Apple & Ingram Micro & Best Buy

Slide 6

Rationale: **Show Slide 6**: Best Buy. Intermediaries exist between Apple and consumers. Specifically, Ingram Micro (wholesale) takes delivery of computers, digital devices, and software from Apple in bulk (logistical function), and then breaks it down in smaller units for retailers, such as Best Buy. Best Buy, in turn, performs other facilitating channel functions, such as sales, transactional, technical support, financing, etc.

- Question 6: Under its Authorized Apple Reseller program, Apple has also established a relationship with MacMall, which sells Apple products online and by telephone through its catalog.

  If you were to purchase an Apple product from **MacMall**, (a) identify the channels members as a producer, wholesaler, and/or retailer and (b) classify the channel strategy used by Apple and its channel members as direct, indirect, and/or strategic channel alliance.

  Answers:

  (a) Channel members are "Producer (Apple)→Retailer (MacMall)→Consumer."

  (b) Channel strategy is "Indirect Channel."

Apple & MacMall

Slide 7

Rationale: **Show Slide 7**: MacMall. An intermediary exists between Apple and consumers. Specifically, MacMall (retailer) takes delivery of computers, digital devices, and software from Apple (logistical function) and performs other facilitating channel functions (sales, transactional, technical support, financing, etc.).

Marketing Lessons. Manufacturers, such as Apple Computer and Microsoft, use multiple channel members and channel strategies to sell their products and services to ultimate consumers. In some cases, such as with Apple, a firm can be both a producer and retailer channel member as well as simultaneously engaging in multiple channel strategies.

Websites. Go to the following websites to learn more about the companies mentioned: Apple's website is www.apple.com; CompUSA's website is www.compusa.com; Micro Center's website is www.microcenter.com; Ingram Micro's website is www.ingrammicro.com; and MacMall's website is www.macmall.com.

CHAPTER 15: MANAGING MARKETING CHANNELS AND WHOLESALING

ICA 15-2: IN-CLASS ACTIVITY

Marketing Channels for Fastenal's Unique Threaded Fasteners[1]

Learning Objectives. To have students identify: (1) the points of difference, (2) target market segments, and (3) marketing channels that might be used for a category of unique threaded fasteners distributed by Fastenal Company.

Definitions. The following marketing terms are referred to in this in-class activity (ICA):

- Marketing Channel: Individuals and firms involved in the process of making a product or service available for use or consumption by consumers or industrial users.

- Points of Difference: Those characteristics of a product that make it superior to competitive substitutes.

- Target Market: One or more specific groups of potential consumers toward which an organization directs its marketing program.

Nature of the Activity. To help students understand the unique nature of the threaded fastener products (points of difference) and their applications and target markets so students can suggest the appropriate marketing channel(s).

Estimated Class Time. 20 minutes.

Materials Needed.

- The ICA15-2.doc Word and ICA15-2.ppt PowerPoint files contained in the ICA15-2 folder of the Instructor's CD #2 from the *Instructor's Survival Kit* box.

- The packet of Fastenal threaded fasteners contained in the *Instructor's Survival Kit* box.

Preparation Before Class. Follow the steps below:

1. Read p. 400 of Chapter 15 and study Figure 15-5: Common marketing channels for business goods and services.

2. Print, read, and if necessary, edit the ICA15-2.doc Word file.

3. Print and/or review the PowerPoint slides from the ICA15-2.ppt PowerPoint file.

4. Skim the Fastenal Appendix D Case D-15 on pp. 650-651 of *Marketing, 8th Edition.*

---

[1] The authors wish to thank Willard D. Oberton, President and CEO of Fastenal Company, and Dr. Robert Hansen, Associate Professor of Marketing, Carlson School of Management, who wrote this ICA.

5. OPTIONAL: Bookmark the Fastenal website (www.fastenal.com) on your classroom computer.

Instructions. Follow the steps below to conduct this ICA:

1. Give students the following mini-lecture on threaded fasteners:

    "The term 'threaded fasteners' is just a name for screws, bolts, and related items used to attach or otherwise secure one item to another item—such as a door hinge to a door. Threaded fasteners, although a common household product, are not often thought of as either an exciting or highly marketable product category. They are often viewed as simply "a commodity"—with a variety of screws and bolts that are easily substitutable for one another and for which the lowest price is a key buying criterion for customers."

2. Ask the students if they have ever seen traditional fasteners, where they have seen them, and what they were used for. Then ask them what is used to secure or install the fasteners. The answer to the last question is screwdrivers; slot screw drivers or Philips head screwdrivers are the most likely answers. But some students may have had experience with other specialty screws or bolts and the special screwdrivers that are needed for them.

3. Pass around the packet of Fastenal threaded fasteners obtained from the *Instructor's Survival Kit* box.

4. **Show Slides 2-4** and give students this background mini-lecture on Fastenal and its unique threaded fasteners:

    "There are common fasteners, like the ones any of us can buy and use in everyday applications, and then there are security fasteners like the ones shown here. If you look at the heads or tops of these fasteners, you should notice that they are not at all similar to the everyday fasteners you have seen and used.

    These fasteners are used where security or tampering issues are critical, where you do not want unauthorized individuals either adjusting or removing the doors or locks held in place by these fasteners. They are used, for example, in public restrooms, parking lots, hospitals, prisons, and other places where people might try to tamper with, remove, or break into locks or doors. The key lies in the head design of the fasteners as they can only be removed using either (a) the same installation device that was used to install the fastener or (b) a special fastener extractor designed specifically to unscrew or remove these fasteners. Note that neither of these tools is intended to be available to a person other than the one who originally installed the security fastener."

5. Next ask students the following questions about fasteners:

- <u>Question 1</u>: What is the main point of difference for these fasteners?

  <u>Answer</u>: The unique security provided by the fasteners by their not being able to be unscrewed with conventional screwdrivers.

- <u>Question 2</u>: Where—or in what application—are these fasteners most likely to be needed?

  <u>Answer</u>: In applications where the doors, locks, or other items held in place should not be able to be removed by burglars or others using conventional screwdrivers.

- <u>Question 3</u>: What kind of organization is most likely to buy them?

  <u>Answer</u>: Buyers are typically industrial customers such as construction, repair and maintenance, or security companies who install and maintain secure doors, locks, etc.

- <u>Question 4</u>: Where or how would these industrial customers purchase these fasteners?

  <u>Answer</u>: These fasteners can rarely be purchased at conventional hardware stores or supply houses used by organizations. So because of security considerations both these fasteners and unique devices to remove them are **not** likely to be available to the general public through conventional outlets but instead are available only from specialized distributors.

- <u>Question 5</u>: What are the problems or challenges facing the company who wants to reach these special customers? What will it take to reach these customers and why should Fastenal do it?

  <u>Answer</u>: The key is that there are fewer of these special customers and they are harder to identify than the typical threaded fastener customer. You can not find these security fasteners at any of the big box home improvement stores but there are available at a few specialty hardware stores and the installation tools are not available at most retail locations. So it will take more effort to target theses customers. And this will take extra effort, which Fastenal is willing to undertake.

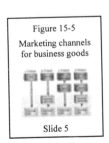

Figure 15-5
Marketing channels for business goods

Slide 5

6. **Show Slide 5**. Customers that use these special threaded fasteners look to two common marketing channels for business goods, as shown in Figure 15-5:

a. Producer→industrial distributor→industrial user channel (B). This describes the channel involving Fastenal, where it acts as an industrial distributor of thousands of fasteners produced by dozens of manufacturers.

b. Producer→agent industrial→user channel (C). As noted in the textbook, the Stoke Fastener Company of California uses agents to call on industrial user customers.

ICA 15-2

7. Conclude with the following mini-lecture:

"Are these specialized fasteners a good business for Fastenal? Even though the fasteners cost roughly 30 percent more for Fastenal to buy from the manufacturer, they sell for a much higher price to those who need security fasteners. As a result, Fastenal's gross margin on security fasteners is approximately 15 percent higher than it is on regular threaded fasteners.

Fastenal can do this because it is the largest distributor of industrial fasteners in the world and sells its products in 1,600 stores throughout North America. Fastenal is able to stock all types of security fasteners somewhere in the distribution system and while each store may not have an on-hand supply of every type of security fastener, each store typically has at least one type in stock for new installations."

Marketing Lesson. Offering specialized fasteners for security applications with a unique point of difference can provide genuine value to industrial customers and significant profit to an industrial distributor in a marketing channel that succeeds in meeting customer needs.

Website. To view the latest lines of Fastenal threaded fasteners, go to www.fastenal.com.

CHAPTER 16: INTEGRATING SUPPLTY CHAIN AND LOGISTICS MANAGEMENT

ICA 16-1: IN-CLASS ACTIVITY

The "Foam Factory" Process Improvement Exercise[1]

Learning Objective. To have students discover the difference between "process improvement," which can lead to a 10 to 20 percent improvement in performing an activity, and "reengineering," a process that can lead to improvements of several hundred percent. Logistics management and order fulfillment are marketing.

Definition. The following marketing term is referred to in this in-class activity (ICA):

- Logistics Management: The practice of organizing the cost-effective flow of raw materials, in-process inventory, finished goods, and related information from point of origin to point of consumption to satisfy customer requirements.

Nature of the Activity. To have the instructor play the role of a production-line manager who leads a student "team" through an exercise that (1) shows how hard it is to change and improve old processes—the process improvement activity—and (2) demonstrates how giving workers real information from the environment can force a shift in thinking that can lead to breakthrough improvements of hundreds of percent—the reengineering process. In this experiment, the "information from the environment" is the speed with which competitive groups have been able to accomplish the task.

Estimated Class Time. 20 minutes.

Materials Needed.

- The ICA16-1.doc Word and ICA16-1.ppt PowerPoint files contained in the ICA16-1 folder of the Instructor's CD #2 from the *Instructor's Survival Kit* box.

- 12 1" × 1" foam cubes (made by cutting up 1-inch insulation foam) plus a small box to hold them. (Alternatively, use 12 small beanbags or 12 toy building blocks).

- A small table in the classroom around which seven students can stand.

- NOTE: Transparencies can be made of the handouts instead of making copies and using the PowerPoint presentation for those instructors who prefer this option.

Preparation Before Class. Follow the steps below:

1. Read material below to be able to conduct the exercise in class. Make sure you understand the movement of the cubes (or beanbags).

2. Print, read, and if necessary, edit the ICA16-1.doc Word file.

---

[1] "The Beanbag Exercise" in Christopher Meyer, *Fast Cycle Time* (New York: The Free Press, 1993), pp. 54 - 57.

3. Print and/or review the PowerPoint slides from the ICA16-1.ppt PowerPoint file.

Instructions. Follow the steps below to conduct this ICA:

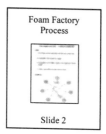

Foam Factory Process

Slide 2

1. Select seven "volunteers" from the class and a "timekeeper" who has a watch with a second hand.

2. **Show Slide 2**: The Foam Factory—A Group Exercise and arrange the seven class members around a table (no chairs) as shown.

3. Read the following instructions to the team (and class):

   a. **Production Run #1: The Old Process**. "You are members of a production line team. You have 5 minutes to read the rules on the transparency and practice passing a foam block (bean bag) or two through the process so you understand it."

   Timekeeper: Time the team as they move the 12 blocks from a loose pile at the start until they are all packed in the box. Typical times to complete the "old process" will be 25 to 35 seconds.

   b. **Production Run #2: An Improved Process**. "Team, you have two minutes to figure out how to improve the process, and to try it again. Try to improve how you did the old process in Production Run #1."

   Timekeeper: Time the team again. Typical times to complete the "improved process" will be 20 to 30 seconds.

   c. **Production Run #3: A Reengineered Process**. "Team, you have just learned that the competition can do this process in 10 seconds. If the company is to remain in business, you must match or beat this time. Please reconsider the rules, and get creative in your redesign. Something has to change! You have five minutes to make your breakthrough."

   Timekeeper: Time the team one last time. Typical times to complete the "reengineered process" will be 7 to 10 seconds.

4. The reengineering breakthrough the team should uncover is to: (1) put all twelve cubes in the center of the table; (2) have six team members place and remove their hands on top of the cubes, thereby having touched or "handled" all of them; and (3) have the seventh team member put all the cubes into the box at once.

Marketing Lessons. Point out how your instructions as their manager influenced the team's behavior and results, and how real data from the environment can have a dramatic impact when shared with the workers. Draw a parallel to actual marketing activities, such as warehousing, order filling, and other supply chain and logistics processes, which are a primary target for process improvement and reengineering efforts. Explain that additional information, such as knowing competitors can perform the activity in 10 seconds, can cause the team to recast the problem and solve it in creative new ways. The team may wish to debate whether its reengineered process meets the meaning of "handle cubes" used in the slide/transparency.

THE FOAM FACTORY—A GROUP EXERCISE

Rules:

1. All cubes go from start pile into the box at the end.

2. All people must handle all cubes.

3. All people must handle cubes in the sequence shown below.

4. Cubes must enter the box one at a time.

Sequence:

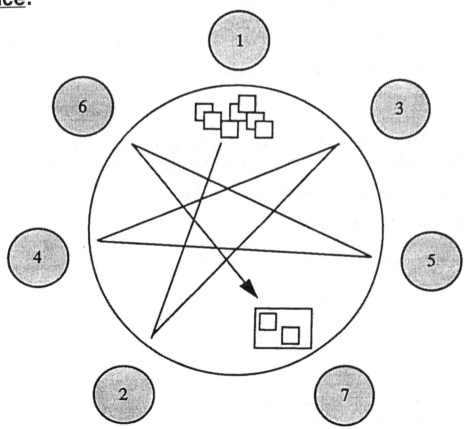

CHAPTER 17: RETAILING

ICA 17-1: IN-CLASS ACTIVITY

Retail Shopping Online: Comparing Prices for a Kodak Digital Camera[1]

Learning Objectives. To have students shop for a digital camera online from a manufacturer, selected retailers, and "bots" to compare their respective prices.

Definitions. The following marketing terms are referred to in this in-class activity (ICA):

- Bots: Electronic shopping agents or robots that comb websites to compare prices and product or service features.

- Online Consumers: The subsegment of all Internet users who employ this technology to research products and services and make purchases.

- Shopping Goods: Items for which the consumer compares several alternatives on criteria, such as price, quality, or style.

Nature of the Activity. To have students access the websites of Kodak, manufacturer of the EasyShare-One zoom digital camera, retailers that may carry this particular brand and model, and shopping agents (or "bots") to experience online retail comparative shopping for this particular product.

Estimated Class Time. 20 minutes, which consists of:

- 5 minutes to explain the nature of this ICA.

- 15 minutes to present summaries by student teams during the next class period.

- [NOTE: Students will spend 30 minutes outside class to complete their assignment.]

Materials Needed.

- The ICA17-1.doc Word and ICA17-1.ppt PowerPoint files contained in the ICA17-1 folder of the Instructor's CD #2 from the *Instructor's Survival Kit* box.

- Copies of the Online Retail Shopping Handout.

- Student access to the Internet.

Preparation Before Class. Follow the steps below:

1. Read pp. 264-265 of Chapter 10, 453-454 of Chapter 17 and 564, 567 of Chapter 21.

2. Print, read, and if necessary, edit the ICA17-1.doc Word file.

---

[1] The authors wish to John Blodgett, Assistant Account Executive of Ketchum Communications on behalf of Kodak, who assisted in the development of this ICA.

3. Print and/or review the PowerPoint slides from the ICA17-1.ppt PowerPoint file.

4. Make copies of the Online Retail Shopping Handout.

5. Familiarize yourself with websites referred to in this ICA.

6. OPTIONAL: Bookmark the Kodak EasyShare (www.kodak.com/go/EasyShare) website on your classroom computer.

Instructions. Follow the steps below to conduct this ICA:

Online Retail Shopping Handout

Kodak EasyShare-One Camera

Slide 2

1. Pass out copies of the Online Retail Shopping Handout to each student.

2. Form students into 4-person teams.

3. **Show Slide 2** and give students the following mini-lecture on the Kodak EasyShare-One zoom digital camera (Source: January 5, 2005 Kodak press release and website information):

In January 2005, Kodak introduced the Kodak EasyShare-One, a new zoom digital camera that allows people to e-mail pictures directly from the camera—anywhere there is a Wi-Fi hot spot (Starbucks, this college/university, etc.) or Wi-Fi-enabled device, such as a computer or Kodak Printer Dock Plus. Other important features include:

a. A 4-megapixel camera with 3X optical zoom lens.

b. A 3" LCD rotating monitor and touch screen to manage the pictures taken.

c. 256 Mb of built-in memory capable of storing 1,500 pictures as well as an optional memory card.

d. Record TV-quality video at 30 frames-per-second, with sound.

e. The MSRP for the Kodak EasyShare-One is $599.95; the Wi-Fi card is $99.95; and the Kodak Printer Dock Plus is $199.95."

4. Explain the nature of this ICA:

"Between now and the next class period, each team will go to the websites listed in the Online Retail Shopping Handout to shop for a Kodak EasyShare-One zoom digital camera. You do NOT have to shop for its accessories, such as the Wi-Fi card or Kodak Printer Dock Plus. Also, ignore any sales taxes or delivery charges.

For each website, attempt to locate the Kodak EasyShare-One zoom digital camera by whatever means you choose. For the shopping 'bots,' write down the identities and prices of the retailers with the lowest and highest prices. If a website does not carry the product, leave the price blank. Finally, call or visit a local digital camera retailer that sells the Kodak EasyShare-One zoom digital camera to obtain a price."

5. Have the students write a 1-page brief that responds to the following questions:

"For each website, attempt to locate the Kodak EasyShare-One zoom digital camera by whatever means you choose. For the shopping 'bots,' write down the identities and prices of the retailers with the lowest and highest prices. If a website does not carry the product, leave the price blank. Finally, call or visit a local digital camera retailer that sells the Kodak EasyShare-One zoom digital camera to obtain a price."

a. Comment on **each** website with respect to its ease of navigation, visual layout, time to find the product, variety of product categories offered, and the price offered for the product. Also, were the shopping "bots" helpful? [¾ page]

b. If you were in the market, would you actually purchase this Kodak EasyShare-One zoom digital camera from one of these online websites? If "Yes," which ones and why? If "No," why not? [¼ page]

Marketing Lesson. Manufacturers, traditional retailers, and online retailers all offer online shopping. In addition, shopping agents or "bots" can assist consumers in locating retailers that carry a desired product item for the lowest price. Consumers can compare prices obtained online with those from traditional "brick & mortar" retailers to get the best possible price, which realistically would include delivery and sales tax charges.

Website. The website for the Kodak EasyShare-One zoom digital camera is www.kodak.com/go/EasyShare.

ONLINE RETAIL SHOPPING HANDOUT

1. For each website, shopping "bot," and local retailer, write down both the name of the retailer (if different from the website) and the price of a Kodak EasyShare-One zoom digital camera. Only write down the price of the digital camera itself. If a website does not carry the Kodak EasyShare-One zoom digital camera, leave the price blank.

	Price of the Kodak EasyShare-One Digital Camera
Website	
Manufacturer	
Kodak (www.kodak.com)	_____
Retailers	
Amazon.com (www.amazon.com)...............................	_____
Best Buy (www.bestbuy.com)	_____
Ritz Camera (www.ritzcamera.com).......................	_____
Ultimate Electronics (www.ultimateelectronics.com)	_____
Local Camera Retailer (name): _____	_____
Shopping "Bots"	
mySimon (www.mysimon.com)	
– Lowest price retailer:...................... _____	_____
– Highest price retailer:...................... _____	_____
Yahoo! (www.shopping.yahoo.com)	
– Lowest price retailer:...................... _____	_____
– Highest price retailer:...................... _____	_____

2. Write a 1-page brief that responds to the following questions:

   a. Comment on **each** website with respect to its ease of navigation, visual layout, time to find the product, variety of product categories offered, and the price offered for the product. Also, were the shopping "bots" helpful? [¾ page]

   b. If you were in the market, would you actually purchase this Kodak EasyShare-One zoom digital camera from one of these online websites? If "Yes," which ones and why? If "No," why not? [¼ page]

3. Hand in your briefs and be prepared to discuss them during the next class period.

CHAPTER 18: INTEGRATED MARKETING COMMUNICATIONS AND DIRECT MARKETING

ICA 18-1: IN-CLASS ACTIVITY

An IMC for a Toro® Snowthrower[1]

Learning Objectives. To have students: (1) suggest elements of an integrated marketing communications (IMC) program and (2) describe how these elements can generate revenues for an innovative consumer product—Toro's Power Max™ snowthrower.

Definitions. The following marketing terms are referred to in this in-class activity (ICA):

- Advertising: Any paid form of nonpersonal communication about an organization, good, service, or idea by an identified sponsor.

- Direct Marketing: A promotion alternative that uses direct communication with consumers to generate a response in the form of an order, a request for further information, or a visit to a retail outlet.

- Integrated Marketing Communications (IMC): The concept of designing marketing communications programs that coordinates all promotional activities—advertising, personal selling, sales promotion, public relations, and direct marketing—to provide a consistent message across all audiences.

- Personal Selling: The two-way flow of communication between a buyer and seller, designed to influence a person's or group's purchase decision, usually in face-to-face communication between the sender and receiver.

- Public Relations: A form of communication management that seeks to influence the feelings, opinions, or beliefs held by customers, prospective customers, stockholders, suppliers, employees, and other publics about a company and its products or services.

- Sales Promotion: A short-term inducement of value offered to arouse interest in buying a good or service.

Nature of the Activity. To have students work in teams to identify integrated marketing communications (IMC) program actions that Toro might take to reach prospective buyers of snowthrowers.

Estimated Class Time. 20 minutes.

Materials Needed.

- The ICA18-1.doc Word and ICA18-1.ppt PowerPoint files contained in the ICA18-1 folder of the Instructor's CD #2 from the *Instructor's Survival Kit* box.

---

[1] The authors wish to thank Scott Wozniak, Marketing Director of Toro, who assisted in the development of this ICA.

- The Toro Snowthrower brochure contained in the *Instructor's Survival Kit* box.

- Copies of the:

  a. Product spec sheet for the Toro Power Max line of snowthrowers. See the enclosed Adobe Acrobat Portable Document Files (.pdf) in the 'pdf' folder within the ICA18-1 folder. [NOTE: You will need the Adobe Acrobat Reader to view and print the PDF documents. To download the latest version, go to www.adobe.com/products/acrobat.]

  b. Toro Power Max Snowthrower IMC Program Handout.

  c. Toro Power Max Snowthrower IMC Program Answers Handout.

- NOTE: Transparencies can be made of the handouts instead of making copies and using the PowerPoint presentation for those instructors who prefer this option.

Preparation Before Class. Follow the steps below:

1. Read pp. 470, 472-475, 481 of Chapter 18.

2. Print, read, and if necessary, edit the ICA18-1.doc Word file.

3. Print and/or review the PowerPoint slides from the ICA18-1.ppt PowerPoint file.

4. Make copies of the:

   a. Product spec sheet for the Toro Power Max line of snowthrowers.

   b. Toro Power Max Snowthrower IMC Program Handout.

   c. Toro Power Max Snowthrower IMC Program Answers Handout.

5. OPTIONAL: Bookmark the Toro website (www.toro.com) on your classroom computer.

Instructions. Follow the steps below to conduct this ICA:

Toro Snowthrower brochure

Slide 2

1. **Show Slide 2** and pass around the Toro Snowthrower Products brochure obtained from the *Instructor's Survival Kit* box. Have students focus on pages 1-2, 6-9.

2. Give the following mini-lecture on an (IMC) program:

   "In the past, organizations designed their advertising program without consulting departments or agencies that had responsibility for sales promotion or public relations. The result was an overall communication effort that was uncoordinated and, in some cases, inconsistent. Today, organizations like Toro use an integrated marketing communications (IMC) program to coordinate all promotional activities—advertising, personal selling, sales promotion, public relations, and direct marketing—to provide a consistent message across all audiences."

3. Give the following mini-lecture about Toro and this ICA:

"Since 1914, The Toro Company has been the leader in providing innovative outdoor maintenance and beautification products for home, recreation, and commercial landscapes around the world. For consumers, Toro offers lines of lawn mowers, yard tools, sprinkler systems, and snowthrowers. This in-class activity focuses on the IMC program developed for the Power Max line of snowthrowers."

4. Form students into 4-person teams.

Toro Power Max
Spec Sheets

5. Pass out copies of the Toro Power Max Snowthrower Spec Sheets to each student.

6. Give the following mini-lecture on the 2004/2005 Toro Power Max snowthrower line:

"According to a news release in November 2004, the first Toro snowthrower was introduced 52 years ago. Today, Toro is the most widely known brand in the snowthrower category. Toro introduced a new line of 5 innovative premium snowthrowers for the winter 2004/2005 under the Power Max brand name. The Power Max line features the following innovations:

Toro Power Max
Auger System

Slide 3

Toro Power Max
Freewheel Steering
& Quick Stick
Chute Control

Slide 4

  a. **Show Slide 3**. The Power Max™ Auger System incorporates an expanded impeller housing, expanded chute base, and a non-stick surface designed to minimize snow build up. Unlike traditional two-stage designs, the revolutionary Power Max Auger System meters snow intake and returns snow that is not immediately thrown back into the auger, virtually eliminating clogging.

  b. **Show Slide 4**. Toro's innovative Freewheel Steering system, which makes turning, reversing, and steering adjustments simple and precise, eliminating the struggles to turn at the end of the driveway or having to wrestle the snowthrower into the garage.

  c. The Quick Stick™ Chute Control, which is like a joystick on a video game, to make snow clearing quick and trouble-free.

These features address key consumers needs identified by Toro consumer research. 'The goal was to make two-stage snowthrower operation easier,' said Scott Wozniak, Toro marketing manager. 'At the same time, we wanted to create a unit that would handle the heaviest snow with ease, including the stuff at the end of the driveway. Power Max snowthrowers can easily handle the toughest snow and features like Quick Stick Chute Control, Freewheel Steering, and the Power Max Auger System keep the operator in complete control of the unit.'"

Toro Power Max
Snowthrower IMC
Program Handout

7. Pass out copies of the Toro Power Max Snowthrower IMC Program Handout to each student.

Toro Power Max
Spec Sheet

Slide 5

8. **Show Slide 5**, have students look at the Toro Power Max snowthrower spec sheet handout (or p. 16 of the brochure), and continue with the following mini-lecture on the Toro Power Max snowthrower line:

"The Power Max line of two-stage snowthrowers includes five models, whose MSRPs range from $899 to $1,699. Power Max snowthrowers are available at local, independent Outdoor Power Equipment (OPE) Toro dealers. The Power Max 826 LE is available at select home improvement retailers, such as Home Depot stores."

9. Give the following mini-lecture on the importance of an IMC program for Toro's Power Max snowthrowers:

"According to Scott Wozniak, 'One unique challenge in marketing durable goods, such as Toro snowthrowers, is the infrequency between purchase cycles for these products. This is especially true with premium outdoor power equipment, where many consumers will enter the market every 7 to 10 years! Depending on the type of product being considered, the amount of time spent researching a purchase can be rather short. These two factors lead to a very small window when consumers will be receptive to the marketing message. Brand plays a vital role in the purchase process and without the weight of a national IMC program, maintaining brand awareness and preference becomes more difficult.'

A truly complete IMC program will include communications that are targeted at both wholesalers and retailers in the channel of distribution as well as those targeted at ultimate consumers. In fact, Toro has developed a major IMC effort directed at its channel members to encourage and support them in their decision to stock and sell the Toro line of Power Max snowthrowers."

Toro Power Max
Snowthrower IMC
Program Handout

Slide 6

10. **Show Slide 6**. Give the students the following instructions:

"In your teams, take 10 to 15 minutes to develop an IMC program for the Toro Power Max snowthrower using the Toro Power Max Snowthrower IMC Program Handout as a guide. As the handout shows:

  a. The target audience is American homeowners who need snow removed from driveways and walkways.

  b. The promotional objectives are to (1) generate awareness and (2) achieve sales of the Toro Power Max snowthrower.

  For each element of the IMC program, suggest a few ideas that Toro could do to accomplish its promotional objectives and explain how these actions could produce sales."

Toro Power Max
Snowthrower IMC
Answers

11. Pass out copies of the Toro Power Max Snowthrower IMC Program Answers Handout to each student.

12. Spend 5 minutes and a sample of teams share their suggestions and actions IMC program for each promotional element of the Toro Power Max snowthrower and compare those with the handout.

13. **Show Slides 7-10** and conclude this ICA with the following mini-lecture:

"Thank you for sharing your ideas for the Toro Power Max snowthrower IMC program. Toro used different mediums to reach target customers for snowthrowers. Its IMC program focused on snow belt markets with good distribution penetration. Mediums reaching a more general audience (Spot TV/radio) promoted the brand whereas more specific media (Internet/in-store point-of-sale) focused on product features, as shown in the following slides:

Toro Power Max
News Release

Slide 7

a. **Show Slide 7: News release**. Dated November 22, 2004, the news release updates the information on the 2004/2005 Toro Power Max snowthrower product line.

b. **The Toro Snowthrower Products Brochure**. A complete product brochure illustrated each series in the Toro line. Two additional pages were devoted to the key features on the new Power Max line. [NOTE: This brochure was shown earlier and passed around in class. Review Slides 3-5, if necessary.]

c. **Show Slide 8: Spot TV ad**. A 30-second ad featuring Toro's "Count On It" theme and in-use product footage. Each segment had a 5 second tag to identify local retail outlets.

d. **Show Slide 9: Radio ad**. A 60 second radio spot featuring innovative Quick Stick chute control and directing consumers to local retailers.

Toro Power Max
TV ad

Slide 8

Toro Power Max
Radio ad

Slide 9

e. **Public Relations**. Focused on 'innovative' Toro features and targeted key publications like *Popular Mechanics*, *This Old House*, *USA Today*, *Consumer Reports*, large metro newspapers (*New York Times*, *Chicago Tribune*), etc.

Toro Power Max
Internet Flash
animation

Slide 10

f. **Show Slide 10: Internet**. The Internet plays a vital role in educating consumers during the purchase process for durable goods. For the Freewheel Steering introduction, a web-animation feature was developed to highlight the key performance benefits of Toro's new Freewheel Steering system. The goal of the animation was to illustrate the superior performance of the Toro system when compared with a 'differential' drive system—commonly used on competitive products.

g. **Show Slides 11-12: In-Store Merchandising Montage**.
A complete point-of-sale/purchase (POP) merchandising kit was developed for dealers highlighting Toro's key 'innovative' features. This kit included the following elements:

Toro Power Max
POP Kit (1)

Slide 11

– The Toro Snowthrower brochure and holder (see above).

– Toro Buying Power Poster that promotes Toro's consumer finance program. Since many two-stage snowthrowers, such as the Power Max, retail at or above $999, consumer retail financing is an important element in the marketing mix.

– Hanging Two-Stage and Single Stage Mobile (3-sided ceiling signage), which tells customers about the products and financing available.

– Power Max Feature Card that is placed on the auger's shelf that highlights the Quick Stick, Auger System, and Freewheel Steering features.

– Power Max Chute Wobbler that adheres to the Power Max chute deflector and 'waves' as customers maneuver the Quick Stick.

Toro Power Max
POP Kit (2)

Slide 12

– Snow Counter Mat Insert that describes the features and Toro's Total Coverage warranty.

– A 30-minute loop videocassette that highlights the key features and benefits of Toro's entire line of snowthrowers.

– Toro Snowthrower Innovation Banner for indoors or outdoors.

– Cooperative ad for newspaper advertising.

Marketing Lesson. An effective IMC program needs to target both retailers and consumers. This becomes especially true when a relatively expensive new consumer product like the Toro Power Max snowthrower is involved.

Website. To view the line of Toro Power Max snowthrowers, go to http://www.toro.com/home/snowthrowers/gastwostage_powermax/index.html.

TORO® POWER MAX™ SNOWTHROWER
IMC PROGRAM HANDOUT

- Target audience—American homeowners where snow removal is required.

- Promotional objectives—(1) create awareness and (2) achieve sales.

ELEMENT OF THE IMC	IMC ACTION	HOW THE ACTION PRODUCES SALES
Advertising		
Personal Selling		
Public Relations		
Sales Promotions		
Direct Marketing		

TORO® POWER MAX™ SNOWTHROWER
IMC PROGRAM ANSWERS HANDOUT

- Target audience—American homeowners where snow removal is required.

- Promotional objectives—(1) create awareness and (2) achieve sales.

ELEMENT OF THE IMC	IMC ACTION	HOW THE ACTION PRODUCES SALES
Advertising	• Advertise innovative Power Max on national and cable (HGTV) TV. • Develop co-operative advertising program with Home Depot (a major Toro retailer), local hardware or lawn & garden stores to run ads on local TV, radio, newspapers, etc.	• Generates consumer awareness about the Power Max and possibly visits to retail outlets or Toro's website. • Long-term: generate actual sales at retail outlets identified in the co-operative ads.
Personal Selling	• Conduct training seminars for retail salespeople. • Have sales brochures and training videotapes available for salespeople.	• Provides retail salespeople with detailed information to answer consumer questions about the Power Max and actually complete a sale.
Public Relations	• Issue press releases and product announcements to gain coverage in magazines, newspapers, and TV news.	• Generates awareness through reading newspapers or magazine articles or watching TV news coverage.
Sales Promotions	• Have attention-getting point-of-purchase displays in Home Depot stores and other Toro dealers.	• Generates consumer awareness for the Power Max in retail outlets where attentive salespeople might actually make a sale.
Direct Marketing	• Put excitement into description of Power Max's capabilities on Toro's website with "Power Max virtual tour." • Let consumers be able to order a Power Max on Toro's website. • Send customers of other Toro products (sprinkler/irrigation) a direct mail piece with coupon.	• Gains awareness and interest among consumers with the Power Max virtual tour. • Generates sales from already loyal Toro customers.

CHAPTER 18: INTEGRATED MARKETING COMMUNICATIONS AND DIRECT MARKETING

ICA 18-2: IN-CLASS ACTIVITY

An IMC for the Hermitage Museum

Learning Objectives. To have students (1) suggest elements of an integrated marketing communications (IMC) program and (2) describe how these elements can generate revenues for a specialized service—Russia's Hermitage Museum, a world-class art museum.

Definitions. The following marketing terms are referred to in this in-class activity (ICA):

- Advertising: Any paid form of nonpersonal communication about an organization, good, service, or idea by an identified sponsor.

- Direct Marketing: A promotion alternative that uses direct communication with consumers to generate a response in the form of an order, a request for further information, or a visit to a retail outlet.

- Integrated Marketing Communications (IMC): The concept of designing marketing communications programs that coordinates all promotional activities—advertising, personal selling, sales promotion, public relations, and direct marketing—to provide a consistent message across all audiences.

- Personal Selling: The two-way flow of communication between a buyer and seller, designed to influence a person's or group's purchase decision, usually in face-to-face communication between the sender and receiver.

- Public Relations: A form of communication management that seeks to influence the feelings, opinions, or beliefs held by customers, prospective customers, stockholders, suppliers, employees, and other publics about a company and its products or services.

- Sales Promotion: A short-term inducement of value offered to arouse interest in buying a good or service.

Nature of the Activity. To have students work in teams to identify integrated marketing communications (IMC) actions the Hermitage Museum might take to reach an American target audience (i.e. market). This ICA shows the wide applicability of marketing concepts because it involves marketing a non-profit service across international boundaries.

Estimated Class Time. 20 minutes.

Materials Needed.

- The ICA18-2.doc Word and ICA18-2.ppt PowerPoint files contained in the ICA18-2 folder of the Instructor's CD #2 from the *Instructor's Survival Kit* box.

- Copies of the:

    a. Web Link: Marketing the Hermitage, a World-Class Art Museum—with a Virtual Tour Handout from p. 23 of *Marketing, 8th Edition.* See the enclosed Adobe Acrobat Portable Document Files (.pdf) in the 'pdf' folder within the ICA18-2 folder. [NOTE: You will need the Adobe Acrobat Reader to view and print the PDF documents. To download the latest version, go to www.adobe.com/products/acrobat.]

    b. An IMC Analysis For The Hermitage Museum Handout.

    c. An IMC Analysis For The Hermitage Museum Answers Handout.

- NOTE: Transparencies can be made of the handouts instead of making copies and using the PowerPoint presentation for those instructors who prefer this option.

Preparation Before Class. Follow the steps below:

1. Read the Hermitage Museum Web Link on p. 24 of Chapter 1 and pp. 470, 472-475, 481 of Chapter 18.

2. Print, read, and if necessary, edit the ICA18-2.doc Word file.

3. Print and/or review the PowerPoint slides from the ICA18-2.ppt PowerPoint file.

4. Make copies of the:

    a. Web Link: Marketing the Hermitage, a World-Class Art Museum—with a Virtual Tour Handout.

    b. An IMC Analysis For The Hermitage Museum Handout.

    c. An IMC Analysis For The Hermitage Museum Answers Handout.

5. Familiarize yourself with the Hermitage Museum website, which is www.hermitagemuseum.org and explore the "Virtual Visit" or the "Virtual Viewings" areas.

6. Review possible answers contained in the An IMC Analysis For The Hermitage Museum Answers Handout.

7. OPTIONAL: Bookmark the Hermitage Museum website (www.hermitagemuseum.org) on your classroom computer.

Instructions. Follow the steps below to conduct this ICA:

Hermitage Museum
Web Link Handout

Slide 2

1. **Show Slide 2** and pass around the Web Link: Marketing the Hermitage, a World-Class Art Museum—with a Virtual Tour Handout.

2. Give the following mini-lecture on an (IMC) program:

   "Today, both for profit and nonprofit, global organizations like The State Hermitage Museum in St. Petersburg, Russia use an integrated marketing communications (IMC) program to coordinate all promotional activities—advertising, personal selling, sales promotion, public relations, and direct marketing—to provide a consistent message across local, regional, and global audiences."

3. Form students into 4-person teams.

Hermitage Museum
Virtual Tour

Slide 3

4. **Spend 1 minute** and have students read the Web Link: Marketing the Hermitage, a World-Class Art Museum—with a Virtual Tour Handout to familiarize themselves with this prestigious institution.

5. **Show Slide 3** and take students on a brief "Virtual Tour" of the Hermitage Museum by going to the Hermitage website, which is www.hermitagemuseum.org.

Hermitage Museum
IMC Handout

Slide 4

6. **Show Slide 4**: An IMC Analysis For The Hermitage Museum Handout. Explain that the top of the handout identifies the:

   a. Target audience or market—Americans with interests in art who may be tourists in Russia or those who never leave the U.S.

   b. Long-term promotional objective—generate revenues for the Hermitage Museum located in St. Petersburg, Russia.

7. Inform students of the difficulty of developing an effective IMC. Point out that some IMC elements don't conveniently fall into a single category. This is the reason the bottom row, "Partnerships with U.S. Art Museums," is filled out on An IMC Analysis For The Hermitage Museum Handout to help students with their IMC plan.

8. **Spend 10 minutes** and have student teams complete the An IMC Analysis For The Hermitage Museum Handout.

9. Have a representative from 3 or 4 student teams share their ideas regarding an IMC analysis of the Hermitage Museum targeted at American consumers.

Marketing Lesson. Developing an effective IMC program requires creativity and attention to detail. This becomes especially true when services offered by institutions like the Hermitage Museum are marketed internationally.

Website. To view the Hermitage Museum website, go to www.hermitagemuseum.org.

AN IMC ANALYSIS FOR THE HERMITAGE MUSEUM HANDOUT

- Target audience or market—Americans with interests in art who may be tourists in Russia or those who never leave the U.S.

- Long-term promotional objective—generate revenues for the Hermitage Museum located in St. Petersburg, Russia.

ELEMENT OF THE IMC	IMC ACTION	HOW THE ACTION PRODUCES SALES
Advertising		
Personal Selling		
Public Relations		
Sales Promotions		
Direct Marketing		
Partnerships with U.S. Art Museums	• Partner with the Guggenheim Museum of NYC to open a "Jewel Box" museum in Las Vegas.	• Short-term: Sales of tickets to U.S.-partnered shows, posters, etc. • Long-term: Encourage Americans to visit the Hermitage in St. Petersburg.

ICA 18-2

AN IMC ANALYSIS FOR THE HERMITAGE MUSEUM
ANSWERS HANDOUT

- Target audience or market—Americans with interests in art who may be tourists in Russia or those who never leave the U.S.

- Long-term promotional objective—generate revenues for the Hermitage Museum located in St. Petersburg, Russia.

ELEMENT OF THE IMC	IMC ACTION	HOW THE ACTION PRODUCES SALES
Advertising	• Advertise in U.S and St. Petersburg Museums.	• Generates ticket sales in the U.S. and among American tourists in St. Petersburg.
Personal Selling	• Have St. Petersburg art experts give guest lectures around the U.S.	• Generates short-term awareness that may lead to longer-term sales.
Public Relations	• Place feature articles in U.S. newspapers. • Arrange for TV interviews with Hermitage art experts.	• Generates awareness through reading newspapers or magazine articles or watching TV news coverage.
Sales Promotions	• Use coupons or price discounts as part of St. Petersburg tour activities. • Develop a contest for a trip to the Museum.	• Generates visits of Americans on a package tour to visit the Hermitage Museum. • Generates interest in a trip to the Hermitage Museum.
Direct Marketing	• Develop online "virtual tour" of the Hermitage Museum.	• Short-term: Could result in sales of posters and art books. • Long-term: Encourage visits by Americans to the Hermitage in St. Petersburg.
Partnerships with U.S. Art Museums	• Partner with the Guggenheim Museum of NYC to open a "Jewel Box" museum in Las Vegas.	• Short-term: Sales of tickets to U.S.-partnered shows, posters, etc. • Long-term: Encourage Americans to visit the Hermitage in St. Petersburg.

CHAPTER 19: ADVERTISING, SALES PROMOTION, AND PUBLIC RELATIONS

ICA 19-1: IN-CLASS ACTIVITY

Harris Ad Track: Measuring the Likeability and Effectiveness of TV Ads[1]

Learning Objective. To have students evaluate the likeability and effectiveness of selected TV ads.

Definitions. The following marketing terms are referred to in this in-class activity (ICA):

- Advertising: Any paid form of nonpersonal communication about an organization, good, service, or idea by an identified sponsor.

- Probability Sampling: Using precise rules to select the sample such that each element of the population has a specific known chance of being selected.

Nature of the Activity. To have students use the Harris Interactive/*USA Today* Ad Track Survey method to indicate whether they like or dislike a TV ad, assess the ad's effectiveness, and state the reasons for their responses.

Estimated Class Time. 15 minutes.

Materials Needed.

- The ICA19-1.doc Word, ICA19-1.ppt PowerPoint, and ICA19-1 Excel spreadsheet files contained in the ICA19-1 folder of the Instructor's CD #2 from the *Instructor's Survival Kit* box.

Preparation Before Class. Follow the steps below:

1. Read p. 482 of Chapter 18 and pp. 497-499 of Chapter 19.

2. Print, read, and if necessary, edit the ICA19-1.doc Word file.

3. Print and/or review the PowerPoint slides from the ICA19-1.ppt PowerPoint file.

4. Print and/or review the Excel spreadsheet from the ICA19-1.xls Excel file.

5. OPTIONAL: Bookmark the Harris Interactive/*USA Today* Ad Track website (www.usatoday.com) on your classroom computer.

---

[1] The authors wish to thank David Krane of Harris Interactive who assisted in the development of this ICA.

Instructions. Follow the steps below to conduct this ICA:

1. Give the following mini-lecture about the Harris Interactive/*USA Today* Ad Track Survey:

   "Since February 2000, Harris Interactive and USA Today have teamed up to provide readers of the national daily newspaper the results of a weekly survey regarding the likeability and effectiveness of a recent TV ad. The results of this collaboration, the Ad Track Survey, is published almost every Monday in the Advertising and Marketing area of the *USA Today's* Money section. Each article contains the following:

   • The identity of the TV ad reviewed by consumers.

   • An environmental scan regarding the product and product class.

   • The results, in graphical format, of the Ad Track Survey, along with the sample size, dates of the survey, and margin of error.

   The findings from the Harris Interactive/*USA Today* Ad Track surveys are based on a nationally representative sample of 2,000 adults, 18 or over. The specific questions are asked of all those who say they have seen the ad ("a lot" or "a few times"). Typically, Harris Interactive surveys between 500 – 1,000 people for each ad. The interviews are conducted online via the Internet. However, this survey is NOT a probability sample. Figures for age, sex, race, education, region, and household income are weighted where necessary to bring them into line with their actual proportions in the population according to the U.S. Census Bureau's latest figures.

   The *USA Today* editorial staff selects the campaigns. Respondents are presented with a written description of the TV ad, which consists of three or four sentences that describe the main feature of the commercial. Each respondent is then asked three questions that measure **awareness** of the ad, **likeability** of the ad, and whether the ad is **perceived as being effective** at selling the particular product or service. Results from previous Ad Track surveys can be found on *USA Today's* website (see www.usatoday.com/money/advertising/adtrack/index.htm)."

2. Open the PowerPoint presentation and Excel spreadsheet for ICA 19-1.

3. Designate two students to be "counters." One student will count the responses from male students and the other will count those from female students. The reasons for doing this are to: (1) replicate the Harris Interactive/*USA Today* Ad Track survey method and (2) determine if there are any differences between the two groups.

4. Give the following mini-lecture:

   "We will now take part in a simulated Harris Interactive/*USA Today* Ad Track Survey. You will be shown three TV commercials. For each ad, you will indicate your responses to a set of questions that I will ask about the ad by raising your hands. You will also be given the opportunity to state the reasons for your responses. Keep your hands raised until your responses have been tallied. I will then input them in an Excel spreadsheet so that we can graphically see how you evaluated the ads and if there are any differences between the men and women in the class."

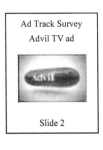

Ad Track Survey
Advil TV ad

Slide 2

5. **Show Slide 2: Advil Liqui-Gels "Speeding Pill" TV ad** [TRT 0:15]. After showing this ad, ask students the following questions and have the designated students write down the counts for males and females:

- Question 1: Have you every seen this TV ad? Your response is either 'Yes' or 'No.'

  Answer: This question ascertains "awareness," one of the advertising objectives from the hierarchy of effects referred to in Chapter 18. Comment on the relative awareness of the ad.

- Question 2: What type of product advertisement is this?

  Answer: This ad is a comparative product advertisement since it compares Advil with Extra Strength Tylenol.

- Question 3: How much would you say you like this ad? [Read the response options below. Have the student "counters" write down the number of responses for men and women in the classroom.]

  a. **Like it a lot.**
  b. **Like it somewhat.**
  c. **Neither like nor dislike.**
  d. **Dislike it.**

  Answer: This question ascertains the "likeability" of the ad.

- Question 4: How effective do you think this ad is in helping the advertiser sell this product? [Read the response options below. Have the student "counters" write down the number of responses for men and women in the classroom.]

  a. **Not at all effective.**
  b. **Not very effective.**
  c. **Somewhat effective.**
  d. **Very effective.**

  Answer: This question ascertains the "effectiveness" of the ad.

Ad Track: Advil

Excel Spreadsheet
ICA19-1.xls

6. **Open the Excel spreadsheet** and perform the following tasks:

- Go to the "AdTrackData" tab of the Excel spreadsheet.
- Type in the responses for "Males [N]" and "Females [N]" in the appropriate cells for the question, "How much do you like this ad?"
- Type in the responses for "Males [N]" and "Females [N]" in the appropriate cells for the question, "How effective do you think this ad is in helping the advertiser sell this product?"

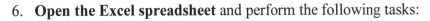

ICA 19-1

- To see the depiction of the results of the Ad Track Survey for the Advil Liqui-Gels "Speeding Pill" TV ad that is similar to the graphs published in *USA Today*, click on the following tabs of the Excel spreadsheet and comment on the results:

    a. **LikeAdChart**. Compares the responses of those students who "Liked the ad a lot" to an Ad Track Survey average of respondents for all ads.

    b. **LikeAdChartMF**. Compares the responses between men and women in the class who "Liked the ad a lot."

    c. **DislikeAdChart**. Compares the responses of those students who "Disliked the ad" to an Ad Track Survey average of respondents for all ads.

    d. **DislikeAdChartMF**. Compares the responses between men and women in the class who "Disliked the ad."

    e. **EffectiveAdChart**. Compares the responses of those students who thought the ad was "Very effective" to an Ad Track Survey average of respondents for all ads.

    f. **EffectiveAdChartMF**. Compares the responses between men and women in the class who thought the ad was "Very effective."

7. **Spend 2 minutes** and ask the students in the class why they liked or disliked the ad and whether the ad was effective in selling the product.

Ad Track Survey
Toro TV ad

Slide 3

8. **Show Slide 3: Toro "Weatherman" TV ad** [TRT 0:30]. After showing this ad, ask students the following questions and have the designated students write down the counts for males and females:

- Question 1: Have you every seen this TV ad? Your response is either 'Yes' or 'No.'

    Answer: This question ascertains "awareness."

- Question 2: What type of product advertisement is this?

    Answer: This ad is a pioneering product advertisement since it tells what the Toro PowerMax snowthrower can do.

- Question 3: How much would you say you like this ad? [Read the response options below. Have the student "counters" write down the number of responses for men and women in the classroom.]

    a. **Like it a lot.**
    b. **Like it somewhat.**
    c. **Neither like nor dislike.**
    d. **Dislike it.**

    Answer: This question ascertains the "likeability" of the ad.

- Question 4: How effective do you think this ad is in helping the advertiser sell this product? [Read the response options below. Have the student "counters" write down the number of responses for men and women in the classroom.]

  a. **Not at all effective.**
  b. **Not very effective.**
  c. **Somewhat effective.**
  d. **Very effective.**

  Answer: This question ascertains the "effectiveness" of the ad.

9. **Open the Excel spreadsheet** and perform the following tasks:

   - Go to the "AdTrackData" tab of the Excel spreadsheet.

   - Type in the responses for "Males [N]" and "Females [N]" in the appropriate cells for the question, "How much do you like this ad?"

   - Type in the responses for "Males [N]" and "Females [N]" in the appropriate cells for the question, "How effective do you think this ad is in helping the advertiser sell this product?"

   - To see the depiction of the results of the Ad Track Survey for the Toro "Weatherman" TV ad that is similar to the graphs published in *USA Today*, click on the following tabs of the Excel spreadsheet:

     a. **LikeAdChart.** Compares the responses of those students who "Liked the ad a lot" to an Ad Track Survey average of respondents for all ads.
     b. **LikeAdChartMF.** Compares the responses between men and women in the class who "Liked the ad a lot."
     c. **DislikeAdChart.** Compares the responses of those students who "Disliked the ad" to an Ad Track Survey average of respondents for all ads.
     d. **DislikeAdChartMF.** Compares the responses between men and women in the class who "Disliked the ad."
     e. **EffectiveAdChart.** Compares the responses of those students who thought the ad was "Very effective" to an Ad Track Survey average of respondents for all ads.
     f. **EffectiveAdChartMF.** Compares the responses between men and women in the class who thought the ad was "Very effective."

10. **Spend 2 minutes** and ask the students in the class why they liked or disliked the ad and whether the ad was effective in selling the product.

Ad Track: Toro

Excel Spreadsheet
ICA19-1.xls

Ad Track Survey
Panasonic TV ad

Slide 4

11. **Show Slide 4: Panasonic "DVR" TV ad** [TRT 0:30]. After showing this ad, ask students the following questions and have the designated students write down the counts for males and females:

- Question 1: Have you every seen this TV ad? Your response is either 'Yes' or 'No.'

  Answer: This question ascertains "awareness."

- Question 2: What type of product advertisement is this?

  Answer: This ad is a pioneering product advertisement since it focuses on what the product is and can do.

- Question 3: How much would you say you like this ad? [Read the response options below. Have the student "counters" write down the number of responses for men and women in the classroom.]

  a. **Like it a lot**.
  b. **Like it somewhat**.
  c. **Neither like nor dislike**.
  d. **Dislike it**.

  Answer: This question ascertains the "likeability" of the ad.

- Question 4: How effective do you think this ad is in helping the advertiser sell this product? [Read the response options below. Have the student "counters" write down the number of responses for men and women in the classroom.]

  a. **Not at all effective**.
  b. **Not very effective**.
  c. **Somewhat effective**.
  d. **Very effective**.

  Answer: This question ascertains the "effectiveness" of the ad.

Ad Track:
Panasonic

Excel Spreadsheet
ICA19-1.xls

12. **Open the Excel spreadsheet** and perform the following tasks:

- Go to the "AdTrackData" tab of the Excel spreadsheet.

- Type in the responses for "Males [N]" and "Females [N]" in the appropriate cells for the question, "How much do you like this ad?"

- Type in the responses for "Males [N]" and "Females [N]" in the appropriate cells for the question, "How effective do you think this ad is in helping the advertiser sell this product?"

- To see the graphical depiction of the results of the Ad Track Survey for the Panasonic "DVR" TV ad that is similar to the graphs published in *USA Today*, click on the following tabs of the Excel spreadsheet:

a. **LikeAdChart**. Compares the responses of those students who "Liked the ad a lot" to an Ad Track Survey average of respondents for all ads.

b. **LikeAdChartMF**. Compares the responses between men and women in the class who "Liked the ad a lot."

c. **DislikeAdChart**. Compares the responses of those students who "Disliked the ad" to an Ad Track Survey average of respondents for all ads.

d. **DislikeAdChartMF**. Compares the responses between men and women in the class who "Disliked the ad."

e. **EffectiveAdChart**. Compares the responses of those students who thought the ad was "Very effective" to an Ad Track Survey average of respondents for all ads.

f. **EffectiveAdChartMF**. Compares the responses between men and women in the class who thought the ad was "Very effective."

13. **Spend 2 minutes** and ask the students in the class why they liked or disliked the ad and whether the ad was effective in selling the product.

Marketing Lessons. Consumers evaluate advertisements all the time, either formally, through surveys like the Harris Interactive/*USA Today* Ad Track survey or Starch Tests, or informally when watching TV. Given the growing popularity of digital video recorders (like the one shown in the Panasonic ad) and the ability of consumers to "skip" over the ads with these devices, advertisers and their agencies must design ads that: (1) accomplish one or more of the hierarchy of effects that translate into advertising objectives (awareness, interest, evaluation, trial, and adoption) and (2) are likable. These two criteria, among others, determine whether an ad is effective. This is why the message content and creativity are so important.

Websites. The Harris Interactive/USA Today Ad Track index of previous surveys is www.usatoday.com/money/advertising/adtrack/index.htm. To view the most current Ad Track survey, go to www.usatoday.com and type "ad track" in the search field. To find out more about Harris Interactive and the Harris Poll, go to www.harrisinteractive.com/about.

CHAPTER 19: ADVERTISING, SALES PROMOTION, AND PUBLIC RELATIONS

ICA 19-2: IN-CLASS ACTIVITY

What Makes a Memorable TV Commercial?[1]

Learning Objective. To have students identify the factors that makes a memorable television commercial.

Definitions. The following marketing terms are referred to in this in-class activity (ICA):

- Advertising: Any paid form of nonpersonal communication about an organization, good, service, or idea by an identified sponsor.

- Commercial: An advertisement broadcast on radio or television.

Nature of the Activity. To have students (1) observe three TV ads in class, (2) classify the type of each TV ad, (3) identify the appeal used, and (4) discuss why the ad was memorable.

Estimated Class Time. 15 minutes.

Materials Needed.

- The ICA19-2.doc Word and ICA19-2.ppt PowerPoint files contained in the ICA19-2 folder of the Instructor's CD #2 from the *Instructor's Survival Kit* box.

Preparation Before Class. Follow the steps below:

1. Read pp. 500-503 of Chapter 19 on designing an advertisement.

2. Print, read, and if necessary, edit the ICA19-2.doc Word file.

3. Print and/or review the slides from the ICA19-2.ppt PowerPoint file.

4. OPTIONAL: Bookmark the Fallon Worldwide (www.fallon.com), Pepsi (www.pepsi.com) and Apple Computer (www.apple.com) websites on your classroom computer.

---

[1] The authors wish to thank Kim Eskro of Fallon Worldwide, Lisa Castaldo of Pepsi, Bob Robinson of Apple Computer, and Robin Grayson of TBWA/Chiat/Day who assisted in the development of this ICA.

Instructions. Follow the steps below to conduct this ICA:

1. Give students this background mini-lecture on the designing good advertising:

   "Designing an advertisement, particularly a television commercial, is both a creative and difficult process. The message conveyed must focus on the key benefits the target audience values while the appeal must generate sufficient interest the target audience will try and then adopt the product or service. Some organizations and their advertising agencies are known for creating effective advertisements. In the next few minutes, you will see three award winning TV ads. While you watch them, ask yourself, 'What makes an ad effective?' and 'Why is this particular ad effective?'"

2. Give students this background mini-lecture on Fallon Worldwide:

   "The Clio Awards hosts the world's largest and most famous advertising awards competition in the international advertising. At a recent Clio Festival, Fallon Worldwide won two Grand Clio Awards, the highest award given, for its BMW *"The Hire"* campaign. Fallon has won several other prestigious advertising awards since it was founded in 1981. Examples of its award-winning ads include Rolling Stone's "Perception/Reality" campaign, MTV's "Jukka Brothers," and the EDS "Cat Herders" TV spot. One of its early TV spots that won acclaim was its "Gold'n Plump Chicken" ad that aired in the early-1980s." This and other ads helped foster the creative reputation that Fallon Worldwide enjoys today.

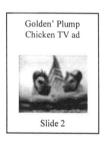

Golden' Plump
Chicken TV ad

Slide 2

3. **Show Slide 2**: "Gold'n Plump Chicken" TV ad. [TRT = 0:30] Have students respond to the following questions:

   - Question 1: Is the "Gold'n Plump Chicken" TV commercial a pioneering (or informational), competitive (or comparative), reminder (or reinforcement), or an advocacy ad?

     Answer: This ad is a competitive ad since it promotes this brand as better than those from "the south."

   - Question 2: What kind of appeal does this ad use?

     Answer: This ad uses a humorous appeal to convey its message to the target audience.

   - Question 3: Why do you think this ad was memorable and worthy of an award?

     Answers: This ad creatively uses humor to motivate target consumers to purchase the Gold'n Plump Chicken brand, which it successfully did.

4. Give students this background mini-lecture on Pepsi:

   "Pepsi Cola has produced several award winning TV ads over the years in its battle with Coca-Cola (as has Coca-Cola) for the hearts and minds of soft drink consumers worldwide. A few of these TV spots are either in the Clio Hall of Fame or cited as one of the best ads ever.

In 1999, *TV Guide* polled advertising agencies to rank the "Fifty Greatest TV Commercials of All Time." The following ad "Pepsi's" Security Camera" TV spot was ranked #21 by those polled by *TV Guide* in its "Fifty Greatest TV Commercials of All Time." Pepsi advertising has won other awards as well."

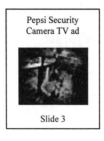

Pepsi Security Camera TV ad

Slide 3

5. **Show Slide 3**: "Pepsi Security Camera" TV ad. [TRT = 0:30] Have students respond to the following questions:

- Question 1: Is the Pepsi "Security Camera" TV commercial a pioneering (or informational), competitive (or comparative), reminder (or reinforcement), or an advocacy ad?

  Answer: This ad is a competitive (comparative) ad because it creatively demonstrates the Coke delivery guy's preference of Pepsi over Coke—his employer!

- Question 2: What kind of appeal does this ad use?

  Answer: This ad uses a humorous appeal (to the tune of "Your Cheatin' Heart") to convey its message to the target audience that Pepsi is better than Coke and that Coke drinkers may feel guilty in trying or switching to Pepsi.

- Question 3: Why do you think this ad was memorable and worthy of an award?

  Answers: This ad creatively uses humor and music **without any dialog** (except the lyrics of the song) to encourage Coke drinkers to boldly, not timidly switch to Pepsi.

6. Give students this background mini-lecture on Apple Computer:

""The last TV spot we're going to view has been voted the best TV commercial ever created by advertising agencies, advertisers, and of course *TV Guide*. It also is a prestigious member in the Clio Hall of Fame because this TV ad changed how advertisers think about the ways ads are created. It set a new standard for cinematic style. Famous Hollywood movie director Ridley Scott (director of such other well-known films, such as *Alien*, *Thelma & Louise*, and Oscar®-winner *Gladiator* and executive producer of Clio Award winner of BMW Films' *Hostage*) directed the TV commercial.

This TV spot cost over $400,000 to make (a huge amount back then) and cost an additional $500,000 to air. The ad aired only once—during Super Bowl XVIII in 1984. However, because of its success, it started the Super Bowl ad extravaganza we see today, when a 30-second TV spot can cost $2.5 million! Finally, the ad was not only a creative success, but also a commercial one as well. After the ad ran, it generated sales of over 500,000 units of the product during the next year. Here now is the best TV commercial ever made:

7. **Show Slide 4**: Apple Computer's "1984" TV ad. [TRT = 1:00] Have students respond to the following questions:

- Question 1: Is the Apple "1984" commercial a pioneering (or informational), competitive (or comparative), reminder (or reinforcement), or an advocacy ad?

  Answer: This ad is a competitive ad because it creatively distinguishes between IBM PC users and the new Macintosh users. In addition, this ad is a pioneering ad since it introduces the Apple Macintosh PC.

- Question 2: What kind of appeal does this ad use?

  Answer: This ad uses a fear appeal. The woman, who is the only character in color, is running away from the police and throws a sledgehammer against the screen to convey to the target audience that she can avoid the negative experience of being a part of the IBM PC culture.

- Question 3: Why do you think this ad was memorable and worthy of an award?

  Answers: This ad was hugely successful on a number of levels because it: (1) sold over 500,000 Macintosh PCs in the first year; (2) established the Super Bowl advertising craze we see today; (3) brought Hollywood production and cinematic flair to a 60-second TV spot; and (4) created brand name recognition for small PC manufacturer at the time.

Marketing Lessons. Over 20,000 TV commercials are created and aired in the U.S. each year. Marketers and advertisers struggle with the problem of creating memorable messages that (1) promotes the idea, product, or service being featured without getting in the way of the message, (2) satisfies the objectives developed for the ad campaign, and (3) falls within a budget that the sponsor can afford.

Websites. To view a list of *Advertising Age's* top 100 campaigns, go to www.adage.com/century/campaigns.html. Unfortunately, the link to *TV Guide's* list of the "Fifty Greatest TV Commercials of All Time" does not now exist. To view current and past Clio award winners and a list of ads that are in its Hall of Fame, go to www.clioawards.com.

CHAPTER 19: ADVERTISING, SALES PROMOTION, AND PUBLIC RELATIONS

ICA 19-3: IN-CLASS ACTIVITY

Recognizing Advertising Slogans

Learning Objective. To have students realize the difficulty advertisers face when trying to help consumers remember their company or brands.

Definitions. The following marketing terms are referred to in this in-class activity (ICA):

- Message: The information sent by a source to a receiver in the communication process.

- Slogan: The verbal or written portion of an advertising message that summarizes the main idea in a few memorable words." From the *Dictionary of Marketing Terms*, 2nd edition, Peter Bennett, Ed. (Lincolnwood: NTC Publishing Group, 1995), p. 264.

Nature of the Activity. To have students identify the company or product associated with an advertising slogan.

Estimated Class Time. 10 minutes.

Materials Needed.

- The ICA19-3.doc Word and ICA19-3.ppt PowerPoint files contained in the ICA19-3 folder of the Instructor's CD #2 from the *Instructor's Survival Kit* box.

- Copies of the Match Each Slogan to the Company or Product Handout.

- NOTE: Transparencies can be made of the handouts instead of making copies and using the PowerPoint presentation for those instructors who prefer this option.

Preparation Before Class. Follow the steps below:

1. Read pp. 500-503 of Chapter 19.

2. Print, read, and if necessary, edit the ICA19-3.doc Word file.

3. Print and/or review the slides from the ICA19-3.ppt PowerPoint file.

4. Make copies of the Match Each Slogan to the Company or Product Handout.

5. OPTIONAL: Bookmark the AdSlogans.com (www.adslogans.com/hof) and SloganSurvey.com (www.slogansurvey.com) websites on your classroom computer.

Instructions. Follow the steps below to conduct this ICA:

1. Give students this background mini-lecture on advertising slogans:

   "Organizations invest billions of dollars in advertising to get you to notice and hopefully buy their products or services. In many instances, the message they create must be reduced to a memorable word or phrase that encapsulates the benefits of brand. These are called 'slogans' or 'taglines,' and are what marketers want you to remember about their brand when you make a purchase decision.

   Marketers have used slogans since the late 1880's when Proctor and Gamble (P&G) used '99 and 44/100% Pure' tagline for its Ivory Soap. Today, many organizations use slogans, but only a few are memorable. According to a 2004 survey conducted by brand strategy firm Emergence, only 5 percent of respondents recognized fewer than half of the slogans tested from 25 of America's most well-known companies. And six of the taglines tested in 2003 have already been replaced."[1]

   What should marketers consider when (or if) to use a slogan?

   - Do not advertise your aspirations (McDonald's 'We Love to See You Smile' or Ford's 'Quality is Job One' because some consumers will try to prove the firm wrong.

   - Give the slogan time to develop. Don't change slogans every year. Give the marketplace time to receive it.

   - Do not use a slogan at all. Instead, focus resources in building a better brand.[2]

2. OPTIONAL: To see some TV commercials and print ads that feature famous slogans, go to www.adslogans.com/hof. The firm has created The Advertising Slogan Hall Of Fame, in which a panel of marketing and advertising executives selects and inducts those slogans that have helped build the brand over time. It also maintains an alphabetical list of slogans. [NOTE: To view the TV ads, you must have Quick Time or Windows Media Player. The ads will be 'streamed' to your computer, which can take time, depending on the speed of your Internet connection.]

Matching Slogans Handout

Slide 2

3. Pass out copies of the Match Each Slogan to the Company or Product Handout to each student.

4. **Show Slide 2**: Match Each Slogan to the Company or Product Handout.

5. **Spend 5 minutes** and have students identify the company or product for each slogan. The answers are:

---

[1] "Advertising A.D.D.: Majority of Taglines Go Unnoticed," 2004 Emergence Slogan Survey. Press release dated October 15, 2004. See http://www.slogansurvey.com/2004surveyreleasefinal.pdf.
[2] Steve McKee, "What's in a Phrase?" *BusinessWeek*, January 14, 2005. See www.businessweek.com.

Company/Product:	Advertising Slogan:	Answer:
1. Target	"Expect More. Pay Less."	I
2. Sprite	"Obey Your Thirst"	T
3. Taco Bell	"Think Outside the Bun"	L
4. Volkswagen	"Drivers Wanted"	F
5. New York Times	"All the News That Fit to Print"	N
6. Sears	"Good Life. Great Price."	Q
7. GE	"Imagination at Work"	A
8. Capital One	"What's in Your Wallet?"	W
9. McDonald's	"I'm Lovin' It"	O
10. Gatorade	"Is it in You?"	K
11. VISA	"It's Everywhere You Want to Be"	S
12. Xerox	"The Document Company"	B
13. DuPont	"The Miracles of Science"	C
14. Allstate Insurance	"You're in Good Hands"	Z
15. Nissan	"Shift"	D
16. Pizza Hut	"Gather 'Round the Good Stuff"	H
17. Panasonic	"Ideas for Life"	G
18. Energizer Batteries	"The Power to Keep You Going, and Going…"	J
19. Ford Motor Co.	"Built for the Road Ahead"	M
20. Microsoft	"Start Something"	Y
21. Wendy's	"It's Better Here"	R
22. Kodak	"Share Moments. Share Life."	E
23. Toyota	"Get the Feeling"	X
24. Coca Cola	"Make it Real"	P
25. Wal-Mart	"Always Low Prices. Always."	U
26. BMW	"The Ultimate Driving Machine"	V

6. Share the following "classic" slogans for students to identify the company or product:

Advertising Slogan:	Company/Product:
A. "The Quicker, Picker Upper"	Bounty
B. "It's the Real Thing"	Coca Cola
C. "Please Don't Squeeze the…"	Charmin Toilet Tissue
D. "Does She or Doesn't She"	Clairol Hair Coloring
E. "Finger-Lickin' Good"	KFC
F. "Good to the Last Drop"	Maxwell House Coffee
G. "Takes a Lickin' and Keeps on Tickin'"	Timex Watches
H. "Just Do It"	Nike
I. "Nobody Doesn't Like…"	Sara Lee
J. "Fly the Friendly Skies"	United Airlines
K. "Breakfast of Champions"	Wheaties
L. "Let Your Fingers Do the Walking"	Yellow Pages
M. "Melts in Your Mouth, Not in Your Hand"	M&M's
N. "M'm M'm Good"	Campbell's Soup
O. "Where's the Beef?"	Wendy's
P. "A Mind is a Terrible Thing to Waste"	United Negro College Fund
Q. "Betcha Can't Eat Just One"	Lay's Potato Chips

Advertising Slogan:	Company/Product:
R. "A Little Dab'll Do Ya"	Brylcreem
S. "Be All That You Can Be"	U. S. Army
T. "Don't Leave Home Without It"	American Express
U. "Because I'm Worth It"	L'Oréal
V. "Ring Around the Collar"	Wisk
W. "The Uncola"	7-Up
X. "When It Rains, It Pours"	Morton Salt
Y. "Capitalist Tool"	Forbes
Z. "You Deserve a Break Today"	McDonald's

Marketing Lesson. One of the challenges of a successful advertising campaign is to break through the clutter with a slogan or ad that is remembered favorably by consumers.

Website. See *Advertising Age's* top 10 slogans at www.adage.com/century/slogans.html.

MATCH EACH SLOGAN TO THE COMPANY OR PRODUCT HANDOUT

SLOGAN		COMPANY/PRODUCT
1. "Expect More. Pay Less."	_____	A. GE
2. "Obey Your Thirst"	_____	B. Xerox
3. "Think Outside the Bun"	_____	C. DuPont
4. "Drivers Wanted"	_____	D. Nissan
5. "All the News That Fit to Print"	_____	E. Kodak
6. "Good Life. Great Price."	_____	F. Volkswagen
7. "Imagination at Work"	_____	G. Panasonic
8. "What's in Your Wallet?"	_____	H. Pizza Hut
9. "I'm Lovin' It"	_____	I. Target
10. "Is it in You?"	_____	J. Energizer Batteries
11. "It's Everywhere You Want to Be"	_____	K. Gatorade
12. "The Document Company"	_____	L. Taco Bell
13. "The Miracles of Science"	_____	M. Ford Motor Company
14. "You're in Good Hands"	_____	N. New York Times
15. "Shift"	_____	O. McDonald's
16. "Gather 'Round the Good Stuff"	_____	P. Coca Cola
17. "Ideas for Life"	_____	Q. Sears
18. "The Power to Keep You Going, and Going…"	_____	R. Wendy's
19. "Built for the Road Ahead"	_____	S. VISA
20. "Start Something"	_____	T. Sprite
21. "It's Better Here"	_____	U. Wal-Mart
22. "Share Moments. Share Life."	_____	V. BMW
23. "Get the Feeling"	_____	W. Capital One
24. "Make it Real"	_____	X. Toyota
25. "Always Low Prices. Always."	_____	Y. Microsoft
26. The Ultimate Driving Machine"	_____	Z. Allstate Insurance

CHAPTER 19: ADVERTISING, SALES PROMOTION, AND PUBLIC RELATIONS

ICA 19-4: IN-CLASS ACTIVITY

Advil® Liqui-Gels® – Valassis Newspouch® Product Sampling Promotion[1]

Learning Objectives. To have students: (1) learn about the practice of product sampling, an important and growing segment of marketing and (2) apply the concepts learned using an actual example of a product sampling promotion developed by a leading firm in the field.

Definitions. The following marketing terms are referred to in this in-class activity (ICA):

- Consumer-oriented Sales Promotion: Sales tools used to support a company's advertising and personal selling efforts directed to ultimate consumers, such as coupons, sweepstakes, and samples.

- Free-standing Insert (FSI): A full-color booklet featuring advertisements with coupons and other promotional offers, inserted in the Sunday newspaper.

- Product Sampling: Offering a free (or at a reduced price) product to consumers in an effort to create awareness, stimulate trial, and induce repeat purchases.

- Sales Promotion: A short-term inducement of value offered to arouse interest in buying a good or service.

Nature of the Activity. To have students (1) learn about the product sampling industry, (2) evaluate the strategy for the Advil® Liqui-Gels® – Valassis Newspouch Product Sampling Promotion, and (3) propose additional sales promotion strategies for Advil® Liqui-Gels®

Estimated Class Time. 30 minutes, which consists of:

- 10 minutes to explain the sales promotion industry, the Advil®/Valassis promotion, and the nature of this ICA.

- 20 minutes to conduct this ICA and present 2-3 summaries of the student teams' evaluation of the Advil/Valassis during the class period.

- OPTIONAL: An additional 15 minutes to complete and discuss an optional activity.

Materials Needed.

- The ICA19-4.doc Word and ICA19-4.ppt PowerPoint files contained in the ICA19-4 folder of the Instructor's CD #2 from the *Instructor's Survival Kit* box.

- The Advil® Liqui-Gels® product sample contained in the Valassis® Newspouch® from the *Instructor's Survival Kit* box.

---

[1] The authors wish to thank Patricia Hudson, Associate Product Manager and Krystal Weber, Public Relation of Valassis and Tim Stauber, Advil Brand Team of Wyeth Consumer Healthcare who assisted in the development of this ICA.

- Copies of the:
  a. Advil® Liqui-Gels®/Valassis Newspouch Product Sample Handout.
  b. Advil® Liqui-Gels®/Valassis Newspouch Product Sample Answers Handout.
  c. OPTIONAL: Other Sales Promotion Strategies for Advil® Handout.

- OPTIONAL: The EduBrandMkt.ppt PowerPoint file contained in the ICA19-4 folder of the Instructor's CD #2 from the *Instructor's Survival Kit* box.

- NOTE: Transparencies can be made of the handouts instead of making copies and using the PowerPoint presentation for those instructors who prefer this option.

Preparation Before Class. Follow the steps below:

1. Read pp. 514-518 of Chapter 19 on sales promotion.

2. Print, read, and if necessary, edit the ICA19-4.doc Word file.

3. Print and/or review the slides from the ICA19-4.ppt PowerPoint file.

4. Make copies of the:
   a. Advil® Liqui-Gels®/Valassis Newspouch Product Sample Handout.
   b. Advil® Liqui-Gels®/Valassis Newspouch Product Sample Answers Handout.
   c. OPTIONAL: Other Sales Promotion Strategies for Advil® Handout.

5. OPTIONAL: Bookmark the Wyeth® (www.wyeth.com), Advil® (www.advil.com) and Valassis (www.valassis.com) websites on your classroom computer.

Instructions. Follow the steps below to conduct this ICA:

1. Pass around the Advil® Liqui-Gels® product sample contained in the Valassis® Newspouch® obtained from the *Instructor's Survival Kit* box.

2. Give students this background mini-lecture on the sales promotion industry:

   "According to *Promo Magazine's 2005 Industry Trend Report*, U.S. marketers spent an estimated $313.2 billion on consumer-oriented sales promotion in 2004, an increase of 8.9% increase over 2003. This change was attributed to economic recovery and an increased confidence in consumer-oriented sales promotion as a marketing strategy. In 2004, spending on product sampling was up 20% to about $1.8 billion."[2]

3. OPTIONAL: For more information on the sales promotion industry, see the Valassis "Educating the Brand Marketers of Tomorrow" PowerPoint presentation.

---

[2] Kathleen M. Joyce, "Riding the Tide," *Promo Magazine's 2005 Industry Trend Report*," (April 1, 2005).

4. Give the following mini-lecture on Valassis:

"Valassis, based in Livonia, MI, is one of the largest full-service marketing firms in the U. S., with 2004 sales of $1 billion. Many of you are familiar with the sales promotion and product sampling techniques developed by Valassis on behalf of its clients. This firm pioneered the coupon booklets that we receive in our local Sunday newspaper, which are called free-standing inserts or FSI's. The FSI is the most popular couponing method, representing 87 percent of all coupons distributed in the United States! Valassis has also created these other product sampling vehicles:

- Newspouch®: A full-color, high impact polybag surrounding the newspaper. It includes a pouch that contains a product sample, informational brochure, and/or coupon attached to the side or end of the bag.

- Brand Bag+™: Similar to the Newspouch, the Brand Bag+ is a full-color polybag "billboard" for a high visibility advertising message. It also has a perforated space at the end of the bag to contain a product sample.

- Newspac®: A full-color, 4-page brochure with an attached sample packet that is placed into the newspaper's promotion section.

- Door Hang Bag: A full-color, high impact polybag hung on a consumer's door knob or handle, which is ideal for distributing bulky or fragile samples and targeting niche consumer groups where newspaper distribution is limited."

5. Give the following mini-lecture on the OTC market for analgesics:

"Many of us have had headaches, backaches, sore muscles, etc. To alleviate these minor aches, we take an "analgesic" or pain reliever that we buy "over-the-counter" (OTC) in grocery, drug, or other stores where nonprescription medications are sold. These pain relievers come in tablet, caplet, gelcap, and liquid filled capsule forms. The three primary types of analgesics sold in the OTC healthcare market based on their principal ingredient are:

- Aspirin: Bayer® (Bayer) and Ecotrin® (GlaxoSmithKline) are the two most popular brands.

- Acetaminophen: Tylenol® (Johnson & Johnson-McNeil) is the most popular brand.

- Ibuprofen: Advil® (Wyeth) and Motrin® (Johnson & Johnson-McNeil) are the two most popular brands.

6. Give the following mini-lecture on Wyeth:

"Wyeth is a global pharmaceutical firm with 2004 sales of $17.4 billion. Its Consumer Healthcare division is the third largest marketer of OTC healthcare products in the world and had $2.5 billion in sales for 2004. In addition to Advil®, the division's other well-known brands include Centrum® vitamins & supplements, Robitussin® cold/cough remedies, and ChapStick® lip balm."

Advil Adult
Product Line

Slide 2

7. **Show Slide 2: Advil® adult product line** and give the following mini-lecture on Advil®:

"The Advil® brand is one of the market leaders in the OTC healthcare market, with over $586 million in global sales for 2004. Advil® is marketed in adult (see slide) and children's versions. In addition to the traditional Advil® formulation, adult medications also include migraine, cold & sinus, allergy, flu & body ache, and multi-symptom formulations. Advil® also comes in tablet, caplet, gelcap, and the new Advil® Liqui-Gels® form. According to its website, Advil® works faster and is stronger than Extra Strength Tylenol. Advil® Liqui-Gels® are sold in five stock keeping units (SKUs): 20 count ($4.29); 40 count ($6.49); 80 count ($9.49); 135 count ($13.49); and 180 count ($16.99)."

8. **Show Slides 3-5: Advil® Liqui-Gels® TV ad** [TRT 0:30], **Internet ad**, and **point of purchase display** while giving the following mini-lecture on the Advil® Liqui-Gels® IMC program:

"In 2004, Advil® began an integrated marketing communication program focused on Advil® Liqui-Gels®. The program included advertising on TV, the Internet, and point of purchase display support at retailers, among others."

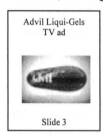

Advil Liqui-Gels
TV ad

Slide 3

Advil Internet ad

Slide 4

Advil POP display

Slide 5

Advil Liqui-Gels
Valassis
Newspouch

Slide 6

Advil/Valassis
Newspouch
Contents

Slide 7

9. **Show Slides 6-7: Advil® Liqui-Gels/Valassis Newspouch** and **Product Sample Promotion Contents** while giving the following mini-lecture on the Advil®/Valassis Product Sample Promotion:

"Due to the increasing popularity of sales promotion as a marketing strategy, Valassis created the Advil® Liqui-Gels® Newspouch promotion in the first quarter of 2005.

• The objectives of the promotion were to generate awareness and trial for the Advil® Liqui-Gels® pain reliever and to defend the Advil® Liqui-Gels® product line against competitive product launches from Tylenol and other private label brands.

• The Newspouch sampling vehicle was used to deliver a 0.34-oz. (2 capsule) sample of Advil® Liqui-Gels® along with a $1.00 off coupon to over 14 million targeted households in the U.S.

• The target audience consisted of households who are medium to heavy users (5+ times during the last 30 days) of the Headache Remedies/Pain Relievers Category and are Advil® Switchers (consumers who switched from other pain relievers like Tylenol)."

Advil Liqui-Gels
Valassis FSI ad

Slide 8

10. **Show Slide 8: Advil Liqui-Gels/Valassis FSI ad** while giving the following mini-lecture:

"Valassis the followed up the Advil® Liqui-Gels® Newspouch promotion with an FSI in 39.5 million newspapers across the U.S. as part of the overall campaign strategy. According to Patty Hudson, Associate Product Manager at Valassis, 'Clients that run a Co-op FSI are typically trying to cover the mass market. It's a cost efficient method to build awareness and grow sales. Newspouch programs are typically smaller in circulation and are higher in cost, which is why reaching their target audience is critical for effectiveness. The Co-op FSI is a great method for building presence in the marketplace on a broad scale.'"

11. Form students into 4-person teams.

Advil/Valassis
Product Sample
Handout

Slide 9

12. Give students the Advil® Liqui-Gels®/Valassis Newspouch Product Sample Handout and/or **show Slide 9**.

13. **Spend 10 minutes** and have student teams complete the Advil® Liqui-Gels®/Valassis Newspouch Product Sample Handout. Ask students to list the advantages and disadvantages of the sales promotion strategy developed for the Advil® Liqui-Gels® Product Sample Promotion using the Valassis Newspouch and $1.00 coupon.

14. **Spend 5 minutes** and have student teams share their responses to the Advil® Liqui-Gels®/Valassis Newspouch Product Sample sales promotion strategy. Write down their responses on either the blackboard or the transparency made from the Advil® Liqui-Gels®/Valassis Newspouch Product Sample Handout.

Advil/Valassis
Product Sample
Answers Handout

15. Give students the Advil® Liqui-Gels®/Valassis Newspouch Product Sample Answers Handout.

16. **Spend 5 minutes** and compare their responses to those identified by both Valassis and Advil® for the Advil® Liqui-Gels®/Valassis Newspouch Product Sample Promotion.

Other Sales
Promotions for
Advil Handout

Slide 10

17. OPTIONAL: Give students the Other Sales Promotion Strategies for Advil® Handout and/or use Slide 10.

18. **Spend 10 minutes** and have student teams complete the Other Sales Promotion Strategies for Advil® Handout. Ask students to (1) identify five other sales promotion strategies and (2) list the advantages and disadvantages of each strategy.

19. **Spend 5 minutes** and have student teams share their responses to the Other Sales Promotion Strategies for Advil® Handout. See pp. 515-518 of the textbook for the answers to this optional activity.

Marketing Lessons. Marketers use product sampling to increase awareness, trial, and adoption of new products, build brand loyalty for existing products, and encourage brand switching, among others.

Websites. For more information about: (1) Valassis, go to www.valassis.com; (2) Wyeth, the maker of Advil®, go to www.wyeth.com; and (3) Advil®, go to www.advil.com, where you may be able to print a coupon for Advil® Liqui-Gels®. To obtain more information about the sales promotion industry, go to www.promomagazine.com.

Advil® Liqui-Gels/Valassis® Newspouch Product Sample Handout

ADVANTAGES	DISADVANTAGES
•	•
•	•
•	•
•	•
•	•

Advil® Liqui-Gels®/Valassis Newspouch Product Sample
Answers Handout

ADVANTAGES	DISADVANTAGES
• Full-color, high impact polybag • Polybag surrounds the newspaper and supersedes the front page providing a competition free environment • Delivered to home subscriber households, thus ensuring Newspouch is "welcomed" into the home • Newspouch can be effective in generating awareness and trial if tracking data are conclusive • Uses Mediamark Research, Inc. (MRI), the leading supplier of syndicated media and product usage survey data, to select target audience • Newspouch is targeted to specific consumers, medium to heavy users of the headache remedy/pain relief category and Advil switchers, increasing the opportunity for trial or purchase • Newspouch contains multiple pieces, including product sample, informational insert and $1.00 off purchase coupon • Artwork effectively conveys product • Newspouch polybag is recyclable • Newspouch polybag has warning to keep away from children • • • • •	• Cost/benefit to marketer: How many trials and adoptions after the samples are delivered? Is further sampling needed to maintain sales? • Ability to reach target audience limited by the number of available newspaper publishers that will accept a polybag • Does not provide the immediate opportunity to purchase that an in-store sampling distribution campaign offers • Does not provide opportunity to ask product questions that an in-store sampling campaign would allow • Bad weather could soil the Newspouch and result in it being thrown away • A Newspouch with a sample can be suspect to consumer theft, thus not reaching the intended consumer • Target audience did not opt into sampling program and therefore trial and repeat purchase behavior may be low • Target consumers may buy their newspapers at newsstands, kiosks, etc. where a Newspouch is not used • Polybag could be dangerous around children if left unattended • • • • •

Other Sales Promotion Strategies for Advil® Handout

STRATEGY	ADVANTAGES	DISADVANTAGES
• #1:	• • •	• • •
• #2:	• • •	• • •
• #3:	• • •	• • •
• #4:	• • •	• • •
• #5:	• • •	• • •

ICA 19-4

CHAPTER 19: ADVERTISING, SALES PROMOTION, AND PUBLIC RELATIONS

ICA 19-5: IN-CLASS ACTIVITY

Product Placement in Movies and TV[1]

Learning Objective. To have students learn about the exploding popularity of product placement or 'brand entertainment' in movies, television programs, and other media as a promotional tool for marketers.

Definition. The following marketing term is referred to in this in-class activity (ICA):

- Product Placement: Using a brand-name product in a movie, television show, video, or commercial for another product.

Nature of the Activity. To have students match a list of movies with a list of products that were used or displayed in these movies.

Estimated Class Time. 10 minutes.

Materials Needed.

- The ICA19-5.doc Word and ICA19-5.ppt PowerPoint files contained in the ICA19-5 folder of the Instructor's CD #2 from the *Instructor's Survival Kit* box.

- Copies of the Match Each Product to the Movies and/or TV Show Handout.

- NOTE: Transparencies can be made of the handouts instead of making copies and using the PowerPoint presentation for those instructors who prefer this option.

Preparation Before Class. Follow the steps below:

1. Read p. 518 of Chapter 19.

2. Print, read, and if necessary, edit the ICA19-5.doc Word file.

3. Print and/or review the slides from the ICA19-5.ppt PowerPoint file.

4. Make copies of the Match Each Product to the Movies and/or TV Show Handout.

5. OPTIONAL: Bookmark the A List Entertainment (www.alistentertainment.com) website on your classroom computer.

---

[1] The authors wish to thank Marcia Levine, President of A List Entertainment, who assisted in the development of this ICA.

Instructions. Follow the steps below to conduct this ICA:

Product Placement Video

Slide 2

1. **Show Slide 2**: A List Entertainment Product Placement Video. [TRT = 3:30]

2. Pass out copies of the Match Each Product to the Movies and/or TV Show Handout to each student.

3. Give students this background mini-lecture on product placement:

"Product placement in movies, TV shows, and other media has exploded. Product placement as a sales promotion strategy 'took off' in 1982 with the placement of Reese's Pieces in the movie *ET: The Extra-Terrestrial*. However, it took another 17 years for product placement to impact television.[2]

Three types of product placement arrangements exist: barter (a product is placed but no fees are paid), gratis (a placement is made for free to assist the character or plot), and paid. In 2005, the value of movie product placements is projected to be $1.42 billion. In television, it is even larger: $2.44 billion. By 2009, total product placement spending for all media could reach $6.9 billion.[3]"

4. Ask students why marketers would place their products in a movie or television show. Responses should include the following:

a. **Increases sales.** Sales of Reese's Pieces, featured in *ET: The Extra-Terrestrial*, exploded by 60 percent while sales of Ray Ban sunglasses increased as a result of being placed in *Top Gun* and *Men in Black*. With respect to TV, Pepsi, GM, and others have repeatedly placed their products in *Survivor* due to increased sales.

b. **Gives a sense of realism.** Characters in movies and TV eat, drink, and wear brand-named products in real life.

c. **Reinforces a character's personality.** Example: James Bond driving an Aston Martin sports car.

d. **Growing use of TiVo and PVRs** (personal video recoreders). Increasingly, viewers of TV programs skip commercials using these devices.

e. **Endorsement value.** Creates an implied endorsement by the characters and the high-profile celebrities who play them.

f. **Brand exposure.** Popular movie and TV shows result in significant exposure of the brand in both domestic and foreign markets.

g. **Audience fragmentation.** Consumers have many more media alternatives (cable TV, video games, the Internet, etc.) to choose from. As a result, the likelihood of viewing a traditional 3-second TV ad is less today.

---

[2] Any Johannes, "TV Placements Overtake Film," *Promo Magazine*, May 1, 2005. See http://promomagazine.com/mag/marketing_tv_placements_overtake.
[3] "Product Placement Spending in Media 2005: Executive Summary," PQ Media, March 2005, pp. 6, 9.

h. **Lower cost CPM**. Product placement is a lower cost alternative in terms of the cost per thousand (CPM). Paid product placements usually cost between $10,000 and $1 million, and average about $50,000.

i. **Growth in 'reality' TV programming**. The success of the 'reality' TV genre has significantly contributed to the growth of product placement. Some reality programs seem to be a 30-minute set of ads!

Matching Product
Placement Handout

Slide 3

5. **Show Slide 3**: Match Each Product to the Movies and/or TV Show Handout.

6. **Spend 5 minutes** and have students identify the product for each product placement. The answers are:

Movies & TV Shows:	Product(s) Placed:	Answer:
1. American Idol	Coca Cola	N
2. ET: The Extra-Terrestrial	Reese's Pieces	H
3. Meet the Fockers	Apple Computer	O
4. Jurassic Park	Ford Explorer	U
5. I, Robot	Audi concept car	Q
6. Top Gun	Ray Ban Sunglasses	A
7. The Matrix	Duracell Batteries	S
8. Forrest Gump	Dr. Pepper	W
9. Good Will Hunting	Dunkin' Donuts	R
10. Men in Black	Ray Ban Sunglasses	A
11. Jerry Maguire	Reebok	E
12. The Apprentice	Dominos	G
13. Batman & Robin	Frito Lay	I
14. Charlie's Angels	Nokia Mobile Phone	B
15. Austin Powers III	MINI Cooper S	J
16. Oprah Winfrey	Pontiac G6	C
17. Seinfeld	Junior Mints	K
18. Friends	7-Up	L
19. Survivor	Chevrolet, Pringles, Reebok	M, E, X
20. Will & Grace	Polo Shirts	V
21. Who Wants to be a Millionaire?	AT&T	D
22. 7th Heaven	Miracle Whip	P
23. ER	Best Buy	T
24. National Treasure	VISA	F

7. Conclude this ICA with the following mini-lecture:

"Because of the growth in product placement in television, Nielsen Media Research has launched the Nielsen Product Placement Report that tracks the brands and TV shows where they are placed. In early 2005, the top brands placed were Coca Cola (American Idol), Everlast (The Contender), and Home Depot (The Apprentice). All three of these are reality TV programs."

Marketing Lesson. The popularity of product placements has grown in recent years because marketers believe that using brands in movies and TV shows is a subtle way of gaining exposure, particularly with younger audiences.

Websites. To more obtain information about product placements, go to A List Entertainment's website, which is www.alistentertainment.com. Another well-known product placement firm is Norm Marshall and Associates, whose website is www.normmarshall.com. To view a list of product placements by movie, go to the brandchannel.com website at www.brandchannel.com/brandcameo_films.asp. At this time, the Nielsen Product Placement Report is not available online.

MATCH EACH PRODUCT TO THE MOVIE AND/OR TV SHOW HANDOUT

MOVIE OR TV SHOW

1. American Idol
2. ET: The Extra-Terrestrial
3. Meet the Fockers
4. Jurassic Park
5. I, Robot
6. Top Gun
7. The Matrix
8. Forrest Gump
9. Good Will Hunting
10. Men In Black
11. Jerry Maguire
12. The Apprentice
13. Batman & Robin
14. Charlie's Angels
15. Austin Powers III
16. Oprah Winfrey
17. Seinfeld
18. Friends
19. Survivor
20. Will & Grace
21. Who Wants to be a Millionaire?
22. 7th Heaven
23. ER
24. National Treasure

PRODUCT PLACEMENT

_____ A. Ray Ban Sunglasses

_____ B. Nokia Mobile Phone

_____ C. Pontiac G6

_____ D. AT&T

_____ E. Reebok

_____ F. VISA

_____ G. Dominos

_____ H. Reese's Pieces

_____ I. Frito Lay

_____ J. MINI Cooper S

_____ K. Junior Mints

_____ L. 7-Up

_____ M. Chevrolet

_____ N. Coca Cola

_____ O. Apple Computer

_____ P. Miracle Whip

_____ Q. Audi concept car

_____ R. Dunkin' Donuts

_____ S. Duracell Batteries

_____ T. Best Buy

_____ U. Ford Explorer

_____ V. Polo Shirts

_____ W. Dr. Pepper

_____ X. Pringles

CHAPTER 19: ADVERTISING, SALES PROMOTION, AND PUBLIC RELATIONS

ICA 19-6: IN-CLASS ACTIVITY

Designing a Publicity Campaign for the Segway® HT[1]

Learning Objectives. To have students (1) understand the elements of the public relations process, (2) learn the importance of publicity in the launch of a product line, and (3) develop a simple publicity campaign for a product.

Definitions. The following marketing terms are referred to in this in-class activity (ICA):

- Public Relations: A form of communication management that seeks to influence the feelings, opinions, or beliefs held by customers, prospective customers, stockholders, suppliers, employees, and other publics about a company and its products or services.

- Publicity: A nonpersonal, indirectly paid presentation of an organization, good, or service.

- Publicity Tools: Methods of obtaining nonpersonal presentation of an organization, good, or service without direct cost. Examples include news releases, news conferences, and public service announcements.

Nature of the Activity. To have students work in teams to develop a simple publicity campaign for one of the Segway® Human Transporter (HT) models.

Estimated Class Time. 30 minutes.

Materials Needed.

- The ICA19-6.doc Word and ICA19-6.ppt PowerPoint files contained in the ICA19-6 folder of the Instructor's CD #2 from the *Instructor's Survival Kit* box.

- Copies of the:
  a. Product spec sheets for the Segway HT i180, Segway p Series, Segway GT, and Segway XT models for Teams 1 – 4 respectively. See the enclosed Adobe Acrobat Portable Document Files (.pdf) in the 'pdf' folder within the ICA19-6 folder. [NOTE: You will need the Adobe Acrobat Reader to view and print the PDF documents. To download the latest version, go to www.adobe.com/products/acrobat.]
  b. Publicity Tools Handout, which is located in the 'pdf' folder or see below.

- NOTE: Transparencies can be made of the handouts instead of making copies and using the PowerPoint presentation for those instructors who prefer this option.

---

[1] The authors wish to thank Eric Fleming, Communications Coordinator of Segway LLC who assisted in the development of this ICA.

Preparation Before Class. Follow the steps below:

1. Read pp. 520-521 of Chapter 19.

2. Print, read, and if necessary, edit the ICA19-6.doc Word file.

3. Print and/or review the PowerPoint slides from the ICA19-6.ppt PowerPoint file.

4. Make copies of the:

   a. Product spec sheets for the Segway HT i180, Segway p Series, Segway GT, and Segway XT models.

   b. Publicity Tools Handout.

5. OPTIONAL: Bookmark the Segway website (www.segway.com) on your classroom computer.

Instructions. Follow the steps below to conduct this ICA:

Segway LLC's
2005 models

Slide 2

1. **Show Slide 2**: Segway HT promotional video [NOTE: Show this video at the beginning of class. TRT 4:45; extra video 1:00.]

2. Form students into 4-person teams based on the following designations: Team 1 is the Segway i180 team; Team 2 is the Segway p Series team; Team 3 is the Segway GT (Golf Transporter) team; and Team 4 is the Segway XT (Cross-Terrain Transporter) team.

Segway HT news
releases for the
i180, p, GT, & XT

3. Pass out the product spec sheets for the Segway HT i180, Segway p Series, Segway GT, and Segway XT models to help student teams complete their Publicity Tools Handout.

4. Give the following mini-lecture on the launch of the Segway HT and subsequent models:

"On December 3, 2001, renowned inventor and entrepreneur Dean Kamen unveiled the Segway® Human Transporter (HT), a self-balancing, two-wheeled personal transportation device. As you saw, users control the speed and direction of the Segway HT by shifting their weight and manually turning the handle bar. Then, in March 2003, Segway introduced new models, including the Segway HT i180, which started at $4,495 and was targeted at both consumers and businesses that wanted extended range and performance on a variety of terrains.

Segway HT
p Series model

Slide 3

[**Show Slide 3**]. In October 2003, Segway introduced the p Series model that is designed to ride on smooth, even surfaces. The p Series, which sells for $3,995, is targeted mainly at consumers and businesses that want a lower cost, smaller Segway HT as an alternative in congested urban areas to short car trips.

In March 2005, Segway upgraded the i Series and introduced two new models:

Segway HT
i180 model

Slide 4

- **[Show Slide 4]** The Segway HT i180 now comes in three new colors (Midnight Blue, Midnight Blue/Solar Yellow, and Midnight Blue/Sport Red). Selling for $4,495, the new i Series models allow both consumers and businesses to further customize their Segway HTs in terms of color, battery, fenders, and wheels.

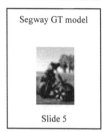

Segway GT model

Slide 5

- **[Show Slide 5]** The Segway GT (Golf Transporter), which sells for $5,495, is specifical   ly designed for golf course use. It has extended range batteries, a golf bag carrier, enhanced traction tires, and a standby key to enable the unit to remain on while hitting a shot. It is designed to replace manual and motorized golf carts.

Segway XT model

Slide 6

- **[Show Slide 6]** The Segway XT (Cross-Terrain Transporter), which sells for $4,995, provides enhanced performance on a variety of terrains with minimal environmental impact. It has knobby tires, study fenders, and extended life batteries that permit a stable ride on uneven, tough terrain. A variety of accessories are available at extra cost, such as a handlebar bag, high-power lights, and hauler that attaches to a trailer hitch."

5. Give the following mini-lecture on public relations and publicity:

"Public relations (PR) is a form of communications management that seeks to favorably influence the image of an organization and its products (or services). Typically, four steps are involved in the PR process: (1) identifying the issues and audience(s) that require a PR campaign, such as launching a new product among target consumers, minimizing the impact of a problem or crisis among employees or the general public, etc.; (2) determining the objectives of the PR campaign, such as generating awareness and/or stimulating sales of a product, enhancing credibility, reducing the impact of a negative situation, etc.; (3) executing the PR campaign using tools, such as publicity; and (4) evaluating the results of the PR campaign. Public relations is becoming an increasingly important part of an organization's integrated marketing communication (IMC) program. The principal reasons are that: (1) PR in general and publicity in particular generates immediate impact and (2) the cost is lower than engaging in an advertising and/or sales promotion campaign.

One of the more frequently used strategies in a PR campaign is the use of publicity. Typical publicity tools include the news release, a news conference, a media or press kit, a special event, etc. When used for a new product, publicity provides information about its uses and benefits to the following publics: (1) target consumers that may purchase the product; (2) media representatives who will report on and analyze the product; (3) governmental agencies that may regulate the product; and (4) employees and shareholders who have a stake in the successful launch of the product."

6. Pass out copies of the Publicity Tools Handout to each student.

Publicity Tools
Handout

Slide 7

7. **Show Slide 7**. Have students take 20 minutes to write down their answers to the following questions on their Publicity Tools Handout:

- Question 1: What are the elements that should be included in a news release for the launch of a new product, such as the Segway HT? Write them down on the Publicity Tools Handout. [**5 minutes**.]

  Answers: **Show Slides 8-10**. Standard news releases should contain the following elements:

Segway HT
News Release (1)

Slide 8

  a. **"News" and "Segway" logo graphics header** (upper right corner). This is part of the design theme for these resources.
  b. **Release date and time**. The new release is usually embargoed from public dissemination until this specified time.
  c. **Contacts**. Name, title, phone number, and e-mail address of the primary/secondary public relation people in the organization (or public relations firm). These people are responsible for answering any media or customer inquiries about the product.
  d. **Catchy headline**. Describes the subject of the news release.
  e. **Location/date**. The city and date of origin of the news release.
  f. **Product description**. A brief of the product, such as its features, benefits, and intended applications and/or targeted customers.

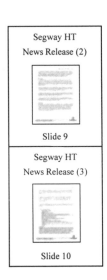

Segway HT
News Release (2)

Slide 9

Segway HT
News Release (3)

Slide 10

  g. **Product specifications**. A detailed description of the product's features.
  h. **Company description**. A brief description of the company that is marketing the product.
  i. **Company contact information**. The address, phone and FAX numbers, and website address of the organization.

- Question 2: What items should be included in a kit for the media and/or potential customers of your Segway model? Write them down on the Publicity Tools Handout. [**5 minutes**.]

  Answers: A media kit include the following:

  a. News release of the product launch (review slides 8-10).
  b. **Show Slide 11**. Company milestones sheet.
  c. **Show Slide 12**. Key personnel bios sheet.
  d. **Show Slide 13**. Product specifications sheet.

Segway HT
Milestones

Slide 11

Segway HT
Key Personnel Bios

Slide 12

Segway HT
i180 Spec Sheet

Slide 13

e. Video (which students saw at the beginning of class) and a Flash animation of how a Segway HT works (see www.segway.com/connect/multimedia.html/).

f. Others as identified, such as Testimonials from consumers, businesses, and universities, FAQs, Price list, Segway in the News, Upcoming events, Downloads, etc.). [NOTE: Go to www.segway.com/aboutus/press_center to find out what other items Segway includes in a typical media kit.]

- Question 3: What other publicity tools would your team develop to inform the media and target consumers about the new Segway HT models? Write it down on the Publicity Tools Handout. [**5 minutes.**]

Answers: The Segway communications team developed the following publicity special events and activities for the new Segway HT models:

a. **Special events**. Hosted an invite-only press event in New York to preview the new product line for writers from men's, science, technology, and design magazines.

b. Developed a secure media center for newspaper writers to preview news releases and product photos.

c. E-mail newsletter.

d. Chat room.

e. News conference.

f. Others to be conducted.

These and other activities generated the following media responses between February 27 and March 29, 2005, the one-month period surrounding the news release of March 1, 2005:

a. **TV**. There were 117 stories and 13.9 million impressions from coverage by national and local TV networks/stations. Fox News, CNN, and MSNBC (on its "Power Lunch" program) aired segments on the products. Also, several news outlets downloaded and aired the B-roll video, resulting in 7.4 million impressions.

b. **Newspapers**. There were 60 stories and 23.2 million impressions. The Associated Press filed 3 stories on its wire, which were syndicated to more than 60 newspapers and online news websites.

c. **Magazines**. There were 3 stories and 11.8 million impressions among consumer and trade magazines, such as *Popular Science's* April 2005 issue. *Golf Course Management*, which is the official publication of the Golf Course Superintendents Association of America, reviewed the Segway GT in its March 2005 issue. Articles in other magazines are pending.

8. **Spend 5 minutes** and have one student from select teams present its publicity tool suggestions regarding the "News Release," "Media Kit," and "Other" elements and actions for their respective Segway HT product.

9. Conclude this ICA with the following statement:

"Public relations in general and publicity in particular are important elements of an organization's marketing strategy. While there is a cost in developing the tools, they are much less expensive than developing an advertising campaign. Also, given the cost and nature of the Segway products, most sales promotion tools (coupons, samples, etc.) are not practical."

Marketing Lessons. Developing an effective PR campaign and publicity program requires creativity and attention to detail. Organizations like Segway LLC either perform this marketing function "in-house" or hire public relations and marketing consulting firms to develop PR strategies and execute PR campaigns that will accomplish the organization's objectives in a more cost-efficient manner than advertising or sales promotion. Increasingly, PR is becoming an integral part of an IMC program for a product or service.

Website. The Segway website is www.segway.com.

Publicity Tools Handout

PUBLICITY TOOL	ELEMENTS TO INCLUDE OR ACTIONS TO TAKE
NEWS RELEASE	<ul><li></li><li></li><li></li><li></li><li></li><li></li><li></li><li></li><li></li></ul>
MEDIA KIT	<ul><li></li><li></li><li></li><li></li><li></li><li></li><li></li><li></li></ul>
OTHER (SPECIAL EVENTS, ETC.)	<ul><li></li><li></li><li></li><li></li><li></li><li></li><li></li></ul>

ICA 19-6

CHAPTER 20: PERSONAL SELLING AND SALES MANAGEMENT

ICA 20-1: IN-CLASS ACTIVITY

Student Perceptions of Selling

Learning Objective. To have students investigate the stereotypes of sales and selling.

Definition. The following marketing term is referred to in this in-class activity (ICA):

- Personal Selling: The two-way flow of communication between a buyer and seller, designed to influence a person's or group's purchase decision, usually in face-to-face communication between the sender and receiver.

Nature of the Activity. To have students take a quick quiz on sales and selling and then compare their attitudes and ideas to actual practice.

Estimated Class Time. 10 minutes.

Materials Needed.

- The ICA20-1.doc Word and ICA20-1.ppt PowerPoint files contained in the ICA20-1 folder of the Instructor's CD #2 from the *Instructor's Survival Kit* box.

- NOTE: Transparencies can be made of the handouts instead of making copies and using the PowerPoint presentation for those instructors who prefer this option.

Preparation Before Class. Follow the steps below:

1. Read pp. 528-530 of Chapter 20 as well as the material below.

2. Print, read, and if necessary, edit the ICA20-1.doc Word file.

3. Print and/or review the PowerPoint slides from the ICA20-1.ppt PowerPoint file.

Instructions. Follow the steps below to conduct this ICA:

1. Explain that the media have reinforced negative stereotypes of personal selling held by society. Not surprisingly, many students hold these same negative opinions. However, many of today's college graduates will begin their marketing career as a sales representative or in a customer service job.

2. Ask students to describe what salespeople do as part of their selling jobs.

3. Ask students if any of them plan on a sales career. For those who say, 'Yes,' ask them why they want to go into sales. Write down these responses on the board or a blank transparency. If no one indicates any interest, ask none would consider a sales career.

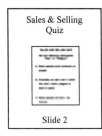

Sales & Selling Quiz

Slide 2

4. **Show Slide 2**: Sales and Selling Quiz and ask the student to respond to discuss the three statements made about selling and give their reasons. The responses should all be fallacious.

5. Respond to the students' comments with the "key observations" from the Sales and Selling Quiz: Some Key Observations:

a. **Sales people push products on people**.

   Observations. The most successful companies and sales forces increasingly are taking a marketing orientation. Consider the following:

   • "We have a simple premise or philosophy, 'Know your customer and his needs.'"—Martin L. Andreas, Senior Vice President, Archer-Daniels-Midland.

   • "We're telling our sales reps, you need to think more broadly than just selling. You need to put on your business hat. I think that works to the advantage of everybody, especially to our customers' advantage. Now sales reps are in partnership with customers, helping them to run their business."—Michael Morley, Vice President and General Manager for U.S. Marketing and Sales, Consumer Imaging Division, Kodak.

   • Bethlehem Steel Corporation's sales philosophy is, "To have a well trained, highly motivated sales force dedicated to developing and satisfying customer needs."

b. **Anybody can get a job in sales. You don't need a degree to work in sales**.

   Observations. Consider the following: "Our salespeople go to colleges and recruit."—David M. Beinner, General Manager of Sales, Bethlehem Steel Corporation. About half its sales force has a technical background.

c. **Sales people are born, not trained**.

   Observations. Knowledge is key for a successful sales person. This means more than valuable sales skills such as listening and probing to understand needs. It means product, industry, and customer knowledge. Consider the following:

   • "Our sales people have to know the big picture. Sometimes that means legislative issues, politics, and trade. We want them to be the best source of information in the industry."—Martin L. Andreas, Senior Vice President, Archer-Daniels-Midland.

   • Kodak sales recruits take 90 days of intensive training before being sent into the field.

Marketing Lesson. Sales and selling will continue to change. After all, if you were a buyer, would you want to waste your time talking to the stereotypical pushy, obnoxious sales person? Selling will continue to emphasize "finding solutions to customers' problems."[1]

---

[1] Sources: Allison Lucas "Portrait of a Salesperson," *Sales and Marketing Management* (June, 1995), p. 13 and Thomas R. Wotruba, "The Evolution of Personal Selling and Sales Management," *Journal of Personal Selling and Sales Management* (Summer, 1995), pp. 1-12.

ICA 20-1

SALES AND SELLING QUIZ

Are the following statements "Fact" or "Fallacy?"

A. Sales people push products on people.

B. Anybody can get a job in sales. You don't need a degree to work in sales.

C. Sales people are born, not trained.

CHAPTER 20: PERSONAL SELLING AND SALES MANAGEMENT

ICA 20-2: IN-CLASS ACTIVITY

Personal Selling Process: News America Marketing[1]

Learning Objectives. To have students utilize the personal selling process to try to sell an in-store media product to a consumer-packaged goods firm to illustrate the kind of sales job many marketing graduates will have right out of college.

Definitions. The following marketing terms are referred to in this in-class activity (ICA):

- Major Account Management: The practice of using team selling to focus on important customers so as to build mutually beneficial, long-term, cooperative relationships.

- Partnership Selling: The practice whereby buyers and sellers combine their expertise and resources to create customized solutions, commit to joint planning, and share customer, competitive, and company information for their mutual benefit, and ultimately the customer.

- Personal Selling Process: Sales activities occurring before and after the sale itself, consisting of six stages:

  a. Prospecting Stage: Is the search for and qualification of potential customers.

  b. Preapproach Stage: Involves obtaining further information about the prospect and deciding on the best method of approach.

  c. Approach Stage: Is the initial meeting between the salesperson and prospect, where the objectives are to gain the prospect's attention, stimulate interest, and build the foundation for the sales presentation itself and the basis for a working relationship.

  d. Presentation Stage: Its objective is to convert the prospect into a customer by creating a desire for the product or service.

  e. Closing Stage: Involves obtaining a purchase commitment from a prospect.

  f. Follow-up Stage: Makes sure the customer's purchase has been properly delivered and installed and difficulties experienced with using the product are addressed.

- Relationship Selling: The practice of building ties to customers based on a salesperson's attention and commitment to customer needs over time.

Nature of the Activity. To have students participate in the personal selling process for one of ten News America Marketing's SmartSource In-Store Media products.

Estimated Class Time. 25 minutes.

---

[1] The authors wish to thank Dawn Knauer, Program Manager of News America Marketing, who assisted in the development of this ICA.

Materials Needed.

- The ICA20-2.doc Word and ICA20-2.ppt PowerPoint files contained in the ICA20-2 folder of the Instructor's CD #2 from the *Instructor's Survival Kit* box.

- Copies of the:

  a. News America Marketing Personal Selling Process Handout.

  b. OPTIONAL: News America Marketing SmartSource In-Store Media product sheets. See the enclosed Adobe Acrobat Portable Document Files (.pdf) in the 'pdf' folder within the ICA20-2 folder. [NOTE: You will need the Adobe Acrobat Reader to view and print the PDF documents. To download the latest version, go to www.adobe.com/products/acrobat.]

- NOTE: Transparencies can be made of the handouts instead of making copies and using the PowerPoint presentation for those instructors who prefer this option.

Preparation Before Class. Follow the steps below:

1. Read pp. 530, 533-539 of Chapter 20.

2. Print, read, and if necessary, edit the ICA20-2.doc Word file.

3. Print and/or review the PowerPoint slides from the ICA20-2.ppt PowerPoint file.

4. Make copies of the:

   a. News America Marketing Personal Selling Process Handout.

   b. OPTIONAL: News America Marketing SmartSource In-Store Media product sheets based on the team designation.

5. OPTIONAL: Bookmark the News America Marketing website (www.newsamerica.com) on your classroom computer.

Instructions. Follow the steps below to conduct this ICA:

1. Give students this background mini-lecture on the in-store media segment of the sales promotion industry:

   "According to *Promo Magazine's 2005 Industry Trend Report*, U.S. marketers spent an estimated $18.5 billion on in-store sales promotion in 2004, an increase of 5% over 2003. In-store marketing includes point-of-purchase (POP) displays, retail merchandising, and in-store media. In-store media accounted for $854 million of the total in-store promotion and consists of the traditional shelf-talkers, coupon dispensers, and other vehicles. In the near future, radio and interactive displays should become more popular as their costs decline.[2]

---

[2] Kathleen M. Joyce, "Riding the Tide," and Betsy Spethmann, "Turning In at the Shelf," *Promo Magazine's 2005 Industry Trend Report*," (April 1, 2005).

2. Give the following mini-lecture on News America Marketing, its in-store media products, and its commitment to the personal selling process:

"News America Marketing is the leading single-source provider of consumer advertising and promotional services. The company's product portfolio, marketed under the SmartSource brand name, consists of the first branded free-standing insert, known as SmartSource Magazine®, various in-store advertising and promotional products, merchandising services, database marketing tools, and online promotions. These products and services allow marketers to deliver a brand message to over 200 million consumers each month via a network of over 1,100 newspapers and 34,500 supermarket, drug store, and mass merchandisers locations across the country, including Albertson's, Kroger, Winn Dixie, CVS, Eckerd, and Rite Aid.[3]

According to News America Marketing, SmartSource in-store media fulfills the following marketing objectives:[4]

   a. Generates awareness, interest, and trial by driving traffic to the brand.
   b. Builds brand equity and loyalty and weakens competitive product offerings.
   c. Breaks the competitive tie at the shelf by offering a sample, coupon, or experience.
   d. Highlights the price point featured for the product.
   e. Provides consumers with additional information.
   f. Introduces consumers to new products or packaging.

News America Marketing prides itself on its practice of **relationship selling**. Its Salespeople are committed to building a long-term relationship with their customers. News America Marketing also goes one step further: it engages in **partnership selling** practices, in which it combines its expertise with that of selected customers to create customized solutions. For large consumer packaged firms, News America Marketing uses **major account management**. Thus, News America Marketing is fully committed to the **personal selling process**, which consists of six stages: (1) prospecting; (2) preapproach; (3) approach; (4) presentation; (5) close; and (6) follow-up."

3. Form students into sets of six (6) 4-person teams, each representing a particular News America Marketing SmartSource in-store media product and step in the personal selling process (**but don't tell them that at this point!**). Students on these teams will act as salespeople for their respective product to a prospective consumer packaged goods client. Each student team's tasks are to:

   a. Identify the marketing objectives of their prospective client that its SmartSource in-store media product can fulfill.
   b. Develop suggestions for each aspect of the personal selling process. During the discussion period, a specified team will only discuss one step of the personal selling process based on its SmartSource in-store media product assignment.

---

[3] News America Marketing press release, "News America Marketing Unveils the Next Generation of In-Store Advertising," November 10, 2004.
[4] SmartSource At A Glance.

4. Pass out copies of the News America Marketing Personal Selling Process Handout to each student.

5. OPTIONAL: Pass out copies of the News America Marketing SmartSource In-Store Media product sheets to each student based on the team designation.

News America Personal Selling Handout

OPTIONAL: News America product sheets

6. **Tell students to take notes** while identifying and describing the six (6) SmartSource in-store media products that represent their respective student team and step in the personal selling process:

a. **Show Slide 2**. Team 1: At-Shelf Sampling^{SM} (Prospecting). Offers trial size products at the shelf.

b. **Show Slide 3**. Team 2: AudioInk^{SM} (Preapproach). Delivers interactive audio messages by 'speaking' to consumers when they touch the medium.

c. **Show Slide 4**. Team 3: Carts$^{®}$ (Approach). Features print advertising on the inside and outside of grocery carts.

At-Shelf Sampling Team: Prospecting

Slide 2

AudioInk Team: Preapproach

Slide 3

Carts Team: Approach

Slide 4

d. **Show Slide 5**. Team 4: Coupon Machine^{SM} (Presentation). Rewards consumers with immediate cents-off savings right at the shelf.

e. **Show Slide 6**. Team 5: Electronic Price Plus^{SM} (Close). Informs consumers of special pricing available at the time.

f. **Show Slide 7**. Team 6: Floortalk$^{®}$ (Follow-up). Stops consumers in their tracks with large-scale floor advertising anywhere in the store.

Coupon Machine Team: Presentation

Slide 5

Electronic Price Team: Close

Slide 6

Floortalk Team: Follow-up

Slide 7

7. **Spend 10 minutes** and have all student teams complete the entire News America Marketing Personal Selling Process Handout. Remind the teams that they must:

   a. Identify the marketing objectives of their prospective client that its SmartSource in-store media product can fulfill.

   b. Develop suggestions on how to accomplish its assigned personal selling process objective.

News America
Personal Selling
Handout

Slide 8

8. **Show Slide 8**. Ask a representative from each team to share their marketing objectives and suggestions based on the following steps in the personal selling process listed below:

- <u>Prospecting</u>: Team 1: At-Shelf Sampling.

  a. **In-store product marketing objectives**. Generate awareness, interest, and trial.

  b. **Personal selling suggestions**. Prospects identified through advertising, referrals, cold canvassing, trade shows, websites, etc.

- <u>Preapproach</u>: Team 2: AudioInk.

  a. **In-store product marketing objectives**. Generate awareness, interest, and trial.

  b. **Personal selling suggestions**. Information sources include, personal observation, other customers, own salespeople, previous sales attempts, etc. Must know customs/norms of country, organization, and if possible, the client.

- <u>Approach</u>: Team 3: Carts.

  a. **In-store product marketing objectives**. Drive traffic to brand. Build brand equity.

  b. **Personal selling suggestions**. Need to make a great first impression, cultivate a warm, business-like relationship, reference common acquaintances and interests, conduct a product demonstration, leave a brochure or other sales materials, etc.

- <u>Presentation</u>: Team 4: Coupon Machine.

  a. **In-store product marketing objectives**. Generate awareness, interest, and trial. Build brand loyalty. Break competitive tie at the shelf. Weaken competitors.

  b. **Personal selling suggestions**. Use suggestive selling, focus on benefits, cost-benefit analysis, probe by asking questions then listen and act on the responses, offer solution to client problems, if client has objections, handle them professionally using one of the techniques described in Chapter 20, etc.

- <u>Close</u>: Team 5: Electronic Price.

  a. **In-store product marketing objectives**. Generate awareness, interest, and trial. Provide information. Break competitive tie at the shelf.

  b. **Personal selling suggestions**. Focus on body language and/or language used to indicate a ready-to-buy decision is forthcoming, ask the client to make a decision on some aspect or term of the sale, ask the client to make decisions on some attribute under the assumption the sales ahs been finalized, offer a time deadline (the offer is good until…), ask specifically for the order, etc.

- <u>Follow-up</u>: Team 6: Floortalk.

  a. **In-store product marketing objectives**. Generate awareness, interest, and trial. Build equity. Break competitive tie at the shelf.

  b. **Personal selling suggestions**. Make sure the product or service has been delivered, ask if you can do anything else to ensure their satisfaction with you and the firm, etc.

Marketing Lessons. Marketers use the personal selling process to develop satisfied, long-term customer relationships. When executed properly, it leads to satisfied customers who may generate additional sales through increased sales and referrals, which leads to the first stage of the process.

Website. To learn more about the marketing services of News America Marketing, go to www.newsamerica.com.

NEWS AMERICA MARKETING
PERSONAL SELLING PROCESS HANDOUT

(1) Marketing objectives fulfilled with the News America Marketing SmartSource In-Store Media product: _____

STAGE	OBJECTIVE	(2) IDEAS TO MEET OBJECTIVE IN THE PERSONAL SELLING PROCESS
Prospecting	Search for and qualify prospects	• • • •
Preapproach	Gather information and decide how to approach the prospect	• • • •
Approach	Gain prospect's attention, stimulate interest, and make the transition to the presentation	• • • •
Presentation	Begin converting a prospect into a customer by creating a desire for the product or service	• • • •
Close	Obtain a purchase commitment from the prospect and create a customer	• • • •
Follow-up	Ensure that the customer is satisfied with the product or service	• • • •

ICA 20-2

CHAPTER 20: PERSONAL SELLING AND SALES MANAGEMENT

ICA 20-3: IN-CLASS ACTIVITY

Expense Account Role-Play

Learning Objectives. To have students: (1) understand the ethical dimensions involved being a sales person within an organization and (2) distinguish between the two different models of ethical behavior in Chapter 4 of the textbook as it applies to salespeople: moral idealism and utilitarianism.

Definitions. The following marketing terms are referred to in this in-class activity (ICA):

- Code of Ethics: A formal statement of ethical principles and rules of conduct.

- Ethics: The moral principles and values that govern the actions and decisions of an individual or group.

- Moral Idealism: A personal moral philosophy that considers certain individual rights or duties as universal, regardless of the outcome.

- Utilitarianism: A personal moral philosophy that focuses on the "greatest good for the greatest number," by assessing the costs and benefits of the consequences of ethical behavior.

Nature of the Activity. To have a few students conduct a role-play by assuming different characters to demonstrate an ethical issue related to salespeople within an organization.

Estimated Class Time. 20 minutes.

Materials Needed.

- The ICA20-3.doc Word and ICA20-3.ppt PowerPoint files contained in the ICA20-3 folder of the Instructor's CD #2 from the *Instructor's Survival Kit* box.

- Three (3) copies of the Expense Account Role-Play Script.

- Three (3) name cards, one for each of the student participants in the role-play.

- NOTE: Transparencies can be made of the handouts instead of making copies and using the PowerPoint presentation for those instructors who prefer this option.

Preparation Before Class. Follow the steps below:

1. Read the material in Chapter 4, pp. 103, 105-106 that discusses (1) corporate culture and codes of ethics and (2) personal moral philosophy and ethical behavior.

2. Print, read, and if necessary, edit the ICA20-3.doc Word file.

3. Print and/or review the PowerPoint slides from the ICA20-3.ppt PowerPoint file.

4. Prepare name cards for each of the characters.

5. Make three (3) copies of the Expense Account Role-Play Script, one for each of the participants, and highlight the particular parts for each character's script.

6. Set up a table and chairs in front of the classroom for the "meeting."

Instructions. Follow the steps below to conduct this ICA:

1. Recruit three students (2 males & 1 female) to play the characters in the role-play. Seat the characters at a table in front of the class and give each the corresponding "script" for his or her character.

2. While the role-playing students are reviewing the scripts, give the following background and then introduce the characters:

"What you are about to see is a reenactment of a real situation. Julia has been with Emco for 6 months and is back at headquarters for her first sales department quarterly review. On the last day of the meeting, Julia finds herself at lunch, seated between two veteran sales representatives, Dan and Mike in the company cafeteria. Listen closely and take note of the dilemma portrayed in this situation. Here are the three characters in our drama:

Character

- Julia: New Emco sales representative.

- Dan: Veteran Emco sales representative.

- Mike: Veteran Emco sales representative.

3. Introduce the cast and his/her job title.

4. Have the students read the expense account role-play script in front of the class.

5. When with the role-play is finished, say:

"So, we now leave Emco's company cafeteria. Let's discuss what we've observed by answering some questions."

6. Ask students the questions below to facilitate the buying center discussion:

- Question 1: What are the relevant facts in the case?

  Answers:

  a. Julia is meeting sales goals with her current expenses.

  b. Dan and Mike perceive Julia's sales and entertainment expenses to be significantly lower than those for the rest of the sales force.

- Question 2: What are some of the ethical issues or questions presented?

  Answers:

  a. Are expenses appropriate to sales objectives/goals?

  b. Should Julia conform to sales force expense norms?

  c. What is the company's code of ethics with regarding this practice?

  d. To what extent does Julia have a responsibility to keep her expenses at a minimum while meeting her objectives?

  e. How did Mike and Dan find out about Julia's sales expenses in the first place?

  f. Do customers expect to be entertained? Is there a culture of "quid pro quo?"

- Question 3: Who are people that are affected by this situation?

  Answer: Julia, Emco's stakeholders (shareholders, other employees, etc.), Emco salesforce (including Dan and Mike), the Emco sales manager, and Emco customers.

- Question 4: What are the alternatives in this situation?

  Answers:

  a. Increase the amount of expenses claimed.

  b. Begin entertaining customers more frequently and more lavishly.

  c. Discuss the situation with the sales manager.

  d. Quit.

- Question 5: What evaluation criteria (from the two ethical perspectives) should be applied to the alternatives?

  Answer: The analysis of the alternatives will depend on the particular personal moral philosophy taken:

  Moral Idealism Perspective:

  a. What does each stakeholder have the right to expect?

  b. Which alternative(s) would you not want imposed on you if you were Julia? Dan and Mike? The sales manager? Customers?

  c. Which stakeholder carries the greatest burden if Julia decides to do nothing?

  d. What is the upper limit on expense budget?

  e. Will exceeding the as yet unknown "average" sales expense may invite scrutiny of past and current sales expenses?

Utilitarian Perspective:

a. Which alternative would provide the greatest benefit to the greatest number?

b. How would costs be measured? How much value should be placed on the:

- Good will of Dan and Mike, the rest of the sales department?

- Benefits of the expenditures to the customer, to the firm, and to Julia's sales performance?

- Costs of bringing this up to the sales manager?

c. Which stakeholder carries the greatest burden if Julia decides to do nothing?

d. What is the practical upper limit on the expense budget?

e. Will exceeding the as yet unknown "average" sales expense may invite scrutiny of past and current sales expenses?

- Question 6: What action should Julia take?

Answers:

a. What alternative would you chose in her situation? Why

b. Which ethical theories make the most sense in this particular situation?

- Could argue for doing nothing. The sales manager has not indicated any problems with Julia's performance or expenses. However, if Julia really should be doing more entertaining and this is an important part of building relationships and selling, she may be negatively affecting a number of stakeholders because she is not operating at her potential.

- Discussing the situation with the sales manager has some merit, but this has the potential for drawing attention to other sales people who are spending more. This gets sales people like Mike and Don "in trouble" or unnecessarily draws attention to Julia's activities. Still, this seems to be the most sensible way to address the situation. Julia could approach the sales manager for feedback on her own performance and not referencing others' expenses.

- Increasing the amount of entertaining expenses without increasing the amount of sales without any real justification would be unethical. This has a negative impact on a number of stakeholders under both models.

Marketing Lesson. A number of stakeholders are affected by the ethical decisions of a company's salespeople. Marketers need to consider the impact of these decisions on organizational and societal stakeholders.

EXPENSE ACCOUNT ROLE-PLAY SCRIPT

Mike: "Julia, the accounting guys are giving us grief about our expenses. You're making us look bad. I've heard that you have the lowest sales expenses of anyone in the whole company."

Dan: "You shouldn't be cutting corners on entertainment with your customers, Julia. And you owe it to yourself when you're on the road to stay in nice hotels and eat well. Pass the pepper, Mike."

Mike: "Yeah. Remember, your expense account is one of the benefits of this job. Say, did you see the game last night? The Chicago Cubs were incredible."

As Mike and Dan continue their conversation (softly ad lib), Julia stands, faces the audience and wonders out loud:

Julia: "Have my sales expenses been too low?"

"Sales for my territory have been steadily growing since I took over the area 6 months ago. I'm meeting my sales goals. I wonder if I should be entertaining my customers more often. Maybe I'd generate more sales if I wined and dined my customers like Mike and Dan. I'm not altogether comfortable asking customers to dinner, although I do frequently take them to lunch.

"I stay in modest hotels while I'm on the road. I usually order room service and work on my call reports in the evenings. Still, I don't feel that I have been miserly with my own personal expenses.

"I wonder if I should discuss the situation with my boss, the sales secretary, or someone in accounting. Or maybe I should find a copy of Emco's Code of Ethics. On the other hand, perhaps that would only draw more attention to the situation and make matters worse. After all, the sales manager has said nothing about my expenses."

[End of the Role-Play]

CHAPTER 21: IMPLEMENTING INTERACTIVE AND MULTICHANNEL MARKETING

ICA 21-1: IN-CLASS ACTIVITY

Interactive Marketing for Hill's Pet Nutrition[1]

Learning Objective. To have students learn about the practice of interactive marketing through product sampling by using an actual example developed by a leading firm in the field.

Definitions. The following marketing terms are referred to in this in-class activity (ICA):

- Customerization: The growing practice of not only customizing a product or service but also personalizing the marketing and overall shopping and buying interaction for each customer.

- Free-standing Insert (FSI): A full-color piece featuring advertisements with coupons and other promotional offers, inserted in the Sunday newspaper.

- Interactive Marketing: Two-way buyer-seller electronic communication in a computer-mediated environment in which the buyer controls the kind and amount of information received from the seller.

- Multichannel Marketing: The blending of different communication and delivery channels that are mutually reinforcing in attracting, retaining, and building relationships with consumers who shop and buy in the traditional marketplace and marketspace.

- Online Consumers: The subsegment of all Internet users who employ this technology to research products and services and make purchases.

- Product Sampling: Offering a free (or at a reduced price) product to consumers in an effort to create awareness, stimulate trial, and induce repeat purchases.

- Promotional Websites: Electronic storefronts principally focused on advertising and promoting a firm's products and services and to provide information on how an item is used and where it can be purchased.

- Transactional Websites: Electronic storefronts principally focused on converting an online browser into an online, catalog, or in-store buyer.

Nature of the Activity. To have students engage in an interactive/multichannel marketing activity for the Hill's® Science Diet® Advanced Protection™ product sample promotion created by VML.

Estimated Class Time. 20 minutes.

---

[1] The authors wish to thank Hill's Pet Nutrition and VML who assisted in the development of this ICA.

Materials Needed.

- The ICA21-1.doc Word and ICA21-1.ppt PowerPoint files contained in the ICA21-1 folder of the Instructor's CD #2 from the *Instructor's Survival Kit* box.

- The Hill's Science Diet Advanced Protection canine product sample contained in the *Instructor's Survival Kit* box.

- Copies of the Hill's Science Diet Interactive Marketing and Product Sample Promotion Handout.

- NOTE: Transparencies can be made of the handouts instead of making copies and using the PowerPoint presentation for those instructors who prefer this option.

Preparation Before Class. Follow the steps below:

1. Read pp. 514-517 of Chapter 19 on sales promotion and 560, 564-565, 568, 572-575 of Chapter 21 on interactive and multichannel marketing.

2. Print, read, and if necessary, edit the ICA21-1.doc Word file.

3. Print and/or review the slides from the ICA21-1.ppt PowerPoint file.

4. Make copies of the of the Hill's Science Diet Interactive Marketing and Product Sample Promotion Handout.

5. OPTIONAL: Bookmark the Hill's Pet Nutrition (www.hillspet.com) and VML (www.vml.com) websites on your classroom computer.

Instructions. Follow the steps below to conduct this ICA:

1. Pass around the Hill's Science Diet Advanced Protection canine product sample contained in the *Instructor's Survival Kit* box.

2. Give students this background mini-lecture on interactive and multichannel marketing:

   "**Interactive marketing** involves two-way buyer-seller electronic communication in a computer-mediated environment in which the buyer controls the kind and amount of information received from the seller. Most adult Internet users have sought online product or service information and actually purchased a product or service online. To varying degrees, these online consumers benefit from **customerization**—the growing practice of not only customizing a product or service but also personalizing the marketing and overall shopping and buying interaction for each customer.

   Two general applications of websites exist based on their intended purpose:

   a. **Transactional websites,** which are essentially electronic storefronts. They convert an online browser into a buyer. They are most common among store and catalog retailers and direct selling companies.

b. **Promotional websites**, which advertise and promote a company's products and provide information on how items can be used and where they can be purchased. They often engage the visitor in an interactive experience involving electronic coupons and other sales promotion alternatives."

3. Give students this background mini-lecture on the interactive marketing segment of the sales promotion industry:

"According to *Promo Magazine's 2005 Industry Trend Report*, U.S. marketers spent an estimated $2.4 billion on interactive/online sales promotion in 2004, an increase of 25% over 2003. For almost 25% of marketers, interactive marketing became one of the top three tactics used by marketers in 2004.[2] For these marketers, cutting edge interactive marketing in 2005 may consist of online video, and multimedia messaging via mobile phone."[3]

4. Give the following mini-lecture on VML:

"VML, based in Kansas City, MO, is the 13th leading interactive marketing agency in the U. S., with 2004 interactive sales of $67 million.[4] As a full-service marketing agency, VML specializes in the integration of online and traditional offline (marketspace and marketplace) communications. Recently, VML was honored for its work on developing Burger King's website that supported its role in NBC's January 2005 season premiere of *The Apprentice*. The website featured a sweepstakes promotion that generated over 600,000 visitors during the promotional period."[5]

5. Give the following mini-lecture on the pet food industry:

"According to the American Pet Products Manufacturers Association (APPMA), the U.S. pet industry expenditures in 2005 is estimated to be $36 billion, with veterinary care, food, and supplies being the top three. In 2005, spending on pet food is expected to reach $14.5 billion. In terms of pet ownership, there are over 44 million dog owners (74 million dogs) and 38 million cat owners (91 million cats).[6]

To satisfy the growing demand for healthier food, the major pet food manufacturers, such as Hill's Pet Nutrition (Science Diet and Prescription Diet), Proctor & Gamble (Iams and Eukanuba), and Nestlé (Ralston-Purina Pro Plan and Purina ONE), have launched all natural, super-premium canine and feline pet food lines. Today, this segment accounts for about 30% of the total pet food market. Recently, a growing number of premium pet food products are being marketed for: (a) behavior modification, such as weight reduction, disease prevention, and skin/hair health; (b) stage in life, such as under 1 year (puppy/kitten), young adult (1 – 6 years), and senior; and (c) emotional well-being."[7]

---

[2] Kathleen M. Joyce, "Riding the Tide," *Promo Magazine's 2005 Industry Trend Report*," (April 1, 2005).

[3] Kathleen M. Joyce, "Digital Bridges," *Promo Magazine's 2005 Industry Trend Report*," (April 1, 2005).

[4] VML press release, February 21,2005.
See http://www.vml.com/q7rd/PortfolioDocuments/Top_50_Interactive.pdf.

[5] VML press release, "VML Creative Receives National Award," February 10, 2005 and Amy Johannes, "Burger King Cooks Up a Winner: Best Overall," *Promo Magazine*, May 1, 2005.

[6] Fact Sheet: Industry Statistics & Trends, American Pet Products Manufacturers Association (APPMA). See http://www.appma.org/press_industrytrends.asp.

[7] Ibid.

Slide 2

Hill's Advanced Protection pet food

6. **Show Slide 2** and pass around the Hill's Science Diet Adult Advanced Protection product sample.

7. Give students this background mini-lecture on the Hill's Science Diet Advanced Protection product for adult dogs (canines) and cats (felines):

   "The corporate mission of Hill's Pet Nutrition is to 'to help enrich and lengthen the special relationships between people and their pets.' Of its many products, Hill's markets the Science Diet Advanced Protection brand for adult dogs and cats. Launched in 2003, Science Diet Advanced Protection is the only brand with an antioxidant formula clinically proven to increase vitality and alertness."

8. Form students into 4-person teams.

9. Ask a student team the following question:

   • Question 1: How could Hill's drive potential consumers of super-premium dog/cat food to try an interactive marketing-delivered product sample?

   Answer: Several options exist: (a) banner ads on a strategic retail partner's websites, such as Petco or PETsMART, that contains the product sample offer and allows interested consumers to then "click-through" to Hill's website; (b) targeted e-mail campaigns to consumers who have previously registered at Hill's or its strategic partners' websites; (c) TV, print, and direct mail that have the Hill's website address mentioned; and (d) special sales promotional offers on Hill's own website.

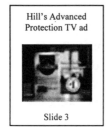

Slide 3

Hill's Advanced Protection TV ad

10. **Show Slides 3-7** and give students this background mini-lecture on the Hill's Science Diet Adult Advanced Protection Interactive Marketing and Product Sample Promotion developed by VML:

    "During the 1st quarter of 2005, VML created the Hill's Science Diet Advanced Protection Interactive Marketing and Product Sample Promotion. An advertising campaign was developed consisting of a TV ad (Slide 3: TRT = 0:15), a FSI (Slide 4), direct mail (Slide 5), print ads (Slide 6), and online ads (Slide 7). The marketing materials promised that consumers would notice an increase in their pet's vitality and alertness within 2 weeks."

Slide 4

Hill's Advanced Protection FSI

Slide 5

Hill's Advanced Protection direct mail

Slide 6

Hill's Advanced Protection print ads

Slide 7

Hill's Advanced Protection online ads

11. Ask a student team the following question:

- Question 2: Why would Hill's create this integrated interactive marketing sales promotion?

  Answer: To: (a) increase brand awareness, promote the product's benefits, and encourage trial of the product; (b) reach target consumers more efficiently and effectively—particularly with direct mail and print ads—based on demographic, geographic, and psychographic parameters; (c) collect information (demographic, behavioral, lifestyle, etc.) from these consumers; and (d) drive consumers to the Hill's website and/or retail strategic partner (such as Petco or PETsMART).

12. Ask a student team the following question:

Hill's Advanced Protection online ads

Slide 7

- Question 3: What is the purpose of an online banner ad?

  Answer: **Show Slide 7.** Online banner ads were placed on targeted sites to reach the Hill's target audience using an animated Flash banner to generate interest and encourage product trial. As you can see, the online ads featured a veterinarian endorsement along with a 'call-to-action' to print an online coupon to save money on the Advanced Protection product.

13. Ask a student team the following question:

Hill's Advanced Protection mini-website

Slide 8

- Question 4: Why would Hill's/VML create a mini-website within the Hill's Pet website for the Hill's Science Diet Advanced Protection products?

  Answer: **Show Slide 8.** The special mini-website was created to: (a) provide product information for dogs and cats; (b) test one's knowledge about the benefits of antioxidants and pet health; (c) learn how the product works; (d) watch (again) the Advanced Protection TV ad; show a competitive comparison; and (f) print a coupon to save money on a future purchase of the product.

14. Ask student teams the following questions:

- Question 5: What kinds of information would Hill's want to capture from consumers interested in a free sample or coupon of super-premium dog/cat food?

Hill's Advanced Protection online registration

Slide 9

  Answer: **Show Slide 9.** The following information would be of interest: (a) contact information of the consumer to send the free sample; (b) demographic information of the dog/cat (name, age, breed, etc.); (c) behavioral information regarding the pet and the food it eats (brand used, product form—dry or canned, dietary issues, such as obesity, sensitive skin or stomach, fur balls, etc.;

and (d) opt-in to receive future communication from Hill's.
[NOTE: The *CAN-SPAM Act* which came into effect on January 1, 2004, sets regulations for when and how businesses can send commercial email messages. Hill's Pet Nutrition diligently adheres to all directives established by the Act.]

- Question 6: Why would Hill's want to collect this information?

  Answer: To be able to develop a personalized and relevant website experience for each consumer, and to create individual for future communication.

15. Ask a student team the following question:

    - Question 7: Why would Hill's want to send an e-mail to users of a competitive pet food product?

Hill's Advanced
Protection
e-mail offer

Slide 10

      Answer: **Show Slide 10.** E-mail marketing provides the ability to target competitive and potential users with product messaging and offers. VML acquired the e-mail addresses of consumers who had purchased competing products in the previous six months, who were then sent an e-mail offer. The inclusion of direct-to-print coupon technology within the e-mail encourages product trial because little effort is required to print a coupon.

16. Ask a student team the following question:

    - Question 8: What other online marketing strategies or tactics could Hill's use to reach new or retain existing customers?

Hill's Advanced
Protection
Pet Chat

Slide 11

      Answer: **Show Slide 11.** One such strategy is an e-newsletter called Pet Chat. This vehicle allows Hill's to communicate with its consumers who have specifically registered (i.e. 'opted-in') to receive information and offers from Hill's. The Hill's e-newsletter is sent regularly to all opted-in e-mail addresses. This is NOT spam—consumers willingly requested this resource and always have the opportunity to 'opt-out' if desired. The August 2004 edition promoted the Advanced Protection product.

17. Ask a student team the following question:

- Question 9: What type of interactive marketing website does the Hill's use? Is it a transactional website or a promotional website?

  Answer: At the time of this ICA, this interactive marketing website is a promotional website. Consumers are directed to the Hill's Advanced Protection mini-website to learn about and the product, interact with the brand, and request a coupon or sample incentive. Consumers are not able to purchase pet food directly on the Hill's website. Instead, the site links to its strategic retail partners (physical store locations and online websites) where consumers can purchase Science Diet products.

Other Sales Promotions for Advil Handout

Slide 12

18. **Show Slide 12** and ask students to list the advantages and disadvantages of the interactive marketing promotion strategy developed for the Hill's Science Diet Advanced Protection Interactive Marketing and Product Sample Promotion. Write down their responses on either the board or the transparency made from the Hill's Science Diet Interactive Marketing and Product Sample Promotion Handout. Compare their responses to those identified by both Hill's Pet Nutrition and VML.

VML's Interactive Marketing Product Sample Promotion for Hill's Science Diet Advanced Protection Adult Pet Food	
Advantages	**Disadvantages**
• 90% of consumers try the product being sampled. • Of those that try, many purchase the brand and adopt the product, switching from a competitor's brand. • Hill's generates a database with demographic, behavioral, and lifestyle information from which to tailor other marketing promotions. • Hill's develops a target profile of its consumers for specific products. • Samples are mailed in a timely fashion. • Coupons, rebates, and other promotions for this or other products are included with the sample to cross-sell these products. • An exchange of value occurs: consumers receive a free sample while Hill's receives qualified prospects for its products. • Hill's Science Diet brand is reinforced in consumers' minds as they use the free sample.	• Not every dog/cat owner has Internet access. • Many pet owners choose to obtain free samples only from physical retail store locations because they want to ask questions about it with an expert. • Some consumers don't want to share personal information about themselves (or their pets) over the Internet for fear of receiving unsolicited e-mails from Hill's or others (spam). [NOTE: Hill's has a policy against this practice!] • Some Internet users use promotional websites but fear transactional websites because they must provide credit card information to buy a product even though it may be a secure transaction. • Some consumers may try but not adopt the product being sampled, thereby increasing marketing and therefore product costs. • The target audience may not be exposed to the promotional offers (banners, links, etc.) on the Internet since they may not visit websites where these offers reside.

Marketing Lesson. Marketers use product sampling via interactive marketing to increase awareness, trial, and adoption of new products and build brand loyalty for existing products.

Websites. For more information, go to the following websites: VML (www.vml.com); Hill's Science Diet (www.hillspet.com or www.sciencediet.com); and the sales promotion industry (www.promomagazine.com).

HILL'S SCIENCE DIET® INTERACTIVE MARKETING AND PRODUCT SAMPLE PROMOTION HANDOUT

ADVANTAGES	DISADVANTAGES
•	•
•	•
•	•
•	•
•	•
•	•
•	•

CHAPTER 21: IMPLEMENTING INTERACTIVE AND MULTICHANNEL MARKETING

ICA 21-2: IN-CLASS ACTIVITY

Buying a BMW Z4 Roadster: Marketplace vs. Marketspace (Part 1)[1]

Learning Objectives. To have students: (1) understand the nature of interactive marketing and electronic commerce, (2) compare the traditional "marketplace" channel with the new "marketspace" channel (Part 1), and (3) experience an interactive marketing website that encourages prospective customers to "build-to-order" a product with the specific features, options, and price they want (Part 2).

Definitions. The following marketing terms are referred to in this in-class activity (ICA):

- Electronic Commerce: Any activity that uses some form of electronic communication in the inventory, exchange, advertisement, distribution, and payment of goods and services.

- Interactive Marketing: Two-way buyer-seller electronic communication in a computer-mediated environment in which the buyer controls the kind and amount of information received from the seller.

- Marketspace: An information- and communication-based electronic exchange environment mostly occupied by sophisticated computer and telecommunication technologies and digitized offerings.

- Multichannel Marketing: The blending of different communication and delivery channels that are mutually reinforcing in attracting, retaining, and building relationships with consumers who shop and buy in the traditional marketplace and marketspace.

Nature of the Activity. To have students compare the traditional marketplace channel for buying a BMW Z4 roadster 3.0i from a BMW Center (dealership) with the new marketspace channel for buying a Z4 roadster 3.0i at BMW's "Build Your BMW" website. The entire activity consists of Part 1 (this ICA) and Part 2 (ICA 21-3).

Estimated Class Time. 20 minutes.

Materials Needed.

- The ICA21-2.doc Word and ICA21-2.ppt PowerPoint files contained in the ICA21-2 folder of the Instructor's CD #2 from the *Instructor's Survival Kit* box.

- The BMW Z4 Roadster brochure contained in the *Instructor's Survival Kit* box.

- Copies of the Using the Six "C" Framework to Suggest Reasons for Buying a BMW Z4 Roadster 3.0i Handout.

---

[1] The authors wish to Teresa Bencivengo, Marketing at BMW, who assisted in the development of this ICA.

- NOTE: Transparencies can be made of the handouts instead of making copies and using the PowerPoint presentation for those instructors who prefer this option.

Preparation Before Class. Follow the steps below:

1. Read pp. 567-574 of Chapter 21.

2. Print, read, and if necessary, edit the ICA21-2.doc Word file.

3. Print and/or review the PowerPoint slides from the ICA21-2.ppt PowerPoint file.

4. Make copies of the Using the Six "C" Framework to Suggest Reasons for Buying a BMW Z4 Roadster 3.0i Handout.

5. Download either the "Expanded Film" version or bookmark the BMW Films (www.bmwfilms.com) webpage of the "streamed" versions of one of *The Hire* Z4 Roadster short films. [NOTE: QuickTime Player or Windows Media Player is required. Consult your institution's technology representative for assistance.]

6. OPTIONAL: Bookmark the BMW (www.bmwusa.com) and BMW Films (www.bmwfilms.com) websites on your classroom computer.

Instructions. Follow the steps below to conduct this ICA:

BMW Films:
The Hire Series

Slide 2

1. OPTIONAL: Show Slide 2 at the beginning of class (or the lecture on interactive marketing). Select and play one of the *The Hire* Series of Internet films featuring the BMW Z4 Roadster. To do this:

   a. Click on the "*The Hire*" graphic to go to the BMW Films website (www.bmwfilms.com).

   b. Click on one of the film titles at the top of the webpage to download the film onto your classroom computer's hard drive ("Hostage" is recommended; TRT = 9:40).

   c. Click on the "View the Film" link.

   d. Complete the brief registration (first name and e-mail address).

   e. Choose the viewing option: (1) "Enhanced Film," which is similar to a DVD experience but has a longer download time; QuickTime or Windows Media Player required) or (2) "Streamed," in which the film is downloaded and played in real time. Select the desired connection speed and a format (Windows Media Player, QuickTime Player or Real Player required) to stream the film selected. [NOTE: make sure the computer has the appropriate Internet access and player before making your selections.]

   f. If you choose to view one of the Hire films, ask students if this Internet multichannel marketing strategy is effective in promoting the BMW Z4 Roadster.

BMW Z4 Roadster
brochure

Slide 3

BMW Z4 Roadster

Slide 4

2. **Show Slide 3** and pass around the BMW Z4 Roadster brochure obtained from the *Instructor's Survival Kit* box.

3. **Show Slide 4** and give students the following mini-lecture on the BMW Z4 Roadster:

"The Z4 Roadster debuted in 2003, replacing the hugely successful Z3 Roadster that was introduced in 1996. According to a BMW press release, 'The new Z4 Roadster does not just replace its predecessor, it takes BMW and the roadster segment to another level.' Wider, longer, and lower in stance, the new Z4 has a soft top and comes in an 'athletic and assertive new design.' Two models are offered: the Z4 Roadster 2.5i at $34,300 and the higher-performing, more extensively-equipped Z4 Roadster 3.0i at $41,300, excluding $695 destination and handling."

4. Give students this background mini-lecture on interactive marketing:

"**Interactive marketing** involves two-way buyer-seller electronic communication in a computer-mediated environment in which the buyer controls the kind and amount of information received from the seller.

Two types of websites exist based on their intended purpose:

   a. **Promotional websites**. These advertise and promote a company's products and provide information on how items can be used and where they can be purchased. As we have just seen in the case of BMW *The Hire* series of Internet-delivered short films not only entertain but also encourage prospective customers to test drive and purchase its Z4 Roadsters. In 2002, *The Hire* Season 1 film series, developed by BMW's advertising agency Fallon Worldwide, won the prestigious Grand Clio Award® for Internet Advertising and the Gold Clio Award® for Cinematography.

   b. **Transactional websites**. These are essentially electronic storefronts that attempt to convert online browsers into buyers. In the case of BMW, it offers its "Build Your BMW" website for prospective customers to customize a BMW Z4 Roadster based on their preferences (model, exterior, interior, package options, accessories, etc.). [NOTE: This will be the subject of ICA 21-3.]

5. Give students this mini-lecture on the BMW "marketplace" channel:

"Like other firms, BMW pursues a multichannel marketing strategy to sell the BMW Z4 Roadster 3.0i to target customers, consisting of the marketplace and marketspace channels. The "marketplace" channel is the traditional dealership that we all are familiar with, which BMW calls a "BMW Center.""

Show Slide 5: BMW Z4 TV ad [TRT = 0:30] **before** and **Show Slide 6**: BMW Z4 print ad while continuing with the mini-lecture:

"To generate awareness and motivate prospective buyers to go to a BMW Center, we see a print ad or TV ad that attracts our attention. For some of us, we see one of our colleagues or classmates driving a Z4 3.0i that stimulates a want. To satisfy this want, we go to the local BMW dealer and check out the Z4 3.0i in the showroom or on the lot.

We are then met by a salesperson, who gives us a brochure (like the one that is currently being passed around) of the Z4 Roadster line and asks us about the Z4 model we are interested in (the Z4 Roadster 3.0i) and the specific features and options we desire (manual transmission, silver exterior paint, etc.). The salesperson then asks if we want to take a test drive of the Z4 3.0i."

Show Slide 7: BMW Z4 3.0i Price List and continue with the mini-lecture:

"After taking the exhilarating test drive, the salesperson asks if we are interested in purchasing the car. If we say, 'Yes,' the salesperson then: (1) quotes us a list or initial price and the prices of the features we want, (2) asks how we want to finance the car (down payment, the type of financing, either loan or lease, and the terms) and about the kind of car we have to trade-in, and (3) informs us of any rebates to reduce the price of the car to arrive at a final price for the car. If we're <u>truly</u> interested, we then begin to negotiate over the final price and terms of the purchase with the salesperson."

6. **Show Slide 8**: BMW Z4 Roadster promotional e-mail and give students this background mini-lecture on the "marketspace" channel:

"BMW also uses an Internet marketing channel to sell its cars. This channel involves the use of both interactive marketing, in which information about the Z4 product line is e-mailed to prospective buyers (in late 2002, the image and accompanying e-mail you see was sent in advance of the car's introduction) and an e-commerce website created so that we are given the opportunity to "build-to-order" the Z4 Roadster 3.0i based on the features and options we select. For BMW's "Build Your BMW" Internet website, prospective buyers can request additional information, have a salesperson from a local dealership contact them to answer any questions or arrange for a test drive, and finance the purchase of their car through BMW Financial Services."

7. Conclude this background mini-lecture:

"Consumers choose to use interactive marketing websites to purchase products because of the convenience, cost, choice, customization, communication, and control they receive. These reasons apply to both the traditional marketplace channel and the new marketspace channel."

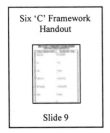

Six 'C' Framework
Handout

Slide 9

8. Pass out copies of the and **Show Slide 9**: Using the Six "C" Framework to Suggest Reasons for Buying a BMW Z4 Roadster 3.0i Handout.

9. Using the six "C" framework, ask students to suggest specific reasons why consumers would choose the traditional marketplace method for purchasing a Z4 Roadster 3.0i and write them on the board or on a transparency made from the Using the Six "C" Framework to Suggest Reasons for Buying a BMW Z4 Roadster 3.0i Handout. Then ask students why they would choose the new marketspace channel for buying a Z4 Roadster 3.0i and write them on the board or on the transparency. Some of the reasons students may suggest are listed below.

Marketing Lesson. Both the marketplace and marketspace channels for buying products are now common, with the latter growing in importance. Students should understand the reasons some consumers may prefer one channel to the other.

Websites. The website for the BMW Z4 roadster 3.0i is www.bmwusa.com. The website to download *The Hire* short film is www.bmwfilms.com.

USING THE SIX "C" FRAMEWORK TO SUGGEST REASONS FOR BUYING A BMW Z4 ROADSTER 3.0i

Traditional "Marketplace" Channel	New "Marketspace" Channel
Convenience: • Local dealer may be available • Relationship with dealer important for after-sale service; expedite repairs • Visually inspect the car before buying	**Convenience:** • Shop anytime and from anywhere • Not dependent upon local dealer availability or hours of operation to compare features & prices
Cost: • May be able to negotiate lower price • May get more value for trade-in • May get better financing terms with one's own local bank	**Cost:** • Usually the same or lower than dealer • Lower due to lower inventory, order processing, communications, and commissions costs • Easier to adjust prices due to market conditions • Search costs lower (save time = money)
Choice: • May have good selection of BMW Z4 roadster 3.0i's on dealer lot • May have more than one dealer in larger metropolitan markets to choose from	**Choice:** • Compare the BMW Center with BMW Virtual Center • Search other websites, such as Carpoint, to compare prices or purchase from other BMW Centers nationwide • Search websites for reviews on BMW Z4 roadster 3.0i
Customization: • Dealers can create direct marketing programs for their local market; know profiles of customers better and therefore target programs more efficiently	**Customization:** • Create the product with only the features and options desired via the "Virtual Center" • Suggest specific features & options to different segments if customer profiles are captured
Communication: • IMC approach to generate awareness, trial, and purchase • Knowledgeable salespeople can be invaluable	**Communication:** • Can request e-mail or telephone response for additional information from an online salesperson • Can receive e-mail notices of product news, special offers, etc. automatically
Control: • Aggressive customers like to dictate the terms of the negotiation process (price, trade-in value, features and options, financing, etc.) • Concern over privacy and security of personal and financial information	**Control:** • Consumers can better dictate the amount of information they receive, the alternatives they wish to evaluate, and the terms of the purchase

BMW of North America

2005 Model Year Retail Prices

Z4 Roadster 3.0i

Base Price USA Port of Entry*	**$41,995**
STEPTRONIC Transmission	1,275
Graphite Finish Trim[1]	150
Fully Automatic Soft Top	750[PP]
Cross Spoke Composite	2,560
Rear Deck Spoiler	220
Sycamore Wood Trim	200
8-Way Power Seats with 3-way Driver Memory	995[PP]
Heated Front Seats	500
Foglights	STD
Xenon Low- and High- Beam Headlights	700
Cruise Control	STD
Aerodynamic Kit	1,164
BMW On-Board Navigation System	1,800
BMW Assist GPS w/ Bluetooth Wireless Technology	750[PP]
Premium Sound System	STD
Metallic Paint	475
Cloth/Leather Combination Upholstery	NA
Leather Upholstery	STD
Extended Leather	1,200
Premium Package (PP)	2,500
Sport Package (SP)	1,200

*Includes $695 destination and handling.

PP = Premium Package   STD = Standard Equipment
SP = Sport Package   NA = Not available or not applicable

[1]Includes door handles, roll bars and steering wheel; also gearshift knob on 3.0i only.

USING THE SIX "C" FRAMEWORK TO SUGGEST REASONS FOR BUYING A BMW Z4 ROADSTER 3.0i

Traditional "Marketplace" Channel	New "Marketspace" Channel
• <u>Convenience</u>	• <u>Convenience</u>
• <u>Cost</u>	• <u>Cost</u>
• <u>Choice</u>	• <u>Choice</u>
• <u>Customization</u>	• <u>Customization</u>
• <u>Communication</u>	• <u>Communication</u>
• <u>Control</u>	• <u>Control</u>

ICA 21-2

CHAPTER 21: IMPLEMENTING INTERACTIVE AND MULTICHANNEL MARKETING

ICA 21-3: IN-CLASS ACTIVITY

Buying a BMW Z4 Roadster: Build Your BMW (Part 2)[1]

Learning Objectives. To have students: (1) understand the nature of interactive marketing and electronic commerce, (2) compare the traditional "marketplace" channel with the new "marketspace" channel (Part 1), and (3) experience an interactive marketing website that encourages prospective customers to "build-to-order" a product with the specific features, options, and price they want (Part 2).

Definitions. The following marketing terms are referred to in this in-class activity (ICA):

- Electronic Commerce: Any activity that uses some form of electronic communication in the inventory, exchange, advertisement, distribution, and payment of goods and services.

- Interactive Marketing: Two-way buyer-seller electronic communication in a computer-mediated environment in which the buyer controls the kind and amount of information received from the seller.

- Marketspace: An information- and communication-based electronic exchange environment mostly occupied by sophisticated computer and telecommunication technologies and digitized offerings.

- Multichannel Marketing: The blending of different communication and delivery channels that are mutually reinforcing in attracting, retaining, and building relationships with consumers who shop and buy in the traditional marketplace and marketspace.

Nature of the Activity. To have students compare the traditional marketplace channel for buying a BMW Z4 Roadster 3.0i from a BMW Center (dealership) with the new marketspace channel for buying a Z4 Roadster 3.0i at BMW's "Build Your BMW" website. The entire activity consists of Part 1 (this ICA) and Part 2 (ICA 21-3).

Estimated Class Time. 20 minutes.

Materials Needed.

- The ICA21-3.doc Word and ICA21-3.ppt PowerPoint files contained in the ICA21-3 folder of the Instructor's CD #2 from the *Instructor's Survival Kit* box.

- The BMW Z4 Roadster brochure contained in the *Instructor's Survival Kit* box.

- Copies of the BMW Z4 Roadster 3.0i Retail Pricing Sheet.

---

[1] The authors wish to Teresa Bencivengo, Marketing at BMW, who assisted in the development of this ICA.

Preparation Before Class. Follow the steps below:

1. Read pp. 567-574 of Chapter 21.

2. Print, read, and if necessary, edit the ICA21-3.doc Word file.

3. Make copies of the BMW Z4 Roadster 3.0i Retail Pricing Sheet.

4. Visit the BMW website at www.bmwusa.com and click on the "Build Your BMW" link.

5. Bookmark the BMW (www.bmwusa.com) website on your classroom computer.

Instructions. Follow the steps below to conduct this ICA:

1. Give students the following mini-lecture for review:

   "Like other firms, BMW pursues a multichannel marketing strategy when selling its products, such as the Z4 Roadster 3.0i, to target its customers. BMW sells its cars both through its traditional dealership network and more recently its Internet website. Previously, we identified the reasons consumers might purchase this vehicle at a local dealer or from its marketing website based on the convenience, cost, choice, customization, communication, and control they receive."

2. Review the students' responses of the Using the Six "C" Framework to Suggest Reasons for Buying a BMW Z4 Roadster 3.0i Handout.

3. Form students into 7 sets of teams. Each team will jointly determine the specific features and options it selects for the BMW Z4 Roadster 3.0i.

4. Pass out copies of the BMW Z4 Roadster 3.0i Pricing Sheet.

5. **Step 1**: Connect to the Build Your BMW website at www.bmwusa.com. Click on the "Z4 Roadster" link and scroll over to the Z4 Roadster 3.0i link and click on it. The Build You BMW webpage for the Z4 Roadster 3.0i (www.bmwusa.com/vehicles/Z4/30i) appears.

6. **Step 2**: To begin the marketspace experience, click on the "Build Your Z4 3.0i" link.

7. **Step 3**: Under the "Build Your BMW" header, have all teams select and write down the "Exterior" and "Interior" color options they want on the BMW Z4 Roadster 3.0i Pricing Sheet based on a consensus of the group. Scroll the cursor over or click on the options to obtain a description.

   a. Some "Interior" color options are not available for a particular "Exterior" color.

   b. See how the selections affect the "Virtual" Z4 Roadster 3.0i on the webpage.

   c. The MSRP (Manufacturer's Suggested Retail Price) changes as options are selected or deleted.

8. Have Team 1 identify its "Exterior" and "Interior" color selections. When finished with the selections, click on either the "Next Step" button or the "Packages/Options" link.

9. **Step 4**: Have all teams select and write down the "Package" and "Options" they want on the BMW Z4 Roadster 3.0i Pricing Sheet based on a consensus of the group.

10. Have Team 2 identify its "Package" and "Options" selections. Again, notice how the screen and MSRP changes. When finished with the selections, click on either the "Next Step" button or the "Accessories" link.

11. **Step 5**: Have all teams select and write down the "Accessories" they want on the BMW Z4 Roadster 3.0i Pricing Sheet based on a consensus of the group.

12. Have Team 3 identify its "Accessories" selections. Again, notice how the screen and MSRP changes. When finished with the selections, click on either the "Next Step" button or the "Summary" link.

13. **Step 6**: Review the selections made.

13. **Step 7—OPTIONAL**: If a printer is available, click on the "View Print-Friendly Format" link.

14. **Step 8**: Click on the "Explore Financing" link to explore monthly payment estimates with BMW Financial Services. Have all teams select and write down the financing options they want on the BMW Z4 Roadster 3.0i Pricing Sheet based on a consensus of the group. [NOTE: To obtain an estimate of the trade-in value of a car, go to the Kelley Blue Book website, which is www.kbb.com.]

    a. Select the "State of Purchase" where you are located.

    b. Input the "Down Payment" and "Trade-in Amount.

    c. Select and write down the financing method ("Lease," "BMW Select," "Traditional Finance," or "Performance Loan"). Under the "Lease" option only, have each team select the "Term" and "Annual Mileage." The "Monthly Payment" is automatically calculated for the BMW Z4 Roadster 3.0i based on the configuration specified on the "Summary" webpage. Have teams compare the leasing option with the other three finance options BMW offers its customers.

15. Have Team 4 identify its "Explore Financing" selections.

16. **Step 9**: Review the features, options, and financing terms that Teams 1 to 4 selected. If you want to change any, go back by clicking on the tab at the bottom of the webpage. When the class is satisfied with its selections, click on the "Save to MyBMW" link. BMW will prompt you to register.

17. OPTIONAL: For an out-of-class assignment, have Team 5 (or other volunteers) go (or telephone) a local BMW dealer. To locate the nearest one, click on the "Locate a Dealer" link at the top of the webpage. Whether in person or on the telephone, have these students kindly ask for a salesperson and explain that you want to obtain prices for the Z4 Roadster 3.0i configuration that is written on the BMW Z4 Roadster 3.0i Pricing Sheet. Tell them that you are doing this for a class project. Have the team write down their findings on the sheet and report them during the start of the next class period.

18. OPTIONAL: Have the following teams obtain prices for the BMW Z4 Roadster 3.0i from one of the following websites. [NOTE: Some of these car-buying websites require that the prospective buyer be a serious purchaser. Try the sites anyway and provide the required information. You may get an e-mail quote or a telephone call from a salesperson at the nearest BMW dealer.]:

    a. Team 6: Autobytel, which is www.autobytel.com.

    b. Team 7: MSN Autos, which is autos.msn.com.

    c. Team 8: Edmunds, www.edmunds.com.

Marketing Lesson. The 21st century will see an expansion of purchases through marketing websites on the Internet. Even complex purchases, like automobiles, can be accomplished through this channel. Thus, as demonstrated in this ICA and ICA 21-2, the new "marketspace" channel for shopping is a viable alternative to the more traditional "marketplace" channel for many of today's consumers.

Websites. The BMW website is www.bmwusa.com. The others are identified above.

BMW Z4 ROADSTER 3.0i PRICING SHEET

	"Z4 Roadster 3.0i" Build Your BMW		BMW Dealer		Autobytel, MSN Autos, or Edmunds
Item	**Price Quote**	**Item**	**Price Quote**	**Item**	**Price Quote**
Base Price:........... _____		Base Price:........... _____		Base Price:........... _____	
Dest. Charge:....... _____		Dest. Charge:....... _____		Dest. Charge:....... _____	
Exterior Color:..... _____		Exterior Color:..... _____		Exterior Color:..... _____	
Interior Color:...... _____		Interior Color:...... _____		Interior Color:...... _____	
Premium Package: _____		Premium Package: _____		Premium Package: _____	
Option #1: .... _____		Option #1: .... _____		Option #1:........... _____	
Option #2: .... _____		Option #2: .... _____		Option #2:........... _____	
Option #3: .... _____		Option #3: .... _____		Option #3:........... _____	
Option #4: .... _____		Option #4: .... _____		Option #4:........... _____	
Option #5: .... _____		Option #5: .... _____		Option #5:........... _____	
Option #6: .... _____		Option #6: .... _____		Option #6:........... _____	
Other Options:..... _____		Other Options:..... _____		Other Options: ..... _____	
TOTAL MSRP:... _____		TOTAL MSRP:... _____		TOTAL MSRP:... _____	
Trade-in Value: ... _____		Trade-in Value:.... _____		Trade-in Value:.... _____	
Down Payment: ... _____		Down Payment: ... _____		Down Payment: ... _____	
Months Financed: _____		Months Financed: _____		Months Financed: _____	
APR: .... _____		APR: .... _____		APR:................... _____	
Monthly Payment: _____		Monthly Payment: _____		Monthly Payment: _____	

CHAPTER 22: PULLING IT ALL TOGETHER: THE STRATEGIC MARKETING PROCESS

ICA 22-1: IN-CLASS ACTIVITY

Line and Brand Extensions: How Far Can General Mills Go?[1]

Learning Objectives. To have students (1) suggest some line and brand extensions and (2) develop some generalizations about when a line or brand extension is or is not likely to work.

Definitions. The following marketing terms are referred to in this in-class activity (ICA):

- Brand Extension: A branding strategy of using a current brand name to enter a completely different product class.

- Brand Name: Any word, device (design, shape, sound, or color), or combination of these used to distinguish a seller's goods or services.

- Line Extension: A branding strategy of using a current brand name to enter a new market segment in its product class.

Nature of the Activity. To have students: (1) suggest new products to extend the Cheerios® brand, (2) assess which line and brand extension ideas make sense and which don't, and (3) suggest some guidelines for developing line and brand extensions.

Estimated Class Time. 20 minutes.

Materials Needed.

- The ICA22-1.doc Word and ICA22-1.ppt PowerPoint files contained in the ICA22-1 folder of the Instructor's CD #2 from the *Instructor's Survival Kit* box.

- The Cheerios® cereal bowl, the Honey Nut Cheerios® cereal bowl, and the Honey Nut Cheerios® Milk 'n Cereal bar from the *Instructor's Survival Kit* box.

- Copies of the Finding Line and Brand Extensions for Cheerios Handout.

Preparation Before Class. Follow the steps below:

1. Read pp. 299-304 of Chapter 11 and pp. 582-583, 591-593, and 595 of Chapter 22.

2. Print, read, and if necessary, edit the ICA22-1.doc Word file.

3. Print and/or review the PowerPoint slides from the ICA22-1.ppt PowerPoint file.

4. Make copies of the Finding Line and Brand Extensions for Cheerios Handout.

---

[1] The authors wish to thank Muffie Taggett and Denise Bosch of General Mills who assisted in the development of this ICA. Cheerios®, Honey Nut Cheerios®, and Fruit Roll-ups® are registered trademarks of General Mills and used by permission.

5. OPTIONAL: Bookmark the General Mills (www.generalmills.com), Cheerios (www.cheerios.com), and Betty Crocker (www.bettycrocker.com) websites on your classroom computer.

Instructions. Follow the steps below to conduct this ICA:

1. Pass around the Cheerios® cereal bowl, the Honey Nut Cheerios® cereal bowl, and the Honey Nut Cheerios® Milk 'n Cereal bar from the *Instructor's Survival Kit* box.

Cheerios
Line extension

Slide 2

2. **Show Slide 2** and give students this background mini-lecture on General Mills and the ready-to-eat (RTE) cereal market:

"In 2004, the U. S. ready-to-eat (RTE) cereal market was $7.6 billion and General Mills had a 31% share of this market, second only to Kellogg's. However, the Cheerios line is the best-selling cereal, with an 11 percent share of the RTE market. This was due in part to the launch of Berry Burst Cheerios®.[2] For the past several years, the growth in the RTE cereal market has remained flat, as consumer demographics and tastes have changed. Some of these changes include:

a. **Fewer people eat breakfast, and those that do want more convenience**. As a result, General Mills introduced its Big G Milk 'n Cereal Bar® product line, which combines cereal, such as Honey Nut Cheerios, with a milk-based layer. It also introduced Go Bags™, which is cereal in a convenient pouch, and Cereal in a Cup.

b. **Consumers are concerned about eating healthier foods**. As a result, General Mills:

- Introduced line extensions of Cheerios with real fruit: Berry Burst Cheerios, which come in three varieties.

- Introduced brand extensions of selected cereals as Milk 'n Cereal Bars.

- Converted all of its cereal lines to whole grains.

- Introduced line extensions of Trix®, Coco Puffs®, and other cereals with 75 percent lower sugar using Splenda® due to the increased incidence of obesity among both children and adults. However, sales of these low-sugar cereals have flattened.[3]

- Introduced brand extensions of Wheaties® and Total® multi-vitamins.

- Introduced new cereal brands Harmony®, a "nutraceutical" cereal that is fortified with higher amounts of folic acid and calcium and targeted at women, and Sunrise®, an organic cereal targeted at those who want all-natural ingredients.

c. **Increased movie tie-ins to promote temporary sales increases**. General Mills created Shrek cereal to help promote *Shrek 2*. Kellogg's has done this for *Spider-Man 2*, *The Incredibles*, *SpongeBob SquarePants*, to name a few."

---

[2] General Mills 2004 Annual Report, pp. 2, 6.
[3] Lee Egerstrom, "Despite Grain-Bashing Diet Fads, Malt-O-Meal Posts 19 Percent Increase in Ready-To-Eat Breakfast Food Sold," *Pioneer Press*, March 10, 2005.

Line/Brand
Extensions Handout

Slide 3

3. Divide the class roughly in half and assign students to one of two sets of teams: the "Line Extension" and the "Brand Extension."

4. Pass out copies of the Finding Line and Brand Extensions for Cheerios® Handout to each student.

5. **Show Slide 4**. Spend 10 minutes and have students from the Cheerios "Line Extension" and the "Brand Extension" teams come up with ideas for products that could extend the Cheerios brand using the Finding Line and Brand Extensions for Cheerios® Handout.

6. Ask representatives of both the Cheerios "Line Extension" and the "Brand Extension" teams for their respective extension ideas and write them on the board.

Cheerios
Brand extensions

Slide 4

7. Ask for a quick show of hands from the students' on their reaction to the question "Does the extension work?" Check either the "Yes" or "No" column on the right side of the Finding Line and Brand Extensions for Cheerios® Handout that corresponds to the **majority** of student votes.

8. **Show Slide 4**. Here are some possible ideas, showing those Cheerios line and brand extensions that are currently (*) offered. [NOTE: Read list below.]

| Brand | Kind of Extension | |
	Line Extension	Brand Extension
Cheerios	• Cheerios* (1941) • Honey Nut Cheerios* (1979) • Apple Cinnamon Cheerios* (1988) • Multi-Grain Cheerios* (1991) • Frosted Cheerios* (1995) • Team Cheerios* (1997) • Strawberry Berry Burst Cheerios* (2003) • Triple Berry Burst Cheerios* (2003) • Strawberry Banana Berry Burst Cheerios* (2004)	• Big G Milk 'n Cereal Bar: Honey Nut Cheerios* • Honey Nut Cheerios Snacks Mix* • Hot Cereal (?) • Private Label Cereal (?) • Honey Nut Cheerios Go Bag* • Honey Nut Cheerios Cereal in a Cup* • T-shirts, Toddler Cereal Containers, Games, etc.* • NASCAR Race Car Sponsorship*

9. Ask the students for their conclusions or guidelines for what might "work" and "not work" in developing line or brand extensions. Some guidelines to discuss are:

   a. Guidelines for line or brand extensions that **do work**:

   - Consumer credibility with the new brand/product under the old brand name umbrella.

   - Potential for significant new incremental sales and profits.

   - Sales don't steal or "cannibalize" those from the original brand.

   - Little risk to the original brand.

   - A perception of high quality for the new brand/product that retains the high consumer regard for the original brand.

   - Others as identified.

   b. Guidelines for line and brand extensions that **don't work** are really the reverse of those just listed. When Frosted Cheerios was introduced, Cheerios marketers had to overcome the concern about guideline "c" above.

Marketing Lessons. Introducing line and brand extensions may look easy but it is a very complex, demanding, and costly process. Firms like General Mills must be concerned that new line extensions do not cannibalize sales from the original or previous extensions. Moreover, new brand extensions should (1) enhance, not diminish the brand equity invested and (2) meet a need of the new market segment-product group being targeted.

Websites. The General Mills website is (www.generalmills.com), the Cheerios website is (www.cheerios.com), and the Betty Crocker website is (www.bettycrocker.com) where you can order Cheerios T-shirts, games, etc.

FINDING LINE AND BRAND EXTENSIONS FOR CHEERIOS® HANDOUT

BRAND	TYPE OF EXTENSION	IDEA FOR EXTENSION OF BASIC BRAND	DOES EXTENSION WORK?	
			YES	NO
Cheerios	LINE	• • • • • • • • • • • •		
	BRAND	• • • • • • • • • • • •		

ICA 22-1

CHAPTER 22: PULLING IT ALL TOGETHER: THE STRATEGIC MARKETING PROCESS

ICA 22-2: IN-CLASS ACTIVITY

Marketing Planning Worksheet

Learning Objective. To have students do a marketing plan that lets them apply the strategic marketing process to highlight the key issues in assessing a marketing opportunity.

Definitions. The following marketing terms are referred to in this in-class activity (ICA):

- Marketing Plan: A road map for the marketing activities of an organization for a specified future period of time, such as one year or five years.

- Strategic Marketing Process: The approach whereby an organization allocates its marketing mix resources to reach its target markets.

Nature of the Activity. To have students complete the marketing planning worksheet for a simple marketing situation that might be either:

1. The one described below.

2. One the instructor selects.

3. The product or service the student or team will use for a marketing plan class project.

   If Choices #1 or #2 are used, this ICA will be used as a means of summarizing the course in conjunction with Chapter 2 of the textbook. Alternatively, the ICA may be used early in the course to help students undertake a preliminary structuring of the product or service used for their marketing plans (Choice #3 above).

Estimated Class Time. 20 minutes.

Materials Needed.

- The ICA22-2.doc Word and ICA22-2.ppt PowerPoint files contained in the ICA22-2 folder of the Instructor's CD #2 from the *Instructor's Survival Kit* box.

- A scenario, like the one below or Choices #2 or #3 described above.

- Copies of the:
  a. Marketing Plan Worksheet.
  b. Marketing Planning Worksheet for Team Development Sessions Handout.

- NOTE: Transparencies can be made of the handouts instead of making copies and using the PowerPoint presentation for those instructors who prefer this option.

Preparation Before Class. Follow the steps below:

1. Read pp. 593-594 of Chapter 22 as well as the material below to use either the scenario below as a basis for the student activity or prepare one of your own.

2. Print, read, and if necessary, edit the ICA22-2.doc Word file.

3. Print and/or review the PowerPoint slides from the ICA22-2.ppt PowerPoint file.

4. Make copies of:

   a. Marketing Planning Worksheet.

   b. Marketing Planning Worksheet for Team Development Sessions Handout.

5. OPTIONAL: Bookmark the McDonald's website (www.mcdonalds.com) on your classroom computer.

Instructions. Follow the steps below to conduct this ICA:

1. Give students this background mini-lecture:

   "A subsidiary of a community health center, specializing in private psychiatric care, has recently expanded into human resource development programs for business and industry. As the first in a series of offerings, the subsidiary is planning to offer an outdoor, adventure-based team development session for employee groups who work together to accomplish tasks. The center's subsidiary activities are intended to generate sufficient revenues to help fund new health programs."

2. Pass out copies of the Marketing Planning Worksheet.

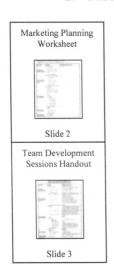

Marketing Planning Worksheet

Slide 2

Team Development Sessions Handout

Slide 3

3. **Show Slide 2**: Marketing Planning Worksheet and **spend 10 minutes** having the students complete the worksheet.

4. Inform students that the Marketing Plan Worksheet provides examples of possible responses to each of the factors involved in developing a marketing plan for the subsidiary of a community health center or any organization.

5. Pass out copies of the Marketing Planning Worksheet for Team Development Sessions Handout.

6. **Show Slide 3**: Marketing Planning Worksheet for Team Development Sessions Handout and discuss the students' ideas and their marketing implications for the choice that was selected from above.

Marketing Lesson. Marketing managers are often faced with a number of alternative opportunities. The Marketing Planning Worksheet enables a marketer to quickly assess the key environmental and marketing factors. While this quick assessment cannot replace an in-depth analysis, it can often screen out impractical ideas.

MARKETING PLANNNING WORKSHEET FOR: _____

FACTOR	ISSUE	MARKETING PLAN
Consumer Analysis/Target Market Analysis	• Who Benefits?	
	• How Do They Benefit?	
	• Who Decides to Buy or Use?	
	• Point of Difference?	
Environmental (Uncontrollable) Factors	• Consumer/Social Factors	
	• Economic Factors	
	• Technological Factors	
	• Competitive Factors	
	• Legal/Regulatory Factors	
Developing the Marketing Plan	• Objective	
	• Research (Collect Info)	
	• Product/Service Offered	
	• Price	
	• Promotion – Advertising	
	– Sales Promotion	
	– Public Relations	
	– Personal Selling	
	• Place/Distribution	
Executing the Marketing Plan	• Budget	
	• Who is Responsible?	
	• Milestone Dates	
Evaluating the Marketing Plan	• Did it Work?	

MARKETING PLANNING WORKSHEET FOR
TEAM DEVELOPMENT SESSIONS HANDOUT

FACTOR	ISSUE	MARKETING PLAN
Consumer Analysis/Target Market Analysis	• Who Benefits?	Employees, work groups, employers
	• How Do They Benefit?	Skill building: problem solving, creative thinking, communication
	• Who Decides to Buy/Use?	Owner, CEO, Director of HR
	• Point of Difference?	Alternative, more experiential approach
Environmental (Uncontrollable) Factors	• Consumer/Social Factors	Perception of need, values to human resource-development
	• Economic Factors	Perceived as too expensive by many small-medium companies
	• Technological Factors	Only 8 - 10 people at one time—requires high technical and safety emphasis
	• Competitive Factors	One competitor—program not as inclusive or safe but its half the cost
	• Legal/Regulatory Factors	None
Developing the Marketing Plan	• Objective	Provide team building workshops to area companies leading to other businesses
	• Research (Collect Info)	Which companies now purchase such programs? What are their characteristics? What companies are considering more progressive management practices?
	• Product/Service Offered	2 hours of orientation and planning, 9-hour course w/ 2 meals, 2 hour debrief session
	• Price	$150
	• Promotion – Advertising	Professional/business journals
	– Sales Promotion	None
	– Public Relations	Professional meeting, free course exhibits, newspaper, TV, radio, fairs
	– Personal Selling	By facilitators and Marketing Director
	• Place/Distribution	4 hours in their office and 9 hours on course
Executing the Marketing Plan	• Budget	$100,000
	• Who is Responsible?	Marketing Director
	• Milestone Dates	Complete model by Aug. 1-2; free days by Oct. 1; Exec. Comm. & Bd. by Sep. 1
Evaluating the Marketing Plan	• Did it Work?	Meeting revenue targets

ICA 22-2

CHAPTER 22: PULLING IT ALL TOGETHER: THE STRATEGIC MARKETING PROCESS

ICA 22-3: IN-CLASS ACTIVITY

Strategic Marketing Trends: *The McKinsey Quarterly*[1]

Learning Objective. To enable students learn about the latest issues and trends in corporate and marketing strategy planning, implementation, and control as they relate to the marketing environment and marketing mix.

Definition. The following marketing term is referred to in this in-class activity (ICA):

- Strategic Marketing Process: The approach whereby an organization allocates its marketing mix resources to reach its target markets.

Nature of the Activity. To have student teams access and comment on selected articles from *The McKinsey Quarterly*, a journal from the well-known management consulting firm to learn about its perspective on corporate and marketing strategy planning, implementation, and control as they relate to the marketing environment and marketing mix.

Estimated Class Time. 30 minutes, which consists of:

- 10 minutes to explain the nature of this ICA.

- 20 minutes to present summaries by student teams during the subsequent class period.

- [NOTE: Students will spend one (1) hour outside class to complete their assignment.]

Materials Needed.

- The ICA22-3.doc Word and ICA22-3.ppt PowerPoint files contained in the ICA22-3 folder of the Instructor's CD #2 from the *Instructor's Survival Kit* box.

- Copies of the:

    a. *The McKinsey Quarterly* Article Selection Handout.

    b. *The McKinsey Quarterly* Handout.

- Student access to the Internet.

Preparation Before Class. Follow the steps below:

1. Print, read, and if necessary, edit the ICA22-3.doc Word file.

2. Familiarize yourself with *The McKinsey Quarterly* website and the set of articles that students may chose to summarize and analyze.

---

[1] The authors wish to thank *The McKinsey Quarterly*, which assisted in the development of this ICA.

3. Develop in-class discussion questions, if desired.

4. Make copies of the:

   a. *The McKinsey Quarterly* Article Selection Handout.

   b. *The McKinsey Quarterly* Handout.

5. OPTIONAL: Bookmark *The McKinsey Quarterly* (www.mckinseyquarterly.com) website on your classroom computer.

Instructions. Follow the steps below to conduct this ICA:

1. Form students into 4-person teams.

2. Pass out copies of *The McKinsey Quarterly* Article Selection Handout and *The McKinsey Quarterly* Handout to each student.

3. Review the Instructions and Assignments sections of *The McKinsey Quarterly* Handout (see below).

4. OPTIONAL: Using your classroom computer, select 1 or 2 articles from *The McKinsey Quarterly* Article Selection Handout to show student teams the process by which they can access the article they select to summarize and analyze.

5. At the beginning of the next class period, select one student from 4 to 5 student teams to give 1 to 2 minute reports on *The McKinsey Quarterly* articles they summarized and analyzed.

6. Have the student teams turn in their 1-page briefs on *The McKinsey Quarterly* articles they summarized and analyzed.

Marketing Lesson. Because the global marketplace continues to undergo a sweeping transformation, many large and medium-size organizations use consulting firms to help them with their corporate and marketing strategy planning, implementation, and control. Students should develop a habit of monitoring the developments in corporate and marketing strategy to proactively respond to these changes. An excellent source is *The McKinsey Quarterly*.

Website. *The McKinsey Quarterly* website is www.mckinseyquarterly.com.

The McKinsey Quarterly Article Selection Handout

In your student teams, choose one of the following articles to read, analyze, and summarize. The articles' title, the chapter in the textbook that it is related to, description, and the website link where it can be accessed on *The McKinsey Quarterly* website are listed below:

Article Selection (Choose 1 only):

1. **New strategies for consumer goods** (Chapters 2, 11, and 22). The industry has already extracted much of the benefit to be had from improving productivity and concentrating on core brands. Meanwhile, its dynamics are changing. What comes next?
   ARTICLE URL: http://www.mckinseyquarterly.com/links/17462

2. **Extreme competition** (Chapters 3 and 7). The forces of globalization, technology, and economic liberalization are combining to make life harder than ever for established companies.
   ARTICLE URL: http://www.mckinseyquarterly.com/links/17460

3. **Customer retention is not enough** (Chapter 5). Defecting customers are far less of a problem than customers who change their buying patterns. New ways of understanding these changes can unlock the power of loyalty.
   ARTICLE URL: http://www.mckinseyquarterly.com/links/17456

4. **Global champions from emerging markets** (Chapter 7). Developing economies have become an invaluable springboard for companies looking to compete successfully abroad.
   ARTICLE URL: http://www.mckinseyquarterly.com/links/17458

5. **Better branding** (Chapter 11). Marketers rely too much on intuition. The key to building brands more scientifically is to combine a forward-looking market segmentation with a better understanding of customers and a brand's identity.
   ARTICLE URL: http://www.mckinseyquarterly.com/links/17452

6. **Playing to win in the business of sports** (Chapter 12). The pressure is on. Making money—not just popularity—is the name of the game.
   ARTICLE URL: http://www.mckinseyquarterly.com/links/17472

7. **The power of pricing** (Chapters 13 and 14). Transaction pricing is the key to surviving the current downturn—and to flourishing when conditions improve.
   ARTICLE URL: http://www.mckinseyquarterly.com/links/17450

8. **Steering customers to the right channels** (Chapter 15). Migrating customers to a new channel can be a pain—for them, the company, and its channel partners. But the rewards can make the effort worthwhile.
   ARTICLE URL: http://www.mckinseyquarterly.com/links/17468

9. **Organizing for CRM** (Chapter 20). Companies should treat a customer-relationship-management solution as a product or service and its users as internal customers—by making it valuable, pricing appropriately, advertising, and providing after-sales support.
   ARTICLE URL: http://www.mckinseyquarterly.com/links/17470

The McKinsey Quarterly Handout

The authors of *Marketing, 8th Edition* want to express our gratitude to McKinsey & Company for granting special access to *The McKinsey Quarterly* so that you can benefit from the organization's current thinking and expertise on the critical strategic trends and issues facing marketers in today's domestic and global marketplace.

Instructions:

❑ Identify what article your team will read, summarize, and analyze from those listed and described in *The McKinsey Quarterly* Article Selection Handout.

❑ Go to *The McKinsey Quarterly* website (www.mckinseyquarterly.com) and type in the entire "Article URL" exactly as specified in the space provided in your browser to access the article.

[NOTE: *The McKinsey Quarterly* has granted complimentary access to these articles. You will need to complete a free, one-time registration to read the full texts. Complimentary access is only available via the exact links specified. If you do not use these links, you may be asked to subscribe when you reach the website.]

❑ Have one team member print the article and make enough copies of it for every student on the team.

Assignments:

❑ Write a 1-page brief that:

1. Identifies and analyzes the main points of the article (½-page).

2. Discusses the implications in terms of marketing strategy, marketing environment, and/or marketing mix (½-page).

❑ At the beginning of the next class period, hand in your 1-page brief.

❑ Be prepared to give a 1 to 2 minute report on the marketing and strategy articles you summarized.

CHAPTER 22: PULLING IT ALL TOGETHER: THE STRATEGIC MARKETING PROCESS

ICA 22-4: IN-CLASS ACTIVITY

Finding Synergies: How Can 3M Enter the Batting Glove Market?[1]

Learning Objective. To have students apply what they have learned about marketing during the term to design a marketing strategy for 3M to enter the batting glove market.

Definitions. The following marketing terms are referred to in this in-class activity (ICA):

- Evaluative Criteria: Factors that represent both the objective attributes of a brand and the subjective ones a consumer uses to compare different products and brands.

- Points of Difference: Those characteristics of a product that make it superior to competitive substitutes.

- SWOT Analysis: An acronym describing an organization's appraisal of its internal **S**trengths and **W**eaknesses and its external **O**pportunities and **T**hreats.

- Synergy: The increased customer value achieved through performing organizational functions more efficiently.

Nature of the Activity. To have student teams learn and apply lessons from 3M's Greptile Grip golf glove to design a marketing strategy for 3M to market batting gloves that covers: (1) evaluative criteria and points of difference; (2) a SWOT analysis; (3) a promotion strategy; and (4) a distribution strategy.

Estimated Class Time. 35 minutes, which consists of:

- 5 minutes to describe the activity.

- 10 minutes of work in teams on the issues.

- 20 minutes of student team presentations (5 teams at 3 minutes each) with discussion.

- [NOTE: Prior to the class meeting, students will review the 3M Greptile Grip golf glove chapter introduction and Video Case 10: 3M Greptile Grip Golf Glove: Great Gripping!

Materials Needed.

- The ICA22-4.doc Word and ICA22-4.ppt PowerPoint files contained in the ICA22-4 folder of the Instructor's CD #2 from the *Instructor's Survival Kit* box.

- The 3M Greptile Grip golf glove contained in the *Instructor's Survival Kit* box.

---

[1] The authors wish to thank George Dierberger, Marketing and International Manager of 3M Sports and Leisure Products, who assisted in the development of this ICA.

- Copies of the 3M's Marketing Strategy for Entering the Batting Glove Market Handout.

- Four blank transparencies and four felt tip pens for the teams to use.

- NOTE: Transparencies can be made of the handouts instead of making copies and using the PowerPoint presentation for those instructors who prefer this option.

Preparation Before Class. Follow the steps below:

1. Read pp. 41-46 of Chapter 2, pp. 260-262, 284-285 of Chapter 10 and pp. 590-592 of Chapter 22.

2. Print, read, and if necessary, edit the ICA22-4.doc Word file.

3. Print and/or review the PowerPoint slides from the ICA22-4.ppt PowerPoint file.

4. Make copies of the 3M's Marketing Strategy for Entering the Batting Glove Market Handout.

5. OPTIONAL: Bookmark the 3M Greptile Grip Golf Glove website (http://cms.3m.com/cms/US/en/2-162/cFilzFX/view.jhtml) on your classroom computer.

Instructions. Follow the steps below to conduct this ICA:

1. Pass around the 3M Greptile Grip golf glove obtained from the *Instructor's Survival Kit* box.

2. Form students into 4 sets of 4-person teams: #1, #2, #3, and #4.

3. Pass out copies of the 3M's Marketing Strategy for Entering the Batting Glove Market Handout to each student.

3M Greptile Grip golf glove

Slide 2

4. **Show Slide 2**: 3M Greptile Grip Golf Glove and give the following background mini-lecture about 3M's microreplication technology golf glove application:

"As you've read, in 2004 3M introduced this Greptile Grip golf glove. The palm of the glove contains 3M's patented microreplication technology that enables golfers to grip their clubs better under hot, humid, or rainy conditions. Given the initial success of the golf glove, 3M is looking for other potential applications for this microreplication technology. Some potential synergies exist by remaining in the sporting goods sector—specifically by offering a 3M batting glove using this technology. Segments exist for various age groups and for both the male baseball/softball and female softball segments. This is a chance for us to take a quick look at this potential opportunity based on what we've learned during the term."

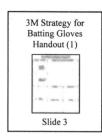

3M Strategy for Batting Gloves Handout (1)

Slide 3

5. **Show Slides 3-4**: 3M's Marketing Strategy for Entering the Batting Glove Market Handout and assign the following responsibilities to the four sets of teams:

- **Team #1**: First identify the important evaluative criteria for batting gloves and then the key points of difference for ballplayers using the glove.

- **Team #2**: Do a SWOT analysis, giving attention to potential (a) marketing and (b) manufacturing/R&D synergies that might exist.

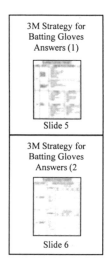

3M Strategy for Batting Gloves Handout (2)

Slide 4

- **Team #3**: Outline a promotion strategy by identifying (a) key segments in the rows, (b) some promotional actions in the columns, and (c) putting a check ($\checkmark$) in the boxes where they link.

- **Team #4**: Outline a distribution strategy by identifying (a) key segments in the rows, (b) some distribution outlets in the columns, and (c) putting a check ($\checkmark$) in the boxes where they link.

6. **Spend 10 minutes** and have the student teams do their assignments. Inform each team that one member must write down and summarize the ideas on a transparency.

7. **Spend 15 minutes** and have one member from 4-5 teams present its team's results written on the overhead transparency in a 3-minute presentation.

3M Strategy for Batting Gloves Answers (1)

Slide 5

8. **Show Slide 5**: 3M's Marketing Strategy for Entering the Batting Glove Market Answers for Team #1 and Team #2. **Spend 3 minutes** discussing among class members about the evaluative criteria, points of difference, and the opportunities and dangers of introducing a 3M batting glove into the market.

3M Strategy for Batting Gloves Answers (2

Slide 6

9. **Show Slide 6**: 3M's Marketing Strategy for Entering the Batting Glove Market Answers for Team #3 and Team #4. **Spend 3 minutes** discussing among class members about the promotion and distribution strategies for introducing a 3M batting glove to the market segments identified.

10. Ask for a quick show of hands from the class to the question, "Do you think the 3M batting glove will succeed in the marketplace—'yes' or 'no'?" Why or why not?

Marketing Lessons. 3M has had success introducing its golf glove into the golf market. So it seems natural to exploit potential marketing and manufacturing/R&D synergies to use its microreplication technology in batting gloves and enter that market. But this analysis should convince students it's not a 'slam dunk' and requires careful strategic market planning, implementation, and eventually—control.

Website. The 3M Greptile Grip Golf Glove website is http://cms.3m.com/cms/US/en/2-162/cFilzFX/view.jhtml.

3M's MARKETING STRATEGY FOR ENTERING
THE BATTING GLOVE MARKET HANDOUT (1)

TEAM	ACTIVITY	MARKETING STRATEGY WORKSHEET	
#1	**Important Evaluative Criteria to Ballplayers**	• • • • •	
	Key Points of Difference to Ballplayers	• • • • •	
#2	**SWOT Analysis**	**Strengths**	**Weaknesses**
		• • • • •	• • • • •
		Opportunities	**Threats**
		• • • • •	• • • • •

ICA 22-4

3M's MARKETING STRATEGY FOR ENTERING
THE BATTING GLOVE MARKET HANDOUT (2)

TEAM	ACTIVITY	MARKETING STRATEGY WORKSHEET					
#3	**Promotion Strategy**	**Ballplayer Market Segment**	**Promotion Action**				
		•					
		•					
		•					
		•					
		•					
#4	**Distribution Strategy**	**Ballplayer Market Segment**	**Distribution Outlets**				
		•					
		•					
		•					
		•					
		•					

3M's MARKETING STRATEGY FOR ENTERING
THE BATTING GLOVE MARKET ANSWERS (1)

TEAM	ACTIVITY	MARKETING STRATEGY WORKSHEET		
#1	**Important Evaluative Criteria to Ballplayers**	• Fit/feel (5.0)* • Durability • Gripping surface in fingers • Gripping surface in palm • Shock absorption • Brand name • Cabretta leather * Ratings are from a student survey using 5-point scale where '5' = 'Very Important'		
	Key Points of Difference to Ballplayers	• Good fit/feel • Provides good gripping • Has effective shock absorption • Others?		
#2	**SWOT Analysis**	**Strengths**		**Weaknesses**
		• 3M name/reputation • Some mfg/R&D synergies • Some marketing synergies • Others?		• 3M brand not strong in sports • No 3M experience in batting glove market • Limited promotional budget • Others?
		Opportunities		**Threats**
		• Large market • Several diverse segments (pro vs. amateur; baseball vs. softball; male vs. female) • Several price points possible • Others?		• Declining baseball/softball participation • Well-entrenched competitors • No distribution in baseball outlets • Others?

3M's MARKETING STRATEGY FOR ENTERING THE BATTING GLOVE MARKET ANSWERS (2)

TEAM	ACTIVITY	MARKETING STRATEGY WORKSHEET					
		Ballplayer Market Segment	**Promotion Action**				
			Profess-ional Endorse-ment	Internet ads	Sports Magazine ads	Point of Purchase Displays	Team/League Endorse-ment
#3	**Promotion Strategy**	• Little Leaguers		✓		✓	✓
		• High school/college males	✓	✓	✓		✓
		• High school/college females		✓	✓		
		• Adult recreation		✓	✓	✓	
		• Professionals	✓				✓
		Ballplayer Market Segment	**Distribution Outlets**				
			Mass Merchan-dise	Sporting Goods Super-stores	Baseball/Softball Specialty Stores	Internet	Team Manager Purchases
#4	**Distribution Strategy**	• Little Leaguers	✓	✓			
		• High school/college males		✓	✓		✓
		• High school/college females		✓	✓		✓
		• Adult recreation	✓	✓		✓	
		• Professionals					✓